THE COMPLETE BOOK OF Baking

THE COMPLETE BOOK OF Baking

Crescent Books
New York

This 1986 edition is published by Ottenheimer Publishers, Inc.,
for Crescent Books, distributed by Crown Publishers, Inc.

First published in Australia by Lansdowne, Sydney
a division of RPLA Pty Limited

Printed in Brazil

Library of Congress Cataloging in Publication Data
Main entry under title:

The Complete book of baking.

Contributors: Ann Creber . . . et al.
Includes index.
1. Baking. I. Joyce, Ray. II. Creber, Ann.

TX763.C625 1986 641.7′1 85-29996
ISBN 0-517-49598-8

h g f e d c b a

Contents

Bread

THE INGREDIENTS

Flours

Most breads are made with plain wheat flour. Wheat flour has a high percentage of gluten—a protein in the wheat structure that stretches and forms the all-important network necessary for bread-making. The gluten is developed through stirring, beating, and kneading the dough.

Hard-wheat flour has gluten added to it. This type of flour absorbs more liquid and will give a larger, lighter loaf.

All-purpose flour is a flour of medium strength (medium gluten percentage) and will give a satisfactory loaf.

Soft-wheat flour is low in gluten and should be mixed with a stronger flour for bread-making, or be kept especially for cake-making.

Rye flour has a good gluten content, but the gluten is slightly different from that found in wheat flour. This flour is often difficult to handle, as it becomes quite sticky. But if used in combination with wheat flour, it gives a very good dough.

Rice flour is high in starch and is an excellent dusting flour when molding a sticky dough. It dries the surface without altering the flour content of the dough.

Potato flour is also used for dusting. It gives a shiny surface to the loaf when mixed with water and brushed over the loaf before baking.

Chick pea or *lentil flour, buckwheat, soy, barley,* or *millet flour* may all be used in combination with plain wheat flour. But first master the art of bread-making, then let your imagination go and experiment with the different flours.

Gluten

In wheat flour and other flours, there are glutenous proteins that form gluten when the dough is made. Gluten is important first because, when developed, it forms the skin of the tiny pockets that hold the gas given off from the yeast. Second, the development or ripening of the gluten plays a major part in the flavor of the dough. Gluten is obtainable from most health food stores. If you wish to increase the gluten content of your flour, add 1 teaspoon of gluten to 1 cup of all-purpose flour. Sift three times to distribute the gluten evenly through the flour.

Wheat germ

Apart from its nutritional value, wheat germ improves the dough, helps to produce a good open crumb in the bread, and prolongs the keeping quality of the loaf.

Wheat germ, millet grain, and cracked wheat may be added to the flour or kneaded into the surface of the dough. These ingredients not only add nutritional value to the loaf, but also interesting texture and flavor. Vary the bread by finally kneading the dough in sesame seeds (toasted or plain), poppy seeds, pumpkin seeds, sunflower seeds, or rock salt, or a combination of these.

Yeast

Yeast is a living plant that produces tiny bubbles of carbon dioxide when combined with moisture, food (in the form of flour), and warmth. This expands the bulk of a dough.

Like any plant it is particular about its environment. It loves a temperature of about 85°F. At a slightly lower temperature it works more slowly, and lower still it hibernates. At a high temperature of about 130°F it expires.

Today's store-bought yeasts are reliable and work very quickly. Two forms are available: compressed, and active dry yeast.

Compressed yeast is available in ⅗-ounce cakes in the dairy section of your food store. The yeast should be firm and moist in consistency, creamy beige in color, and sweet-smelling.

The yeast should keep well in the refrigerator for about 2 weeks.

It may also be frozen. Store in a freezer bag or plastic container labeled and dated. Yeast in good condition will keep successfully for about 3 months. Allow the yeast about 15 minutes to thaw before using. Then dissolve the cake in warm water for 5 minutes before combining it with the other ingredients.

Dry yeast is sold in ½-ounce packages or 4-ounce jars; 1 scant tablespoon equals 1 package of dry yeast. When rising dry yeast, sprinkle it over a little very warm water and leave for 10 to 15 minutes. Whisk for a few seconds and add to the dough as described in the recipe. When substituting dry yeast for compressed yeast, use 1 package of dry for 1 cake of compressed yeast.

Butter

Fat is seldom added to everyday bread, other than in the form of oil or milk.

When a dough or batter is to be enriched with butter, the butter is usually worked in after the straight dough has risen for the first time. This is because the fat globules, in coating the flour grains, make them sticky and makes the action of the yeast more difficult in the dough. But once the yeast has done its work and spread evenly through the dough, the addition of fat presents less of a problem.

Oil

Oil added to the dough makes it exceptionally easy to handle, although only a very small amount is used.

Olive oil is by far the best to add, for the flavor is superb. But for an alternative oil and flavor, use peanut oil, sunflower seed oil, or even sesame seed oil.

Milk

Milk added to dough (in the proportion of 1 part milk to 3 parts water) improves the texture of the loaf and gives a softer crust—although oil or fat will do the same.

Salt

The addition of salt is all-important, for bread made without salt is unpalatable. Salt retards the yeast action and prevents the dough from overfermenting or developing a sour taste if a slow rising is necessary. If a fast rising is necessary, it is possible to increase the quantity of yeast a little and keep the salt content constant. Salt helps the retention of moisture in the dough, but too much salt makes the crust very hard.

If coarse salt crystals are used, these first must be dissolved in warm water, for once the crystals are mixed with the flour, nothing will dissolve them. Fine cooking salt, of course, may be added to the flour. Rock salt kneaded into the surface of the dough gives a good crunchy crust.

Sugar

Unlike salt, sugar stimulates the yeast. Always add the sugar to the yeast with the other ingredients, for if added directly it will overstimulate and exhaust the yeast.

THE PROCESS OF BREAD-MAKING

Sponging

Sponging speeds up the rising of dough and gives a lighter dough. The yeast, warm liquid, and flour are mixed together and allowed to "sponge" in one of the following ways:

- A well is made in the weighed and sifted flour. The yeast mixture is added to the center. A light batter is formed then covered thickly with some of the flour. This is left to "sponge." When the foaming liquid breaks through the flour, the "sponge" is ready.
- Yeast, flour, and water are mixed together in a small bowl, left to 'sponge' until foaming, then added to the weighed flour.
- Yeast is mixed with a little warm liquid and flour and formed into a small ball. This ball is then dropped into a bowl of warm water. When the ball rises in the liquid, it is ready. This is then sifted out and added to the dough.

Kneading

The dough should be kneaded with a regular rhythmic action, using the heel of the hand to push, then the cupped hand to draw the dough back again. The other hand turns the dough at the same time. This action distributes the yeast evenly throughout the dough and develops the gluten in the dough. The dough should be smooth and elastic—when a finger is pressed into it the depression should disappear quickly.

Rising

The dough is left in a warm draft-free place to rise until doubled in bulk.

Shaping

The dough is turned out of the bowl onto a floured surface and kneaded lightly to the required shape.

Proving

When the dough has been shaped and placed into its baking pan, it is allowed to "prove" or rise until it is almost doubled in bulk.

It is then scored, brushed with a glaze, and sprinkled with seeds, or is left natural.

Baking

Bread is usually baked in a hot oven to quickly kill the yeast and set the loaf. Some recipes require the temperature to be lowered after 15 minutes.

When cooked, the crust should be a good rich color, and the base of the loaf when tapped with your knuckles should sound hollow.

1. Sponging, well method

2. Sponging, ball method

3. Kneading

4. Rising

5. Shaping

6. Proving

Milk Bread

Yield: 1 loaf

4 cups flour

1 teaspoon salt

1½ cups milk

2 teaspoons sugar

1 cake fresh compressed yeast

½ stick butter

Sift the flour and salt into a large warmed bowl.

Warm half of the milk to lukewarm with the sugar.

Cream the yeast in a small bowl and pour it over the warm milk and sugar. Stir until the yeast has dissolved.

Make a well in the center of the flour and pour in the milk-sugar and yeast mixture. Stir in sufficient surrounding flour to make a light batter. Sprinkle the top of the batter with a little flour. Let the bowl stand in a warm place until the batter looks spongy and is full of bubbles.

Warm the rest of the milk with the butter, and pour this onto the sponge in the bowl. Mix to a soft dough (using extra flour or extra warm milk if necessary). Place the dough on a lightly floured surface and knead until the dough is smooth and elastic. Rinse out the bowl and lightly grease it with butter. Return the dough to the bowl. Turn the dough over so that the top is lightly greased, and cover loosely with a cloth or with plastic wrap. Leave to rise in a warm place until doubled in bulk.

Preheat the oven to 450°F.

Punch the dough down with your fist and knead it lightly on a floured surface. Shape the dough into a loaf shape and place it on a lightly greased baking sheet or in a greased bread pan. Let prove in a warm place for about 30 minutes or until the loaf has risen to almost the required shape.

Bake in very hot oven for 45 minutes or until the crust resounds when tapped. If the base is slightly damp, leave it out of its pan and return it to the oven for a few minutes. Cool on a wire rack.

Bread Knots

Yield: 12 knots

½ quantity Milk Bread dough (see recipe on left)

1 egg, beaten

poppy seeds, sesame seeds, caraway seeds, or a little grated cheddar cheese

Make Milk Bread dough according to the directions given in the recipe. Leave the dough to rise in the bowl until doubled in bulk.

Preheat the oven to 450°F.

Punch the dough down and knead it lightly on a floured surface. Divide the dough into 12 equal portions. Roll each into a sausage shape about 6 inches long, and then tie each into a knot. Place apart on a greased baking sheet. Leave in a warm place to prove and double in size.

Brush with beaten egg to glaze, and sprinkle with poppy seeds, sesame seeds, caraway seeds, or cheddar cheese.

Bake for 10 to 15 minutes or until golden brown.

Crescent Rolls

Yield: 8 rolls

½ quantity Milk Bread dough (see recipe on left)

soft butter

1 egg, beaten

sesame seeds or caraway seeds

Make Milk Bread dough according to the directions given in the recipe. Leave the dough to rise in the bowl until doubled in bulk.

Preheat the oven to 450°F.

Punch the dough down and knead it lightly on a floured surface. Roll the dough into a circle ¼ inch thick, and spread the top with soft butter. Cut into eight wedges. Roll up each wedge, rolling from the wider edge toward the point. Shape each into a crescent, stretching the dough gently. Place on a greased baking sheet and leave in a warm place to prove.

Brush with beaten egg to glaze, and sprinkle with sesame seeds or caraway seeds.

Bake for 10 to 15 minutes or until golden brown.

Whole-Wheat Bread

Yield: 1 loaf

2 cups all-purpose white flour

2 cups whole-wheat flour

2 teaspoons salt

1 cake fresh compressed yeast

1⅔ cups lukewarm water

sesame seeds or poppy seeds

Mix the flours together in a large warmed bowl and add the salt.

Cream the yeast and add a little of the lukewarm water. Sprinkle with a little flour and let stand in a warm place until it becomes frothy.

Make a well in the flour. Add the yeast mixture and the remaining water. Mix with a wooden spoon until the dough comes cleanly away from the sides of the bowl. Turn out onto a lightly floured surface and knead for about 10 minutes. Return the dough to the rinsed-out bowl. Cover with a damp cloth and set aside in a warm place until doubled in bulk.

Preheat the oven to 425°F.

Punch the dough down and knead lightly for about 3 minutes. Place in a greased $9 \times 5 \times 3$-inch loaf pan. Cover with a cloth and let stand in a warm place to prove.

Brush the top of the loaf with lukewarm water and score the surface in two or three places with a sharp knife. Sprinkle with sesame or poppy seeds.

Bake for 35 to 45 minutes or until the bottom of the loaf sounds hollow when you turn the loaf out of its pan and tap it with your knuckles. Cool on a wire rack.

Household Bread

Yield: 4 loaves

4 pounds all-purpose white flour (or a mixture of whole-wheat flour with wheat germ or rye flour)

1½ tablespoons salt

1 tablespoon sugar

2 cakes fresh compressed yeast

5 cups warm water

Sift the flour, salt, and sugar into a large warmed bowl.

Cream the yeast with the warm water. Make a well in the center of the flour and pour the water–yeast mixture into this. Mix until a fairly liquid batter has formed. Sprinkle the surface of the batter thickly with some of the surrounding flour.

Leave the bowl covered in a warm place until the frothing batter breaks through. This "sponging" should take about 30 minutes.

Beat in the surrounding flour, first using a wooden spoon, then your hands. Lift the dough out onto a floured surface and knead the dough until smooth and elastic (about 10 to 15 minutes). Return the dough to the rinsed-out bowl and cut a cross in the top of the dough. Cover and place in a warm place for about 2 hours, or leave overnight in a cool place.

Preheat the oven to 400°F.

Punch the dough down and knead it lightly. Divide the dough into fourths, and form into the required shapes. Put into four greased bread pans, or, if cottage loaves or braids, place onto greased baking trays. Leave the loaves to prove.

Bake in a hot oven until a deep golden brown, for about 40 minutes to 1 hour. Cool on a wire rack.

Cloverleaf Rolls

Yield: 24 rolls

1 quantity Milk Bread dough ***(see recipe on page 12)***

melted butter

poppy seeds

Make Milk Bread dough according to directions given in the recipe. Leave the dough to rise in the bowl until doubled in bulk.

Preheat the oven to 450°F.

Punch the dough down, turn out onto a lightly floured surface, and knead until smooth. Divide the dough evenly into 24 pieces. Then divide each piece into thirds and form into small balls.

Lightly grease muffin trays for 24 muffins. Into each cup place three balls, forming a three-leafed clover pattern. Leave the trays in a warm place until the rolls prove and double in bulk.

Brush with melted butter to glaze and, if desired, sprinkle with poppy seeds.

Bake for 15 to 18 minutes or until golden brown.

Farmhouse Loaves

Yield: 2 loaves

2 cakes fresh compressed yeast

2 cups warm water

2 tablespoons honey

3 cups all-purpose white flour

3 cups whole-wheat flour

1 tablespoon salt

grated cheddar cheese plus caraway seeds for sprinkling

Mix the yeast with about half a cup of the warm water. Stir the honey into the remaining 1½ cups of warm water.

Sift the flours together with the salt into a large warmed bowl. Make a well in the center of the flour and into this pour the yeast mixture and the honey and water. Gradually draw in the surrounding flour and mix until it is a smooth dough (add extra water, if necessary, to make a manageable dough). Turn the dough out onto a lightly floured surface and knead until smooth and elastic (about 7 minutes).

Rinse the bowl clean and lightly grease it with a little butter or oil. Return the dough to the bowl and turn it once so that the top surface is oiled. Cover and leave in a warm place until doubled in bulk.

Preheat the oven to 400°F.

Punch the dough down and leave it for 10 minutes. Turn the dough out onto a lightly floured surface and knead lightly. Divide the dough in half and form into two loaves of the shapes required—place into two greased bread pans. If making cottage loaves or braids, place on greased baking sheets. Leave the loaves in a warm place to prove until doubled in bulk.

Sprinkle with grated cheese and caraway seeds.

Bake for 40 to 45 minutes or until the crust is golden brown and the loaf sounds hollow when tapped with the knuckles. Leave to cool on a wire rack.

Cottage Loaves

Yield: 2 loaves

1 quantity Farmhouse dough (see recipe above)

extra flour (rice flour, if desired), for dusting

Make the dough according to the directions given in the recipe for Farmhouse Loaves. Let the dough rise and double in bulk.

Preheat the oven to 400°F.

Punch the dough down and knead it lightly on a floured surface. Divide the dough in half. From each of these two pieces, break off about a quarter of the dough. Knead each piece into a round shape, two large and two small.

To assemble each cottage loaf, place a small round of dough on top of a larger round, using a little milk or water to stick. Then briefly plunge a floury wooden spoon handle or finger right down into the center of the dough.

Place the shaped bread onto a greased baking sheet and cover with a large bowl inverted, or with a cloth. Let rise for about 30 minutes. Just before baking, dust with extra flour.

Bake for 45 minutes or until the bread sounds hollow when tapped with the knuckles.

Cracked-Wheat Bread

Yield: 2 loaves

1 cup finely ground cracked wheat

3 cups boiling water

½ stick butter

1 tablespoon salt

3 tablespoons honey

1 tablespoon molasses

¾ cup milk

2 cakes fresh compressed yeast

¼ cup water

4 cups all-purpose white flour

2 cups whole-wheat flour

Mix the cracked wheat and boiling water together in a saucepan and cook for about 10 minutes, or until most of the moisture is absorbed. Stir in the butter, salt, honey, molasses, and milk.

Cream the yeast with the water until dissolved.

Sift the flours into a large warmed bowl and stir in the cracked-wheat mixture. Mix, using your hands, until thoroughly combined. Stir in the yeast mixture, and add more warm water, if necessary, to form a manageable dough. Lift the dough out onto a floured surface and knead until smooth.

Rinse out the bowl and lightly oil it. Return the dough to the bowl and turn once so that the surface is lightly greased. Cover and leave in a warm place until doubled in bulk.

Preheat the oven to 400°F.

Punch the dough down and knead it lightly. Divide the dough in half and place in lightly greased deep bread pans. Leave to prove until well risen.

Bake for 40 minutes or until crusty golden brown. Remove each loaf from its pan, and, if the base is slightly damp, return the bread to the oven for 5 minutes. Cool on a wire rack.

Right: **Farmhouse Loaves (see above left).**

Country Oatmeal Bread

Yield: 1 loaf

¾ cup boiling water
½ cup rolled oats
3 tablespoons butter
¼ cup molasses
2 teaspoons salt
1 cake fresh compressed yeast
½ cup warm water
2¾ cups strong white flour
1 egg
1 egg white, slightly beaten
¼ cup rolled oats for sprinkling
¼ teaspoon coarse salt for sprinkling

Combine the boiling water with the rolled oats, butter, molasses, and salt. Let cool to lukewarm.

Cream the yeast and dissolve it in the ½ cup of warm water.

Sift the flour into a large warmed bowl and make a well in the center. Stir in the dissolved yeast, then the egg, then the cooled rolled-oats mixture. Using a wooden spoon, stir to combine thoroughly. Turn out onto a lightly floured surface and knead until smooth.

Return the dough to a rinsed-out bowl and leave covered in a warm place until doubled in bulk (about 1 to 1½ hours).

Preheat the oven to 375°F.

Punch the dough down and lightly knead it into a round. Grease the inside of a deep round cake pan or a large 2-pound fruit can, and place the dough in the pan. Brush its surface with the beaten egg white and sprinkle with the remaining ¼ cup of rolled oats and salt. Leave in a warm place until almost doubled in bulk.

Bake for 1 hour or until the crust is brown and the loaf sounds hollow when you turn it out of the pan and tap it with your knuckles. If browning too quickly, cover with a piece of brown paper or aluminum foil. When cooked, remove the loaf from the pan and cool on a wire rack.

French Bread

Yield: 2 long loaves

1 cake fresh compressed yeast
1 tablespoon butter, softened
1 teaspoon sugar
1¼ cups warm water
4 cups flour
1 teaspoon salt

Place the yeast, butter, and sugar into a bowl. Stir in the warm water until the butter melts and the yeast is liquified.

Sift flour and salt into a large warmed bowl. Stir in the liquid ingredients. Gather the dough into a mass and turn it out onto a floured surface. Knead for 3 to 4 minutes, until the dough is smooth and elastic.

Grease the rinsed-out mixing bowl with a little butter or oil, and place the dough in the bowl. Turn the dough over so that the top is smeared with butter or oil. Cover with a sheet of plastic wrap and leave in a warm place for about 1 to 1½ hours. The dough will rise to two and a half times its original bulk and should be light and spongy.

Preheat the oven to 375°F.

Punch the dough down and turn it out onto a floured surface. Roll it out to an oblong shape 12 × 8 inches. Check during rolling to make sure the dough is not sticking, flouring the surface again if necessary. Using a very sharp knife, cut the dough cleanly in half lengthwise; do not drag the knife through the dough. Roll up each loaf tightly from the long side. Seal the ends and roll lengths slightly to make a good shape. Place the loaves on a greased baking sheet, and leave to prove in a warm place for about 20 minutes.

Make slashes across the loaf at intervals and brush the surface with water.

Bake for 40 minutes or until golden brown and crisp. Remove from the baking sheet and cool on a wire rack.

Sourdough Starter

2 teaspoons active dry yeast
2 cups lukewarm water
2 cups flour

Dissolve the yeast in warm water in a large glass bowl. Gradually stir in the flour, then beat until smooth. Cover the bowl with a tea towel and let stand overnight in a warm place. Bubbles should appear on the surface, but if after 24 hours none have appeared, discard and start again.

Stir the mixture well and cover with plastic wrap, and return to a warm draft-free place. Let stand until foamy (about 2 to 3 days).

When the sourdough starter has become foamy, stir it well and pour into a clean glass jar. Cover well and store in the refrigerator. When a clear liquid has risen to the top, the starter is ready to use. Stir before using.

The starter can be stored in the refrigerator for several weeks and used for several batches of bread. To replenish your supplies, discard all but 1 cup of the starter, because any excess (unless reactivated) may become rancid. Add 1 cup of starter to 1 cup of flour and 1 cup of lukewarm water, then proceed as before.

Always allow the starter to warm to room temperature before adding it to dough.

Sourdough Bread

Yield: 2 loaves

4 cups flour

2 teaspoons salt

1 cup Sourdough Starter (see recipe, page 16)

1½ cups warm water

2 teaspoons molasses or honey

Next morning:

1½ to 2 cups flour

2 tablespoons butter

2 small eggs

Sift the flour and salt into a large warmed bowl. Make a well in the center of the flour and stir in 1 cup of sourdough starter, the water, and molasses or honey. Mix thoroughly and let stand overnight uncovered in a warm place.

Next morning: Preheat the oven to 400°F.

Stir down any crust that may have formed and add the 1½ to 2 cups of flour.

Soften the butter and mix it into the dough with the eggs.

Turn the dough out onto a well-floured surface and knead until smooth and elastic. Shape the dough into two loaves and place on greased baking sheets or in greased bread pans. Brush lightly with a little extra butter. Leave the loaves to prove until almost doubled in bulk.

Bake for 45 to 50 minutes. Cool on a wire rack.

Quick Sourdough Rye Bread

Yield: 2 loaves

6 cups strong wheat flour

4 cups rye flour

¾ teaspoon salt

2½ cups warm water

1½ cakes fresh compressed yeast

1 teaspoon caraway seeds

Measure out half of the wheat flour, half of the rye four, and half of the salt. Mix together in a large bowl. Mix in enough of the warm water to make a soft dough, at first using a wooden spoon, then your hand. Place the dough in a clean bowl and let stand in a warm place for about 12 to 16 hours or until it has an agreeably sour smell.

Mix together the remaining flours and salt. Dissolve the yeast in some of the remaining water and stir into the flour, adding more warm water to make a soft dough.

Incorporate the soured dough with the new dough, and knead until it is smooth and elastic. Return the dough to a clean warmed bowl. Leave in a warm place for about 1½ hours or until doubled in bulk.

Preheat the oven to 400°F.

Punch the dough down and turn it out onto a floured surface. Knead the caraway seeds into the dough and shape it into two cigar or torpedo shapes. Place on a greased baking sheet and leave to prove for 1½ hours.

Prick the loaves with a fork in four or five places before placing them in the oven.

Bake for about 1 hour in the hot oven, reducing the temperature after 20 minutes or so to moderately hot, 375°F. Cool on a wire rack.

Note: If you wish to have the characteristic shiny crust of rye bread, mix a little potato flour or rice flour with boiling water, and brush this over the loaves just before baking and again about halfway through baking.

Rye Bread

Yield: 2 loaves

2 cakes fresh compressed yeast

1½ cups warm water

¼ cup molasses

⅓ cup sugar

1 tablespoon fennel seeds

1 tablespoon anise seeds

2½ cups rye flour

2½ cups all-purpose white flour

2 tablespoons butter

Cream the yeast with the warm water in a large bowl. Stir in the molasses, sugar, fennel seeds, and anise seeds. Sift the rye flour over and beat until a smooth dough. Gradually add the all-purpose flour and mix to a smooth dough, holding back some of the flour if the dough is getting too stiff. Soften the butter and work into the dough. Turn the dough out onto a floured surface and knead until smooth.

Rinse out the bowl and return the dough to the bowl. Let rise in a warm place until doubled in bulk. This will be slower than normal, as the dough is quite a heavy one.

Preheat the oven to 375°F.

Punch the dough down and knead the dough into a round. Divide it in half and knead each into a long oval shape—the shape of a cigar. A sprinkling of rice flour or potato flour will help if the dough is sticky.

Place the shaped loaves onto greased baking sheets and let prove until almost doubled in bulk.

Make four diagonal slashes in the tops of the loaves and bake for 30 to 35 minutes. Cool on a wire rack.

Corn Bread

Yield: 2 loaves

2 cakes fresh compressed yeast

2 cups warm water

2 teaspoons salt

½ cup light corn syrup or molasses

4 tablespoons oil or melted butter

1 cup cornmeal

5 to 5½ cups flour

Cream the yeast and dissolve it in the warm water in a large mixing bowl. Add the salt, corn syrup or molasses, oil (or melted butter), cornmeal and half of the flour. Beat using a wooden spoon until smooth. Add more of the remaining flour, if required, to produce a manageable dough.

Turn the dough out onto a floured surface and knead until smooth and elastic, about 10 minutes. Rinse out the bowl and lightly grease it with oil or butter. Return the dough to the bowl and turn it to grease the top. Cover and set in a warm place until doubled in bulk.

Preheat the oven to 375°F.

Punch the dough down and turn it out onto a lightly floured surface. Knead lightly and divide the dough in half. Shape each into a round, or into a loaf shape if baking in bread pans. Place on greased baking sheets or in two greased bread pans, and let prove for about 30 minutes.

Bake for 35 to 40 minutes or until the loaves sound hollow when tapped. Turn out onto a wire rack to cool.

Flowerpot Loaves

Use new terra-cotta flowerpots. Scrub them clean but don't use detergent, just hot clean water. Leave the pots upside down to dry thoroughly.

When it is time to bake the loaves, oil the inside of each pot well or line it with aluminum foil. Fill the pot (whether it be a flowerpot, casserole, or serving dish) more than half full with the dough. Let prove in a warm place until the dough has risen.

Brush the top of the dough with beaten egg glaze, or with water or milk warmed to room temperature, or leave it lightly floured. Score the surface if you like. Sprinkle with poppy seeds, sesame seeds, or caraway seeds.

Bake in a preheated oven at 400°F for about 45 minutes, depending on the size of the pot, until the loaf sounds hollow when you turn it out of the pot and tap it with your knuckles. Cool on a wire rack, then return the bread to the pot to serve.

Right: **Clockwise from right: Olive and Feta Cheese Bread (see p. 24); Bacon Loaf (see p. 23); Flowerpot Loaves (see above).**

AUX

Challah Braids

Yield: 2 loaves

1½ cakes fresh compressed yeast
1⅓ cups lukewarm water
3 eggs
1 tablespoon sugar
1 tablespoon sea salt
5 cups flour
½ stick butter, softened
1 egg yolk, mixed with a little water
poppy seeds (optional) for sprinkling

Cream the yeast and dissolve it in the lukewarm water. Beat the eggs, sugar, and sea salt together.

Sift the flour into a large warmed bowl. Make a well in the center and pour over the yeast and egg mixtures. Add the softened butter. Beat, gradually drawing in the surrounding flour, until the dough is smooth.

Turn the dough out onto a floured surface and knead until smooth and elastic, adding more flour if necessary; kneading should take about 5 to 7 minutes.

Rinse out the bowl and lightly grease with a little butter or oil. Return the dough to the bowl and turn it over so that the greased surface is on top. Cover and set in a warm place until doubled in bulk.

Preheat the oven to 400°F.

Punch the dough down and divide into six equal portions. Roll each portion into a long sausage shape about 1 inch thick. Braid three of the strands together and then the other three. Pinch the ends to seal. Place the two loaves on lightly greased baking sheets and leave in a warm place to prove.

Brush the surface with egg yolk mixed with a little water and sprinkle with poppy seeds. Bake for 35 to 40 minutes or until the bottom of the loaf sounds hollow when tapped. Cool on a wire rack.

Potato Bread

Yield: 16 rolls or 1 loaf

2 medium-sized potatoes, to yield ¾ cup when mashed
4 cups flour
1 tablespoon salt
1 cake fresh compressed yeast
1¼ cups milk and water mixed

Peel and cook the potatoes in boiling salted water until tender. Drain and set over heat to dry the potatoes. Mash or sieve the potatoes until smooth.

Sift the flour and salt into a large warmed bowl.

Cream the yeast and stir in the warm milk and water until the yeast has dissolved.

Rub the mashed potatoes while still warm into the flour (as you would rub butter in), until well mixed. Make a well in the center and add the yeast mixture. Stir until it forms a soft dough. Turn out and knead the dough until smooth and elastic.

Rinse the bowl out and lightly butter it. Return the dough to the bowl and turn it to grease the top. Cover and set in a warm place until doubled in bulk. This will take a little more time than with other bread recipes.

Preheat the oven to 400°F.

Punch the dough down and turn it out onto a working surface. Knead lightly and, if making rolls, divide into 16 portions. Knead each into a smooth ball, pulling the dough into itself to make a smooth top. Place on a lightly greased baking sheet. Cover loosely with a cloth, and leave to prove.

When well risen and well shaped, bake for 15 to 20 minutes or until golden brown. Cool on a wire rack.

For the loaf: Shape the dough into the required shape and place in a deep straight-sided pan. Cover with a damp cloth or a piece of plastic wrap and leave to prove for about an hour.

Bake for 45 minutes or until the crust is brown and the loaf sounds hollow when tapped. Take care not to let the crust get too brown and harden. Cool on a wire rack.

Pocket Bread

Yield: 6 "pockets"

1 cake fresh compressed yeast
1⅓ cups warm water
3 to 3½ cups flour
1 teaspoon salt
pinch of sugar
1 tablespoon olive oil
cornmeal for dusting

Dissolve the yeast in a little of the warm water.

Sift half of the flour into a warmed bowl. Stir in the salt, sugar, oil, the remaining warm water, and the dissolved yeast. Beat until smooth, adding enough of the remaining flour to make a soft dough.

Turn the dough onto a lightly floured surface, knead until smooth and elastic, about 10 minutes.

Rinse out the bowl and lightly grease it. Return the dough to the bowl and turn it once so that the greased surface is on top. Cover and leave in a warm place until doubled in bulk (about 1 hour).

Preheat the oven to 500°F.

Punch the dough down and divide it into six equal parts. Shape into balls and leave in a warm place to rise (about 30 minutes).

Sprinkle the working surface with cornmeal and on this roll out each ball into a circle about ⅛ inch thick. Place on ungreased baking sheet and leave to prove for 15 minutes.

Bake for 10 minutes or until puffed and lightly browned.

Cool on wire trays and keep in a sealed plastic bag until ready to use.

Naan

Yield: 8 loaves

2 cakes fresh compressed yeast
¾ cup warm water
1 tablespoon sugar
¼ cup yogurt or buttermilk
1 egg
½ stick butter or ghee, melted
3½ cups all-purpose white flour
2 teaspoons salt

Cream the yeast and stir in the warm water.

Mix together the sugar, yogurt (or buttermilk), egg, and melted butter (or ghee).

Sift the flour and salt into a warm mixing bowl and make a well in the center. Stir in the yeast and water mixture, then the yogurt and sugar mixture. Use a wooden spoon at first, then, as the dough gets stiffer, use your hands. Turn the dough out of the bowl onto a lightly floured surface and knead until smooth and elastic.

Rinse out the bowl and lightly oil it. Return the dough to the bowl and cover it loosely with a cloth. Leave in a warm place until doubled in bulk.

Preheat the oven to 450°F.

Punch the dough down and leave it for 10 minutes.

Divide the dough into eight balls. Pat each into a round shape and then pull the dough to form an oval shape which is slightly thinner in the center than at the edges. Each oval should be about 7 inches long and about 4 inches wide.

Place the heavy flat baking sheets in the hot oven to heat them. When very hot, carefully remove them, place two loaves on each, and quickly return to the oven. Bake for about 10 minutes or until golden and puffed.

Variation: The Naan may be brushed with a little melted butter or ghee and sprinkled with poppy seeds before baking.

Almond and Orange Buns

Yield: about 8 buns

½ cake fresh compressed yeast

¼ cup sugar

1 tablespoon lukewarm water

½ cup milk

½ stick butter, cut into small pieces

3 cups flour

¼ teaspoon salt

1 egg, lightly beaten

½ cup raisins

¼ cup orange juice

2 teaspoons olive oil

3 tablespoons chopped blanched almonds

1 tablespoon grated orange rind

1 egg yolk, beaten with 2 tablespoons milk

Dissolve the yeast and a pinch of sugar in the lukewarm water and set it aside for 15 minutes or until it becomes frothy.

Put the milk in a saucepan, add the butter, and heat until the butter dissolves. Set it aside to cool to lukewarm.

Sift the flour and salt into a mixing bowl and add the remaining sugar. Make a well in the flour and add the yeast mixture, the beaten egg, and the milk–butter mixture. Stir with a wooden spoon until the dough comes away from the sides of the bowl, then knead with your hands until the dough is smooth and elastic—this will take about 10 minutes. Rinse and dry the bowl, return the dough to it, cover with a towel, and leave in a warm place for about 1½ hours or until the dough has doubled in bulk.

Meanwhile, soak the raisins in the orange juice for about 15 minutes or until they are plumped up.

When the dough has risen sufficiently, punch it down and add the olive oil, the drained raisins, the almonds, and orange rind. Knead the dough for a few minutes, long enough to distribute the fruit and nuts evenly, then divide it into eight equal pieces. Form the pieces of dough into balls, place them on a greased baking sheet, cover with a towel, and set aside in a warm place for 30 to 40 minutes or until the dough has doubled in bulk.

Preheat the oven to 400°F. Brush the dough balls with the egg and milk mixture, and bake them for 20 to 25 minutes or until they are golden brown. Allow to cool on wire racks.

Cranberry Bread

Yield: 1 large loaf

1½ cups fresh or canned cranberries

⅓ cup sugar

1 cup finely chopped walnuts

grated rind of 1 orange

1 cake fresh compressed yeast

1 cup lukewarm milk

4 cups flour

1 teaspoon salt

½ teaspoon grated nutmeg

½ teaspoon ground cinnamon

1 stick butter

1 egg

Glaze:
2 tablespoons sugar

1 tablespoon milk

If you are using canned cranberries, drain them. Chop the cranberries in a blender or food processor; do not puree them. Put them into a bowl with the sugar, walnuts, and orange rind.

Put the yeast into a small bowl with a pinch of sugar and 2 tablespoons of the warmed milk and set it aside in a warm place until it starts to become frothy.

Sift the flour, salt, nutmeg, and cinnamon into a large warmed bowl. Make a well in the flour and add the yeast mixture, cranberry mixture, melted butter, egg, and the remaining milk. Using your hands, draw the flour into the liquid and continue mixing until the dough comes away from the sides of the bowl.

Turn it out onto a floured board and knead for 8 to 10 minutes or until the dough is smooth and elastic. Return the dough to the rinsed-out bowl, cover with a towel, and leave in a warm place for 1 to 1½ hours or until it has doubled in bulk.

Punch the dough down and knead again for 3 or 4 minutes, then form it into a rectangle and place it in a greased 2-pound loaf pan. Cover with a towel and leave in a warm place for 35 minutes or until the dough has risen to the top of the pan.

Preheat the oven to 400°F. Bake for 15 minutes, then reduce the temperature to 350°F and bake for a further 35 minutes. Remove the bread from the pan and rap the underside of the loaf with your knuckles. If it feels soft, return it to the oven, upside down—and without the pan, for an additional 5 minutes.

To make the glaze: Combine the sugar and milk in a small saucepan and cook over low heat, stirring constantly, until the sugar dissolves. Simmer for a few minutes to thicken the glaze slightly. As soon as the bread is cooked, paint the top and sides with the glaze and cool on a wire rack.

Bacon Loaf

Yield: 1 loaf

8 ounces bacon
½ ounce fresh compressed yeast
¼ cup warm water
¼ cup warm milk
1½ teaspoons sugar
1 teaspoon salt
2 eggs
3 cups flour
1 tablespoon olive oil
½ cup diced Emmentaler cheese

Chop the bacon coarsely. Fry until crisp; reserve the fat.

Cream the yeast with the warm water and milk.

Mix the sugar, salt, and eggs together.

Sift the flour into a large warm bowl and make a well in the center. Stir in the yeast mixture, then the egg mixture, and then the reserved bacon fat and the olive oil. Gradually draw in the surrounding flour until it forms a manageable dough. Add more liquid if necessary. Knead the dough in the bowl until smooth and elastic. Cover and leave in a warm place until double in bulk.

Preheat the oven to 400°F.

Punch down the dough. Gently work in the diced cheese and fried bacon. Shape into a smooth round and place into a shallow 8-inch cake pan. Leave in a warm place until almost double in bulk.

Bake for 30 minutes or until golden brown. Serve warm.

Onion Bread

Yield: 1 loaf

½ ounce fresh compressed yeast
1 cup warm water
3 cups flour
1 teaspoon sugar
2 teaspoons salt
3 tablespoons olive oil
3 large Spanish or brown onions
pinch of salt and sugar to season the onions

Cream the yeast with the warm water.

Sift the flour with the sugar and salt into a warm bowl. Stir in the dissolved yeast and water. Gradually draw in the surrounding flour to form a soft dough. Add a little more liquid if necessary. Turn the dough out onto a floured surface and knead until smooth.

Rinse out the bowl and return the dough to the bowl. Cover and leave in a warm place until double in bulk.

Preheat the oven to 400°F.

Punch down the dough. Knead in 2 tablespoons of the olive oil.

Halve, peel, and thinly slice the onions. Sauté them gently in the remaining tablespoon of olive oil until they are soft. Season to taste with salt and a little sugar. Set aside to cool.

Turn the dough out of the bowl and knead into a long sausage shape. Coil it into a ring and place it onto a baking tray. Secure the ends together. Leave to rise until almost double in bulk.

Spread the cooled sautéed onions over the dough.

Bake for 15 minutes, then lower the heat to 375°F and bake for 20 minutes or until golden brown. Serve bread hot or cold, sliced, with butter.

Garlic Bread

Yield: 1 loaf

1 long loaf of French bread
4 cloves garlic, peeled
pinch of salt
1½ to 2 sticks butter

Preheat the oven to 375°F.

Slash the bread diagonally at ¾-inch intervals, almost through to the base of the loaf.

Crush the garlic with a good pinch of salt until a smooth paste is formed.

Soften the butter in a small bowl and add the crushed garlic. Mix well, using a metal spoon or plastic spatula. Spread the garlic butter between the slices of bread. Smear any remaining butter on the top. Wrap the bread in aluminum foil.

Bake for 15 minutes. Open the foil for the last 5 minutes to allow the crust to crisp.

Anchovy Loaf

In place of the garlic butter, use 6 mashed anchovy fillets. Soak the anchovies in milk for a few minutes to remove excess salt. Mix the anchovies with 1½ to 2 sticks of butter, then proceed as above.

Cheese Bread

Yield: 2 loaves

2 cakes fresh compressed yeast
½ cup warm water
1½ cups warm milk
1 tablespoon salt
2 tablespoons sugar
¼ cup olive oil
1 egg
6 cups flour
1½ cups grated cheddar cheese
1 teaspoon caraway seeds
extra grated cheese for sprinkling

Cream the yeast with the warm water.

Mix together the milk, salt, sugar, oil, and egg.

Sift the flour into a large warmed bowl and stir in the yeast and water, and then the milk mixture. Sprinkle on the grated cheese and caraway seeds. Add a little more liquid if necessary to form a manageable dough. Turn the dough out onto a lightly floured surface and knead until smooth and elastic.

Rinse the bowl clean and lightly oil it. Return the dough to the bowl and turn it once to oil the surface. Cover and leave in a warm place until doubled in bulk.

Preheat the oven to 400°F.

Punch the dough down and knead it lightly. Divide the dough in half and shape into the required shape—place in greased bread pans or onto greased sheets. Let prove in a warm place until well risen.

Bake for 40 minutes or until golden brown. If desired, the loaves may be sprinkled with extra cheese and returned to the oven for 5 minutes, until the cheese has melted. Cool the loaves on a wire rack.

Olive and Feta-Cheese Bread

Yield: 1 loaf

2 cups all-purpose white flour
2 cups whole-wheat flour
1 teaspoon salt
1 cake fresh compressed yeast
1⅔ cups lukewarm water
2 ounces feta cheese, crumbled
⅓ cup black olives, pitted and sliced
1 tablespoon olive oil

In a large warmed bowl, mix together the flours and salt.

Cream the yeast with a little of the water and flour, and set is aside for about 10 minutes or until it becomes frothy.

Make a well in the flour and add the yeast mixture, then the remaining water. Mix with a wooden spoon until the dough comes away from the sides of the bowl, then knead with your hands for about 10 minutes or until the dough is smooth and elastic. Cover the bowl with a cloth and set it aside in a warm place until the dough doubles in bulk.

Preheat the oven to 425°F.

Punch the dough down and add the feta cheese, olives, and oil. Knead until they are well distributed throughout the dough. Oil a 9 × 5 × 3-inch bread pan and put the dough into it. Cover with a cloth and let rise to the top of the pan. Depending on the warmth in the room, this will take 30 minutes to 1 hour.

Bake the bread in the hot oven for 25 minutes, then reduce the temperature to moderately hot, 375°F, and bake for an additional 20 minutes.

Remove the loaf from the pan and tap the base with your knuckles. If it sounds hollow, the loaf is cooked. If it is soft, return it to the oven for another 5 minutes without the pan. Cool on a wire rack.

Spiced Braided Loaves

Yield: 2 loaves

2 cakes fresh compressed yeast

⅓ cup sugar

¾ cup warm water

1 tablespoon salt

4 tablespoons butter, softened

1¼ cups warm milk

1 tablespoon ground cinnamon, or a mixture of cinnamon, nutmeg, and allspice

6 cups flour

Glaze:
1 egg yolk, beaten with 1 tablespoon water

Dissolve the yeast and sugar in the warm water and set aside. Add the salt and butter to the warm milk. When the butter has melted, stir in the yeast mixture. Pour this liquid into a warmed bowl and add the spices.

Add the flour, a cup at a time, beating well between each addition (you may not need all the flour). Knead the dough until it is smooth and elastic—this will take about 8 minutes. Form the dough into a ball and put it back into the rinsed-out and buttered bowl. Cover with a thick towel and leave in a warm place until it has doubled in bulk.

Punch down the dough and knead it for a couple of minutes. Then divide the dough into six pieces. Shape each piece into a ball and then into a long sausage shape with tapered ends. Press the ends of three strands together and braid them, finishing off neatly by pressing the ends together. Do the same with the remaining three strands.

Place the loaves, with a space between them, on a buttered baking sheet. Cover loosely with a towel, and leave them to rise for 30 minutes or until they have doubled in bulk.

Preheat the oven to 425°F. Paint the loaves with the egg yolk and water mixture (the mixture should be no colder than room temperature). Bake them for 15 minutes, then reduce the oven temperature to 350°F for an additional 20 to 25 minutes or until the loaves are golden brown and the base sounds hollow when rapped with the knuckles. Allow to cool on wire racks.

Fruit and Nut Bread

Yield: 1 loaf

3 cups flour

⅓ cup brown sugar

pinch of salt

1 teaspoon mixed spice (ground cinnamon, grated nutmeg, powdered ginger, and allspice)

1 cake fresh compressed yeast

⅔ cup warm milk

½ stick butter, melted and cooled

½ cup raisins

½ cup currants

⅓ cup candied peel

1 cup chopped Brazil nuts

Glaze:
⅔ cup milk

6 tablespoons sugar

Put the flour, sugar, salt, and spices into a large bowl. Make a well in the center. Dissolve the yeast in a little of the milk and pour it into the flour. Add the butter and the remaining milk and mix together.

Knead the dough until it feels soft and elastic, adding more flour or warm water if necessary. Put the dough back into the bowl, cover with a cloth, and leave in a warm place until the dough has doubled in bulk (about 1½ hours).

Add the fruit and nuts and knead again until well mixed. Grease a small loaf pan with butter, and put the dough into it, pressing it down well. Cover with a cloth and leave it in a warm place until the dough comes to the top of the pan (about 30 minutes).

Preheat the oven to 400°F.

Bake for 35 to 45 minutes or until the loaf has shrunk slightly in the pan and is brown on top. Remove from the pan. Turn it upside down and tap it lightly with your knuckles. If it feels soft, return it to the oven, upside down, without the pan for an additional 5 minutes.

To make the glaze: Put the milk and sugar into a saucepan and bring to a boil, stirring constantly until the sugar has dissolved. Boil for 3 to 5 minutes or until the glaze has thickened slightly.

As soon as the loaf is cooked, paint it with the sugar-and-milk glaze and leave it on a wire rack to cool.

Fan-Tans

Yield: about 15 rolls

1 cake fresh compressed yeast

¾ cup warm milk

4 cups flour

¼ cup sugar

¼ teaspoon salt

¾ stick butter, melted

2 eggs, lightly beaten

Glaze:
1 egg, beaten with 1 tablespoon milk

Put the yeast in a bowl with a pinch of sugar and 2 tablespoons of the warm milk. Set the bowl aside until the mixture is puffed up and frothy.

Sift the flour into a large warmed bowl with the sugar and salt. Make a well in the center and add the yeast mixture, the remaining milk, two-thirds of the melted butter, and the eggs.

Using your hands, mix the flour into the liquid until the dough comes away cleanly from the sides of the bowl. Add more milk if the dough is too stiff. Turn out onto a floured board and knead for about 5 minutes or until it is smooth and elastic.

Rinse and dry the bowl and grease it lightly. Form the dough into a ball and return it to the bowl. Cover it with a towel, and set it aside in a warm place for 2 hours or until it has doubled in bulk.

Knead the dough again for a few minutes and leave it to rest 10 minutes. Then roll out the dough into a rectangle about ⅛ inch thick. Using a pastry brush, brush the dough with the remaining melted butter. Cut the dough into strips about 1½ inches wide. Pile five strips on top of each other and press down lightly so that they stick together. Cut the strips into pieces about 2 inches long.

Place the pieces on a greased baking sheet, cover with a towel, and leave in a warm place until they have doubled in bulk.

Preheat the oven to 425°F.

Brush the top of each Fan-Tan with the glaze.

Bake for 20 to 25 minutes or until they are golden brown. Allow to cool on a wire rack before serving.

Pretzels

Yield: 48 pretzels

1 cake fresh compressed yeast

¼ teaspoon sugar

1 cup lukewarm milk

2 tablespoons butter, melted and cooled

3 cups flour

½ teaspoon salt

1 tablespoon caraway seeds (optional)

1 egg, lightly beaten

2 teaspoons coarse sea salt

Dissolve the yeast and sugar in 2 tablespoons of the lukewarm milk. Set it aside until it froths. Stir the melted butter into the remaining milk.

Sift the flour and salt into a warmed bowl (add half the caraway seeds, if using them) and make a well in the center. Pour in the yeast mixture and the milk–butter mixture and stir with a wooden spoon until well mixed. Then turn out onto a floured board and knead with your hands until the dough is smooth and elastic. This will take 8 to 10 minutes.

Return the dough to the rinsed-out and lightly greased bowl, cover with a towel and leave it in a warm place for about an hour or until it has doubled in bulk.

Punch the dough down and knead again, this time for about 4 minutes. Using your hands, form the dough into a sausage, about 12 inches long. Cut the dough into 48 equal pieces and roll each piece out into a sausage about 6 inches long.

To form them into pretzels, hold one end of the dough strip in each hand and form into a circle. Make a knot in the dough, and press the ends back on to the circle of dough.

Preheat the oven to 375°F. Half fill a large saucepan with water and bring to boil. Add the pretzels, a few at a time so that you don't crowd the pan, and cook them until they rise to the surface (this will take about 1 minute). Remove them from the pan with a slotted spoon and drain them in a colander. Cook the remaining pretzels in the same way.

Place the pretzels on greased baking sheets and brush them with beaten egg. Sprinkle with coarse sea salt and, if you desire, the remaining caraway seeds. Bake the pretzels for 15 minutes or until they are golden brown and crisp. Allow to cool on wire racks.

Right: **Pretzels** **(see above).**

English Muffins

Yield: about 12 muffins

1 egg

1¼ cups warm milk

2 tablespoons butter, melted and cooled

1 cake fresh compressed yeast

4 tablespoons warm water

4 cups flour

1 teaspoon salt

Beat the egg in a bowl and add the milk and butter. Cream the yeast with the warm water and set aside.

Put the flour and salt into a bowl and warm it in a low oven. Make a well in the center and pour in the yeast mixture and then the egg–milk–butter mixture. Mix well and then knead thoroughly, adding more flour or warm water if necessary. The dough should be soft and smooth. Cover the bowl with a thick towel and leave it in a warm place for about 1½ hours or until it has doubled in bulk.

Preheat the oven to 450°F. Roll the dough out on a floured board into a circle about ½ inch thick and cut into rounds with a biscuit cutter about 2 inches in diameter.

Place the muffins on a floured baking sheet and bake for 8 minutes, then turn them over and bake the other side for 6 or 7 minutes, until they are well risen.

Traditionally, muffins are toasted on the outside, then they are pulled apart and buttered.

Herb Bread

Yield: 2 loaves

2 cakes fresh compressed yeast

2 cups warm water

6 cups flour

3 teaspoons salt

3 teaspoons sugar

1 tablespoon olive oil

1 teaspoon dried marjoram

½ teaspoon dried thyme

4 tablespoons fresh chopped parsley

Cream the yeast with the water.

Sift the flour into a large warmed bowl with the salt and sugar. Make a well in the center and add the dissolved yeast and water. Pour over the olive oil and sprinkle over the herbs. Gradually draw in the surrounding flour, first with a wooden spoon, then with your hands. Turn the dough out onto a floured surface and knead until smooth and elastic.

Rinse out the bowl and lightly oil it. Return the dough to the bowl and turn it once to oil the top surface of the dough. Cover and leave in a warm place until doubled in bulk.

Preheat the oven to 400°F.

Punch the dough down and lightly knead. Divide it in half and shape into loaves. Place into greased bread pans or onto greased baking sheets. Leave in a warm place until nearly doubled in bulk.

Brush the top surfaces with milk or egg glaze and sprinkle with extra herbs or poppy seeds. Bake for 40 minutes or until the loaf sounds hollow when tapped with the knuckles. Cool on a wire rack.

Variations: In place of the herbs use 2 teaspoons of caraway seeds and dill seeds; or 2 teaspoons of grated nutmeg, 2 teaspoons of dill, and 1 tablespoon of fresh sage. When using fresh herbs, be sure to triple the amounts suggested for dry herbs.

Flat Armenian Bread

Yield: 10 large rounds

1½ cakes fresh compressed yeast

2½ cups lukewarm water

6 cups all-purpose white flour

1 stick unsalted butter

3 teaspoons sugar

2½ teaspoons salt

1½ tablespoons sesame seeds

Cream the yeast and dissolve it in about ½ cup of the lukewarm water. Sprinkle with a little flour and leave in a warm place until bubbling.

Melt the butter and add sugar and salt, stirring until dissolved. Allow it to cool a little.

Sift the flour into a large warmed bowl and make a well in the center. Pour the yeast mixture into the well in the flour, then the melted butter mixture, and then gradually the remaining lukewarm water. Not all the water may be needed. Beat, gradually incorporating the flour until the dough is smooth and soft. Beat for about 10 minutes. Cover loosely and leave in a warm place to rise, until doubled in bulk.

Preheat the oven to 350°F.

Turn the dough out onto a floured surface and divide into 10 equal parts. Knead each lightly into a ball, then roll out each ball into a circle as thinly as possible. Place two on a greased baking sheet. Sprinkle with a little water and then sprinkle with a pinch or two of sesame seeds.

Bake in the coolest part of the oven for about 20 minutes or until the bread is a pale golden brown. Transfer to a wire rack.

Sprinkle and bake the remaining eight rounds, two at a time, as above.

Croissants

Yield: 12 croissants

½ cake fresh compressed yeast
3 tablespoons warm water
3 teaspoons sugar
2 cups flour
1½ teaspoons salt
⅔ cup warm milk
2 tablespoons vegetable oil
1 stick unsalted butter
Glaze: ***1 egg***
1 teaspoon water

Put the yeast, water, and 1 teaspoon of sugar into a bowl and set aside until it is puffed up and frothy.

Sift the flour into a bowl. Dissolve the remaining sugar and the salt in the milk. Make a well in the flour and pour in the yeast mixture, the milk mixture, and the oil. Blend together with your hands, scraping all the dough from the sides of the bowl. Knead it on a lightly floured board for about 5 minutes. (It will be very sticky.)

Return the dough to the rinsed-out and dried bowl and cover with a towel. Set it aside in a warm place until it has risen to about three times its original volume. Depending on the temperature, this will take 3 to 4 hours.

Knead it slightly on a lightly floured board, then press it out into a rectangle about 12 × 8 inches. Fold it into thirds horizontally and return it to the bowl. Cover again and leave to rise until double in bulk.

Remove the dough from the bowl and place it on a lightly floured plate. Cover the dough and plate with plastic wrap and refrigerate for 30 minutes.

Meanwhile, put the butter into a bowl of cold water and knead it with your hands until it is soft and spreadable—but not oily.

Put the dough onto a lightly floured board and push it out into a rectangle about 14 × 8 inches; it is easiest to have one of the shorter sides nearest you. Using your hands, spread the butter over the far two-thirds of the dough, leaving a ¼-inch border all around; fold the unbuttered third of the dough up to the middle, then fold the top third down over it.

Lightly flour the surface of the dough. Swivel it around 90° so that the shortest side is nearest you. Roll it out carefully into a rectangle about 14×16 inches and again fold one third over, then the other third. If the butter starts to become oily, refrigerate the dough immediately.

Sprinkle the dough lightly with flour, wrap it in greaseproof paper, and chill it in the refrigerator for 1 hour.

Remove dough from the refrigerator and let stand for about 10 minutes. Then roll it into a rectangle 14 × 6 inches and fold it again into thirds. Once more, turn the dough, roll it out again and fold it again. Wrap it in greaseproof paper and chill it for 2 hours.

Remove the dough from the refrigerator and let stand for 10 minutes. Roll the dough out into a rectangle about 20 × 5 inches, cut in half and chill one half. Cut the other half into three pieces, roll out each piece into a square, and cut it in half diagonally, making two triangles. Starting with the base of the triangle, roll it up toward the point, stretching the point slightly as you do so. Curve the roll into a crescent shape and place on a buttered baking sheet. Do the same with the remaining dough.

Cover the dough crescents with plastic wrap and set aside in a warm place until they have risen to double their original size.

Preheat the oven to 475°F. Beat the egg with the water and brush this glaze over the croissants. Bake for 12 to 15 minutes or until they are golden brown. Cool slightly on a wire rack before serving.

Bagels

Yield: 24 bagels

1 cup milk
½ stick butter
5 teaspoons powdered sugar
1 cake fresh compressed yeast
1 egg, separated
½ teaspoon salt
3½ cups flour
poppy seeds, for sprinkling

Bring the milk to a boil, remove it from the heat and add the butter and sugar, stirring until the butter has melted and the sugar has dissolved. Set the milk mixture aside to cool to lukewarm.

Add the yeast to the cooled milk mixture and set it aside in a warm place until it starts to froth.

Add the egg white (unbeaten) and the salt to the milk mixture, stirring well. Then add the flour, a little at a time, stirring constantly until the dough is smooth. Knead the dough on a floured board for about 15 minutes or until it is smooth and elastic. Put it into a greased bowl, cover with a towel, and set aside for 1 to 1½ hours or until it has doubled in bulk.

Punch down the dough and divide it into 24 equal pieces. Form each piece into a ball and place your finger in the middle of it to make a hole. Widen the hole with your finger until it makes up about one-third of the ball's diameter. Set the bagels aside, covered with plastic wrap, for about 10 minutes or until they start to rise.

Meanwhile, bring a large pan of water to a boil. When boiling, add the bagels, a few at a time. Cook for about 15 seconds or until they puff up, and then remove them immediately with a slotted spoon and place them on a greased baking sheet. Continue cooking the rest of the bagels in the same way.

Preheat the oven to 400°F. Mix the leftover egg yolk with a little cold water and paint it over the tops of the bagels. Sprinkle with poppy seeds and bake for about 20 minutes or until brown and crisp. Remove from the oven and allow to cool on wire racks.

Brioches

Yield: about 12 brioches

3 tablespoons lukewarm water

1 cake fresh compressed yeast

1 teaspoon sugar

2 cups flour

additional 2 teaspoons sugar

1 teaspoon salt

3 large eggs, beaten

1½ sticks unsalted butter

Glaze:
1 egg, beaten with 1 teaspoon of water

Pour the warm water into a small bowl and add the yeast and 1 teaspoon of sugar. Set the bowl aside until the yeast dissolves.

Put the flour, 2 teaspoons of sugar, and the salt into the bowl of a food processor and add the yeast mixture and eggs. Process for a few minutes, stopping the machine and scraping down the sides when necessary. The dough will start out very sticky, but will become more elastic the longer you process it.

Put the butter into a bowl of cold water and squeeze it in your hands until it is soft. Divide it into six pieces and drop them one by one into the food processor, adding each piece only after the previous piece has been absorbed by the dough. By the time all the butter has been added, the dough should be elastic, though it will still be a bit sticky.

Put the dough into a clean bowl and cover with a towel. Set it aside to rise to triple its bulk. If the butter starts to melt and the dough looks oily, put the bowl in the refrigerator from time to time. It will take about 4 hours to rise.

Turn the dough out onto a lightly floured board and form it into a rectangle about 10 × 5 inches. Fold it into thirds, as if you were making puff pastry, then press it out again, and again fold it into thirds. Put the dough back into the bowl, cover, and leave it to rise to double its bulk. This will take about 1½ hours.

Form the dough into a round, put it on a plate and cover it with foil. Put it in the refrigerator for about 30 minutes—if you don't do this, the dough will be too sticky to form into balls.

Grease individual brioche molds or muffin tins with butter. Take three-quarters of the dough and form little balls, each of which will half fill a mold. Using two fingers, make a hole in the center of each ball of dough, wider at the top than at the bottom.

Make smaller balls with the remaining dough and form each one into a teardrop shape. Put the pointed end into the prepared hole so that each brioche has a little topknot in the center. Set aside for the dough to rise again, until it has doubled in volume.

Preheat the oven to 475°F. Just before baking, brush the surface of each brioche with the egg glaze. Using scissors, clip at intervals under the small ball of dough (this will ensure that it rises properly in the oven).

Bake for 15 minutes. Allow to cool on wire racks.

If you wish to freeze them, allow to cool, then wrap carefully in plastic or foil and put in the freezer. Thaw for 10 minutes or so in an oven preheated to 350°F.

Sally Lunns

Yield: 2 cakes

3 cups flour

½ teaspoon salt

1 cup milk

2 tablespoons butter

1 cake fresh compressed yeast

1 teaspoon sugar

1 egg

Glaze:
2 tablespoons sugar

1 tablespoon milk

Sift the flour and salt into a heatproof bowl and put it in a low oven to warm it. Put two 7-inch cake pans in the oven at the same time to warm them.

Heat the milk and butter together until the butter melts, then allow it to cool to lukewarm.

Put the yeast and sugar into a bowl and add a little of the warm milk–butter mixture to it. Set aside for 5 minutes or until it dissolves.

Beat the egg and add it to the milk–butter mixture, then add the yeast mixture. Make a well in the flour and pour in the milk mixture. Beat well with a wooden spoon, adding more flour if the mixture is too sticky. With floured hands, knead the dough for about 4 minutes, until it feels smooth and elastic.

Divide the dough in half, butter the warm cake pans and put half the dough into each, pressing down well around the edge. Cover the pans with a towel and leave them in a warm place to rise—it should only take half an hour for the dough to rise to the tops of the pans.

Preheat the oven to 400°F. Bake the cakes for 15 to 20 minutes or until they are light brown on top and a toothpick inserted into the center comes out clean.

While they are cooking, make the glaze. Put the sugar and milk into a small saucepan and heat gently, stirring constantly, until the sugar dissolves. Let it simmer for a minute or two to thicken it slightly.

As soon as you take the cakes from the oven, turn them out onto wire racks and spread them with the glaze. Or you can ice them, once they've cooled, with lemon or pink icing.

Variations: Add raisins or any type of dried fruit; spices such as cinnamon, nutmeg, and allspice can be mixed into the flour. Grated or finely sliced apple gives the cakes an interesting texture and flavor.

Hot-Cross Buns

Yield: 20 buns

1¼ cups milk

2 cakes fresh compressed yeast

4 cups flour

2 teaspoons salt

⅓ cup brown sugar

2 teaspoons mixed spice (ground cinnamon, nutmeg, ginger, allspice, coriander)

½ stick butter, melted and cooled

2 eggs

2 tablespoons dried currants

1 tablespoon candied peel

2 tablespoons powdered sugar

Cross:
small quantity Shortcrust Pastry ***(see recipe, page 150)***
or
4 tablespoons self-rising flour

2 tablespoons cold water

Glaze:
2 tablespoons milk (taken from the 1¼ cups above)

2 tablespoons powdered sugar

Warm the milk and put a tablespoon of it into a cup with the yeast and a pinch of sugar. Stir and let stand for 15 minutes or until frothy.

Put the flour, salt, sugar, and spices together in a bowl and mix well. Make a well in the center and pour in the yeast mixture, the melted butter, the eggs, and a little of the milk. Knead the dough, adding more milk if necessary, until the dough is smooth and stiff and comes away easily from the sides of the bowl. You may not need all the milk to achieve this (2 tablespoons of it will be required later for the glaze).

Add the dried fruit and knead well so that it is evenly distributed. Cover the bowl with a towel and leave in a warm place for at least 2 hours or until it has doubled in bulk.

Knead the dough again until it feels elastic. Divide the dough into 20 even portions and form each portion into a ball. Place them on well-greased baking sheets, cover with a towel, and leave in a warm place until they have doubled in bulk. In warm weather this will take about 30 minutes.

Preheat the oven to 375°F. To make a cross on the top of each bun, use one of three methods.

- Score a cross with a sharp pointed knife.
- Cut shortcrust pastry into short strips, moisten one side with water, and stick the strips in cross shapes on the tops of the buns.
- Mix the self-rising flour with the water, beating until smooth. Put the mixture into a small funnel made with greaseproof paper and pipe a cross on top of each bun.

Place the buns on a buttered baking sheet and bake in the preheated oven for 15 to 20 minutes, turning the baking sheet around once during cooking.

Meanwhile, make the glaze. Boil the milk and powdered sugar together until they become thick and syrupy. Take the buns out of the oven and brush them immediately with the glaze, giving them two coats.

Tsoureki

Yield: 1 large loaf

2 cakes fresh compressed yeast

¼ cup warm water

½ cup lukewarm milk

½ teaspoon sugar

1 cup flour

3 eggs

additional ¾ cup sugar

grated rind of 1 lemon or ½ teaspoon caraway seeds

additional 4 cups flour

1 stick melted butter, cooled

sesame seeds

1 extra egg, for glaze

In a large warmed bowl, dissolve the yeast in the warm water. Add the milk, the ½ teaspoon of sugar, and the cup of flour. Stir the batter well, cover the bowl with a thick towel and set it aside in a warm place to rise for about 1 hour.

Beat the eggs with the ¾ cup of sugar and lemon rind or caraway seeds in an electric mixer or over a pan of hot water until the mixture is thick.

Add the egg mixture to the batter. Add the 4 cups of flour and the butter. Mix until the dough comes away from the sides of the bowl (add more flour if it is too sticky).

Knead it on a floured board until it is smooth and elastic—this will take about 5 minutes. Put the dough back into the rinsed-out and dried mixing bowl, cover with a towel and set aside in a warm place until it has doubled in bulk. This can take 2 or 3 hours, because the dough is so rich.

Punch the dough down, knead it again and divide it into three pieces. Roll each piece out on a floured board into a long, thin sausage. Sprinkle the sesame seeds on a plate, roll the sausages in them loosely.

Generously grease a baking sheet. Place the dough on it, cover, and leave to rise to double its bulk.

Preheat the oven to 400°F. Beat the egg with a little cold water and brush this over the dough. Bake for 15 minutes, then reduce the temperature to 350°F and bake for an additional 30 to 35 minutes.

The bread emerges from the oven brown and shiny. Cool it on a wire rack.

Panettone

Yield: 1 large loaf

¾ stick butter, softened

1 cake fresh compressed yeast

¼ cup lukewarm water

4 cups flour

⅓ cup sugar

1½ teaspoons salt

¾ cup lukewarm milk

3 eggs, lightly beaten

½ cup candied peel

¾ cup raisins

2 teaspoons grated lemon rind

2 tablespoons melted butter

Grease the inside of a 2-pound coffee can with some of the softened butter. Line the bottom and sides with greaseproof paper, allowing it to extend above the top of the can by about 1 inch. Grease the paper well and place the can on a baking sheet.

Put the yeast, a pinch of sugar, and the water into a bowl and set it aside in a warm place until it is puffed up and frothy.

Sift the flour, sugar, and salt into a large warmed mixing bowl. Make a well in the center and pour in the yeast mixture and the milk. Using your hands, gradually draw the flour into the liquid and continue mixing until the dough comes away cleanly from the sides of the bowl.

Turn the dough out onto a floured board and knead it well until it is smooth and elastic. Place the dough in the rinsed-out and dried bowl, cover with a thick towel, and set aside in a warm place until the dough has doubled in bulk.

Add the remaining softened butter, the eggs, candied peel, raisins, and lemon rind. Knead again for about 5 minutes. Put the dough back into the bowl, cover, and set aside in a warm place for about 1 hour.

Preheat the oven to 400°F. Put the dough into the prepared coffee can, cover, and leave for 30 minutes or until it has risen slightly. Using a pastry brush, coat the top of the dough with some of the melted butter.

Bake the Panettone for 30 minutes. Reduce the temperature to 350°F and bake for an additional 30 minutes. Take the bread out of the oven and brush the top with the remaining melted butter. Allow it to cool in the can for 20 minutes, then remove, peel off the paper, and cool the Panettone completely on a wire rack.

Stollen

Yield: 1 large loaf

1 cake fresh compressed yeast

1 tablespoon lukewarm water

1 stick butter

¾ cup milk, scalded

4 cups flour

¾ cup sugar

1 teaspoon salt

½ teaspoon ground cinnamon

¼ teaspoon ground mace

¼ teaspoon ground cardamom

2 eggs, lightly beaten

1 cup chopped candied peel

½ cup raisins

½ cup chopped walnuts

Icing:
2 tablespoons butter, melted

1½ cups confectioners' sugar

2 tablespoons water

¼ teaspoon vanilla extract

walnut halves, for decoration

Put the yeast, a pinch of sugar, and the water into a bowl. Stir it and set it aside in a warm place until it is puffed up and frothy.

Stir the butter into the scalded milk until it has melted, then set aside to cool to lukewarm.

Sift the flour, sugar, salt, and spices into a large warmed bowl. Make a well in the center and pour in the yeast mixture, the milk–butter mixture, and the eggs.

Using your hands, gradually draw the flour into the liquid and continue mixing until the dough comes away cleanly from the sides of the bowl. Add more flour or milk as necessary. Turn the dough out onto a floured board and knead well until it is smooth and elastic.

Rinse out and dry the bowl and return the dough to it, sprinkling flour lightly over the top. Cover with a thick towel and set it aside in a warm place until the dough has doubled in bulk. This will take 1 to 1½ hours.

Knead the dough again for a few minutes, then add the dried fruit and nuts and continue kneading until they are evenly distributed throughout the dough. Shape the dough into an oval and place it on a greased baking sheet. Cover with the towel and set aside in a warm place for about 45 minutes or until it has risen by about half.

Preheat the oven to 400°F. Bake the Stollen for 15 minutes, then reduce the temperature to 350°F and bake for an additional 30 minutes. Remove the bread from the oven and rap the underside with your knuckles. If it is hard and sounds hollow, the Stollen is cooked. If not, return it to the oven, upside down, and bake for another 5 minutes. Leave it to cool on a wire rack.

To make the icing: Beat the butter, sugar, and water together until they are well blended, then add the vanilla extract.

When the Stollen is cool, spread the icing generously over the top and sides, and decorate with walnut halves. Serve sliced and spread with butter.

Tea Cakes & Breads

Basic Rich Butter Cake

Yield: 1 cake

2 cups flour

1½ teaspoons baking powder

1½ sticks butter

1 cup powdered sugar

3 eggs, beaten

3 tablespoons milk

½ teaspoon vanilla extract

Preheat the oven to 350°F. Grease a deep-sided 8-inch-round cake pan, and line it with greaseproof paper.

Sift the flour and baking powder together.

In a large bowl, cream the butter and sugar until light and fluffy. Add the eggs gradually, beating well after each addition. Mix in half the flour and half of the milk; combine well. Add the remaining flour and milk and the vanilla extract, and mix well. Turn into the cake pan and level the top.

Bake for 1 hour in the moderately hot oven. It is great served warm with a little butter.

Chocolate Butter Cake

To the batter for Basic Rich Butter Cake, add 2 tablespoons of cocoa and mix well.

Butter Cake with Peaches

To the batter for Basic Rich Butter Cake, add 2 tablespoons of fresh wheat germ and ½ cup of chopped dried peaches.

The peaches should be soaked in boiling water for 15 minutes, then drained and patted dry with a paper towel before being added to the mixture.

Walnut Butter Cake

To the batter for Basic Rich Butter Cake, add ½ cup finely chopped walnuts and ½ teaspoon of grated nutmeg.

When baked, brush the hot cake with melted butter.

Then sprinkle the hot cake with a mixture of 2 teaspoons of brown sugar, 2 tablespoons of finely crushed walnuts, and a pinch of grated nutmeg.

Orange Butter Cake

In the preparation of the batter for Basic Rich Butter Cake substitute orange juice for the milk and add the grated rind of 1 orange.

When baked, top the cake with Warm Glacé Icing (see recipe, page 102). Serve with clove-spiced tea.

Butter Cake with Crumble Topping

Before baking the batter for Basic Rich Butter Cake, cover it with crumble topping. Rub together ¼ cup whole-wheat flour, 2 tablespoons butter, 2 tablespoons brown sugar, ¼ cup oatmeal, 1 tablespoon grated coconut, and 1 teaspoon ground cinnamon. Lightly pat this mixture onto the batter. Then proceed with baking, as above.

Sand Cake

Yield: 1 cake

1 stick butter

1 teaspoon grated lemon rind

1 cup sugar

3 eggs

1 cup flour

½ cup ground rice

1 teaspoon baking powder

¼ teaspoon grated nutmeg

4 tablespoons dry sherry

2 teaspoons lemon juice

confectioners' sugar, for sprinkling

Preheat the oven to 350°F. Grease an 8 × 4-inch loaf pan, and line it with greaseproof paper.

In a large bowl, beat together the butter and lemon rind, then gradually beat in the sugar. Add the eggs, one at a time, beating well after each.

Sift together the flour, ground rice, baking powder, and nutmeg, and add this to the butter–sugar–eggs mixture. Mix well. Fold in the sherry and lemon juice. Turn into the pan.

Bake for 45 to 50 minutes. When cooked, remove from pan and cool on a wire rack. When cool, dust the surface with sifted confectioners' sugar. Serve at the "English" tea time, 5 p.m., with strong tea or black coffee enriched with a few drops of sweet sherry.

Coconut Cake

Yield: 1 cake

3½ cups flour

pinch of salt

4 teaspoons baking powder

2 sticks butter

1¼ cups powdered sugar

½ cup flaked coconut

⅓ cup grated solidified coconut milk

4 eggs, beaten

¾ cup milk

Preheat the oven to 350°F. Grease an 8-inch cake pan and line it with greaseproof paper.

Sift the flour, salt, and baking powder into a large bowl. Rub in the butter until mixture resembles fine bread crumbs. Stir in the sugar, coconut, and grated solidified coconut milk. Gradually mix the eggs and milk into the flour mixture. Turn it into the cake pan and smooth the top.

Bake for 1½ to 1¾ hours. Turn out onto a wire rack to cool. The cake can be decorated with Warm Glacé Icing (see recipe, page 102) and sprinkled with shredded coconut.

Pineapple Coconut Cake
To the batter for Coconut Cake, add ½ cup of chopped candied pineapple and ¾ teaspoon of ground clove.

Gingerbread

Yield: 1 cake

4 cups flour
3 level teaspoons ground ginger
3 teaspoons baking powder
1 teaspoon baking soda
1 teaspoon salt
1½ cups brown sugar
1½ sticks butter
½ cup molasses
½ cup light corn syrup
2½ cups milk
1 large egg, beaten

Preheat the oven to 350°F. Grease a deep-sided, 8-inch-square cake pan and line it with greaseproof paper.

Sift the dry ingredients, except the sugar, into a large bowl.

Warm the sugar, butter, molasses, and syrup in a saucepan over low heat until the butter has just melted. Stir this into the dry mixture, together with the milk and beaten egg. Beat thoroughly and pour into the cake pan.

Bake in the center of the oven for 1½ hours. Remove from the oven and allow to cool in the pan for 15 minutes. Then turn out onto a wire rack. When cold, wrap in foil without removing the paper. Store for 4 or 5 days before cutting into squares.

Serve with a hot mug of cocoa. It tastes even better with a thin lemon icing.

Raisin Cakes

Yield: 2 cakes

1 stick butter
½ cup sugar
2 eggs
1 tablespoon grated citrus (orange or lemon) rind
1 cup raisins
2 cups self-rising flour
⅔ cup milk

Preheat the oven to 350°F. Grease two shallow loaf pans and line the base with greaseproof paper.

Cream the butter and sugar, until light and creamy. Add eggs one at a time, beating well after each addition. Beat in the citrus rind, then mix in the raisins. Add the sifted flour alternately with the milk, and mix well. Turn into the pans.

Bake for 30 to 35 minutes. Turn out, and cool on wire rack.

Variation: Mix in sliced dried apricots and a few slivered almonds before baking.

Light Fruit Cake

Yield: 1 cake

2½ cups flour
1 teaspoon baking powder
2 sticks butter
1 cup powdered sugar
4 eggs, beaten
½ cup raisins
½ cup currants
¼ cup mixed peel
2 tablespoons milk

Preheat the oven to 325°F. Grease a deep-sided 8-inch-round cake pan, and line it with greaseproof paper.

Sift together the flour and baking powder.

In a large bowl, beat together the butter and sugar until light and fluffy. Add the beaten eggs gradually, beating well after each addition. Mix in the fruit, then the flour, and then the milk. Turn out into the cake pan.

Bake for 1¾ hours. Remove from the pan and cool on a wire rack.

Cinnamon Tea Cake

Yield: 1 cake

1 egg, separated
½ cup sugar
½ teaspoon vanilla extract
½ cup milk
1 cup self-rising flour
1 stick butter, melted
Topping: ***1 tablespoon melted butter***
1 tablespoon sugar
½ teaspoon ground cinnamon

Preheat the oven to 375°F. Grease a 7-inch cake pan

Beat the egg white until stiff, then add the yolk. Gradually beat in the sugar.

In a small bowl, add the vanilla to the milk, then add this a little at a time to the egg and sugar mixture. Lightly stir in the sifted four and the melted butter. Pour into the cake pan.

Bake for 20 to 25 minutes. Remove from the pan and, while still hot, brush with melted butter and sprinkle with sugar and cinnamon.

Serve warm or (just as good) cold, spread with unsalted butter.

Madeira Cake

Yield: 1 cake

2 sticks butter
grated rind of ½ lemon
½ teaspoon ground cinnamon
1¼ cups powdered sugar
5 eggs
3¼ cups flour
2 teaspoons baking powder
pinch of salt
½ cup milk
½ cup slivered blanched almonds
2 tablespoons candied citrus peel

Preheat the oven to 350°F. Grease a deep-sided, 8-inch-round cake pan, and line it with greaseproof paper.

Cream the butter with the lemon rind and cinnamon, and add sugar gradually. Beat until the mixture is light and soft.

In a separate bowl, beat the eggs one at a time with some of the flour, then sift in the remaining flour with the baking powder and salt. Fold this into the butter–sugar mixture with the milk. Turn into the pan, and arrange the almonds and candied peel on the top.

Bake for 1 hour, then reduce the heat to 325°F and bake for another 15 minutes. Turn out onto a wire rack to cool.

Coffee Cake

Yield: 1 cake

1¾ cups flour
1 teaspoon baking powder
½ teaspoon baking soda
½ teaspoon salt
¼ teaspoon grated nutmeg
¾ cup sugar
1 stick butter
½ cup oatmeal
⅓ cup wheat germ
1 egg
¾ cup raisins, chopped a little
⅔ cup milk
3 tablespoons instant coffee powder
confectioners' sugar, for sprinkling

Preheat the oven to 350°F. Grease an 8-inch-square cake pan.

Sift together the flour, baking powder, baking soda, salt, nutmeg, and sugar.

In a separate bowl, rub the butter into the oatmeal and wheat germ, then add this to the flour mixture. Add the egg and raisins, and mix well.

Warm the milk a little and dissolve the coffee in it. Blend this into the mixture and stir well. Pour into the cake pan.

Bake for about 35 minutes. Serve warm, cut into squares and dusted with confectioners' sugar.

Right: **Clockwise from top: Light Fruit Cake (see p. 37); Coconut Cake (see p. 36); Fresh Apple Cake (see p. 42); Cinnamon Tea Cake (see above left).**

Walnut-Crumble Apricot Cake

Yield: 1 cake

16 dried apricots

1 stick butter

⅔ cup powdered sugar

2 eggs

2 cups self-rising flour, sifted

½ cup milk

Topping:
½ cup self-rising whole-wheat flour

¼ cup brown sugar

¼ cup chopped walnuts

½ teaspoon ground cardamom

4 tablespoons butter

Soak the apricots in boiling water for 20 minutes.

Preheat the oven to 350°F. Grease an 8-inch springform pan.

Cream the butter and sugar until light and fluffy. Add the eggs one at a time, beating between each addition. Gently fold in the flour one-third at a time, alternately with the milk. Pour the batter into the cake pan.

Drain the apricots thoroughly, then arrange them on top of the batter.

To prepare the crumble topping: Mix all the dry ingredients together and then rub in the butter. Spread the crumble mixture over the apricots. Cover with foil.

Bake for 40 minutes. Gently remove the foil and bake for about 30 minutes more. Serve warm or cold.

Lemon Yogurt Cake

Yield: 1 cake

1 stick butter

¾ cup powdered sugar

3 eggs

finely grated rind of 1 lemon

¾ cup plain yogurt

2 cups self-rising flour, sifted

½ cup sliced dried apricots

Preheat the oven to 325°F. Grease an 8×6-inch loaf pan.

Cream the butter and sugar until light and fluffy. Add the eggs one at a time, beating well between each. Gently fold in the lemon rind, yogurt, sifted flour, and dried apricot slices. Spoon the mixture into the pan.

Bake for 1¼ hours. Turn out onto a wire rack to cool.

The cake is made even more delicious by topping with a yogurt icing. Mix 1 tablespoon of plain yogurt with ½ cup of confectioners' sugar, spread this over the cake, and sprinkle with finely grated lemon rind.

Coffee and Peppermint Cake

Yield: 1 cake

1½ sticks butter

1 cup powdered sugar

2 cups flour

1½ teaspoons baking powder

3 eggs

3 tablespoons milk

4 tablespoons instant coffee powder

5 drops peppermint extract

Preheat the oven to 350°F. Grease a deep-sided, 8-inch-round cake pan and line it with greaseproof paper.

Cream the butter and sugar until light and fluffy.

Into a separate bowl, sift the flour and baking powder together. To the butter and sugar, add the eggs gradually, beating after each.

Warm the milk and dissolve the coffee in it.

To the butter–sugar–egg mixture, add half of the flour and half of the coffee-milk. Combine well. Add the remaining flour and milk and the peppermint extract; mix well. Turn into the cake pan and smooth over the top.

Bake for 1 hour. Turn out onto a wire rack to cool. Serve with hot chocolate or a chocolate liqueur.

Fresh Pear and Bran Cake

Yield: 1 cake

½ cup finely chopped walnuts

¾ cup brown sugar

1 teaspoon ground cinnamon

2 teaspoons wheat bran

1½ cups thinly sliced pear

½ teaspoon lemon juice

1 stick butter

2 eggs

1¼ cups whole-wheat flour

1½ teaspoons baking powder

½ cup sour cream

½ teaspoon milk

Preheat the oven to 350°F. Grease a deep loaf pan. Four bowls are needed for the preparation.

Combine the walnuts, ¼ cup of sugar, cinnamon, bran, pear slices, and lemon juice.

In a large bowl, cream the butter and remaining ½ cup of sugar together. Beat in the eggs, one at a time.

Sift together the flour and baking powder.

Combine the sour cream and milk.

Into the butter–sugar–egg mixture, stir the sifted dry ingredients alternately with the sour-cream mixture. Pour half of this batter into the pan. Spread the fruit and nut mixture over this, then spread the rest of the batter.

Bake for 50 minutes. Turn out of the pan onto a wire rack to cool.

Glazed Banana Bread

Yield: 1 loaf

2 cups self-rising whole-wheat flour

2 tablespoons wheat germ

½ teaspoon baking soda

3 tablespoons butter

¾ cup powdered sugar

6½ ounces cottage cheese

2 eggs

1 cup mashed bananas (very ripe bananas!)

Preheat the oven to 350°F. Grease an 8×6-inch loaf pan.

Sift the flour, wheat germ, and baking soda together into a bowl, adding any coarser bits left in the sieve.

In a separate bowl, cream the butter, sugar, and cottage cheese together. Add the eggs, one at a time, beating between each addition. Fold in the flour mixture and the mashed banana alternately. Pour into the pan.

Bake for 1 hour. Turn out onto a wire rack to cool.

If you like, spread Warm Glacé Icing (see recipe, page 102) over the loaf and top with a few slices of fresh banana cut diagonally and brushed with lemon juice. With or without icing, it is wonderful with mint tea.

Turkish Fig Bar

Yield: 1 cake

1 stick butter

1 cup brown sugar

½ cup milk

1 teaspoon vanilla extract

3 egg yolks

2 cups self-rising flour

¾ teaspoon baking powder

pinch of salt

1 teaspoon grated nutmeg

3 egg whites, stiffly beaten

Fig Filling:
1 cup chopped dried figs

2 tablespoons honey

1 tablespoon finely grated lemon rind

2 cups water

2 teaspoons cornstarch

Prepare the filling first. Simmer the figs, honey, and lemon rind in water for 10 minutes. Mix the cornstarch with a little cold water to dissolve it, then add it to the simmering figs. Cook until it becomes very thick.

Preheat the oven to 350°F. Lightly grease a large loaf pan.

Blend the butter and sugar together well. Add the milk, vanilla, and egg yolks and mix well. Sift in the flour, baking powder, salt, and nutmeg, beating well. Fold in the stiffly beaten egg whites.

Spread half of the batter in the pan. On this, spread the filling, then cover with the rest of the batter.

Bake for 35 to 45 minutes. Turn out of the pan onto a wire rack to cool.

Fresh Apple Cake

Yield: 1 cake

1 cup brown sugar
2 eggs
½ cup vegetable oil
1 teaspoon vanilla extract
3 tablespoons milk
3 cups diced fresh apple (about 4 apples, cored)
2 cups whole-wheat flour
1 teaspoon baking powder
½ teaspoon salt
½ teaspoon ground cinnamon
½ teaspoon grated nutmeg

Preheat the oven to 350°F. Grease and flour a 9-inch-square cake pan.

Beat together the sugar and eggs until thick and light. Beat in the oil and vanilla and milk. Stir in the diced apple.

In a separate bowl sift together the flour, baking powder, salt, and spices, then fold this into the apple mixture. Pour into the cake pan.

Bake for 45 minutes. Serve warm, perhaps with hot custard or with a yogurt and honey mix.

Chocolate Prune Cake

Yield: 1 cake

1 cup whole prunes
1 stick butter
1 cup brown sugar
2 eggs
1 cup self-rising flour
1 cup self-rising whole-wheat flour
½ cup cocoa
½ teaspoon ground clove
½ cup prune-cooking water

Preheat the oven to 350°F. Grease an 8×6-inch square pan.

Gently simmer the prunes in 2 cups of water for 8 minutes. Cool, and drain, saving the liquid. Remove the pits.

Beat the butter and sugar until creamy. Add the eggs, and beat until well mixed. Sift in the flours, cocoa, and ground clove. Add the prunes and stir in, adding ½ cup of the prune-cooking liquid. Pour into the pan.

Bake for 40 minutes. Allow to cool in the pan.

The cake can later be iced with a chocolate icing (see recipe, page 102).

Chocolate Prune Cake with Walnuts

To the batter for Chocolate Prune Cake, add ½ cup of chopped walnuts.

Ice with a coffee icing (see recipe, page 102) and sprinkle with walnut meal.

Orange-Blossom Cake

Yield: 1 cake

1 stick butter
1¼ cups brown sugar
1 cup milk
3 egg yolks
4 teaspoons orange-blossom water
2 cups whole-wheat flour
2 teaspoons baking powder
½ teaspoon salt
½ teaspoon ground clove
1 cup slivered blanched almonds
1 cup currants
2 tablespoons coarsely grated orange rind
3 egg whites, stiffly beaten

Preheat the oven to 350°F. Grease a large loaf pan.

Blend the butter and sugar together well. Add the milk, egg yolks, and orange-blossom water.

Into a separate bowl, sift together the flour, baking powder, salt, and ground clove, then add this to the mixture and beat well. Add the almonds, currants, and orange rind; mix well. Fold in the stiffly beaten egg whites. Spread into the pan.

Bake for 35 to 45 minutes. Turn out of the pan onto a wire rack.

The cake can be glazed while hot (see recipe, page 121), or after it has cooled it can be coated with a thin icing and sprinkled with finely chopped mixed peel. Serve with black China tea.

Right: **Clockwise from top right: Chocolate Prune Cake (above left); Orange-Blossom Cake (see above); Lemon Yogurt Cake (see p. 40).**

Greek Coconut Cake

Yield: 1 cake

1 stick butter
1 cup sugar
4 eggs, beaten
2 cups flaked coconut
1 cup self-rising flour
Syrup: ***1½ cups sugar***
1¼ cups water
fresh grated rind of ½ lemon

Preheat the oven to 450°F. Grease a deep-sided 8-inch-square cake pan.

Cream the butter and sugar until light and fluffy. Add well-beaten eggs; beat well. Fold in the coconut and sifted flour; mix well. Spread the mixture in the cake pan.

Bake for 15 minutes or until the top is golden brown, then reduce the heat to 300°F and bake for another 25 minutes.

Allow to cool for 5 minutes in the pan, then pour over the prepared syrup. Allow the cake to become cold in the pan before turning it out.

Syrup: Stir the sugar, water, and lemon rind in a saucepan over low heat until the sugar has dissolved. Increase the heat to bring it to a boil, then reduce the heat and simmer for 5 minutes. Pour hot over cake.

Pineapple Bread

Yield: 1 loaf

2 cups whole-wheat flour
1 teaspoon baking powder
½ teaspoon salt
1 cup raisins
1 cup chopped walnuts
1 egg
½ cup honey
2 tablespoons vegetable oil
1 tablespoon vanilla extract
1 teaspoon baking soda
1 cup finely chopped pineapple

Preheat the oven to 350°F. Grease a loaf pan.

Sift the dry ingredients into a bowl. Add the raisins and walnuts.

In a separate bowl beat together the egg, honey, oil, and vanilla, then add this to the flour mixture.

Dissolve the baking soda with the pineapple, and stir it into the batter. Pour into the pan.

Bake for 1 hour. Turn the bread out onto a wire rack to cool.

Prune Health Loaf

Yield: 1 loaf

½ stick butter
¾ cup brown sugar
6½ ounces cottage cheese
finely grated rind of 1 lemon
2 eggs
½ cup halved and pitted prunes
1 tablespoon lemon juice
2 cups self-rising whole-wheat flour
2 tablespoons wheat germ
1 teaspoon mixed spice (cinnamon, nutmeg, allspice)

Preheat the oven to 325°F. Grease an 8×6-inch loaf pan.

Cream together the butter and sugar until light and fluffy. Blend in the cottage cheese and lemon rind. Add the eggs one at a time, beating well between each addition. Fold in the remaining ingredients, and pour the mixture into the pan.

Bake for 1 hour. Turn out of the pan and allow to cool on a wire rack. Serve sliced, with butter

Soda Bread

Yield: 1 loaf

4 cups flour
4 level teaspoons baking powder
1 teaspoon salt
2 tablespoons margarine
2 teaspoons powdered sugar
1 cup buttermilk
¼ cup milk

Preheat the oven to 400°F. Flour a baking sheet.

Sift the flour, baking powder, and salt into a bowl. Rub in the margarine until the mixture resembles bread crumbs.

Mix in the sugar. Make a depression in the center and add the buttermilk and milk. Mix to a soft dough with a broad-bladed knife (add a little more milk if necessary). Turn out onto a floured surface and knead lightly. Shape into a round and flatten slightly. Place on the baking sheet, and mark the top with a knife into six equal triangles for easy breaking when baked.

Bake for about 30 minutes. Cool on a wire rack, and serve with butter and/or cream cheese.

Spiced Banana Scones

Yield: 12 scones

2 cups self-rising flour

pinch of salt

¾ stick butter

⅔ cup milk

an additional 2 tablespoons butter, melted

1 ripe banana

2 tablespoons brown sugar

½ teaspoon ground cinnamon

½ teaspoon grated nutmeg

Preheat the oven to 425°F. Lightly grease a baking sheet.

Sift the flour and salt into a bowl. Rub in the butter until the mixture resembles fine bread crumbs. Add the milk, and mix to a soft dough. Turn out onto a floured surface, knead lightly, and then roll out to about ¼ inch thick. Cut into 12 rounds and brush the surface of each with melted butter.

Peel and mash the banana with a little brown sugar, and spread this over half of each round. Fold over and press the edges together firmly. Brush the tops with melted butter and sprinkle thickly with the sugar, cinnamon, and nutmeg. Place on the baking sheet, sugar side up.

Bake for 10 to 15 minutes. Serve warm, and don't allow them to dry out.

Damper

Yield: 1 loaf

4 cups self-rising flour

2 teaspoons salt

2 tablespoons butter

1 tablespoon sugar

1½ cups water

1 egg yolk

1 tablespoon milk

Preheat the oven to 375°F.

Sift the flour and salt into a bowl. Rub in the butter. Then mix in the sugar. Make a well in the center of the mixture. Pour in the water and, using your hand, mix to a soft dough. Turn out onto a floured surface and knead until smooth.

Grease a 6- to 8-cup casserole dish with butter. Place the dough in the casserole rounded side up and cut a cross in the top. Beat the egg yolk and milk together, then brush this over the dough; it will give the damper a beautiful golden glaze. Cover with a well-greased lid or a buttered piece of aluminum foil.

Bake for about 45 minutes. Uncover for the last half of the cooking. Leave for a few minutes before turning out of the dish. Serve in thick slices.

Easy Fruit Bread

Yield: 1 loaf

4 cups self-rising flour

1 teaspoon grated nutmeg

½ stick butter

1 cup brown sugar

1½ cups raisins

1⅔ cups currants

⅓ cup mixed peel

1 egg

1½ cups milk

1 cup light corn syrup

Preheat the oven to 375°F. Grease a large loaf pan.

Mix all the ingredients together well with an electric beater. Pour the mixture into the pan.

Bake for 1 hour. Turn out onto a wire rack to cool.

Lemon and Apricot Bread

Yield: 1 loaf

¾ stick butter

1 cup sugar

2 eggs

1½ cups flour

1½ teaspoons baking powder

¼ teaspoon salt

½ cup milk

1 tablespoon grated lemon rind

1 tablespoon lemon juice

½ cup raisins

½ cup chopped dried apricots

Topping:
2 tablespoons lemon juice

½ cup sugar

Preheat the oven to 375°F. Grease a large loaf pan.

Melt the butter, and mix it in a bowl with the sugar. Add the eggs one at a time and beat well. Add the sifted flour, baking powder, and salt, alternately with the milk. Mix well. Fold in the lemon rind, lemon juice, raisins, and apricots. Pour into the pan and level the surface.

Bake for 50 to 60 minutes.

To prepare the topping: Stir the lemon juice and sugar in a saucepan oyer low heat until the sugar dissolves. While the bread is still hot, spoon the topping over it. Allow to cool in the pan.

Pumpkin Nut Bread

Yield: 1 loaf

1½ cups pumpkin puree

½ cup honey

½ cup brown sugar

½ cup vegetable oil

½ cup chopped dates

½ cup chopped walnuts

½ teaspoon salt

½ teaspoon ground cinnamon

½ teaspoon ground clove

2 teaspoons baking powder

1 cup all-purpose white flour

1¼ cups whole-wheat flour

2 tablespoons wheat germ

Peel, chop, and cook the pumpkin, then mash or puree enough to make 1½ cups of puree.

Preheat the oven to 350°F. Grease a deep loaf pan.

In a large bowl, combine the honey, brown sugar, vegetable oil, pumpkin puree, dates, walnuts, salt, cinnamon, cloves, and baking powder. Mix well.

Stir in the remaining ingredients, then pour the mixture into the pan.

Bake for about 1 hour. Cool in the pan for 20 minutes, then turn out onto a wire rack.

Right: **Clockwise from top: Pumpkin Nut Bread (see above); Lemon and Apricot Bread (see above left); Butter Cake with Crumble Topping (see p. 36).**

Whole-Wheat Pound Cake

Yield: 1 cake

2 sticks butter
2 cups brown sugar
3 eggs, lightly beaten
1 teaspoon grated lemon rind
2¼ cups sifted whole-wheat flour
1 teaspoon baking powder
½ teaspoon salt
1 cup plain yogurt with 1 teaspoon vanilla extract mixed in

Preheat the oven to 325°F. Grease a 10-inch loaf pan. Dust with flour and shake out the excess.

Cream the butter until light. Gradually beat in the sugar. Add the beaten eggs, and mix thoroughly. Mix in the lemon rind, then the flour, baking powder, salt, and yogurt. Spread into the cake pan.

Bake for 65 minutes. Let cool in the pan for 15 minutes, then transfer to a wire rack.

Good with thick Citrus Frosting (see recipe, page 102).

Note: Instead of all whole-wheat flour, half all-purpose and half whole-wheat flour can be used.

Whole-Wheat Date Scones

Yield: 15 scones

1 cup self-rising flour
1½ cups self-rising whole-wheat flour
2 teaspoons fresh wheat-germ
pinch of salt
¼ teaspoon grated nutmeg
1 teaspoon ground cinnamon
½ teaspoon grated lemon rind
½ stick butter
4 ounces dates, chopped
2 tablespoons honey
1 egg
½ cup milk

Preheat the oven to 450°F. Grease a baking tray. Sift the dry ingredients into a large bowl. Add the lemon rind. Rub in the butter until the mixture resembles fine bread crumbs. Add the dates; mix lightly. Make a depression in the center.

In a separate bowl combine the honey, egg, and milk. Pour this into the well in the larger bowl. Mix to a soft dough. Turn out onto a floured surface and knead lightly. Pat out to ¾ inch thick and cut into 15 rounds. Place close together on the baking tray. Brush the tops with extra milk.

Bake for 12 to 15 minutes. Serve warm, or let cool on a wire rack.

Ginger Fig Scones

Yield: 10 to 12 scones

2 cups self-rising flour
pinch of salt
1 teaspoon dry ground ginger
1½ ounces margarine
1 cup thinly sliced dried figs
4 tablespoons water, mixed with 4 tablespoons milk
milk for glazing

Preheat the oven to 450°F. (Do not grease the baking tray.)

Sift the flour, salt, and ginger together into a bowl. Rub in the margarine. Add the sliced figs and then the milk–water mixture to make a soft dough. Turn out onto a floured surface and knead lightly. Pat out to ¾ inch thick and cut into 10 to 12 rounds. Set the rounds close together on the baking tray. Brush with milk.

Bake near the top of the oven for about 10 minutes. Allow to cool on a wire rack.

Caraway Raisin Scones

Using the basic recipe for Ginger Fig Scones, replace the ginger with 2 teaspoons of caraway seeds and ½ teaspoon of ground caraway. Replace the figs with 1 cup raisins.

Gem Scones

Yield: 10 scones

2 tablespoons butter
2 tablespoons sugar
1 egg
pinch of salt
½ cup milk
1 cup self-rising flour

Preheat the oven to 400°F. Heat the muffin tins in the oven.

Cream the butter and sugar. Add the egg, salt, and milk, and mix well. Lightly fold in the sifted flour.

Grease the hot muffin tins. Spoon the batter into them, filling each cup three-quarters full.

Bake for 10 to 15 minutes. Serve warm.

Variations: The basic batter for gem scones is simple to make, and the flavor can be varied in many ways. These are just a few:

Add ½ cup of raisins to the batter.

For a delicious savory flavor, add 2 tablespoons of chopped fresh dill, ½ teaspoon of paprika, 2 tablespoons of grated Parmesan cheese, and about 1 extra tablespoon of milk. Mix well into the batter.

Another variation—add 2 tablespoons of coconut to the batter. Then, when filling the muffin tins with batter, place 1 drop of marmalade in the center of each scone before baking.

Paprika Scone Round

Yield: 1 loaf

½ cup flour
1⅓ cups whole-wheat flour
3 level teaspoons baking powder
1 teaspoon salt
1 teaspoon paprika
sprinkle of ground dried chilies
1 teaspoon dried marjoram
¼ cup brown sugar
½ stick margarine
⅔ cup milk

Preheat the oven to 450°F. Lightly flour the baking sheet.

Sift all the dry ingredients together into a bowl. Rub in the margarine until the mixture resembles bread crumbs. Mix in enough of the milk to give a light dough. Mix with a broad knife blade so as not to remove the air between the particles. This would result in a heavy scone.

Turn out onto a floured surface; knead lightly. Shape into a round. Mark the top surface with a knife blade into six equal triangles.

Bake near the top of an oven for about 15 minutes. Serve warm. Cut into the six pieces and butter each liberally. Good with Romano cheese and a five o'clock sherry.

Cakes

Modern Cake-Making Techniques

With few exceptions, the methods used for the mixing of the various types of cakes fall into one of the following categories.

- *Rubbing* the shortening through the dry ingredients—this method produces a fairly dry, coarse cake that is usually used for inexpensive luncheon loaves and slices.
- *Creaming* the shortening and sugar together before the addition of the eggs and other ingredients—this method is used for light, medium, and rich butter cakes, with or without added fruits, nuts, etc., as desired.
- *Beating* of the eggs (or egg whites) and sugar until thickened and increased in volume before folding in the dry ingredients—this method makes the light-textured sponge varieties with little or no shortening added.
- *Mixing* of the melted shortening (or oil) with the other liquid or moist ingredients before the addition of the flour—this is an extremely popular quick-and-easy method for a large number of modern cakes suitable for all occasions.

Differences in texture and appearance are mainly due to the method chosen for combining the balanced ingredients before the cake is baked.

Secrets of Success

When it comes to turning out a blue-ribbon cake every time, creative instinct is not enough. The straight and narrow path of correct proportions, careful attention to techniques, and a reliable baking oven are of the utmost importance.

Here is a list of the basic steps to be considered for successful cake-making.

- Use a recipe from a reliable source.
- Weigh or measure ingredients accurately.
- Use the size of cake pan recommended.
- Line and/or grease the cake pan as instructed.
- Check the oven manufacturer's instructions to ensure the correct oven temperature, shelf position, etc.
- Follow the steps in the recipe carefully—beating, whisking, folding, etc., as instructed.
- Avoid opening the oven door during at least the first three-quarters of the baking time. Then open it only sparingly to ascertain the final baking time required.
- Allow the cake to "settle" in the pan before turning it out onto a wire cake rack to cool away from any drafts.
- Do not ice the cake until it is completely cold.

Greasing Cake Pans

Most cake pans—even the so-called nonstick cake pans—need to be lightly greased on the inside before adding the cake mixture, so that the baked cake will turn out easily onto a rack or cooler without leaving part of the base, corners, or sides adhering to the pan. Greasing should be done by evenly brushing or spreading a light layer of softened or melted shortening over the inside surface of the pan. Heavily salted shortenings should be avoided, as the salt content may cause sticking problems. Allow the shortening to reset before spooning in the cake mixture.

Note: Some cakes, particularly the light "chiffon" or "angel" cake varieties are baked in ungreased or oiled pans but this will always be mentioned in the recipe instructions.

Flouring Cake Pans

An extra precaution against sticking may be taken by lightly dusting the freshly greased surface of the cake pan with flour. Sprinkle 1 to 2 teaspoons of flour into the base of the pan and, while slightly tilting the pan to all sides, gently tap the outside to distribute the flour. Tip out any excess and allow the shortening to reset before use.

A second method is to spread a mixture of softened shortening and flour lightly over the inside surface of the pan and allow it to set before adding the cake mixture.

Lining Cake Pans

The precaution of lining cake pans before using for baking cakes can have two purposes.

1. To ensure that cakes—particularly high-ratio sugar cakes—do not stick in the pans and break when turned out. Using greaseproof (not wax-coated) paper, cut strips to fit the sides and/or base of the pan neatly, press over the freshly greased inside surface, and grease again. When cooked and turned out, the paper will adhere to the cake and may be carefully peeled away.
2. Two, three, or even four layers of paper—or 1 to 2 layers of aluminum foil with an inner layer of greaseproof—may be used for large, heavily fruited cakes that require long, slow baking. This thicker lining is allowed to protrude 1 or 2 inches above the top of the pan and acts as an insulator so that the outside of the cake does not become too browned and hard before the center is cooked. Very large cakes may also be further protected by a sheet of foil or paper placed loosely over the top for the first half or two-thirds of the baking time so that the top does not become too hard and crusted.

Testing During Baking

Browned cakes are not necessarily cooked cakes. Test carefully to avoid disappointment.

- Firm yet springy to the touch—a gentle pressure with 1 or 2 fingertips on the surface will give a good indication for the lighter cakes.
- Slight shrinkage from the sides of the cake pan—again, this applies to lighter cakes and sponges.
- Insert a very fine skewer through the thickest section of the cake—no moist cake mixture should remain on the skewer on removal from firmer or larger cakes. Note that cake mixture on the skewer is not to be confused with particles of dried fruits, etc., from the richer cakes and loaves.

If in doubt, leave a little longer. A slightly overcooked cake is better than one that sinks in the middle after removal from the oven.

Reasons for Unsuccessful Cakes
- *Cakes sinking in the middle*
Too much sugar, too little flour. Too much raising agent, too much liquid. Incompletely cooked.
- *Surface cracking on cakes*
Too much flour, too little liquid. Too high an oven temperature. Too small a cake pan.
- *Excessively moist or "soggy" cakes*
Too much liquid, too much sugar. Ingredients insufficiently mixed. Too slow an oven temperature. Incompletely cooked.
- *Coarse cake texture*
Undermixing or overmixing of ingredients. Too much raising agent. Too much shortening (butter, margarine, etc.).
- *Rising and sinking while in the oven*
Too much liquid, too much raising agent. Too frequent/too soon opening of the oven door. Slamming the oven door to close it.
- *Hard, crusty top and sides*
Oven temperature too hot. Cake is overbaked.
- *Sticky, moist top*
Cake is underbaked. Contains too much sugar. Paper or foil placed on top creates steaming.
- *Heavy, compact texture*
Too little raising agent. Too much mixing after adding flour. Ingredient balance needs adjustment.

Note: Apart from the above-mentioned problems that may account for unsuccessful cake-baking, high altitude can affect the action of certain agents in cake-making. The quantities of some ingredients may need to be altered—such as additional liquids, less raising agents, etc.

Cake-Making Ingredients
Only the best-quality, fresh ingredients can make a good cake:
- *Butter or margarine* should not show any signs of rancidity or foreign odors or flavors from incorrect storage.
- *Eggs* should be fresh. Store them in the refrigerator, but allow them time to warm to room temperature before use in cake-making.
- *Sugars* should be stored correctly and not allowed to absorb extra moisture. Use the specified type for best results.
- *Flours* that are freshly packaged retain their correct moisture content. Self-rising flours kept too long lose some of the rising ability.
- *Liquids,* such as water, milk, fruit juices, and wines, should be used at room temperature unless otherwise stated. Use accurate measures.
- *Flavoring ingredients,* such as ground spices, dried fruits, coffee, chocolate or cocoa, should be as fresh as possible. Experienced cake-makers can sometimes alter a recipe by varying these ingredients, being sure to substitute others of a similar type and texture.

All ingredients should be assembled, cake pans prepared, and ovens set for preheating, before commencing to mix a cake.

Freezing Cakes
Before the advent of the freezer, the life of a cake was limited to the time it was able to be kept fresh when stored in an airtight container. Storage in the home freezer has increased that life to 3 to 6 months or more, depending on the type of cake and its filling and/or frosting.

For most practical purposes it is easier to freeze and store unfilled and undecorated cakes. But sometimes, when entertaining a large number of people, freezing the complete cake is more convenient.

Wrap unfilled, undecorated cakes while fresh (but not hot) in plastic wrap, freezer bags, or aluminum foil. Exclude as much air as possible before sealing, and freeze quickly to avoid the formation of too many ice crystals that can cause the cake to become overmoist when thawed.

Filled, frosted and decorated cakes should be placed uncovered in the freezer to freeze quickly. Once firm, remove them from the freezer, wrap and seal securely and return them to the freezer as quickly as possible for storage.

Uncooked cake batters already prepared and in the greased cake pan can be frozen. To cook, unwrap the cake pan and place it in the refrigerator to partially defrost before baking in the oven.

Defrosting Frozen Cakes
Plain cakes should be unsealed and left at room temperature, with the wrapping loosened but not completely removed, for 1 to 3 hours according to size.

Filled and decorated cakes may be unwrapped and allowed to thaw in the refrigerator for several hours or overnight.

Microwave ovens, with a defrosting versatility, are extremely handy for the quick and easy thawing of cakes. However, these are then likely to become stale sooner than traditionally thawed cakes.

The most successful fillings and icings or frostings for freezer cakes are those with a reasonably high content of shortening (butter, margarine, etc.). Water icings tend to become brittle and, unless properly thawed, may cause moistness to develop immediately under the surface.

Quantity cake-baking, coupled with the use of a freezer for storing, is the most convenient and economical way to keep a supply of homemade confections on hand for use at short notice.

Covering the Cake with Icing
Rich fruit cakes made for various celebrations, such as weddings, birthdays, christenings, and anniversaries, are usually covered with two types of icing:
- *Almond or Mock Almond Paste* (see recpies, page 102). This undercoat or foundation icing not only provides the basic shape for the cake but also adds flavor and helps the cake keep longer.
- *Fondant Covering Paste* (see recipe, page 111. The outer or final covering icing not only gives a professional finish to the cake but also provides a smooth, attractive background for the applied decorations. For those who prefer to dispense with the almond paste because of cost or personal taste, a double

thickness of fondant paste may be used. Allow the undercoat to become firm and dry—a period of 2 to 3 days—before applying the final fondant covering.

If the cake has been stored:

- Carefully peel away the paper lining from the cake, taking particular care not to damage corners or edges.
- If the cake has risen slightly in a dome, cut it off with a sharp knife to level it, and turn it upside down onto a board. The cake must sit firm and straight.
- Brush over the top and sides to remove any loose cake crumbs.
- Using small pieces of the almond paste (or fondant undercoat), patch up any cracks, holes or broken edges so that a good shape is produced for the final covering.
- Brush over the entire surface of the cake with lightly beaten egg white, let it stand for 20 to 30 minutes, then brush over again and lift the cake onto a clean sheet of aluminum foil or greaseproof paper. The Almond or Mock Almond Paste and the Fondant Covering Paste can be made beforehand. Keep almond paste and fondant paste in airtight containers to prevent surface drying. Just before use, knead until soft and pliable again.

The techniques for covering the cake apply to both almond paste and fondant paste:

- Measure the exterior of the cake with a ruler or flexible tape measure in one motion, going up one side of the cake, across the top, and down the other side, thus giving an approximate size for the covering.
- Roll out the paste to a round or square shape slightly smaller than the measurement obtained—the paste will stretch slightly when it is placed on the cake. Lift the paste continually from the board so that it does not stick underneath. If using sifted confectioners' sugar on the board, use as little as possible because it may make the paste too firm and dry.
- Carefully lift the paste onto the prepared cake, using a rolling pin for assistance in centering the paste so that it falls evenly down the sides of the cake.
- Dust the palms of each hand with powdered sugar. Starting on the top of the cake, smooth the paste over the cake with a light swirling motion.
- Cup the palms and smooth the paste over the edge and sides, paying particular attention to the corners of square cakes. Avoid putting too much pressure on the paste because it will show handprints.
- Trim away any excess paste at the base of the cake with a large sharp knife. Brush away any excess sugar and paste crumbs from around the base (not over the cake).
- Set aside to dry for 2 to 3 days before applying the final coating.

The techniques above apply to both almond paste and fondant paste. For fondant covering:

- After rolling out the paste on a lightly coated board, carefully prick any air bubbles in the surface with a very fine needle. Smooth over gently.
- Once the fondant paste has been lifted onto the cake, a light dusting of cornstarch on the palms of the hands before smoothing over will give an extra smoothness and shine to the surface.
- After the fondant paste has dried sufficiently, remove the cake from its foil or paper base and lift it onto its final plate or foil-covered board ready for decoration. To prevent slipping during movement and/or transport, spread a little Royal Icing under the cake (see recipe, page 102).

Decorations for Celebration Cakes

For handmade decorations two types of icing can be used:

- *Modeling Fondant* (see recipe, page 114). A smooth pliable dough paste used for hand-modeling flowers, leaves, etc., to be used as the decorative feature on the cake.
- *Royal Icing* (see recipe, page 102). A thin smooth icing that is filled into a piping bag with shaped nozzles for simple or elaborate pipework, and small flower and leaf designs.

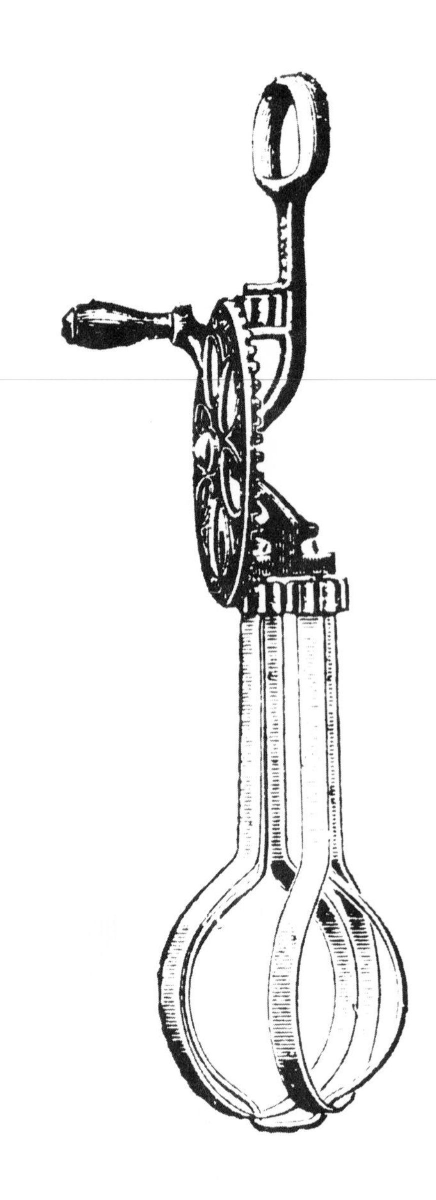

Continental Cream Sponge

Yield: 1 layer cake

2 eggs

1 cup powdered sugar, slightly warmed

1 teaspoon vanilla extract

2 cups flour

2 teaspoons baking powder

¼ teaspoon salt

1¼ cups cream, lightly whipped

Hungarian Hazelnut Filling (see recipe, page 112)

confectioners' sugar, for topping

Preheat the oven to 325°F. Grease and flour a 9-inch-square pan.

Beat the eggs until very frothy. Gradually add the warmed powdered sugar, beating each addition until well dissolved. Then add the vanilla extract with the last addition of sugar.

Sift the flour, baking powder, and salt together. Sift about half of this over the egg–sugar mixture and fold in gently. Gently fold in about half of the lightly whipped cream. Repeat the flour and cream addition with the remaining mixtures—do not overmix. Spoon into the pan.

Bake for 55 to 60 minutes. Turn out carefully onto a cake rack to cool.

When cold, cut in half and sandwich together with the Hungarian Hazelnut Filling between the layers; dust sifted powdered sugar over the top. Chill slightly before serving in slices.

Jelly Roll

Yield: 1 jelly roll

¾ cup self-rising flour

pinch of salt

3 eggs

¾ cup powdered sugar

1 tablespoon hot water

3 to 4 tablespoons warm jam

whipped cream

powdered sugar for dredging

Grease a 15×11×1-inch jelly-roll pan and line with greased greaseproof paper.

Set oven temperature at 400°F. Sift the flour with the salt. Place the eggs and sugar in a bowl and stand over a pan of gently simmering, not boiling, water. Whisk well until the mixture is very thick and creamy.

Remove the bowl from the heat and continue whisking until the mixture is cool. Fold in the flour as lightly as possible, then the hot water. Pour the mixture into the prepared pan. Bake for 7 to 10 minutes, until pale golden. Do not overcook, as it makes rolling up difficult.

Quickly turn the sponge out onto a tea towel, well sprinkled with powdered suger. Trim off the crisp edges, roll in the towel, cool, then unroll.

Spread with jam and whipped cream. Roll up. Sprinkle with a little more powdered sugar before serving.

Spiced Honey Sponge

Yield: 1 layered sponge cake

3 eggs, separated

½ cup powdered sugar

1 teaspoon vanilla extract

¾ cup self-rising flour

2 tablespoons cornstarch

1 teaspoon mixed spices (cinnamon, ginger, nutmeg, allspice)

¼ teaspoon salt

¼ cup milk, scalding hot

1 tablespoon honey

1 tablespoon butter

whipped sweetened cream, for filling

confectioners' sugar, for topping

mixed spices, for topping (cinnamon, nutmeg, allspice)

Preheat the oven to 350°F. Grease and flour two 7-inch layer-cake pans.

Beat the egg whites until stiff peaks form; gradually add the sugar, beating well after each addition. Fold in the egg yolks and vanilla extract.

Sift the dry ingredients twice. Then sift this again over the egg mixture, and fold in lightly.

Combine the milk, honey, and butter. Slowly pour this down the side of the bowl into the egg–flour mixture, folding in very lightly. Pour into the prepared pans.

Bake for 22 to 25 minutes. Remove from the oven and allow to stand for 1 to 2 minutes before carefully turning out onto a fine mesh cake rack to cool.

When cold, join the two layers with the whipped cream, and dust the top with sifted confectioners' sugar and mixed spices.

Basic or Foundation Butter Cake

1 stick butter or margarine, softened

½ cup sugar

1 teaspoon vanilla extract

2 eggs

2 cups self-rising flour

¼ teaspoon salt

½ cup milk

The following proportions make a softer cake more suited to larger cakes, loaves, layer cakes, etc.

1 stick butter or margarine, softened

¾ cup powdered sugar

1 teaspoon vanilla extract

3 eggs

2 cups self-rising flour

¼ teaspoon salt

¼ cup milk

The mixing methods are the same. Either can be made for the following sizes of cake pans. The baking temperatures and times vary according to the size (and depth) of cake and added flavoring ingredients.

Two 7-inch layer-cake pans: 350°F for 25 to 30 minutes.
One 11×7-inch or 9-inch pan: 350°F for 40 to 45 minutes.
One 7- to 8-inch ring pan: 350°F for 35 to 40 minutes.
Two 9½×2½-inch pans: 350°F for 30 to 35 minutes.
One 9×4½-inch deep-sided loaf pan: 325°F for 55 to 60 minutes.
One 8-inch deep-sided cake pan: 325°F for 55 to 60 minutes.
Twenty-four small or twenty large muffin tins: 375°F for 15 to 17 minutes.

Preheat the oven to the temperature specified for the size of the cake pan(s). Grease the cake pan(s) well.

Beat the butter and sugar with the vanilla until light and creamy. Add the eggs one at a time, beating well after each addition.

Sift the flour and salt together. Sift and fold into the butter–sugar–eggs mixture in alternate batches with the milk, adding about a third of each at a time; mix lightly but thoroughly.

Spoon into the greased cake pan(s) and bake in the preheated oven according to temperature and times above. Remove from the oven and allow to stand for 3 to 7 minutes before turning out onto a cake rack to cool.

Flavored Variations:

Chocolate: Before mixing, heat the milk and add 2 tablespoons of cocoa to it. Allow to cool before use.

Mocha: Before mixing, heat the milk and add 2 tablespoons of cocoa and 1 teaspoon of instant coffee powder. Allow to cool before use.

Raisin: Add ⅓ to ½ cup raisins and 1 teaspoon mixed spices with the flour.

Cherry Almond: Add 2 tablespoons of chopped candied cherries and 2 tablespoons of slivered almonds with the flour.

Date: Add ⅓ to ½ cup of chopped dates and 1 teaspoon grated lemon rind with the flour.

Banana: Add ¾ to 1 cup of mashed banana with the flour and 1 teaspoon of baking soda dissolved in the milk.

Orange: Add 2 teaspoons of grated orange rind with the flour and substitute orange juice for the milk.

Coconut: Add ⅓ to ½ cup of flaked coconut with the flour and an extra 1 to 2 tablespoons of milk.

Marble Cake

Divide the cake mixture into three portions. Add 2 tablespoons of melted chocolate to one portion; color the second portion with pink food coloring; and leave the third portion plain.

Spoon alternate portions into the prepared deep-sided cake pan and swirl lightly with a fine knife blade to produce a marbled effect. Bake as above.

Rainbow Cake

Prepare 2 quantities of cake mixture. Grease three 8-inch layer pans.

Divide the cake mixture into three portions. To one portion, add 2 tablespoons of cocoa that has been dissolved in 3 tablespoons of hot milk or water and allowed to cool; color the second portion with pink food coloring and add 1 teaspoon of strawberry extract; and leave the third portion plain.

Place each portion into one of the prepared cake pans and bake as above.

When cold, sandwich together in chocolate, pink, and white formation, using jams (jelly) as the filling. Ice with Warm Glacé Icing (see recipe, page 102).

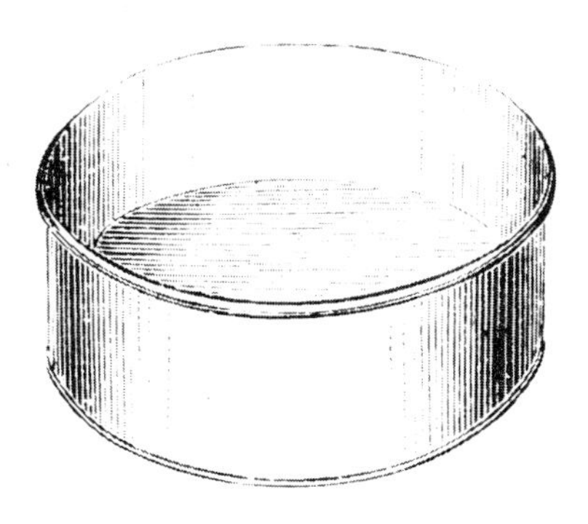

Pecan Prune Rolls

Yield: 2 nut-roll cakes

1¼ cups prunes, pits removed
1 cup water
1 stick butter or margarine, softened
1 cup sugar
2 tablespoons grated orange rind
2 cups flour
2 teaspoons baking powder
¼ teaspoon salt
½ teaspoon baking soda
¼ cup orange juice or milk
½ cup chopped pecans

Preheat the oven to 350°F. Thoroughly grease and flour two 8×3-inch nut-roll pans with perforated lids (or some perforated aluminum foil to cover the tops).

Simmer the prunes in the water for 3 to 4 minutes. Set aside to cool, then remove the prunes and chop finely, reserving ½ cup of the prune liquid.

Beat the butter, sugar, and orange rind until light and fluffy. Gradually add the ½ cup of prune liquid, beating thoroughly. Sift the dry ingredients over the butter cream and fold in lightly. Add the prunes, orange juice, and pecans, and mix well. Spoon the mixture into the two pans and attach the perforated lids—or cover each with a rectangle of perforated aluminum foil.

Stand the nut-roll pans upright in the oven and bake for 35 to 40 minutes. Remove from the oven remove the lids, and allow to stand for 5 to 6 minutes before carefully turning out onto cake racks to cool.

Walnut Date Rolls
Substitute dates and walnuts for the prunes and pecans, and use grated lemon rind instead of the orange rind.

Blue Ribbon Sponge Sandwich

Yield: 2 sponge layers

3 eggs
½ cup powdered sugar
1 cup flour
1 tablespoon cornstarch
2 teaspoons baking powder
¼ teaspoon salt
2 teaspoons butter or margarine
¼ cup very hot water
½ teaspoon vanilla extract

Preheat the oven to 350°F. Grease two deep 7-inch layer-cake pans and dust lightly with flour.

Separate the eggs and place the whites in a clean, dry glass bowl; beat with an electric beater, hand beater, or egg whisk to stiff white foam. Add the powdered sugar 1 tablespoon at a time and beat well after each addition—the sugar must be completely dissolved. Fold in the egg yolks lightly and gently.

Sift the flour with the cornstarch, baking powder, and salt twice. Then sift this again over the egg mixture. (Don't mix it in yet.)

Melt the butter in the hot water, add the vanilla extract, and carefully pour down the side of the bowl into the egg mixture. Now, using a metal spoon and with a gentle folding motion, mix the dry ingredients and the liquid through the eggs and sugar. Pour the mixture gently into the two cake pans, being careful to avoid knocking or banging either the bowl or the pans. Spread lightly to even the surface.

Bake for 22 to 25 minutes, preferably both pans on the same oven shelf so that both sponges will be evenly cooked and browned. Remove from the oven and allow to stand for 1 minute—out of a draft—then turn carefully onto a fine mesh cake rack or a tea towel over a cake rack to cool.

Topping and Filling Variations:
Plain Sponge: Fill with raspberry jam and dust the top with sifted confectioners' sugar.
Cream Sponge: Fill with fresh whipped cream or Mock Cream (see recipe, page 112) and dust the top with powdered sugar.
Lemon Sponge: Fill with Lemon Butter Cream (see recipe, page 117) and dust the top with powdered sugar.
Toffee Sponge: Fill and top the sponge with fresh whipped cream and decorate with Toffee Topping (see recipe, page 110).
Strawberry Sponge: Fill and top with fresh whipped cream and decorate the top with whole or sliced strawberries.

Right: **Blue Ribbon Sponge Sandwich (see above).**

Rich Chocolate Butter Cake

Yield: 1 cake

2-inch strip of vanilla pod

½ cup milk, hot

6 ounces pure baking chocolate, chopped

1½ sticks butter, softened

¾ cup powdered sugar

4 eggs, separated

1 cup flour

½ cup cornstarch

1 teaspoon baking powder

½ teaspoon baking soda

Frosting:
4 squares (4 ounces) fruit and nut chocolate

2 tablespoons butter

¼ cup evaporated milk

½ cup confectioners' sugar, sifted

Soak the vanilla pod in hot milk for 30 minutes.

Preheat the oven to 350°F. Line the base of a deep-sided 8-inch cake pan, and grease it well.

Discard the vanilla pod, and add the chocolate to the now vanilla-flavored milk. Over a very low heat, stir in 2 tablespoons of the butter until well blended. Allow to cool.

Beat the remaining butter with the sugar until light and fluffy. Add the cooled chocolate mixture and beat well. Add the egg yolks one at a time and mix in lightly.

Sift the dry ingredients together, then sift them over the butter–chocolate mixture and fold in lightly. Beat the egg whites until they form stiff peaks, then gently fold into the mixture—do not overmix. Turn into the cake pan.

Bake for 60 to 80 minutes. Remove from the oven and allow to stand for 5 to 6 minutes before carefully turning out onto a cake rack to cool.

When cold, wrap a "collar" of greaseproof paper around the cake, allowing the top edge of the paper to stand about 1 inch above the surface of the cake.

Frosting: Chop the block of chocolate into small pieces, and melt it with the butter in a heatproof bowl placed over hot—not boiling—water. Remove from the heat, and stir in the evaporated milk and powdered sugar. Quickly pour onto the top of the cake. Allow the frosting to set before removing the greaseproof paper. Let stand overnight before cutting into slices.

Almond Butter Ring

Yield: 1 fluted ring cake

¼ cup flaked almonds, for coating

2 sticks butter, softened

2½ cups powdered sugar

1 teaspoon vanilla extract

½ teaspoon almond extract

5 eggs

2½ cups flour

½ teaspoon baking powder

½ teaspoon baking soda

¼ teaspoon salt

¾ cup sour cream

Preheat the oven to 325°F. Grease a 9-inch fluted ring cake pan and scatter the almonds over the surface, pressing on lightly; dust a little flour over all, shaking out all surplus.

Beat the butter, powdered sugar, vanilla extract, and almond extract until very light and frothy. Add the eggs one at a time; beat well after each addition.

Sift the dry ingredients together, then sift over the butter–egg mixture and fold in. Add the sour cream and fold in lightly but thoroughly. Spoon the cake mixture into the prepared cake pan.

Bake for 1½–1¾ hours. Remove from the oven and allow to stand for 5 to 6 minutes before turning out onto a cake rack to cool.

If desired, dust the cake lightly with sifted confectioners' sugar before serving.

Cherry Crystal Ring

Yield: 1 ring cake

¾ stick butter or margarine, softened

½ cup sugar

2 eggs

1½ cups self-rising flour, sifted

½ packet (2 ounces) cherry-flavored gelatin dessert

½ cup milk

Warm Glacé Icing (see recipe, page 102)

¼ cup sliced candied cherries

¼ cup flaked coconut, colored pink

Preheat the oven to 350°F. Thoroughly grease an 8-inch ring pan.

Beat the butter and sugar until creamy. Add the eggs one at a time, beating well after each addition. Fold in alternate batches of sifted flour, gelatin crystals, and milk, about a third of each at a time; mix lightly but thoroughly. Spoon into the ring pan.

Bake for 35 to 40 minutes. Remove from the oven and allow to stand for 2 to 3 minutes, then turn out onto a cake rack to cool.

When cold, ice with the Warm Glacé Icing and decorate with the cherry slices and coconut. If desired, the remaining ½ packet of cherry-flavored gelatin crystals may be used instead of the pink coconut.

Cherry Seed Cake

Yield: 1 fluted ring cake

2 sticks butter or margarine, softened

¼ teaspoon salt (optional)

1½ cups flour

4 eggs, separated

1 cup powdered sugar

1 to 2 tablespoons caraway seeds

⅔ cup candied cherries

extra ⅔ cup flour

1 teaspoon baking powder

Warm Glacé Icing (see recipe, page 102)

Preheat the oven to 325°F. Thoroughly grease and flour an 8- to 9-inch fluted ring pan.

In a large bowl, beat the butter until creamy, adding the salt if desired. Gradually add the sifted flour, beating well after each addition.

Beat the egg whites until still. Gradually add the sugar, beating well. Add the egg yolks and caraway seeds and beat for 1 to 2 minutes. Very lightly and gently, combine this into the butter–flour mixture. Slice the cherries into 3 or 4 rings, and fold them in.

Sift the extra flour with the baking powder, then sift over the mixture in the bowl and fold in carefully. Spoon into the well-greased and floured fluted ring pan.

Bake for 75 to 80 minutes. Remove from the oven and allow to stand for 4 to 5 minutes before turning onto a wire cake rack to cool.

When cold, drizzle the Warm Glacé Icing over, allowing it to run down between the flutes or grooves in the cake.

Frosted Banana-Cream Cake

Yield: 1 cake

1 stick butter or margarine, softened

1 cup sugar

1 teaspoon vanilla extract

½ teaspoon ground cinnamon (or nutmeg)

2 eggs, beaten

1 cup mashed ripe banana

¼ cup milk

2 cups flour

1½ teaspoons baking powder

1 teaspoon baking soda

¼ teaspoon salt

¼ cup chopped walnuts

Cinnamon Cream Frosting:
1 cup sour cream

¼ cup brown sugar

½ to 1 teaspoon ground cinnamon (or nutmeg)

Preheat the oven to 350°F. Line and grease an 11×7-inch pan.

Beat the butter, sugar, vanilla extract, and cinnamon (or nutmeg) until light and fluffy. Add the eggs, then the mashed banana and milk, beating well between each addition.

Sift the dry ingredients together, then sift over the butter–banana mixture and fold in. Add the walnuts and mix through. Turn into the pan.

Bake for 35 to 40 minutes. Remove from the oven and allow to stand for 5-to 6 minutes before turning out onto a cake rack to cool.

Frosting: Combine all the ingredients, beating well. Spread over the cake and allow to firm before slicing.

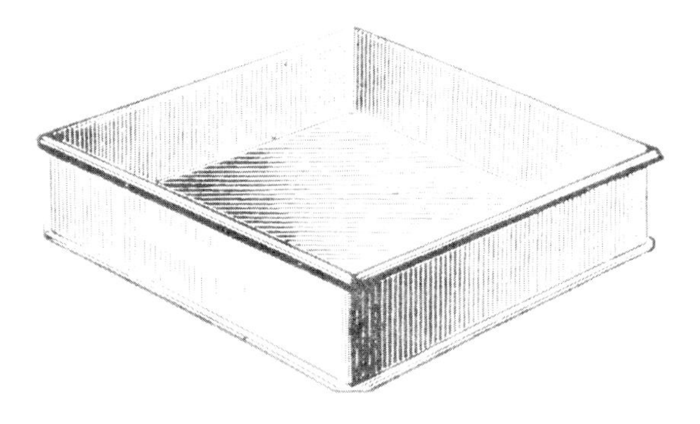

Continental Butter Ring Cake

Yield: 1 fluted ring cake

2 sticks unsalted butter, chopped

3 eggs, separated

1 cup sugar, very slightly warmed

1½ tablespoons brandy

⅞ cup milk

2 cups flour

3 teaspoons baking powder

½ cup chocolate drink powder

confectioners' sugar, for topping

Preheat the oven to 325°F. Grease and flour an 8-inch fluted ring pan.

Heat the butter until it is fully melted and beginning to color slightly; remove from the heat and set aside to cool.

Beat the egg whites in a clean dry bowl, preferably glass, until stiff peaks form. Beat the egg yolks and fold them in, then add the sugar, brandy, and milk; beat for 5 to 6 minutes.

Sift the flour and baking powder together, then sift again over the egg mixture and fold in lightly—do not overmix. Spoon half of the mixture into the fluted ring pan.

Sift the drinking chocolate over the remaining mixture and fold in lightly. Spoon this into the ring pan; and with a fine skewer, swirl the two mixtures to produce a marbled effect.

Bake for about 1¼ hours. Remove from the oven and allow to stand for 3 to 4 minutes; then turn onto a cake rack to cool.

Dust liberally with sifted powdered sugar before serving.

Classic Madeira Butter Cake

Yield: 1 cake

2 sticks butter or margarine, softened

1 cup powdered sugar

1 teaspoon vanilla extract

4 eggs

2 cups flour

1½ teaspoons baking powder

2 tablespoons chopped mixed peel

extra 1 tablespoon sugar, for topping

Preheat the oven to 325°F. Line the base of a deep-sided 8-inch cake pan and grease it well.

Beat the butter and sugar with the vanilla extract until very light and fluffy. Add the eggs one at a time, beating well between each addition. Sift the flour and baking powder over the mixture and stir gently to mix through. Spoon into the cake pan, and scatter the chopped peel and extra sugar evenly over the top.

Bake for 1¼ to 1½ hours. Remove from the oven and allow to stand for 8 to 10 minutes before turning out onto a wire cake rack to cool.

Note: Some recipes instruct that the mixed peel should be scattered over the surface of the cake about 30 minutes before the cake is finished baking If this is desired, care must be taken to do this quickly without removing the cake from the oven, or there is a considerable risk of the cake sinking in the center.

One-Bowl Butter Cake Supreme

Yield: 1 cake

1 cup self-rising flour

¼ cup custard powder

¼ teaspoon salt

1 cup powdered sugar

2 eggs

½ cup milk

1 teaspoon vanilla extract

1 stick butter, softened

Preheat the oven to 325°F. Line and grease a deep-sided 7-inch cake pan.

Sift the flour, custard powder, salt, and powdered sugar into a large bowl. Make a well in the center and break in the eggs. Add the milk, vanilla extract, and butter. Beat for 8 to 10 minutes (if using an electric mixer, set on medium speed) until the mixture is very smooth. Pour into the cake pan.

Bake for 1¼ hours. Remove from the oven and allow to stand for 3 to 4 minutes before turning out carefully onto a cake rack to cool. When cold, ice and decorate as desired.

Variation:

Citrus: Add 2 teaspoons of grated orange or lemon rind to the dry ingredients.

Choc-Coffee: Add 2 tablespoons of cocoa and 1 teaspoon of instant coffee powder to the dry ingredients, plus 1 extra tablespoon of milk.

Right: **Clockwise from top right: Almond Butter Ring (see p. 60); Rich Chocolate Butter Cake (see p. 60); Frosted Banana Cream Cake (see p. 61).**

Frosted Peanut-Butter Cake

Yield: 1 four-layer cake

¾ stick butter or margarine, softened

1½ cups sugar

1 teaspoon vanilla extract

⅓ cup peanut butter—creamy type

2 eggs

2¼ cups flour

3 teaspoons baking powder

¼ teaspoon salt

1 cup milk

Filling and Frosting:
¾ stick butter or margarine, softened

½ cup peanut butter—crunchy type

1 teaspoon vanilla extract

½ cup evaporated milk

2 to 2½ cups confectioners' sugar

2 tablespoons cocoa

Preheat the oven to 350°F. Line the bottom and grease two 8-inch layer-cake pans.

Beat the butter and sugar until creamy. Add the vanilla and peanut butter and beat well. Beat in the eggs one at a time.

Sift the flour, baking powder, and salt together. Add to the butter–sugar–eggs mixture by sifting and folding in alternate batches of the flour and the milk, about a third of each at a time; mix lightly but thoroughly. Spoon the mixture into the layer-cake pans.

Bake for 25 to 30 minutes. Remove from the oven and allow to stand for 2 to 3 minutes before turning out onto cake racks to cool. When cold, slice each cake in half horizontally, to make four layers.

Filling and Frosting: Beat the butter, peanut butter, and vanilla until creamy. Add the evaporated milk and beat thoroughly. Gradually add the sifted powdered sugar and cocoa, beating until a soft spreading consistency is obtained.

To Assemble: Use about two-thirds of the filling and frosting mixture for filling. Spread the mixture between the four cake layers, re-forming the cake, and gently pressing to adhere. Spread the remaining mixture on top of the cake, swirling or roughing it to an attractive design. Chill before cutting, especially in warm weather.

California Orange Cake

Yield: 1 cake

1 stick butter or margarine, softened

1 cup sugar

1 egg, beaten

½ teaspoon vanilla extract

2 cups flour

1 teaspoon baking powder

1 teaspoon baking soda

¼ teaspoon salt

1 teaspoon ground cinnamon

1 cup sour milk

1 large orange, just ripe

1 cup chopped walnuts or pecans

1 cup raisins

½ to ¾ cup flaked coconut, for topping

Preheat the oven to 350°F. Line the base of a 9-inch-square cake pan and grease well.

Beat the butter and sugar until creamy. Add the egg and vanilla and beat well.

Sift the dry ingredients together, then sift again over the butter cream and fold in, alternately with the sour milk.

Peel the orange, removing as much of the white membrane as possible; chop very finely and mix in a bowl with the chopped nuts and raisins. With a slotted spoon, spoon out one-quarter to one-third of this mixture and mix it into the cake mixture, folding lightly. To the remaining orange–nuts–raisins mixture, add the coconut, and set aside until after baking.

Spoon the cake mixture into the cake pan, and bake for 40 to 45 minutes. Remove from the oven and allow to stand for 5 minutes.

Preheat the broiler. Carefully spread the reserved orange–nuts–raisins mixture over the top of the cake, and place under the broiler to toast lightly. Remove from heat and allow to stand for another 5 minutes. Then carefully turn out onto a cake rack that has been covered with greaseproof paper. Reverse the cake to top side uppermost and allow to cool.

Latticed Apple Cake

Yield: 1 cake

1½ sticks butter or margarine, softened

¾ cup sugar

1 teaspoon grated lemon rind

4 eggs

2¼ cups flour

2 teaspoons baking powder

Topping:
1 cup drained cooked (or canned) apples

1 to 2 tablespoons sugar (optional)

¼ quantity Almond Paste
(see recipe, page 105)

½ cup apricot jam (apricot jelly)

1 to 2 tablespoons confectioners' sugar

Preheat the oven to 350°F. Grease and flour an 8-inch springform pan.

Beat the butter and sugar with the lemon rind until creamy. Add the eggs one at a time, beating well after each addition. Sift the flour and baking powder over the cream mixture and fold in. Spread into the springform pan and level the surface.

Bake for 35 to 40 minutes. Remove from the oven and leave in the pan for 5 to 6 minutes before adding the topping.

Topping: Sweeten the apples with the sugar, if desired. Roll out the Almond Paste to about ¼ inch thick and cut into ¾-inch strips.

Carefully spread the apples over the still-warm cake and arrange a lattice pattern of Almond Paste strips on top. Drop a little apricot jam between the lattice pieces.

Return to the oven for another 15 to 20 minutes. Remove from the springform pan and allow to cool; dust with powdered sugar before serving.

Chocolate Roll

Yield: 1 roll

2 eggs

butter, sugar, and flour (each to equal the weight of the two eggs)

1 teaspoon baking powder

1 tablespoon cocoa

1 teaspoon vanilla extract

2 tablespoons warm water

Mock Cream Filling
(see recipe, page 112)

sugar and cocoa, for rolling and topping

Preheat the oven to 400°F. Line and grease a 12 × 10-inch jelly-roll pan.

Separate the eggs. Beat the butter and sugar to a cream, add the egg yolks, and beat well.

Sift the flour, baking powder, and cocoa three times; add to the butter cream and fold in. Then add the combined vanilla and warm water, and fold this in also.

Whisk the egg whites to soft peaks and fold very gently into the cake mixture—do not overmix. Turn into the prepared pan. Bake for 17 to 20 minutes.

Soak a clean cloth in boiling water, wring it out, and lay it on the work surface. Cover it with greaseproof paper, then sprinkle sugar over the surface of the paper. Turn the chocolate roll out of the pan and onto the paper and peel away the lining. Carefully roll the cake in the paper; cover it loosely with the hot cloth and allow to cool.

When cold, unroll it and discard the paper. Spread the Mock Cream Filling, re-roll and dust with combined sugar and cocoa.

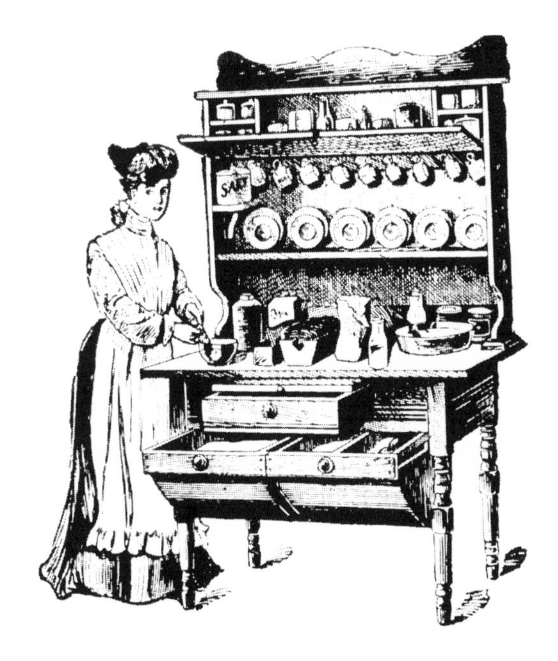

Sherried Chocolate Ring

Yield: 1 fluted ring cake

½ cup boiling water
½ cup chopped dried apricots
½ cup chopped raisins
¼ cup sweet sherry
1 stick butter or margarine, softened
¾ cup powdered sugar
2 eggs
3 ounces pure baking chocolate, melted
2 cups self-rising flour
¼ teaspoon salt
¼ teaspoon baking soda
½ cup milk
Honeyed Chocolate Frosting (see recipe, page 109)

Pour the boiling water over the apricots in a bowl; allow to stand a few minutes, then pour off the liquid. Add the raisins and sweet sherry to the apricots, and set aside for 1 hour.

Preheat the oven to 325°F. Thoroughly grease and flour an 8-inch fluted ring pan.

Beat the butter and sugar until creamy. Add the eggs one at a time, beating well after each addition. Then beat in the cooled chocolate. Sift the dry ingredients over the butter–chocolate mixture; fold in lightly. Add the apricot–raisin mixture and the milk, and fold in lightly but thoroughly to combine. Spoon into the fluted ring pan.

Bake for 55 to 60 minutes. Remove from the oven and allow to stand for 5 to 6 minutes before turning out onto a cake rack to cool.

When cold, drizzle the Honeyed Chocolate Frosting over the top and allow it to run unevenly down the flutes or grooves in the cake.

Hazelnut Coffee Cake

Yield: 1 cake

1½ sticks butter or margarine, softened
¾ cup powdered sugar
1 teaspoon instant coffee powder
1 tablespoon honey
4 eggs
1 tablespoon whiskey coffee cream liqueur
1¼ cups ground hazelnuts
1 cup self-rising flour
Coffee Fudge Frosting (see recipe, page 106)

Preheat the oven to 350°F. Grease and flour a deep-sided 8-inch springform cake pan or fluted ring pan.

Beat the butter and sugar until creamy. Add the instant coffee powder and the honey, and beat until light and fluffy. Add the eggs one at a time, beating well after each addition. Beat the liqueur in well, and fold in the hazelnuts.

Sift the flour, then sift again over the butter–hazelnut mixture and fold in lightly. Spoon into the springform pan.

Bake for 45 to 50 minutes. Remove from the oven and allow to stand for 5 to 6 minutes before loosening the cake-pan ring. When cold, place the cake on a serving platter and cover with the Coffee Fudge Frosting.

Right: **Hazelnut Coffee Cake (see above).**

Whisked Chocolate Slice

Yield: 1 cake

1½ cups flour
2 tablespoons cocoa
¾ cup sugar
¼ teaspoon salt
1 teaspoon baking powder
⅓ cup corn oil
1 tablespoon vinegar
1 teaspoon vanilla extract
1 cup lukewarm water
Chocolate Butter Cream (see recipe, page 116)

Preheat the oven to 350°F. Line and grease a 9-inch pan.

Sift the flour, cocoa, sugar, salt, and baking powder twice, then sift into the mixing bowl and make a well in the center.

Mix the oil and vinegar with the vanilla and water; beat to combine. Pour into the flour–cocoa mixture. Using a flat egg whisk, beat as quickly and lightly as possible to combine—do not overbeat. Turn into the prepared pan.

Bake for 30 to 35 minutes or until springy to the touch. Remove from the oven and allow to stand for 5 to 6 minutes before turning out onto a cake rack to cool.

Cover with Chocolate Butter Cream and, when set, cut into slices or shapes for serving.

Chocolate Velvet Cake

Yield: 1 cake

2¼ cups flour
2 teaspoons baking powder
½ teaspoon baking soda
3 eggs
1 teaspoon vanilla extract
1¼ cups sugar
1 cup mayonnaise
4 ounces pure baking chocolate, melted
Chocolate Peppermint Gloss (see recipe, page 109)

Preheat the oven to 350°F. Line the base of an 11×7-inch pan, and grease it well.

Sift the flour, baking powder, and baking soda together 2 or 3 times.

Combine the eggs, vanilla, and sugar in the bowl of an electric mixer and beat at high speed until thick and fluffy. Add the mayonnaise and the cooled chocolate, and beat at half speed until well blended. Add the sifted dry ingredients, and fold in, using a metal or wooden spoon. Pour into the pan.

Bake for 50 to 55 minutes. Remove from the oven and allow to stand for 8 to 10 minutes before turning out onto a cake rack to cool. When cold, ice with the Chocolate Peppermint Gloss.

Special Crusted Chocolate Cake

Yield: 1 deep cake

1 stick butter or margarine, softened
1⅔ cups brown sugar
2 eggs, separated
4 ounces pure baking chocolate, melted
1 cup chopped raisins
2½ cups flour
3 teaspoons baking powder
½ teaspoon cinnamon
½ cup sour milk
¼ cup brandy, warmed
1 to 2 tablespoons white sugar, for topping

Preheat the oven to 350°F. Line and grease a deep-sided 8-inch cake pan.

Beat the butter and 1⅓ cups of the sugar until light and fluffy.

Beat the egg yolks with the remaining ⅓ cup of sugar, then beat the two mixtures together. Add the cooled chocolate and the raisins, and mix thoroughly.

Sift the dry ingredients together.

Combine the sour milk and brandy. Add alternate batches of the milk–brandy and flour mixtures to the butter–chocolate mixture.

Beat the egg whites until soft peaks form, and fold very lightly into the cake mixture—do not overmix. Spoon into the cake pan and sprinkle the white sugar over the top.

Bake in the preheated oven for 40 minutes, then lower the temperature slightly and bake for another 40 to 45 minutes. Remove from the oven and allow to stand for 8 to 10 minutes before carefully turning out onto a cake rack to cool.

Caribbean Coffee Cakes

Yield: 2 filled cakes

1½ cups sugar

¾ cup boiling water

1½ sticks butter or margarine, softened

1 teaspoon rum extract

3 eggs, separated

3 cups flour

3 teaspoons baking powder

¼ teaspoon salt

2 tablespoons whole milk powder

½ cup lukewarm water

whipped sweetened cream, for filling

confectioners' sugar, for topping

Preheat the oven to 350°F. Line and grease two 8-inch cake pans.

In a small, heavy-based saucepan, place ½ cup of the sugar and heat slowly, stirring constantly until the sugar has dissolved; discontinue stirring and allow the sugar to heat until a rich brown syrup forms and begins to smoke. This will take 7 to 10 minutes.

Remove from the heat and carefully, very gradually stir in the boiling water. Set aside to cool and measure out ½ cup, discarding the remainder.

Beat the butter with the remaining 1 cup of sugar and the rum extract until creamy. Add the egg yolks one at a time, beating well after each addition.

Sift the flour, baking powder, and salt together. Into the butter–sugar–egg mixture, fold in alternate batches of the flour mixture, the cooled syrup-water, and the milk mixed with the lukewarm water.

Beat the egg whites until soft peaks form, and gently fold into the cake mixture. Spoon into the two cake pans.

Bake for 25 to 30 minutes. Remove from the oven and allow to stand for 1 to 2 minutes before carefully turning out onto fine mesh cake racks to cool. When cold, cut each cake in half horizontally. Rejoin with a whipped-cream filling, and dust sifted powdered sugar over the top.

Chocolate Fudge Cake

Yield: 1 layer cake

3 ounces pure dark baking chocolate, chopped

1½ sticks butter or margarine, softened

1½ cups brown sugar

1 teaspoon vanilla extract

3 eggs

1 cup sour cream

2 tablespoons cocoa

½ cup hot water

1 tablespoon plum jam (plum jelly)

2½ cups self-rising flour

2½ cups cream, whipped

Chocolate Caraque (see below)

Preheat the oven to 350°F. Line the bottoms of two 9-inch pans and grease them well.

Melt the chocolate in a bowl over hot—not boiling—water. Allow to cool.

Beat the butter, brown sugar, and vanilla until very creamy. Add the eggs one at a time, beating well after each addition, then beat in the sour cream.

Blend the cocoa with the hot water and plum jam, and add to the butter cream with the melted chocolate. Beat well to combine. Sift the flour over the top and fold in lightly but thoroughly—do not overmix. Spoon into the two pans.

Bake for 30 to 35 minutes before turning out onto cake racks to cool.

When cold, fill with the whipped cream, sandwich together, and cover the top and sides with whipped cream, sweetened if desired with a little sugar. Decorate with Chocolate Caraque and rosettes of whipped cream and allow to firm before slicing.

Chocolate Caraque

Melt 3½ ounces dark chocolate over a pan of simmering water. Leave to cool and thicken then melt again. Spread it very thinly over a marble slab, a laminated countertop, or the back of a flat baking sheet. Leave until just beginning to harden, then, using a sharp flexible knife, curl off splinters of chocolate.

Orange Raisin Loaf

Yield: 1 loaf cake

1 cup chopped raisins
¼ cup chopped walnuts or pecans
2 teaspoons grated orange rind
⅓ cup orange juice
1¼ cups self-rising flour
1 cup self-rising whole-wheat flour
½ teaspoon baking soda
¼ teaspoon salt
1 stick butter or margarine, softened
1 cup brown sugar
1 cup plain yogurt
2 eggs, beaten

Combine the raisins, walnuts, and orange rind with the orange juice and set aside for 20 minutes, stirring occasionally.

Preheat the oven to 325°F. Line and grease a 9½ × 4-inch loaf pan.

Sift the flours, baking soda, and salt together, returning the whole-grain pieces from the sieve.

Cream the butter and brown sugar well. Add the yogurt and eggs, and mix all together. Fold in alternate batches of the flour and raisin–walnut mixtures, about a third of each at a time; mix lightly but thoroughly to combine. Turn into the loaf pan.

Bake for 55 to 60 minutes. Remove from the oven and allow to stand for 5 to 6 minutes before carefully turning out onto a cake rack. When cold, store in an airtight container for 1 to 2 days before cutting into slices.

Currant Tea Loaf

Yield: 1 loaf cake

½ cup sugar
1 cup currants
1 cup warm strong tea
2½ cups self-rising flour
1 teaspoon mixed spices (cinnamon, nutmeg, allspice)
¼ teaspoon salt
1 to 2 teaspoons grated lemon (or orange) rind

Combine the sugar and currants in a large bowl; pour the tea over the top and set aside, stirring occasionally, for at least 1 hour.

Preheat the oven to 350°F. Line and grease an 8 × 3-inch loaf pan.

Sift all the remaining ingredients together, then sift again over the currant mixture and stir until well mixed—do not overmix. Spoon the mixture into the loaf pan.

Bake in the preheated oven for 20 minutes, then reduce the temperature to 300°F, and bake for another 40 to 45 minutes. Remove from the oven and allow to stand for 8 to 10 minutes before turning out onto a cake rack to cool.

Store in an airtight container for 1 day before cutting into slices and serving, buttered if desired.

Cider Honey Cake

Yield: 1 loaf cake

1 cup flour
1 cup whole-wheat flour
1 teaspoon mixed spices (cinnamon, nutmeg, allspice)
¼ teaspoon salt
¼ teaspoon ground ginger
½ cup raisins
2 tablespoons chopped mixed peel
¼ cup brown sugar
1 stick butter or margarine, melted
⅔ cup honey
1 teaspoon baking soda
5 ounces sparkling cider
1 egg, beaten

Preheat the oven to 325°F. Line and grease a 9 × 4½-inch loaf pan.

Sift the flours with the spices, salt, and ground ginger, returning the whole-grain pieces from the sieve. Combine with the raisins, peel, and brown sugar in a bowl, making a well in the center.

Combine the hot melted butter with the honey, and pour into the well in the flour mixture.

Dissolve the baking soda in the cider, and quickly add this and the beaten egg to the bowl. Beat all the ingredients together with a flat egg whisk until mixed thoroughly. Turn into the loaf pan.

Bake for 55 to 60 minutes. Remove from the oven and allow to stand for 5 to 6 minutes before carefully turning out onto a cake rack. When cold, store in an airtight container for 1 to 2 days before slicing.

Spread slices with honey and lemon-flavored butter, if desired.

Right: **Cider Honey Cake (see above).**

Ginger Chocolate Cake

Yield: 1 cake

1 cup chopped crystallized ginger
1 cup brown sugar
1 stick butter or margarine, chopped
1 tablespoon cocoa
¾ cup water
1 teaspoon baking soda
¼ cup milk
2 cups flour
1 teaspoon baking powder
1 teaspoon ground ginger
1 egg, beaten
Chocolate Warm Glacé Icing (see recipe, page 102)
extra ⅓ cup chopped ginger, for topping

Preheat the oven to 350°F. Line the base of a 9-inch pan and grease it well.

Place the ginger, brown sugar, butter, cocoa, and water into a small saucepan; bring slowly to a boil, simmer for 3 to 4 minutes, then set aside to cool.

Turn the mixture into a bowl. Dissolve the baking soda in the milk and add to the bowl. Sift the dry ingredients over the top and fold in lightly. Add the egg and mix thoroughly. Spoon into the prepared pan.

Bake for 35 to 40 minutes. Remove from the oven and allow to stand for 4 to 5 minutes before turning out onto a cake rack to cool.

When cold, cover the top with the Chocolate Warm Glacé Icing, and scatter the extra chopped ginger over the surface.

Crumble-Top Coffee Cake

Yield: 1 cake

1 egg
½ cup sugar
⅓ cup corn oil
1 teaspoon vanilla extract
1½ cups flour
3 teaspoons baking powder
¼ teaspoon salt
½ cup minute (quick-cooking) oats, finely crushed
½ teaspoon mixed spices, optional
1 cup raisins
Topping:
⅓ cup brown sugar
½ cup self-rising flour
1 teaspoon mixed spices
½ stick butter or margarine, melted and cooled

Preheat the oven to 375°F. Line the bottom of an 8-inch-square cake pan and grease well.

Combine the egg, sugar, corn oil, and vanilla in a bowl and beat briskly for 2 to 3 minutes. Sift the flour, baking powder, salt, crushed oats, and spices over the egg–oil mixture (including the residue oats from the sifter) and fold in lightly—do not overmix. Turn into the cake pan and scatter the raisins evenly over the top.

Topping: Combine all the topping ingredients and press through the holes of a colander or coarse strainer over the top of the cake mixture.

Bake in the preheated oven for 15 minutes, then reduce the oven temperature to 350°F and bake for another 30 to 35 minutes. Remove from the oven and allow to stand for 3 to 4 minutes before turning out, then reverse the cake carefully onto a cake rack to cool.

Tomato Raisin Loaf

Yield: 1 loaf cake

1 stick butter or margarine, softened
¾ cup powdered sugar
1 teaspoon grated lemon rind
2 eggs
1 cup skinned, chopped tomatoes
½ cup chopped raisins
¼ cup chopped nuts
1½ cups self-rising flour
½ cup whole-wheat flour
1 teaspoon mixed spices (cinnamon, nutmeg, allspice)
¼ teaspoon salt

Preheat the oven to 350°F. Line the base of a 9 × 4-inch loaf pan and grease it well.

Beat the butter, sugar, and lemon rind until creamy. Add the eggs one at a time, beating well after each addition.

Press the tomatoes through a sieve to remove the seeds; add the pulp to the butter-cream, and add the raisins and nuts. Sift the dry ingredients over the butter–tomato mixture and fold them in. Spoon into the loaf pan.

Bake for 35 to 40 minutes. Remove from the oven and allow to stand for 5 to 6 minutes before carefully turning out onto a cake rack to cool. Store in an airtight container for 2 to 3 days before slicing.

Note: Other similar recipes to this use canned tomato puree or soup. If using either of these in place of the fresh tomatoes, add a little more mixed spice to counteract the bland flavor.

Moist Ring Cake

Yield: 1 ring cake

1¼ cups flour
1 teaspoon baking soda
1 teaspoon baking powder
1 teaspoon mixed spices (cinnamon, nutmeg, allspice)
1 cup brown sugar
⅔ cup corn oil
2 eggs
2 teaspoons grated lemon rind
1 tablespoon lemon juice
½ cup well-drained crushed pineapple
1 cup shredded carrot
¼ cup chopped salted nuts
Cream Cheese Frosting: *2 ounces packaged cream cheese, softened*
1 cup confectioners' sugar, sifted
2 to 3 tablespoons sweet sherry
½ to 1 teaspoon mixed spices

Preheat oven to 350°F. Grease and flour a 7- to 8-inch ring pan.

Sift the flour with the other dry ingredients into a bowl; add the brown sugar and toss through, then form a well in the center. Add the corn oil, eggs, lemon rind, and lemon juice, then the pineapple, carrot, and chopped nuts, and beat all together with a flat egg whisk for 2 to 3 minutes.

Pour the mixture into the pan and bake for 35 to 40 minutes. Remove from the oven and allow to stand for 2 to 3 minutes before turning out onto a cake rack to cool.

Beat the cream cheese until smooth. Gradually add the powdered sugar, beating well. Add sufficient sweet sherry to produce a spreading consistency; flavor with mixed spices, as desired.

When the ring cake is cool, spread the Cream Cheese Frosting roughly over the top. Allow the frosting to become firm before cutting.

One-Egg Gingerbread

Yield: 1 cake

4 cups flour

4 teaspoons baking powder

5 teaspoons ground ginger

¼ teaspoon salt

1 teaspoon baking soda

1 cup molasses

1½ sticks butter or margarine, chopped

1½ cups brown sugar

1 egg, beaten

1¼ cups milk, warmed

lemon-flavored Warm Glacé Icing (see recipe, page 102)

⅓ cup chopped crystallized ginger

Preheat the oven to 350°F. Line and well grease an 11 × 10-inch pan.

Sift the flour, baking powder, ground ginger, salt, and baking soda into a bowl.

Place the molasses, butter, and brown sugar into a saucepan and heat slowly until the sugar is dissolved—do not overheat; cool and stir well.

When barely warm, add to the flour mixture and fold in. Lastly add the beaten egg and milk, and beat lightly to combine—do not overmix. Pour into the baking pan.

Bake for 50 minutes, then lower oven temperature slightly and bake for another 30 to 35 minutes. Let cake stand for 8 to 10 minutes before turning it out onto a cake rack to cool.

When cold, ice with the lemon-flavored Warm Glacé Icing and decorate with the chopped ginger.

Apricot Nut Loaf

Yield: 1 loaf cake

½ cup chopped dried apricots

sweet sherry

1 egg

1 cup sugar

¾ stick butter or margarine, melted

2 cups flour

3 teaspoons baking powder

½ teaspoon baking soda

¼ teaspoon salt

½ cup orange juice

1 cup chopped walnuts

Soak the dried apricots in sufficient sweet sherry to cover for 1 hour.

Preheat the oven to 325°F. Line and grease an 8 × 4-inch loaf pan. Drain the apricots well, and reserve ¼ cup of the liquid.

Beat the egg until frothy. Gradually add the sugar, beating until well mixed. Stir in the cooled butter. Sift the flour, baking powder, baking soda, and salt over the egg–sugar mixture, and fold through in alternate batches with the orange juice and reserved apricot liquid. Add the walnuts and fold in lightly. Turn into the prepared loaf pan.

Bake for 75 to 80 minutes. Remove from the oven and allow to stand for 5 to 6 minutes before turning out onto a cake rack to cool. Store in an airtight container for 1 to 2 days before cutting into slices.

Buttered Cottage Twists

Yield: 2 cakes

- ***2 eggs***
- ***1 cup sugar***
- ***½ cup cottage cheese***
- ***½ cup corn oil***
- ***1 teaspoon grated lemon rind***
- ***1 teaspoon vanilla extract***
- ***4 cups flour, sifted***
- ***1 teaspoon baking soda***
- ***½ cup milk***
- ***2 to 3 tablespoons sesame seeds***
- ***butter or margarine, for spreading***

Preheat the oven to 400°F. Grease a 9½ × 2½-inch pan.

Reserve one egg white for glazing. Combine the other egg white and the yolks with the sugar, and beat until fluffy. Add the cottage cheese, oil, lemon rind, and vanilla, and beat well. Fold in the sifted flour and baking soda, add the milk, and mix to a soft dough—use a little extra milk if the mixture seems too firm.

Turn onto a lightly floured board; divide the dough into fourths and knead each to a thin strip about 12 inches long. Taking two of the strips, twist loosely together and lift into the prepared pan. Repeat with the other two strips. Allow space between the two twists—the mixture will rise during baking. Lightly beat the reserved egg white and brush this over the twists; sprinkle the sesame seeds on top.

Bake for 8 to 10 minutes, then reduce the temperature to 350°F, and bake for another 25 to 30 minutes. Turn out and serve warm in buttered slices.

Whole-Wheat Carrot Cake

Yield: 1 cake

- ***1 cup sugar, very slightly warmed***
- ***¾ cup corn oil***
- ***2 eggs***
- ***1½ cups grated carrot***
- ***1 cup whole-wheat flour***
- ***1 teaspoon baking powder***
- ***½ teaspoon ground ginger***
- ***½ teaspoon grated nutmeg***
- ***¼ teaspoon salt***
- ***¾ cup chopped raisins***
- ***½ cup chopped walnuts***
- ***1 teaspoon grated orange rind***
- ***Cream Cheese Frosting (see recipe, page 108)***

Preheat the oven to 350°F. Line and grease an 8 × 4½-inch loaf pan.

Beat the sugar and corn oil together until well mixed. Add the eggs one at a time, beating well after each addition; then add the grated carrot and mix well.

Sift the dry ingredients together. Place the raisins, walnuts, and orange rind in another bowl, and sift the flour mixture over them; toss well to mix. Fold this into the sugar–carrot mixture, mixing lightly but thoroughly. Spoon into the loaf pan.

Bake for 35 to 40 minutes. Remove from the oven and allow to stand for 3 to 4 minutes before turning out onto a cake rack to cool.

Buttermilk Fruit Loaf

Yield: 1 loaf cake

½ cup brown sugar

¼ cup honey

½ stick butter or margarine, softened

1 egg, beaten

1½ cups flour

1 teaspoon baking powder

½ teaspoon baking soda

¼ teaspoon salt

¾ cup raisins

1 cup buttermilk

¾ cup minute (quick-cooking) oats

Preheat the oven to 325°F. Line and grease a 9 × 4½-inch loaf pan.

Combine the brown sugar, honey, and butter in a bowl and beat until soft and creamy. Add the beaten egg and mix well. Sift the flour, baking powder, baking soda, and salt over the butter mixture and fold in. Add the raisins and stir.

Mix the buttermilk and oats together, and fold this into the mixture in the bowl; fold thoroughly to combine. Spoon into the loaf pan.

Bake for 55 to 60 minutes. Remove from the oven and allow to stand for 10 to 12 minutes before turning out onto a cake rack to cool. Store in an airtight container for 1 to 2 days before cutting into slices.

Raspberry Peanut Squares

Yield: 1 9-inch-square slab

2 cups self-rising flour

¼ teaspoon salt

1 cup powdered sugar

1 stick butter or margarine, chopped

1 cup chopped peanuts

3 tablespoons raspberry jam (raspberry jelly)

2 eggs, beaten

2 teaspoons lemon juice

¾ cup milk

confectioners' sugar, for topping

Preheat the oven to 350°F. Line the base of a 9-inch-square pan and grease it well.

Place the flour, salt, and sugar in the bowl of a food processor, using the cutting blade; add the butter and process for a few seconds, then tip the mixture into a bowl. Add the peanuts, raspberry jam, beaten eggs, lemon juice, and milk, and beat with a flat egg whisk for 1 to 2 minutes. Pour into the pan.

Bake for 40 to 45 minutes. Remove from the oven and allow to stand for 3 to 4 minutes before turning out carefully onto a cake rack to cool.

Sift a little powdered sugar over the top and cut into squares for serving.

Apple Cake

Yield: 1 cake

2 large green cooking apples, peeled and cored

½ cup light corn syrup

¾ stick butter or margarine, softened

½ cup brown sugar, loosely packed

1 egg

½ teaspoon baking soda

½ cup sour milk

2 cups flour, sifted

1 teaspoon mixed spices (cinnamon, nutmeg, allspice)

½ cup chopped dates

Slice the apples thinly and place with the corn syrup into a small nonstick saucepan; cover and cook over very low heat until the apples are soft, then set aside to cool.

Preheat the oven to 350°F. Line the base of a 7- to 8-inch cake pan and grease it well.

Beat the butter and sugar until creamy. Add the egg and beat well. Dissolve the baking soda in the sour milk, and beat this in too. Fold in alternate batches of sifted flour and spices, cooked apple mixture, and chopped dates, about a third of each at a time. Spoon into the cake pan.

Bake for 55 to 60 minutes. Remove from the oven and allow to stand for 5 to 6 minutes before turning out onto a cake rack to cool. Serve freshly baked. Cut into slices and spread with butter, if desired.

Spiced Buttermilk Cake

Yield: 1 cake

1 stick unsalted butter, softened

1 cup powdered sugar

1 egg

2¼ cups flour

1 teaspoon baking soda

1 teaspoon ground cinnamon

1 teaspoon ground cardamom

1 teaspoon ground cloves

½ cup chopped raisins

1 cup buttermilk

Preheat the oven to 350°F. Line the bottom and grease a 9-inch-square cake pan.

Beat the butter until very white. Gradually add the sugar, beating well after each addition. Add the egg and beat well.

Sift the dry ingredients together, then sift again over the raisins and toss to mix.

Add alternate batches of the flour–raisin mixture and the buttermilk to the butter cream, about a third of each at a time; fold in lightly but thoroughly—do not overmix. Spoon the mixture into the cake pan, spreading evenly.

Bake for 50 to 55 minutes. Remove from the oven and allow to stand for 5 to 6 minutes before turning out onto a cake rack to cool. When cold, cut into slices or squares for serving.

Cherry Lemon Ring

Yield: 1 ring cake

1¾ cups self-rising flour

¼ cup cornstarch

1 tablespoon whole milk powder

2 to 3 teaspoons grated lemon rind

1 cup sugar

1 stick butter or margarine

3 eggs

½ cup water, lightly flavored with lemon juice

⅔ cup chopped cordial cherries

lemon-flavored Warm Glacé Icing (see recipe, page 102)

Preheat the oven to 350°F. Thoroughly grease a fluted 8-inch ring pan.

Sift the dry ingredients into a bowl, add the lemon rind and sugar and toss to mix. Make a well in the center.

Heat the butter until just melted and allow to cool.

Combine the eggs and water and beat well; add to the flour mixture, then add the cooled butter, and beat with a flat egg whisk for 4 to 5 minutes.

Scatter the chopped cherries over the base and sides of the greased ring pan; press on lightly. Pour the cake mixture into the pan.

Bake for 45 to 50 minutes. Remove from the oven and allow to stand for 5 to 6 minutes before turning out carefully onto a cake rack.

When cold, drizzle lemon-flavored Warm Glacé Icing over the top, allowing it to run into the flutes down the sides. When set, cut into slices.

Apricot Cream Bars

Yield: 2 cakes

1½ cups canned apricot nectar

½ cup chopped dried apricots

1⅓ cups chopped raisins

2 tablespoons butter or margarine

2 teaspoons grated lemon rind

¾ cup sugar

1 egg

⅓ cup fresh cream

2¾ cups flour

2 teaspoons baking soda

¼ teaspoon salt

1 to 2 tablespoons lemon juice, as required

Preheat the oven to 350°F. Line the bases of two 9 × 3-inch pans.

Combine the apricot nectar, dried apricots, and raisins in a saucepan and bring slowly to a boil. Simmer for 2 to 3 minutes, then add the butter and lemon rind and allow to cool.

Beat the sugar and egg together until the sugar is dissolved. Add the cream and beat lightly.

Sift the dry ingredients over the egg–cream mixture, and fold this in lightly, alternately with the cold apricot–raisin mixture. Add sufficient lemon juice to make a moist cake mixture. Turn into the two pans.

Bake for 40 to 50 minutes. Remove from the oven and allow to stand for 5 to 6 minutes before turning out onto cake racks to cool. Store in an airtight container for 2 to 3 days before slicing.

Genoise Gâteau

Yield: 1 layer cake

Cake:
4 eggs
½ cup sugar
½ teaspoon vanilla extract
1 cup flour
½ teaspoon baking powder
¼ teaspoon salt
½ stick butter or margarine, melted
Meringues:
3 egg whites
½ cup sugar
1 cup flaked coconut
2 teaspoons cornstarch
Filling:
10 ounces heavy cream, chilled
2 tablespoons confectioners' sugar
1 to 2 tablespoons brandy

Cake: Preheat the oven to 375°F. Grease well an 8-inch cake pan.

Beat the eggs, sugar, and vanilla in a heatproof bowl over a saucepan that contains hot—not boiling—water, for only 1 minute. Remove the saucepan from the heat and continue to beat the mixture, using an electric hand beater or rotary whisk, until the mixture is pale, thick, and foamy (about 6 to 8 minutes). Remove the bowl from the saucepan and continue beating for 2 to 3 minutes or until the mixture cools to warm.

Sift the flour, baking powder, and salt together, then sift again over the egg mixture; fold about half through. Drizzle the cooled butter over, and fold very lightly and gently until just combined—do not overmix. Pour into the cake pan.

Bake for 25 to 30 minutes or until springy to the touch. Remove from the oven and allow to stand for 4 to 5 minutes before carefully turning out onto a fine mesh cake rack to cool.

Meringues: Preheat the oven to 300°F. Grease two baking sheets and dust lightly with cornstarch.

Beat the egg whites in a clean dry bowl—preferably glass—until a stiff white foam. Gradually add the sugar, beating well after each addition so that the sugar is dissolved. Combine the coconut and cornstarch and fold into the mixture. Spread in two 8-inch circles on the prepared baking sheets.

Bake for 35 to 40 minutes. Remove from the oven and allow to cool on the baking sheets, then carefully run a broad knife or metal spatula underneath to loosen.

Filling: Beat the chilled cream until softly foaming; then add the confectioners' sugar and brandy and beat until thick. Chill well before using.

To assemble: Carefully cut the cake in half horizontally. On the bottom half, spread one-quarter of the filling. Place one meringue circle on this and spread another quarter of the filling over the meringue.

Place the second cake layer on this and spread the remaining filling over. Place the second meringue circle on the top; press down very gently to adhere all layers. Chill before cutting into slices.

Variation: Add chopped, well-drained fresh or dried fruits through the filling.

Grapefruit Cream Cake

Yield: 1 cake

¾ stick butter or margarine, softened
¾ cup powdered sugar
⅓ cup grapefruit marmalade
2 teaspoons grated orange rind
½ cup chopped nuts
2 eggs, separated
2 cups flour
2 teaspoons baking powder
2 teaspoons whole milk powder
¼ teaspoon salt
⅓ cup water
Filling:
1 cup heavy cream, whipped
2 to 3 teaspoons confectioners' sugar
2 to 3 teaspoons grated orange rind
¼ cup chopped nuts

Preheat the oven to 350°F. Thoroughly grease and flour an 8-inch tube pan.

Beat the butter and sugar until creamy. Gradually beat in the marmalade and orange rind, then add the chopped nuts and mix well. Mix the egg yolks into the butter cream. Then fold in the sifted dry ingredients and the water.

Beat the egg whites to a soft foam, and fold lightly into the cake mixture. Spoon into the pan.

Bake for 50 to 55 minutes. Remove from the oven and allow to stand for 4 to 5 minutes before turning out onto a cake rack to cool.

When the cake is cold, combine the ingredients for the filling and fill the center; decorate as desired. Chill before cutting into slices.

Right: **Clockwise from top right: Latticed Apple Cake (see p. 65); Golden Oat Cake (see p. 87); Chocolate Roll (see p. 65); Apricot Nut Loaf (see p. 74).**

Meringue Genoise

Yield: 1 layer cake

Cake Mixture:
2 cups flour

¼ teaspoon salt

1 teaspoon baking powder

1 stick butter or margarine

8 eggs at room temperature

1 cup sugar

1 teaspoon almond extract

Syrup:
½ cup water

1 cup sugar

2 to 3 tablespoons apricot brandy liqueur

Meringue:
¼ cup water

¾ cup sugar

4 egg whites

Filling and Topping:
¾ cup apricot jam (apricot jelly)

½ cup flaked almonds

¼ cup powdered sugar

Cake: Sift the flour, salt, and baking powder three times onto a sheet of waxed paper.

Heat the butter in a small saucepan until just melted; set aside to cool. Break the eggs into a large heatproof bowl. Add the sugar and extract and place the bowl over a large saucepan containing gently simmering water. Lift the saucepan off the heat and whisk the egg–sugar mixture briskly until thick, foaming, and at least doubled in bulk (approximately 8 minutes). Lift the bowl off the saucepan and beat for another 3 to 4 minutes; scatter the flour lightly over the surface and fold in very lightly.

Drizzle the butter around the edge of the mixture and fold in gently—do not overmix.

Carefully spoon equal portions of the mixture into two greased and floured 8-inch cake pans. Bake in a moderately hot oven (375°F) for 35 to 40 minutes.

Allow the cakes to remain in the pans for 3 to 4 minutes before turning onto a rack to cool.

Syrup: Place the water and sugar into a small heavy-based saucepan and bring slowly to a boil, stirring to dissolve the sugar. Allow to boil, without stirring, for 2 to 3 minutes, then remove from heat. Allow to cool and add the liqueur.

Meringue: Bring the water and sugar to a boil in a small saucepan; boil for 1 minute, then allow to cool.

Beat the egg whites to a stiff foam. Slowly add the sugar syrup, beating constantly to a thick, white meringue.

To Assemble: Preheat the oven to 425°F.

Sandwich the two cakes together with about half the apricot jam. Spread the remainder over the top.

Place the cake on an ovenproof platter and cover all over with the meringue; scatter the almonds over the surface and then sprinkle liberally with the sugar.

Place in the preheated oven for 7 to 8 minutes to form a crust on the meringue. Remove from the oven and allow to cool before serving.

Chocolate Cream Torte

Yield: 1 layer torte

Meringues:
6 egg whites

1½ cups sugar

¼ teaspoon salt

½ teaspoon cream of tartar

1 teaspoon almond extract

1 cup flaked coconut

Filling:
⅔ cup semisweet chocolate pieces

1 cup marshmallows, chopped

¾ cup evaporated milk

¾ cup heavy cream, chilled

Preheat the oven to 300°F. Grease three baking sheets and lightly dust with cornstarch.

Beat the egg whites in a clean, dry bowl—preferably glass—until a stiff white foam. Gradually add half the sugar, beating well after each addition so that the sugar is dissolved.

Combine the remaining sugar with the salt and cream of tartar; scatter this over the egg-white mixture and fold in very gently, adding the almond extract for flavor. Spread into three 7-inch circles on the prepared baking sheets. Scatter the coconut over each circle.

Bake for 30 to 35 minutes. Carefully loosen on the baking sheets with a broad knife or metal spatula and set aside to cool.

Filling: Combine the chocolate pieces with the marshmallows and evaporated milk in a heatproof bowl placed over hot—not boiling—water; heat, stirring frequently until well blended. Remove from the heat and allow to cool.

Whip the cream until thickened and fold into the chocolate mixture. Chill before using.

To assemble: Place one of the meringues on a serving plate and spread half of the chocolate filling over; top with a second meringue and again spread with filling.

Arrange the third meringue on the top and gently press down to adhere, being careful not to crack the crisp layers. Chill for at least 6 hours before serving.

Variation: Use finely chopped nuts in place of the coconut, and flavor the filling with rum or brandy extract or a little concentrated liqueur.

Rich Mocha Cream Gâteau

Yield: 1 layer cake

12 ounces pure dark baking chocolate, chopped

1 cup milk

½ stick butter or margarine, softened well

1¾ cups flour

1 teaspoon baking powder

2 teaspoons instant coffee powder

½ teaspoon baking soda

¼ teaspoon salt

1 cup powdered sugar

3 eggs, beaten

2 teaspoons rum or brandy extract

Filling:
10 ounces heavy cream, chilled

1 tablespoon confectioners' sugar

Frosting:
6 ounces pure dark baking chocolate, chopped

2 sticks unsalted butter, softened

2 egg yolks

1 teaspoon instant coffee powder

1 teaspoon rum or brandy extract

1¼ to 1½ cups confectioners' sugar, sifted

Preheat the oven to 350°F. Line the bottoms of two 9-inch layer pans, and grease well.

Place the chocolate into a heatproof bowl over hot—not boiling—water and allow to melt; set aside to cool slightly. When cool, combine with the milk and softened butter.

Sift the dry ingredients, including the sugar, into a large bowl and make a well in the center; add the combined chocolate, milk, and butter and beat for 1 to 2 minutes. Add the beaten eggs and extract, and beat for 2 minutes. Spoon into the layer pans.

Bake for 25 to 30 minutes. Remove from the oven and allow to stand for 2 to 3 minutes, then carefully turn out onto cake racks to cool. When cold, slice each cake in half horizontally—making four layers.

Filling: Whip the cream and powdered sugar until thickened. Chill well.

Frosting: Melt the chocolate in a heatproof bowl over hot—not boiling— water. Allow to cool to room temperature.

Gradually blend the cooled chocolate into the creamed butter, then add the egg yolks and coffee powder and beat well. Flavor with the extract and generally add sufficient powdered sugar to mix to a smooth spreading consistency.

To Assemble: Spread the whipped cream between the four cake layers and re-form into a gâteau, pressing gently to adhere. Spoon half the frosting onto the top of the gâteau and use the remainder for decoration in swirls or rosettes, as desired. Chill before serving, particularly in warm weather.

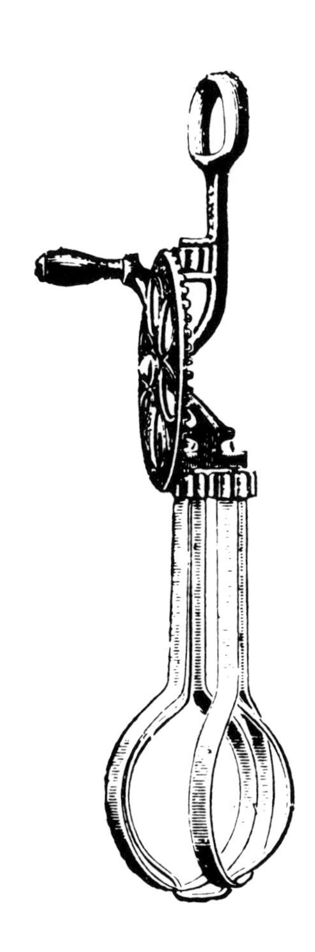

For a Perfect Fruit Cake

Cake Pan Linings

The larger and richer the cake, the longer it needs to bake. Greater protection is therefore needed to prevent the outsides of the cake from overcooking, overbrowning, and drying out.

• For a 6- to 8-inch cake pan, line with one layer of good quality thick aluminum foil, then line again with one to two layers of greaseproof paper and grease well.

• For a 9- to 11-inch cake pan, line with two layers of good quality thick aluminum foil, then line again with two layers of greaseproof paper and grease well.

• For the very large cake pan, line as above but place another layer of aluminum foil around the outside of the pan and secure it, then place the pan on a double thickness of foil on the actual oven shelf for baking.

Larger cakes may also require a sheet of foil over the top of the cake for the first 1 to 3 hours to prevent overbrowning, but care should be taken not to lay it too close to the cake surface or steaming may cause a moist or soggy top layer.

The final shape of the baked cake depends on the careful lining of the cake, particularly in square corners and around the bottom edges.

Cake, Size and Quantities

Cake Required	*Rich Fruit Cake*	*Cake-Pan Size*
Single layer:		
Small	1 quantity	10–11 inches
Large	1¼ quantities	12 inches
Two layers:		
Small	1 quantity	10–11 inches
Large	1¼ quantities	12 inches
Small	1¼ quantities	6–6½ inches 10 inches
Large	1¾ quantities	7–8 inches 12 inches
Three layers:		
Small	1¾–2 quantities	7–8¼ inches 9–91/2inches 12–13 inches

Note that square cake pans require slightly more mixture to fill than round ones. And for better visual balance, square cakes should be slightly deeper, especially for layered and decorated varieties.

Cake Size, Baking Temperature, Time

Oven temperature thermostats are not always accurate, so unless you are sure of the correctness of your oven it may be wise to have it checked before embarking on the mammoth task of cooking a very large fruit cake for a special occasion. Check the oven position recommended in the manufacturer's instructions.

Cake Size	*Oven Temperature*	*Baking Time*
6–6½ inches	325°F	2–2½ hours
7½–8 inches	300°F then turn to 275°F	2 hours + 1½–2 hours
9½–10 inches	300°F then turn to 275°F	2½ hours + 2–2½ hours
11½–12 inches	300°F then turn to 275°F	3 hours + 3–3½ hours
12½–13 inches	300°F then turn to 275°F	3 hours + 3½–4 hours

Note that deep cakes will take longer to cook.

Do not disturb the cake for at least half to three-quarters of the baking time, then check the cake's progress, without holding the oven door open any longer than is necessary.

Start testing for doneness about 10 minutes before the minimum stated baking time. A very fine skewer pierced diagonally through the cake center (preferably into a crack if visible) should be clear of moist cake mixture upon removal. Do not confuse dried fruits with uncooked cake mixture.

The cooked cake mixture should be firm to the touch of a finger in several surface spots. Some experienced cake bakers say there is a distinct humming sound from an uncooked rich fruit cake. If in doubt, leave for 5 to 10 minutes or turn off the oven and leave for 10 to 15 minutes.

Upon removal from the oven, if the surface of the cake appears a little dry, brush with a little extra liquor before covering; brush again if required after cooling and before final wrapping for storage.

. Cut greaseproof strips to line sides of pan

2. Brush strips with melted butter

. Line pan with buttered greaseproof paper

4. Cream butter and sugar; beat in eggs

. Smooth top of cake mixture

6. Rich Fruit Cake (see p. 84)

Rich Fruit Cake

Yield: 1 11-inch deep cake

1½ pounds (5 cups) raisins
1½ pounds (5 cups) white seedless raisins
2½ cups currants
8 ounces mixed peel
8 ounces candied cherries
¾ cup dried apricots
1¼ cups pitted dates
or use 5¼ pounds mixed dried fruits (instead of above ingredients)
⅔ cup port, Marsala, or sweet sherry
4 ounces blanched almonds, chopped
4 sticks butter, softened
2⅔ cups brown sugar
2 tablespoons light corn syrup
2 teaspoons grated lemon rind
8 eggs
5 cups flour
1 cup self-rising flour
½ teaspoon ground dried ginger
½ teaspoon ground cinnamon
½ teaspoon grated nutmeg
½ teaspoon baking soda
½ teaspoon salt
extra port, Marsala, or sweet sherry, as required

Combine the fruits in a nonmetal bowl, chopping those that require it into small pieces (or put all the fruits in batches through a food processor and chop coarsely). Add the liquor and stir well to mix. Set aside for 10 to 12 hours, stirring from time to time.

Preheat the oven to 300°F. Line a deep-sided 10- to 11-inch cake pan, and grease it thoroughly.

Add the almonds to the fruit and stir through.

In a very large bowl, beat the butter and brown sugar until creamy. Add the corn syrup and lemon rind, and beat thoroughly. Add the eggs one at a time, beating well after each addition. At this stage it will be more practical to dispense with the beating implement and use a clean hand for further mixing.

In a separate bowl, sift the flours with the spices, baking soda, and salt. Sift half of this into the butter–egg mixture; add half the fruit mixture, and mix. Add the remaining flour and fruit mixtures and fold in, mixing lightly but thoroughly to blend all the ingredients together. Add extra liquor if required.

Spoon the mixture into the lined and greased cake pan and smooth the surface with a wet hand.

Place in the preheated oven and bake for 1 hour. Then reduce the temperature to 250 to 275°F and continue baking for about 4 more hours, depending on the size and depth of the cake.

Remove from the oven, cover loosely, and allow to cool slowly in the cake pan. When quite cold, turn out carefully and wrap for storing. It should be stored for 2 to 3 weeks before icing and decorating.

Festive Fruit Wreath

Yield: 1 fluted ring cake

1 cup chopped dried apricots
1 cup chopped walnuts or pecans
1½ cups chopped raisins
1½ tablespoons brandy
1½ tablespoons orange juice
1 stick butter or margarine, softened
¾ cup powdered sugar
3 eggs, separated
1 cup flaked coconut
½ cup crushed and drained pineapple
1 cup self-rising flour
1 cup flour

Combine the apricots, walnuts, and raisins with the brandy and fruit juices and set aside for 5 to 6 hours, stirring occasionally.

Preheat the oven to 325°F. Thoroughly grease and flour a 9-inch fluted ring pan.

Beat the butter and sugar until creamy. Add the egg yolks and beat well. Mix in the coconut and drained pineapple.

Sift the flours together over the butter–coconut mixture and lightly fold in. Beat the egg whites until stiff and add with the dried fruit mixture. Mix lightly—do not overmix. Turn into the fluted ring pan and stand it on a baking sheet.

Bake in the preheated oven for 1 hour, then reduce the temperature to 275°F and bake another 50 to 60 minutes, covering the top of the cake with a sheet of aluminum foil to avoid overbrowning. Leave to cool in the pan.

Golden Fruit Cake

Yield: 1 cake

½ cup powdered sugar

½ cup light brown sugar

2 eggs

½ cup corn oil

1 cup cooked and mashed pumpkin (about 12 ounces when raw)

2 tablespoons light corn syrup

1 cup self-rising flour

1 cup flour

½ teaspoon ground cinnamon

¼ teaspoon grated nutmeg

¼ teaspoon ground ginger

1 tablespoon whole milk powder

1½ cups chopped raisins

¼ cup water

Preheat the oven to 350°F. Line the bottom and grease a 9 x 5-inch oblong cake pan.

Combine the sugars, eggs, and oil in a large bowl and beat with an electric hand mixer or rotary whisk for 2 minutes. Add the pumpkin and corn syrup and beat for another 2 minutes; then remove the beaters or whisk.

Sift the flours, spices, and milk powder together. Sift again over the sugar–pumpkin mixture; using a wooden spoon, fold in lightly. Then add the raisins and water and fold again. Turn into the cake pan.

Bake for 1 hour, then reduce the temperature slightly and bake for 20 to 30 minutes. Remove from the oven and allow to stand for 8 to 10 minutes before turning out onto a cake rack to cool. Let it stand overnight before slicing.

Mincemeat Pecan Ring

Yield: 1 ring cake

½ stick butter or margarine, softened

½ cup powdered sugar

¼ teaspoon lemon extract

1 egg

¾ cup prepared mincemeat

¼ cup pecans, chopped

1½ cups flour

2 teaspoons baking powder

½ teaspoon baking soda

¼ teaspoon salt

½ cup milk

Pecan Butter-Cream Topping: Vienna Butter Cream ***(see recipe, page 117)***

½ cup chopped pecans

¼ teaspoon lemon extract

Preheat the oven to 350°F. Thoroughly grease a 7-inch ring pan.

Cream the butter and sugar until light and fluffy. Add the lemon extract and egg, and beat well. Stir the mincemeat and chopped pecans through the mixture. Sift the dry ingredients over and fold in, adding the milk in two or three batches. Spoon into the ring pan.

Bake for 45 to 50 minutes. Remove from the oven and allow to stand for 5 minutes before turning out onto a cake rack to cool.

Topping: While the Vienna Butter Cream is still soft, fold in the pecan nuts and flavor with lemon extract.

When the cake is cold, spread the butter-cream topping over and swirl or "rough up" to an attractive design. Allow to set before cutting.

Malted Raisin Cake

Yield: 1 cake

3 cups flour

1 teaspoon baking powder

½ teaspoon baking soda

¼ teaspoon salt

½ cup milk, heated

⅓ cup light corn syrup

½ cup malt extract

1 tablespoon lemon juice

1½ cups raisins

½ cup chopped walnuts

2 eggs, beaten

Preheat the oven to 300°F. Line the base of a 12 × 8-inch baking pan, and grease well.

Sift the dry ingredients into a large bowl.

Into the hot milk, stir the syrup and malt extract, add the lemon juice, and mix well to blend.

Toss the raisins and walnuts through the flour mixture. Add the malt–milk mixture and the beaten eggs, and beat until thoroughly combined—do not overmix. Turn into the baking pan.

Bake for 1¼ hours. Remove from the oven and stand for 8 to 10 minutes before turning out onto a cake rack to cool. When cold, store overnight in an airtight container before cutting into slices and spreading with butter or margarine, if desired.

Spiced Raisin Cakes

Yield: 20 to 24 little cakes

2 cups self-rising flour

¼ teaspoon salt

1 teaspoon mixed spices (cinnamon, nutmeg, ginger, allspice)

¼ cup brown sugar

½ cup raisins

2 tablespoons butter or margarine

1 tablespoon light corn syrup

2 eggs, beaten

¾ cup milk

Preheat the oven to 400°F. Grease deep-sided muffin tins.

Sift the flour, salt, and spices into a bowl. Add the brown sugar and raisins, and mix.

Melt the butter and blend with the corn syrup. Beat into the eggs and add the milk to blend. Stir into the flour–raisin mixture quickly and lightly until just combined. Spoon into the deep muffin tins, filling them two-thirds full.

Bake for 17 to 20 minutes. Turn out onto cake racks to cool. Store in an airtight container until ready for use.

Fruit and Vegetable Cake

Yield: 1 cake

2 eggs

½ cup brown sugar

¼ cup honey

⅜ cup corn oil

1½ cups flour

3 teaspoons baking powder

1 teaspoon mixed spices (cinnamon, nutmeg, allspice)

¼ teaspoon salt

¾ cup raisins

¼ cup chopped walnuts

1 cup shredded raw zucchini

Preheat the oven to 350°F. Line and grease an 8½ × 5-inch cake pan.

Place the eggs in the small bowl of an electric mixer and beat until thick and frothy. Add the sugar, honey, and oil, and continue beating for 2 to 3 minutes.

Sift the flour, baking powder, spices, and salt into a large bowl and make a well in the center. Add the egg–sugar mixture and stir through lightly with a wooden spoon. Add the raisins, walnuts, and shredded vegetable, and combine thoroughly. Turn into the cake pan.

Bake for 55 to 60 minutes. Remove from the oven and allow to stand for 8 to 10 minutes before carefully turning out onto a cake rack to cool. Store in an airtight container for 1 to 2 days before cutting into slices.

Note: Small, young zucchini can be shredded with their skins intact. Larger, older vegetables should be peeled and have their seeds removed first.

Choc-Coffee Rounds

Yield: 24 to 26 little cakes

1 stick butter or margarine, softened

¾ cup brown sugar

2 eggs, beaten

1 teaspoon vanilla extract

2 ounces baking chocolate, melted

2 cups flour

½ teaspoon baking soda

¼ teaspoon salt

1 teaspoon baking powder

¾ cup sour cream

½ cup chopped walnuts

Choc-Coffee Cream (see recipe, page 116)

Preheat the oven to 375°F. Grease shallow muffin tins.

Cream the butter and sugar until light and fluffy. Beat in the eggs and vanilla, then stir in the cooled chocolate.

Sift the flour, baking soda, salt, and baking powder together. Add to the chocolate mixture in alternate batches with the sour cream. Lightly fold in the walnuts. Fill the muffin tins two-thirds full.

Bake for 15 to 17 minutes. Carefully turn out onto cake racks to cool.

Frost with the Choc-Coffee Cream and allow to set.

Poppy-Seed Layer Cake

Yield: 1 four-layer cake

⅓ cup poppy seeds

⅓ cup milk

½ stick butter or margarine, softened

1 cup sugar

3 eggs, separated

⅓ cup evaporated milk

2 cups flour

3 teaspoons baking powder

¼ teaspoon salt

Mocha Custard Filling (see recipe, page 113)

confectioners' sugar, for topping

Preheat the oven to 350°F. Line the bottoms and grease two 8-inch layer pans. Soak the poppy seeds in the milk to soften slightly.

Beat the butter until creamy; gradually add the sugar, beating well. Add the egg yolks, then the evaporated milk and the poppy seed–milk mixture, beating constantly. Fold in the sifted flour, baking powder, and salt, mixing lightly. Spoon the mixture into the two layer pans.

Bake for 35 to 40 minutes or until springy to the touch. Remove from the oven and allow to stand for 3 to 4 minutes before turning out onto cake racks to cool.

When cold, cut each cake in half—horizontally—for filling. Assemble the cakes, spreading the Mocha Custard Filling between the layers. Dust sifted confectioners' sugar over the top, and chill until the filling is firm enough for cutting.

Golden Oat Cake

Yield: 1 cake

1½ cups self-rising flour

½ teaspoon salt

⅔ cup brown sugar

2 teaspoons grated orange rind

1¼ cups minute (quick-cooking) oats

2 eggs

1 cup milk

1 cup corn oil

Topping:
⅓ cup brown sugar

2 tablespoons minute (quick-cooking) oats

1 tablespoon corn oil

½ cup crushed and drained pineapple

2 tablespoons chopped candied cherries

2 tablespoons chopped walnuts

Preheat the oven to 350°F. Line the base of a 9-inch-square cake pan and grease well.

Sift the flour and salt into a bowl. Add the brown sugar, orange rind, and oats and toss to mix thoroughly.

Beat the eggs; add the milk and corn oil and mix well. Pour onto the flour–oats mixture and stir to combine all ingredients thoroughly—do not overmix. Turn into the cake pan.

Bake for 45 to 50 minutes. Combine the topping ingredients and, briefly removing the cake from the oven, quickly but carefully scatter over the top of the cake. Lower the oven temperature to 325°F and bake for another 15 to 20 minutes. Serve warm.

Rock Cakes

Yield: 24 to 26 small cakes

2 cups self-rising flour
¼ teaspoon salt
½ teaspoon mixed spices (cinnamon, nutmeg, coriander, ginger)
¾ stick butter or margarine, chopped
⅓ cup powdered sugar
2 tablespoons mixed dried fruits
1 tablespoon chopped dried peel
1 egg, beaten
2 to 3 tablespoons milk
extra butter, for spreading

Preheat the oven to 375°F. Prepare cookie sheets by greasing them well.

Sift the flour, salt, and spices into a bowl; add the butter and rub through with the fingertips until fine. Mix in the sugar.

Combine the dried fruits and peel with the egg; add this to the mixture, with sufficient milk to mix to a stiff consistency. Pile in heaped spoonfuls about 2 inches apart on the cookie sheets.

Bake for 15 to 17 minutes. Turn onto cake racks to cool. Before serving, split each rock cake and spread with butter if desired.

Variations:

Sugar Tops: Before baking, sprinkle the tops with sugar or coffee crystals.

St. Clements: Add 2 teaspoons of grated orange rind and 1 teaspoon of grated lemon rind instead of the dried peel.

Whole-Wheat: Substitute half of the white flour with whole-wheat flour, and use brown sugar instead of powdered sugar.

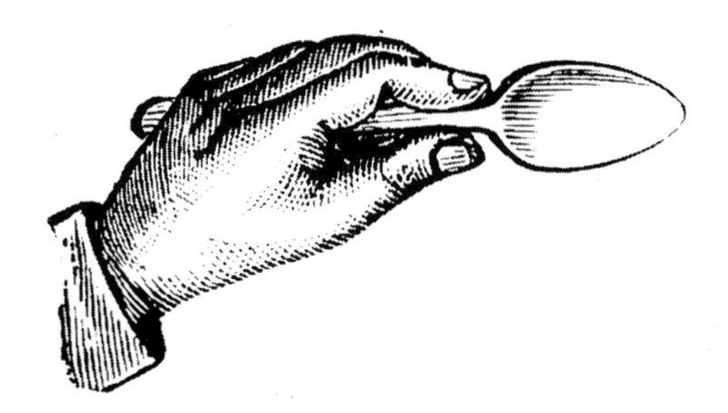

Coco-Lemon Cakes

Yield: 20 to 24 little cakes

2 cups self-rising flour
¼ teaspoon salt
¾ stick butter or margarine, chopped
⅓ cup powdered sugar
⅓ cup flaked coconut
2 teaspoons grated lemon rind
1 egg
2 tablespoons milk
1 teaspoon vanilla extract
extra flaked coconut, for topping

Preheat the oven to 375°F. Grease the muffin tins.

Sift the flour and salt into a bowl; rub in the butter with the tips of the fingers until fine. Add the sugar, coconut, and lemon rind, and mix thoroughly.

Beat the egg with the milk and vanilla, and mix into the flour–coconut mixture. (Should the coconut be dry, a little extra milk may be required.) Fill each muffin tin cup two-thirds full; sprinkle a little extra coconut over the top.

Bake for 20 to 22 minutes. Turn out onto cake racks, and serve warm or cold.

Spicy Apple Drops

Yield: 20 to 24 little cakes

1 package cake mix for butter cake
1 egg
water or milk
½ to ¾ cup cooked apple pulp
½ teaspoon ground cinnamon
½ teaspoon grated nutmeg
melted butter or margarine
1 tablespoon sugar
extra 1 teaspoon mixed cinnamon and nutmeg

Preheat the oven to 375°F. Grease muffin tins.

Make up the cake mix according to directions on the package, using the egg and slightly less water or milk than required, to give a firmer batter.

Flavor the apple pulp with the combined cinnamon and nutmeg.

Spoon about 2 teaspoons of cake mixture into each muffin tin cup. Add about 1 teaspoon of the spiced apple pulp, being careful not to touch the sides of the pan. Top with more cake mixture to fill each cup two-thirds full.

Bake for 12 to 15 minutes, until golden brown and just firm to the touch. Remove from the pans and, while still warm, brush the tops with melted butter. Quickly sprinkle with the combined sugar and extra spices. Allow to cool.

Raisin Bran Cakes

Yield: 28 to 30 little cakes

1 stick butter or margarine, softened

½ cup sugar

1 egg

1 cup bran cereal

1 cup milk

1 cup self-rising flour

1 teaspoon mixed spices (cinnamon, nutmeg, ginger, allspice)

¼ teaspoon salt

½ to ¾ cup raisins

Preheat the oven to 375°F. Grease deep-sided muffin tins.

Beat the butter and sugar to a cream. Add the egg, beating thoroughly.

Soak the bran cereal in the milk until well absorbed; then mix with the butter–egg mixture. Sift the flour, spices, and salt together and fold into the butter–bran mixture with the raisins. Fill the muffin tins two-thirds full.

Bake for 12 to 15 minutes or until cooked and golden brown. Turn out onto a cake rack to cool.

Coffee Nut Cakes

Yield: 26 to 30 little cakes

3 cups self-rising flour

¼ teaspoon salt

¾ cup brown sugar

½ cup chopped walnuts

¼ cup chopped dates or raisins

1 egg

3 tablespoons butter or margarine, melted

1¼ cups black coffee, cold

Preheat the oven to 375°F. Grease deep-sided muffin tins.

Sift the flour and salt into a bowl; mix in the sugar, walnuts, and dates. Make a well in the center.

Beat the egg, cooled butter, and black coffee together; pour this into the flour–fruit mixture and beat lightly but thoroughly to combine. Fill the muffin tins two-thirds full.

Bake for 20 to 22 minutes. Turn out onto cake racks to cool, then serve freshly baked—with or without icing, as desired.

Jaffa Gems

Yield: 24 to 30 gem cakes

1 stick butter or margarine, softened

½ cup sugar

2 ounces coarsely grated chocolate

3 teaspoons grated orange rind

2 eggs

2 cups self-rising flour

¼ teaspoon salt

⅓ cup milk

Orange Glacé Icing (see recipe, page 102)

coarsely grated chocolate, for topping

Preheat the oven to 375°F. Heat the gem irons in the oven.

Beat the butter and sugar to a cream. Add the grated chocolate and orange rind, and beat well. Then beat in the eggs one at a time.

Sift the flour and salt together, and fold into the butter–chocolate mixture alternately with the milk.

Quickly grease the heated gem irons and fill them two-thirds full with cake mixture.

Bake for 15 to 17 minutes. Turn out onto a cake rack to cool.

Ice the tops with Orange Glacé Icing and sprinkle with grated chocolate for decoration.

Chocomallows

Yield: 16 to 18 cakes

¾ stick butter or margarine, softened
⅓ cup powdered sugar
2 eggs, beaten
1½ cups self-rising flour
2 tablespoons cocoa
¼ teaspoon salt
½ teaspoon ground cinnamon
2 tablespoons evaporated milk
2 teaspoons lemon juice
Chocolate Glacé Icing (see recipe, page 102)
Marshmallow: 1 cup orange juice
1 cup sugar
¼ teaspoon cream of tartar
1 tablespoon gelatin
2 teaspoons lemon juice
about 1 cup flaked coconut

Preheat the oven to 400°F. Heat the gem irons in the oven.

Beat the butter and sugar until light and fluffy. Add the eggs and beat well. Into a separate bowl, sift the flour, cocoa, salt, and cinnamon together. Combine the evaporated milk and lemon juice in a small bowl and set aside for 5 minutes.

Fold the dry ingredients into the butter mixture in alternate amounts with the soured milk.

Quickly grease the well-heated gem irons and fill two-thirds full with the cake mixture.

Bake for 14 to 16 minutes. Turn out onto cake racks, and, when cold, level the tops and coat all over with Chocolate Glacé Icing; allow to set.

Marshmallow: Have clean gem irons on hand. Combine the orange juice, sugar, cream of tartar, and gelatin in a small heavy-based saucepan, bring slowly to a boil, then allow to boil for 10 minutes.

Remove from the heat and allow to cool. Turn into a large bowl and add the lemon juice. When the mixture is about the consistency of unbeaten egg whites, beat with an electric mixer or rotary whisk until the mixture has thickened and increased in volume.

Quickly fill wetted gem irons, and chill until set. Unmold, and coat the rounded surface with the coconut, leaving the level tops uncoated.

To Assemble the Chocomallows: To join the chocolate and marshmallow rounds, slowly pass a heated metal spatula over the uncoated marshmallow surface to slightly dissolve, then quickly press the marshmallow against the level chocolate surface of the little cake to adhere. Allow to set before serving.

Thistledowns

Yield: 38 to 40 small gem cakes

2 cups flour
3 teaspoons baking powder
¼ cup powdered sugar
¼ teaspoon salt
⅓ cup corn oil
1 egg, beaten
2 tablespoons nonfat milk powder
1 cup water
confectioners' sugar for topping

Preheat the oven to 400°F. Heat the gem irons in the oven.

Sift the flour with the baking powder, sugar, and salt twice, then sift into a bowl and make a well in the center.

Combine the corn oil with the egg. Beat the milk powder into the water. Then beat the two mixtures together. Pour into the flour mixture and mix very lightly with a flat egg whisk until just smooth. Allow to stand for 15 to 20 minutes, undisturbed.

Quickly grease and flour the heated gem irons, and fill them half full with the cake mixture—use one movement for the filling, without "topping up" with extra mixture.

Bake for 12 to 15 minutes. Carefully turn out onto cake racks, dust the tops with sifted powdered sugar, and serve very fresh.

Right: **Clockwise from top: Date and Peanut Ragamuffins (see p. 92); Apricot Crunchies (see p. 92); Spice and Sugar Swirls (see p. 96); Nut Pumpkin Gems (see p. 92).**

THE ABSOLUTE

Golden Ginger Gems

Yield: 16 to 18 gem cakes

½ stick butter or margarine, softened

1¼ cup sugar

1 teaspoon ground ginger

2 tablespoons light corn syrup

1 egg

1½ cups flour

2 tablespoons chopped crystallized ginger

1 teaspoon baking soda

½ cup milk

Preheat the oven to 375°F. Place large-cavity gem irons in the oven to heat them.

Beat the butter and sugar with the ground ginger until light and fluffy. Add the corn syrup, then the egg, and beat well. Fold in the sifted flour and chopped ginger. Dissolve the baking soda in the milk, and add to the mixture to make a soft dough.

Quickly grease the heated gem irons and fill two-thirds full.

Bake for 12 to 15 minutes. Turn out onto cake racks, and serve warm or cold.

Nut Pumpkin Gems

Yield: 18 to 20 gem cakes

½ stick butter or margarine, softened

¼ cup powdered sugar

½ teaspoon cinnamon

¾ cup cooked (or canned) mashed pumpkin, cold

1 egg

2½ cups self-rising flour

½ cup chopped walnuts

½ cup milk

extra butter or margarine, for spreading

Preheat the oven to 425°F. Heat the gem irons in the oven.

Beat the butter and sugar until light. Add the cinnamon, pumpkin, and egg and beat thoroughly. Fold in alternate batches of sifted flour, walnuts, and milk, about a third of each at a time, to make a soft dough.

Quickly grease the heated gem irons and fill them two-thirds full with the mixture.

Bake for 12 to 15 minutes. Turn out onto cake racks and serve warm or cool, split and spread with butter.

Apricot Crunchies

Yield: 20 to 24 little cakes

½ cup lightly crushed cornflakes

2 cups self-rising flour

½ teaspoon salt

3 tablespoons sugar

2 tablespoons butter or margarine, melted

1 egg, beaten

½ cup milk

½ cup chopped dried apricots

extra ½ stick butter or margarine, melted

3 tablespoons brown sugar

½ cup chopped nuts

Preheat the oven to 400°F. Grease small muffin tins, and lightly coat the insides with the cornflakes.

Sift the flour, salt, and sugar into a bowl.

Combine the melted butter, egg, milk, and apricots, and add to the flour mixture; mix into a soft dough. Turn onto a lightly floured board, pat out to 1 inch thick, and cut into 20 to 24 pieces. Dip each piece in the extra melted butter, then toss in a mixture of the combined brown sugar and nuts. Place one piece into each muffin-tin cup.

Bake for 17 to 20 minutes. Turn out to cool on cake racks and eat while very fresh.

Date and Peanut Ragamuffins

Yield: 10 to 12 muffins

½ stick butter or margarine, softened

¼ cup sugar

1 egg

1 cup self-rising flour

½ cup chopped dates

2 tablespoons chopped salted peanuts

1½ tablespoons orange juice

½ teaspoon baking soda

1 tablespoon boiling water

Preheat the oven to 375°F. Grease deep-sided muffin tins.

Beat the butter and sugar until creamy. Add the egg and mix thoroughly, then fold in the sifted flour.

Combine the dates, peanuts, and orange juice in a bowl and mix well to separate the dates. Add to the butter mixture and fold in.

Dissolve the baking soda in the boiling water. Quickly sprinkle over the mixture and mix in lightly but thoroughly. Spoon into the muffin tins, filling them two-thirds full.

Bake for 17 to 20 minutes. Turn out onto cake racks to cool, and serve while very fresh.

St. Clements Cakes

Yield: 20 to 24 little cakes

1 stick butter or margarine, softened

⅔ cup powdered sugar

2 teaspoons grated orange rind

1½ cups self-rising flour

2 eggs, beaten

3 tablespoons milk

Syrup:
½ cup powdered sugar

2 tablespoons orange juice

2 tablespoons lemon juice

Preheat the oven to 375°F. Place individual paper baking cups in the muffin tins.

Beat the butter and sugar with the orange rind until light and fluffy. Add alternate batches of the sifted flour, eggs, and milk, about a third of each at a time. Fill the muffin tins two-thirds full.

Bake for 17 to 20 minutes. Remove from the oven and top with the syrup.

Syrup: Combine the sugar with the orange juice and lemon juice in a small saucepan, and heat slowly until the sugar is dissolved; then boil for 5 minutes.

Slowly spoon the syrup over each of the little cakes while they are still hot. Set aside to cool on cake racks.

Crusted Date Squares

Yield: 16 squares

½ stick butter or margarine, softened

⅓ cup powdered sugar

1 egg

1 cup flour

1 teaspoon baking powder

¼ teaspoon baking soda

¼ teaspoon salt

2 to 3 tablespoons orange juice

Filling:
¾ cup chopped, pitted dates

2 to 3 teaspoons grated orange rind

1 teaspoon grated lemon rind

¼ teaspoon mixed spices (cinnamon, nutmeg, ginger, allspice)

⅔ cup combined orange and lemon juice

Topping:
1 cup cornflakes, lightly crushed

⅔ cup flaked coconut

1 to 2 tablespoons brown sugar

Preheat the oven to 375°F. Thoroughly grease a 9- to 10-inch-square pan.

Beat the butter and sugar to a cream. Add the egg and beat well. Sift the dry ingredients together, and then fold into the butter cream with sufficient orange juice to make a fairly firm mixture. Spread into the pan.

Filling: Combine the dates with the fruit rinds, spices, and fruit juices in a small saucepan and heat slowly, stirring constantly, until the mixture forms a paste. Remove from the heat and allow to cool. When cool, spread onto the cake mixture as evenly as possible.

Topping: Mix the cornflakes, coconut and brown sugar together and sprinkle over the date filling; pat down lightly with a broad knife or spatula.

Bake for 20 to 25 minutes. Mark into squares while hot, and allow to cool in the pan. Turn out and store in an airtight container until ready for use.

Caramel Layer Cake

Yield: 1 layer cake

1½ cups powdered sugar

½ cup hot black coffee—plus water, as required

2 cups flour

3 teaspoons baking powder

½ teaspoon salt

1 stick butter or margarine, softened

2 eggs, beaten

Caramel Frosting:
2 tablespoons sugar

3 ounces butter or margarine

3 ounces evaporated or creamy milk

1 teaspoon vanilla extract

3 cups confectioners' sugar, sifted

Mock Cream Filling:
(see recipe, page 112)

Preheat the oven to 350°F. Line and grease the bottoms of two 8- or 9-inch layer-cake pans.

Spoon ¼ cup of the sugar into a small heavy-based saucepan and dissolve over low heat, without stirring. Allow to boil to a rich brown caramel (smoke fumes will appear). Remove from the heat and slowly but very carefully add the hot coffee, stirring until all lumps dissolve. Return to a low heat if the mixture cools before the lumps dissolve. Let the liquid cool, then pour into a measuring cup and add enough water to make 7½ ounces.

Sift the flour, baking powder, and salt together twice and set aside.

Beat the butter with the remaining 1¼ cups of powdered sugar until creamy. Add the beaten eggs and beat thoroughly, then beat in about half of the caramel liquid. Fold in the sifted flour alternately with the remaining caramel liquid, mixing lightly to combine. Spoon into the cake pans.

Bake for 25 to 35 minutes, until springy to the touch. Remove from the oven and let stand for 1 to 2 minutes before turning out onto fine-mesh cake racks to cool.

Caramel Frosting: Place the sugar into a small heavy-based saucepan and heat to form a caramel (as for the cake mixture, above).

Heat the butter and milk until just beginning to boil, then carefully stir into the caramel until the lumps dissolve (as above). Add the vanilla. Pour into a heatproof bowl and let cool. Gradually add the confectioners' sugar. Beat until the mixture obtains a creamy spreading consistency.

To Assemble: Spread the Mock Cream Filling onto one of the cake layers. Place the second layer on top, and press gently to adhere.

Spread half the Caramel Frosting over the top layer. Place the remaining Caramel Frosting into a pastry bag with a rose tube, and pipe rosettes around the outer edge to decorate.

In warm weather, chill slightly before cutting into slices.

Snow Cake

Yield: 2 cakes

3 ounces butter or margarine, softened well

1 cup powdered sugar

1 teaspoon vanilla extract

1¾ cups flour

2 teaspoons baking powder

¼ teaspoon salt

½ cup milk

2 egg whites

Vienna Butter Cream
(see recipe, page 117)

2 or 3 ripe passion fruits

Preheat the oven to 350°F. Line the bases of two 7-inch layer-cake pans, and grease well.

Place the butter, sugar, and vanilla into a bowl. Sift in the flour, baking powder, and salt. Add the milk. Beat for 1 to 2 minutes with an egg whisk.

Beat the egg whites until soft peaks form; very gently fold into the cake mixture. Spoon into the two cake pans.

Bake for 25 to 30 minutes or until springy to the touch. Remove from the oven and let stand for 1 to 2 minutes before turning out onto a cake rack to cool.

When cold, frost each cake with the Vienna Butter Cream. Cut the passion fruits in half and spoon the pulp over the top.

Right: **Clockwise from top: Snow Cake (see above); California Orange Cake (see p. 64); Poppy-Seed Layer Cake (see p. 87).**

Spice and Sugar Swirls

Yield: 10 to 12 little swirls

2 cups self-rising flour

½ teaspoon salt

1 tablespoon sugar

½ stick butter or margarine

⅔ cup milk

1 egg, beaten

Filling:
2 tablespoons butter or margarine, melted

2 tablespoons brown sugar

1 teaspoon ground cinnamon

¾ cup chopped walnuts

Topping:
½ stick butter or margarine, melted

2 tablespoons brown sugar

2 tablespoons chopped walnuts

Preheat the oven to 425°F. Grease the muffin tins.

Sift the flour, salt, and sugar into a bowl. Melt the butter, add the milk and beaten egg, and stir into the flour mixture with a knife blade to mix to a soft dough. Turn onto a lightly floured board and pat out into a rectangle about 1 inch thick.

Combine the filling ingredients and sprinkle over the dough. Roll the rectangle of dough up loosely, and cut into 10 to 12 slices. Into each muffin-tin cup, place one slice—on its side so that the swirl is showing. Drizzle the melted butter over, and sprinkle with brown sugar and walnuts.

Bake for 15 to 17 minutes. Turn out onto cake racks, and serve warm.

Candy Cups

A recipe especially for microwave cooking

Yield: 12 little cakes

1 stick butter or margarine, softened

½ cup sugar

1 egg

1 cup milk

2 cups self-rising flour

1 tablespoon cocoa

peppermint candy stick, crushed, for topping

Combine the butter, sugar, egg, milk, sifted flour, and cocoa in a bowl, and whisk with a rotary beater or flat egg whisk until all ingredients are blended well—do not overmix.

Place six double-thickness paper baking cups into individual small custard cups or similar nonmetal dishes. Spoon in the cake mixture to fill each container three-quarters full. (Set the remaining mixture aside for the second batch.) Arrange on the glass tray or base of a microwave oven and heat for 4 to 5 minutes—according to directions given in oven's instruction booklet.

Remove from the oven and allow to stand for 4 to 5 minutes, then liberally sprinkle the top of each little cake with crushed peppermint candy. Allow to cool.

Repeat the heating procedure with the remaining mixture.

Note: A package of chocolate cake mix may replace the above cake recipe, if desired.

Micro Minis

A recipe especially for microwave cooking

Yield: 14 to 18 little cakes

¾ cup self-rising flour

1 tablespoon chocolate-drink powder

1½ tablespoons instant pudding mix

1 teaspoon milk powder

⅓ cup sugar

1 egg

1 tablespoon water

¾ stick butter or margarine, melted

Toppings:
flaked coconut, chocolate sprinkles, finely chopped nuts

Sift the dry ingredients (including sugar) into a bowl and make a well in the center. Add the egg, water, and cooled butter, and beat with a flat egg whisk for 2 minutes.

Place double-thickness paper baking cups into small custard cups or similar nonmetal dishes (or use the special microwave muffin pans and fill each half full with the cake mixture. Sprinkle one of the above toppings over each container of mixture and cook in batches of 6 to 8 according to manufacturer's instruction, for 2 to 2½ minutes—do not overcook.

Sprinkle a little more topping over each cake while the surfaces are still moist, if desired, and set aside to cool.

Fairy Cakes

Yield: 48 little cakes

2 sticks butter or margarine, softened

1 cup sugar

2 teaspoons vanilla extract

4 eggs, beaten

4 cups self-rising flour

¼ teaspoon salt

1 tablespoon skim-milk powder

1 cup water

Warm Glacé Icing
(see recipe, page 102)

Preheat the oven to 375°F. Line muffin tins with paper baking cups.

Beat the butter and sugar to a cream. Add the vanilla and beat well. Add the eggs gradually and beat thoroughly.

Sift the flour, salt, and milk powder, then sift again over the butter–egg mixture and fold in lightly. Add the water and fold in. Spoon the mixture into muffin tins, filling them two-thirds full.

Bake one or two dozen at a time for 17 to 20 minutes.

Icing and Decoration: When cold, ice the tops of the little cakes with pastel-colored Warm Glacé Icing and sprinkle pastel nonpareil over the surface.

Icings, Fillings & Glazes

Icings

Icings are confectioners' sugar and a liquid that set smoothly in a thin layer on top of the cake. Varying degrees of hardness may be obtained, depending on the mixing method or the amount and use of a shortening in the ingredients.

Icings are suitable for sponges, butter cakes, etc., where a simple coating is required. Flavoring and coloring can be added.

Frostings

Frostings are thicker sugar-based mixtures that are beaten to produce a soft, fluffy or meringue-like consistency, applied in thicker roughened or swirling patterns for a more luscious special-occasion effect. Flavorings and colorings, with a minimum of feature ingredients may be added as desired.

Frostings are suitable for layered sponges, butter cakes, shaped ring cakes, and for more elaborate or special-occasion use.

Creams

Most creams have a larger proportion of shortening or cream content than frostings. With added flavorings and colorings, plus small amounts of extra ingredients, they may also be used as fillings because they do not set too hard.

Creams are suitable for sponges, butter cakes, layered tortes, or gâteaux. Many need refrigeration storage, particularly during warmer weather.

Glazes

Glazes are heated mixtures of sugar and liquid, thin enough to be spooned or drizzled over the surface of the cake and absorbed. The sugar content is often supplied by the addition of jam, jelly, or honey. A flavored liqueur addition to the liquid is popular.

Glazes are suitable for dessert-style cakes that are served moist and for layer cakes, etc.

Fillings

These are thick, creamy mixtures whose main purpose is to hold together the layers of sponges, butter cakes, and the richer, more special-occasion and dessert-style confections. A filling may also be made from a frosting recipe with added fruits, nuts, marshmallows, chocolates, creams, liqueurs, or flavorings. Many need refrigeration storage.

Fillings are suitable for all types of sponges, butter cakes, and rolled cakes, to provide flavor and texture contrast.

Toppings

Crunchy or crumble-style toppings are usually used on the simple coffee cakes and loaves, sprinkled over the surface before or after baking. Care must be taken in turning out these cakes from their baking pans, to prevent damaging the textured surface.

Toppings are suitable for firm plain-style cakes to provide extra flavor and contrast interest.

Pastes and Fondants

These are firmer coverings of a dough-like consistency—rolled out flat and lifted onto the cake, then hand-molded into shape to set firmly for further finishing and decoration.

These are suitable for the rich fruit cakes used for weddings, birthdays, or other celebrations.

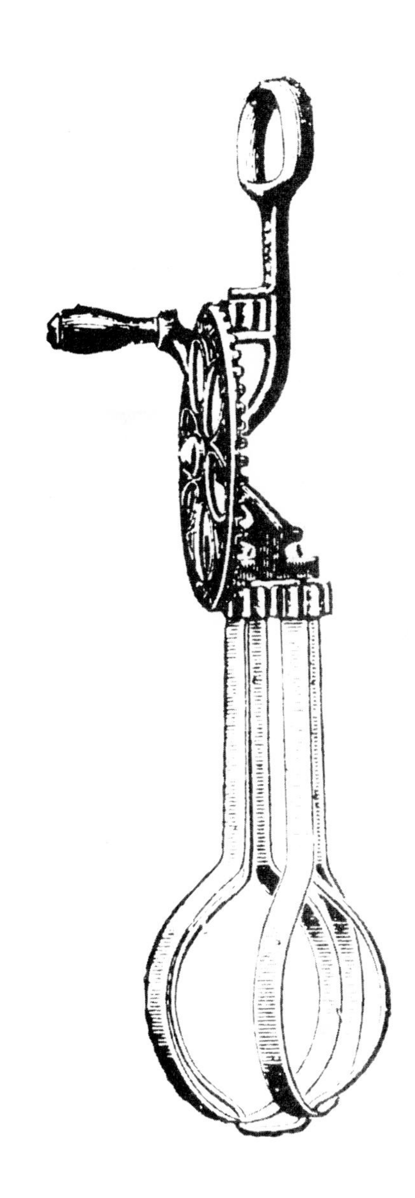

ICINGS

Warm Glacé Icing

Yield: Icing to cover the top of a 7- to 8-inch cake

1½ cups confectioners' sugar

1 tablespoon butter or margarine

1 to 2 tablespoons water, boiling

Method 1

Sift the confectioners' sugar into a bowl; make a well in the center.

Melt the butter in about 1½ tablespoons of boiling water. Add this to the sugar, and stir to smooth consistency. Add drops of boiling water, as required, to blend to creamy consistency. Pour at once onto the cake, and smooth over with a broad knife or spatula.

Allow to set before cutting.

Method 2

Sift the confectioners' sugar into a bowl; make a well in the center. Add the butter and 1½ tablespoons of boiling water, and stir to a paste. Place the bowl over hot water and stir until the butter melts and the icing is warmed. Add drops of boiling water, if required, to produce a creamy consistency. Pour at once onto the cake, and smooth over with a broad knife or spatula.

Allow to set before cutting.

Note: To smooth the icing on the cake more easily, dip a broad knife or spatula into boiling water to heat, shake off excess water, and lightly wipe the whole blade over the icing to even out. Do not wipe again, as blemishes would remain on the quickly setting surface.

Variations:

Citrus: Use orange juice or lemon juice instead of water and add drops of orange or yellow food coloring.

Chocolate: Add 1 to 2 tablespoons cocoa or drinking chocolate to the confectioners' sugar.

Coffee: Blend 1 to 2 teaspoons of instant coffee powder into the boiling water in Method 1.

Mocha: Add 1 tablespoon of cocoa and 1 teaspoon of instant coffee powder to the sugar in Method 2.

Pastel: Color the icing with a few drops of pink, green, or blue food coloring.

Royal Icing

Yield: ½ to ¾ cup

1 egg white

1¼ cups confectioners' sugar, finely sifted

½ teaspoon lemon juice, strained

Place the egg white in a clean, dry bowl (preferably glass) and beat lightly with a dry wooden spoon to break up but not become frothy.

Gradually add the sugar 1 to 2 tablespoons at a time, beating thoroughly after each addition to dissolve the sugar. As the mixture begins to thicken, add the sugar in smaller and smaller quantities.

When the mixture reaches the consistency of thick cream, add the lemon juice and continue beating for 1 to 2 minutes before adding more sugar as required—depending on size of egg white used.

Beat until the mixture will stand in short stiff peaks; cover the bowl with a damp—not wet—cloth until ready for use, beating again to smooth out if necessary. Use as required for pipe decoration work. Store tightly covered.

Note: Although the hand beating is tiresome, it produces a better icing than that made with electric mixers, which tend to incorporate too much air and produce a soft "marshmallow" result.

1. Brush sides and top of cake with lightly beaten egg white. Roll out two-thirds of the Almond Paste into a long strip and use to cover sides of cake.

2. Roll out remaining Almond Paste into a square the size of the top of the cake and carefully lift onto cake.

3. Smooth top and sides of cake, sealing edges by pressing Almond Paste together, using a little egg white if necessary. Brush Almond Paste with egg white.

4. Sprinkle a work surface liberally with sifted powdered sugar or cornstarch. Roll out Covering Fondant and use to cover cake.

5. Smooth Covering Fondant over top and sides of cake, rubbing corners and edges well. Cut off excess fondant.

6. Place a spoonful of Royal Icing on the center of a covered cake board. Center the cake on the board. Leave fondant to set for at least 24 hours before decorating.

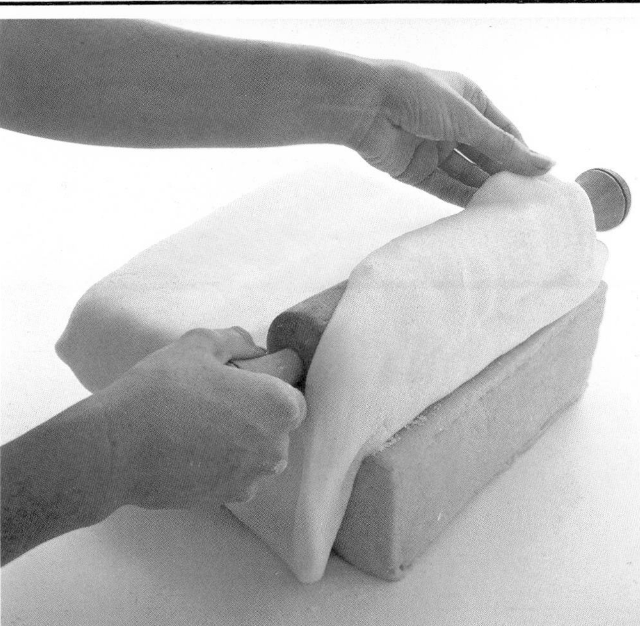

4

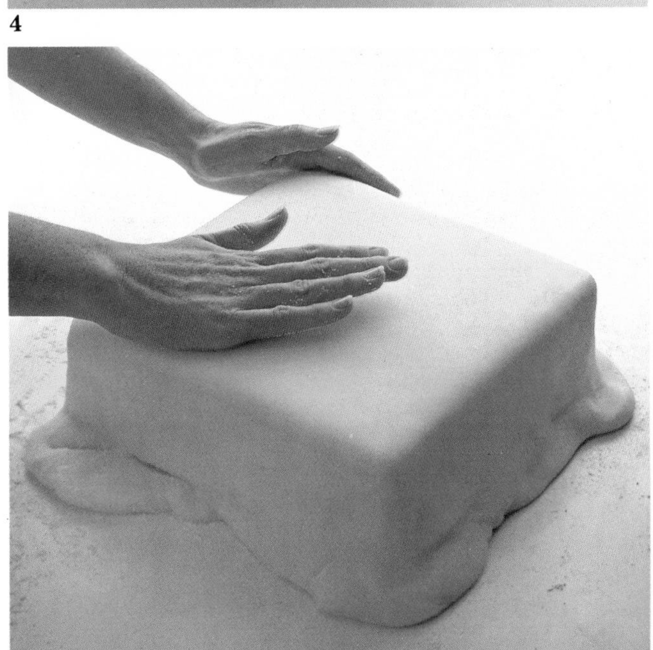

5

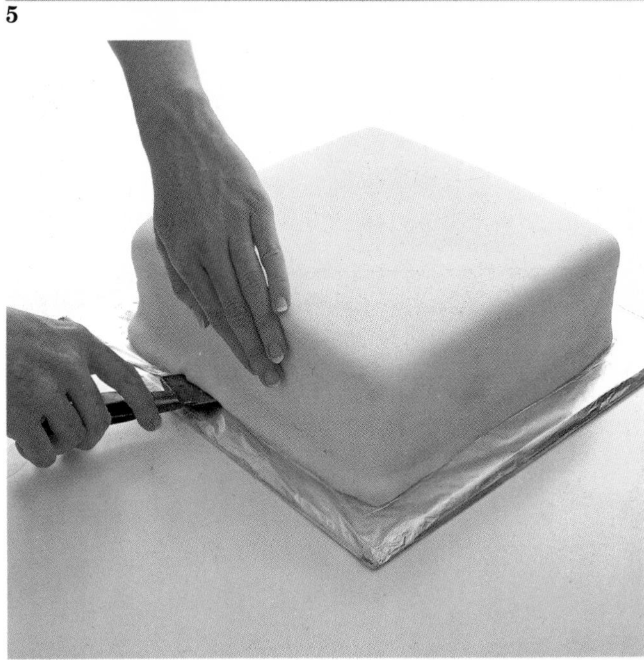

6

Rich Mocha Icing

Yield: Icing to cover the top of an 8- to 9-inch cake

¾ stick butter or margarine, softened
1½ cups confectioners' sugar, sifted
4 tablespoons chocolate-drink powder
2 tablespoons cocoa
2 teaspoons instant coffee
2 tablespoons boiling water
1 teaspoon vanilla extract or brandy extract

Cream the butter with half of the sugar.

Combine the chocolate, cocoa, and instant coffee in a small bowl; add the boiling water and blend to a soft paste, adding the vanilla or brandy extract.

Gradually beat the chocolate mixture into the buttered cream, then add the remaining sugar and beat well.

Quickly pour over the cake and smooth around the top edge; or allow it to drizzle down the sides, if desired. Allow to set before cutting.

Boiled White Icing

Yield: Icing to cover the tops and sides of two 8-inch cakes

2 cups sugar
1 cup water
2 egg whites
pinch of salt
few drops of lemon juice
1 teaspoon vanilla extract

Put the sugar and water into a saucepan over low heat and stir until the sugar has dissolved. Bring to a boil and cook until the syrup measures 240°F on a sugar thermometer or until a spoonful of the mixture forms a soft ball when dropped into iced water. Remove from the heat.

Beat the egg whites with the salt until they are frothy. Pour the hot but not boiling syrup into the egg white, beating constantly. (The easiest way to do this is in an electric mixer.) Add the lemon juice and vanilla.

Set the icing aside for a few minutes so that it begins to harden, then use immediately.

Satin Icing

Yield: Icing to cover the top of a 10-inch-square cake

¼ cup sugar
¼ cup evaporated milk
1 teaspoon light corn syrup
1 tablespoon butter or margarine
1½ cups confectioners' sugar, sifted
1 teaspoon almond extract

Combine the sugar, evaporated milk, corn syrup, and butter in a heatproof bowl; stir over boiling water until the butter has melted and all ingredients are well blended. Remove from the heat.

Gradually add the powdered sugar, beating well after each addition. Flavor with the almond extract, and spread over the cake. Allow to set before cutting.

Note: Should the icing seem a little thin, add an extra spoonful of sugar and beat well before using.

Mock Maple Icing

Yield: Icing to cover the top of an 8- to 9-inch cake

2 teaspoons butter or margarine
3 teaspoons light corn syrup
1½ cups confectioners' sugar, finely sifted
1 to 2 tablespoons lemon juice

Combine the butter and corn syrup in a heatproof bowl and melt over boiling water. Remove from the heat.

Gradually add three-quarters of the sugar, beating well. Add alternate batches of the remaining sugar and the lemon juice until the desired consistency is obtained.

Quickly pour over the cake and smooth around the top edge; or allow it to drizzle down the sides, if desired. Allow to set before cutting.

PASTES

Almond Paste—Marzipan

Yield: Paste to cover the top and sides of an 8-inch fruit cake

4½ cups confectioners' sugar

2¼ cups ground almonds

3 egg yolks

2 tablespoons sweet sherry

1 tablespoon lemon juice

Sift the sugar into a bowl and add the ground almonds; mix thoroughly and make a well in the center.

Beat the egg yolks, sweet sherry, and lemon juice together. Pour into the sugar mixture and gradually work into a firm smooth paste with one hand, kneading well.

Lightly sprinkle a board or work surface with a little extra powdered sugar, lift the mixture onto the board, and knead with both hands to a firm smooth dough—do not add too much extra sugar unless the dough is very soft. Cover tightly until ready for use, then re-knead gently before rolling out and applying to the cake as required.

Mock Almond Paste

Yield: Paste to cover the top and sides of an 8-inch fruit cake

3 cups confectioners' sugar

2⅔ cups flaked coconut

2 egg whites, lightly beaten

2 tablespoons corn syrup, warmed

almond, vanilla, or peppermint extract

Sift the sugar into a bowl and add the coconut; mix thoroughly and make a well in the center.

Add the egg whites, corn syrup, and 1 to 2 teaspoons of the desired flavoring, and beat with a wooden spoon to mix in as much of the sugar mixture as possible before the paste becomes too thick to handle. Remove the spoon and work with one hand to form a firm, smooth paste.

Lift onto a board that is lightly sprinkled with powdered sugar, and knead with both hands to a firm pliable dough—do not add too much sugar unless the dough is very soft. Cover tightly until ready for use, then re-knead gently before rolling out and applying to the cake as required.

FROSTINGS

Snow Frosting

Yield: Frosting to cover the top and sides of a 7- to 8-inch cake

2 egg whites

4 tablespoons water

1⅓ cups sugar

½ teaspoon baking powder

Place the unbeaten egg whites and the water into a heatproof glass bowl and sprinkle the sugar over the top. Place the bowl over a saucepan containing boiling water, and beat constantly until the mixture foams and begins to thicken—approximately 12 minutes.

Scatter the baking powder over the surface and continue beating until the mixture thickens further and begins to "crust" in the base of the bowl.

Remove from the heat and beat while cooling, for 1 to 2 minutes. Spoon over the top of the cake, allowing the mixture to fall over the sides; spread quickly all over the cake, and swirl into an attractive design with a knife or spatula. Allow to set before cutting.

Note: This frosting does need a little care in preparation: first to beat to the correct consistency before spooning over the cake and then to work quickly to swirl attractively before the frosting hardens.

Variations:

Citrus: Substitute half the amount of water with orange juice or lemon juice, and color with orange or yellow food coloring.

Chocolate Marble: (*See photograph, opposite page.*) Drizzle 2 to 3 tablespoons of melted chocolate over the completed frosting on the cake and swirl through with a fine knife or skewer for a marbled effect.

Coffee: (*See photograph, opposite page.*) Blend 1 to 2 teaspoons of instant coffee powder into the water before cooking, plus a little brandy or rum extract for flavor.

Nut Crunch: Quickly fold in ½ cup of finely chopped almonds or coconut before spooning the frosting over the cake. Or scatter nuts over the frosting on the cake before it hardens.

Cherry: Quickly fold in ½ cup of chopped candied cherries and color the frosting pale pink with food coloring, just before spooning it over the cake.

Butter Nut Frosting

Yield: Frosting to cover the top of an 11 × 7-inch cake

4 ounces cream cheese

⅓ cup peanut butter, crunchy style

1 teaspoon vanilla extract

1¼ cups confectioners' sugar, sifted

Allow the cream cheese to soften at room temperature for about 30 minutes. Place in a bowl with the peanut butter, and mix to combine. Add the vanilla, and gradually beat in the sugar to form a thick spreading cream. If the mixture seems too stiff, a little milk or cream may be added and blended through. Spread onto the cake and allow to become firm before cutting.

Coffee Fudge Frosting

Yield: Frosting to cover the top and partially cover the sides of an 8- to 9-inch fluted ring cake

⅔ cup evaporated milk

1 cup sugar

½ stick butter or margarine

1 teaspoon coffee extract

2 teaspoons Kahlua

Place the evaporated milk, sugar, butter, and coffee extract into a nonstick saucepan and heat slowly until the sugar is dissolved; stir gently to blend.

Bring to a boil; then boil steadily until, when a teaspoon of mixture is dropped into a glass of cold water, a soft ball is formed—about 5 minutes.

Take the saucepan from the heat and stand it in a large (heatproof) bowl containing ice water, to immediately retard further cooking. Beat constantly with a wooden spoon until the mixture begins to thicken. Remove the saucepan from the bowl.

Add the liqueur, and continue beating to a soft whipped-cream consistency. Pour onto the cake, allowing the frosting to drizzle down the sides. Allow to set before cutting.

Note: Cooking to the correct stage and the constant beating are the keys to success in making this creamy frosting.

Right: **Clockwise from top left: Snow Frosting (above); Coffee Frosting (above); Chocolate Marble Frosting (above).**

Sour-Cream Frosting

Yield: Frosting to cover the top of a 12 × 7-inch cake

1 cup sour cream, chilled

1 tablespoon lemon juice

¼ cup brown sugar, firmly packed

1 to 2 teaspoons ground cinnamon

Beat the sour cream and lemon juice together, and chill for 10 to 15 minutes to thicken.

Beat in the brown sugar. Spoon onto the cake, and swirl or mark with a knife to decorate; sprinkle cinnamon over the top. Chill, to firm again before cutting.

Cream-Cheese Frosting

Yield: Frosting to cover the top of an 8- to 9-inch cake

3 ounces packaged cream cheese

½ stick butter or margarine

1 teaspoon grated lemon rind

1½ cups confectioners' sugar, sifted

Allow the cream cheese and butter to stand at room temperature until softened. Place in a bowl with the lemon rind and beat until creamy. Gradually add the sugar, beating well between each addition.

Spread onto the cake, using a knife to swirl into an attractive design. Allow to become firm before cutting.

Variations:

Cinnamon: Add ½ teaspoon of ground cinnamon to the butter–cheese mixture. Or sprinkle the cinnamon over the frosting on the cake.

Chocolate: Melt 2 ounces of baking chocolate and blend into the butter–cheese mixture; flavor with vanilla extract before covering the cake.

Carrot: Fold in ½ cup of freshly grated carrot before covering the cake.

Sherry Nut: Beat 1½ tablespoons of sweet sherry into the butter–cheese mixture; fold in ½ cup of ground hazelnuts after adding the sugar.

Strawberry: Fold in 1 cup of chopped strawberries, taking care not to break up the fruit pieces.

Caramel Walnut Frosting

Yield: Frosting to cover the top of an 8- to 9-inch cake

¾ stick butter or margarine

½ cup brown sugar

3 tablespoons milk

1 cup confectioners' sugar, sifted

½ cup coarsely chopped walnuts

Melt the butter in a small nonstick saucepan. Add the brown sugar, and stir carefully to blend so that the mixture does not come too far up the sides of the pan. Remove the spoon and bring to a full rolling boil. Lower the heat and cook, again stirring constantly but carefully, for 2 minutes.

Add the milk and cook, stirring until the mixture once again comes to a boil. Remove from the heat, and cool to lukewarm.

Gradually beat the powdered sugar into the mixture, beating until the mixture is smooth and starts to thicken.

Fold in the walnuts, and spread onto the cake. Allow to become firm before cutting.

Crunchy Butterscotch Frosting

Yield: Frosting to cover and fill an 8- to 9-inch double-layer cake

4 ounces packaged cream cheese

2 tablespoons cream or evaporated milk

¼ teaspoon salt

3 cups confectioners' sugar, sifted

1 cup crushed butterscotch or toffee

Allow the cream cheese to stand at room temperature until softened. Beat until creamy; gradually add the cream and salt and beat well.

Add the powdered sugar in three or four batches, beating well after each addition. Fold in the crushed toffee or butterscotch.

Use as a filling between the layers and to cover the cake. Decorate the top with extra toffee pieces, if desired.

Note: As the crushed toffee may soften on prolonged contact with the moist frosting, the cake will need to be kept refrigerated or chilled unless eaten within a day or two.

Honeyed Chocolate Frosting

Yield: Frosting to cover the top of a 10-inch cake

¼ stick butter or margarine

1 tablespoon honey

3 ounces chocolate, grated

1½ cups confectioners' sugar, sifted

2 to 3 teaspoons lemon juice

Combine the butter, honey, and chocolate in a double boiler and heat over hot—not boiling—water until well blended. Remove from the heat and allow to cool slightly.

Gradually add the powdered sugar, beating well; flavor with lemon juice.

Spoon over the cake and swirl or mark into an attractive design. Allow to set before cutting.

Chocolate Peppermint Gloss

Yield: Frosting to cover the top and sides of a 9-inch ring cake

½ cup sugar

2 tablespoons cornstarch

1 cup hot milk

2 ounces chocolate, coarsely grated

¼ teaspoon salt

1½ ounces unsalted butter, chilled

½ to 1 teaspoon peppermint extract

Mix the sugar and cornstarch in a small nonstick saucepan. Stir in the hot milk and add the grated chocolate, beating briskly to form a smooth sauce. Cook over a low heat, stirring constantly, until the sauce thickens. Add the salt, and remove from the heat.

Cut the butter into small pieces and add to the sauce gradually, beating well between each addition. Flavor with drops of the peppermint extract, as desired.

Spread onto the cake while icing is hot; smooth over where required and allow to set before cutting.

Rocky-Road Frosting

Yield: Frosting to cover the top of a 9- to 10-inch cake

4 ounces unsweetened cooking chocolate

24 to 26 marshmallows, halved

½ stick butter or margarine, chopped

¼ cup water or sweet sherry

1½ cups confectioners' sugar, sifted

½ cup candied cherries, halved

½ cup walnuts, halved or quartered

Coarsely chop the chocolate and place in a heavy saucepan with half the quantity of marshmallows, the butter, and water; place over low heat and stir slowly but constantly until well blended. Remove from the heat and allow to cool to lukewarm.

Gradually add the powdered sugar, folding in lightly. Fold the cherries and walnuts through and fold in the remaining marshmallows.

Spoon onto the cake and "rough up" the surface with a knife. Allow to set before cutting.

Halving the marshmallows: Dip the blades of kitchen scissors frequently in either hot water or cooking oil to prevent marshmallows constantly sticking while cutting.

TOPPINGS

Pine–Nut Topping

Yield: Topping to cover the top of a 10-inch-square cake

½ stick butter or margarine
2 ounces peanut butter
1 cup brown sugar
1½ cups finely chopped salted peanuts
½ cup crushed, well-drained pineapple

Melt the butter and peanut butter in a saucepan over low heat. Add the sugar, peanuts, and pineapple and mix all together. Spread over the top of the cool—not cold—cake, and place on the rack of the broiler. Grill under low heat until the topping is bubbling and beginning to brown. Remove from heat and allow to cool before cutting.

Toffee Topping

Yield: Topping to decorate the top of an 8-inch cake

1 cup sugar
⅓ cup water, boiling

Dissolve the sugar in the water in a small saucepan over a very low heat. Bring to a boil, then increase the heat and allow to boil rapidly until the syrup turns a pale gold color.

Meanwhile grease the bottom of an 8-inch shallow cake pan.

When the syrup colors to a little lighter than desired, remove from the heat and allow the bubbles to subside; quickly but carefully pour into the prepared cake pan. Set aside, undisturbed, until the toffee begins to set.

Decoration 1: As the toffee sets, mark into serving-sized wedges (eight to ten wedges) with a well-greased round-ended knife. When completely set, carefully lift the wedges out and decorate, cartwheel fashion, on cream-topped sponge or light butter cake.

Decoration 2: Allow the toffee to completely set in the cake pan. With the handle of a knife, sharply tap the toffee surface to shatter into pieces, then lift out and scatter over a cream-topped sponge or light butter cake.

Coconut Topping

Yield: Topping to cover the top of a 9-inch cake

⅔ cup brown sugar
¾ stick butter or margarine, melted
¼ cup cream or evaporated milk
1½ cups flaked coconut
1 teaspoon vanilla extract

Combine all the ingredients in a bowl and mix well. Spread over the top of the warm cake, and place on the rack of a broiler pan. Grill under low heat until the topping surface is bubbling and beginning to brown. Remove from the heat and allow to cool before cutting.

Streusel Topping

Yield: Topping to cover the top of an 8-inch cake

¾ stick butter or margarine, softened
1 tablespoon brown sugar
1 cup chopped walnuts
1 teaspoon ground cinnamon
1 teaspoon grated orange rind
½ cup chopped candied cherries
orange juice

Beat the butter and brown sugar until creamy. Add the walnuts, cinnamon, and orange rind, and beat. Fold in the cherries and add sufficient orange juice to form a firm yet crumbly mixture.

Quickly sprinkle over the top of a half-baked, firm-textured cake without removing it from the oven; close the oven door and continue baking for the required time.

Remove the cake from the oven and allow to stand for 5 to 7 minutes in the pan. Turn out onto a rack covered with a clean cloth, then turn back onto another rack and allow to cool before cutting.

Right: **From top: Streusel Topping (see above); Pine Nut Topping (see above left); Coconut Topping (see above).**

FILLINGS

Chocolate Liqueur Filling

Yield: Fills a 4-egg chocolate sponge roll

¾ cup cream

½ stick butter or margarine

12 ounces baking chocolate, chopped

2 tablespoons coffee rum liqueur

Place the cream and butter in a nonstick saucepan and heat until boiling rapidly. Add the chocolate and stir until the chocolate has melted and is blended through. Remove from the heat and allow to cool.

Beat the mixture vigorously with an electric hand beater until it begins to thicken. Add the liqueur and continue beating until the filling is sufficiently thick to spread onto the sponge roll. Roll up and chill before cutting.

The richness of the chocolate filling requires no other covering to the roll than a light dusting of confectioners' sugar or a whipped unsweetened cream.

Hungarian Hazelnut Filling

Yield: Fills an 8-inch cake, sliced into three layers

1¼ cups cream

½ cup powdered sugar

¾ cup finely chopped hazelnuts

6 egg yolks

2 to 3 teaspoons brandy or rum

Place the cream, sugar, and hazelnuts into a small nonstick saucepan; bring slowly to a boil. Simmer over low heat until the mixture is thick—approximately 10 minutes.

Remove from the heat, pour the mixture into a heatproof bowl (warmed slightly), and stir until cold.

Add the egg yolks one at a time and beat in thoroughly; flavor with brandy or rum. Spread onto the layers of cake, rejoin the layers, and cover the outside of the cake as desired.

A simple chocolate flavored Vienna Butter Cream would complement the richness of this filling (see recipe, page 117).

Lemon-Sauce Filling

Yield: 1½ to 1¾ cups

½ cup sugar

2 tablespoons cornstarch

⅔ cup water

2 egg yolks (optional)

2 tablespoons butter or margarine, chopped

3 teaspoons grated lemon rind

½ cup lemon juice

Combine the sugar and cornstarch in a small, nonstick saucepan; gradually blend in the water. Heat slowly until boiling, stirring constantly. Lower the heat and simmer for 1 to 2 minutes, stirring frequently.

(If a richer mixture is desired, add the egg yolks at this stage and beat in briskly.)

Remove from the heat and add the butter; stir until melted through. Then stir in the lemon rind and lemon juice.

Mock Cream Filling—Boiled

Yield: 1½ to 1¾ cups

1¼ cups milk

2 tablespoons cornstarch

½ stick butter or margarine

1 teaspoon vanilla extract

2 tablespoons confectioners' sugar

Blend 3 tablespoons of the milk with the cornstarch.

Heat the remaining milk in a small, nonstick saucepan, until boiling. Gradually add the blended cornstarch and stir briskly until smooth. Lower the heat and simmer for 1 to 2 minutes, then remove from the heat and allow to cool.

Beat the butter, vanilla, and sugar until creamy. Gradually add the milk mixture, beating well between each addition.

Use as a filling for sponges or light layer cakes.

Note: A richer cream may be made by substituting half the milk with cream or evaporated milk.

Variations:

Chocolate: Beat 2 tablespoons of grated chocolate into the hot milk mixture before cooling.

Mocha: Add 1 tablespoon of cocoa and 1 teaspoon of instant coffee powder to the cornstarch while blending with the milk.

Mock Cream Filling—Washed

Yield: 1 cup

1 stick butter, softened

½ cup sugar

1 tablespoon hot milk

vanilla extract

Beat the butter and sugar together until the mixture is very white and fine; care should be taken to constantly incorporate any mixture clinging up the sides of the bowl so that all the creaminess is of the same consistency.

Carefully pour ice-cold water over the mixture, let it stand for 1 minute, then pour it off and beat thoroughly. Repeat this "washing" process two or three times, until the mixture is very smooth and no sugar crystals remain undissolved.

Add the hot milk and vanilla, and beat through. Use to fill sponges, sponge rolls, and light layer cakes.

Mocha Custard Filling

Yield: 1¾ to 2 cups

3 tablespoons custard powder

2 tablespoons cocoa

1 teaspoon instant coffee powder

4 tablespoons sugar

¼ teaspoon salt

1½ cups milk

2 tablespoons butter or margarine

vanilla extract or brandy extract

Combine the custard powder, cocoa, instant coffee powder, sugar, and salt in a small nonstick saucepan; gradually blend in the milk. Heat slowly, stirring constantly, until bubbling. Remove from the heat, and beat in the butter. Flavor as desired, cover, and chill. Use to fill recess sponges, pie crusts, meringues, etc.

Note: Extra richness may be added to this filling by doubling the quantity of butter to ½ stick.

Pineapple Ginger Filling

Yield: 2½ to 3 cups

1 tablespoon custard powder

¼ teaspoon ground ginger

1¼ cups milk

4 egg yolks

1 tablespoon light corn syrup

1 tablespoon lemon juice

2 tablespoons butter or margarine, chopped

2 ounces crystallized ginger, chopped

1 cup crushed, well-drained pineapple

Combine the custard powder and ground ginger in a nonstick saucepan; blend in the milk and bring slowly to a boil, stirring constantly.

Beat the egg yolks, corn syrup, and lemon juice together, then beat into the milk mixture with the butter pieces. Stir over low heat for 1 to 2 minutes, until mixture has a thick custard consistency. Allow to cool.

Fold in the ginger and pineapple, and chill before using. Use to fill meringues, pie crusts, layer tortes, etc.

Date and Walnut Filling

Yield: 1½ cups

1½ cups pitted, chopped dates

½ cup lemon juice

1 teaspoon grated lemon rind

¼ cup chopped walnuts

1 tablespoon brown sugar

Combine the dates and lemon juice in a small nonstick saucepan and stir over low heat until the dates have softened and the mixture is thick. Remove from the heat, add the lemon rind, walnuts, and brown sugar, and stir. Allow to cool before using to fill spiced or fruited layer cakes, etc.

Note: This filling may be extended in volume by adding 2 to 3 ounces cream cheese, Ricotta cheese, or natural yogurt.

FONDANTS

Covering Fondant

Yield: Fondant to cover the top and sides of an 8-inch fruit cake

1 ounce water
2 teaspoons gelatin
⅓ ounce vegetable shortening
1 tablespoon sugar water
1 teaspoon glycerin
3 cups confectioners' sugar
food coloring (optional)

Combine the water and gelatin in a heatproof bowl and place over boiling water until well blended. Add the shortening and sugar water and stir to combine, then add the glycerin.

Sift all but ½ cup of the sugar into a bowl, and make a well in the center. Add the lukewarm gelatin mixture. Stir with a wooden spoon until as much of the sugar is incorporated as possible before the paste becomes too thick to handle. Remove the spoon and work with one hand to form a soft, smooth paste. Add drops of food coloring to obtain desired pastel shade.

Lift onto a board that is liberally sprinkled with the reserved ½ cup powdered sugar, and knead with both hands until smooth and pliable without stickiness. Cover tightly until ready for use, then re-knead gently before rolling out and applying to the cake as required.

Modeling Fondant

Yield: about 1½ pounds mixture

½ cup sugar
1 tablespoon sugar water
2½ tablespoons water
¼ teaspoon cream of tartar
½ teaspoon glycerin
2½ teaspoons gelatin
extra 1 ounce water, warmed
1 ounce vegetable shortening, chopped
2½ cups confectioners' sugar
food coloring (optional)

Place the sugar, sugar water, water, cream of tartar, and glycerin into a small, heavy-based saucepan and heat slowly until the sugar is dissolved; bring slowly to a boil.

Boil the sugar syrup until it registers 240°F on a sugar thermometer—or when a little dropped into a glass of cold water forms a soft ball. Remove from the heat.

Dissolve the gelatin in the warmed water, and add to the sugar mixture when the bubbles subside; allow the mixture to cool for 5 to 6 minutes, then add the chopped shortening and allow it to melt through.

Turn into a large bowl and gradually beat in three-quarters of the sifted sugar to form a thick paste. Cover with a damp—not wet—cloth and set aside for at least 12 hours.

Turn onto a board and knead in the remaining powdered sugar. Add drops of food coloring, as desired.

1. To make hyacinths, color Modeling Fondant with food coloring. Using cornstarch lightly on fingertips, take a small piece of Modeling Fondant about the size of a pea and roll between the fingers to form a cone shape. Insert knitting needle (dipped in cornstarch) and hollow center out finely. Using scissors, cut to form six petals. Cut petals to a point and curl backward.

2. Insert moistened hooked wire through the flower and secure at base using thumb and forefinger. One bud and two flowers may be twisted together to form a spray.

3. To make frangipani, roll out sufficient Modeling Fondant thinly to cut five petals at the same time with a petal cutter. Moisten petals and press them together to form a fan. Pick up petals and with the back of the flower facing you, lap right side over left and press firmly to join flower. Twist base with fingers.

4. Place flower in egg carton and curl each petal by placing small pieces of foil between them. Leave to dry. Make a green cone and, when completely dry, place a small amount of Royal Icing inside cone to attach flower. To color flower, use nontoxic chalk powder (mixture of lemon and light orange) and lightly dust with dry brush.

5. Extension Work. Using a No. 3 pipe and Royal Icing, pipe scallops around the base of the cake, allowing each row to dry before piping the next. You will need 4 or 5 rows of scallops to support the bridgework. Change to No. 00 pipe and drop threads from the top to the scallops. Make sure each line is straight and evenly spaced.

6. For lace pieces and embroidery work, Royal Icing is used with a No. 00 pipe.

2

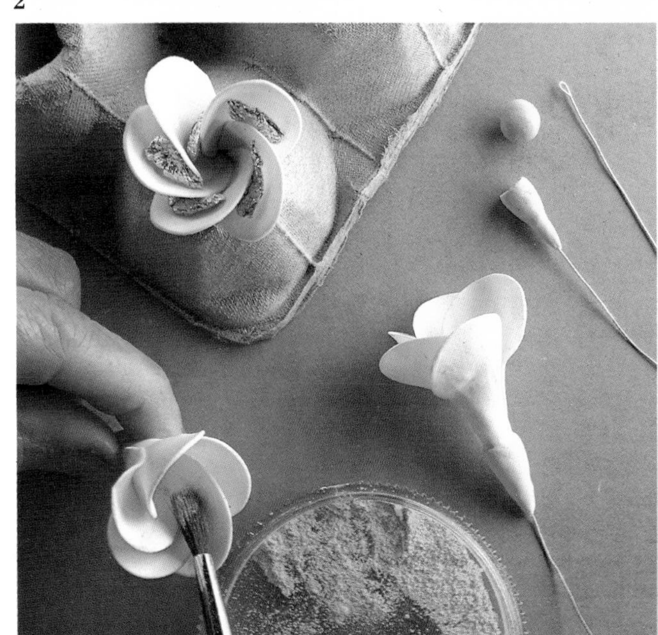

4

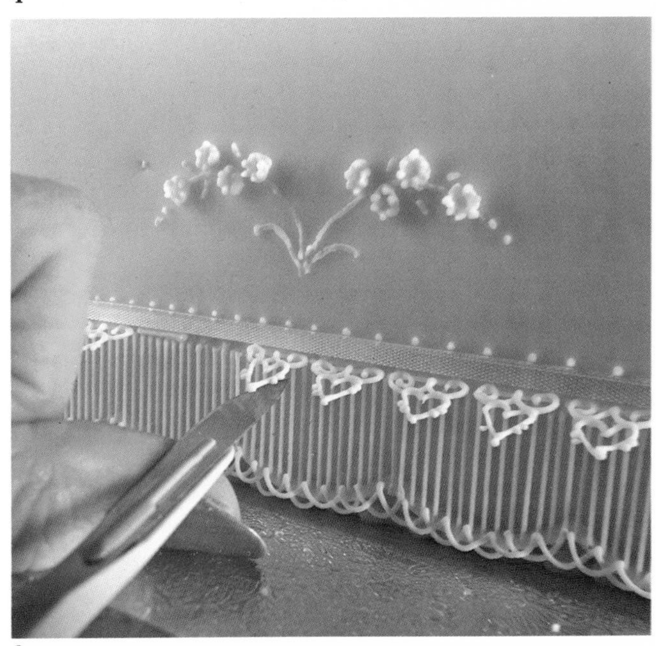

6

CREAMS

Chocolate Butter Cream

Yield: Cream to cover and fill an 8- to 9-inch double-layer cake

¾ stick butter or margarine
1 cup semisweet chocolate pieces
½ cup sour cream
1 teaspoon vanilla extract or rum extract
2½ to 2¾ cups confectioners' sugar

Combine the butter and chocolate pieces in a heat-proof bowl over hot—not boiling—water, and stir until blended. Remove from the heat and allow to cool slightly.

Stir in the sour cream and vanilla, and gradually work in the sifted sugar to form a soft, spreading consistency. Beat well.

Use as a filling between the layers and to cover the cake. Swirl or peak the top into an attractive design. Allow to become firm before cutting.

Choc-Coffee Cream

Add 2 teaspoons of instant coffee powder that has been blended to a paste with a little hot water to the melted chocolate mixture before adding the sour cream.

Brandied Coffee Cream

Yield: Cream to cover and fill a 9-inch double-layer cake

2 sticks butter, softened
1 tablespoon instant coffee powder
3 tablespoons milk, heated
¼ teaspoon salt
3 cups confectioners' sugar, sifted
1 to 2 tablespoons brandy

Beat the butter until creamy. Dissolve the instant coffee powder in the heated milk and add to the butter, beating well. Add the salt. Gradually beat in 2 cups of the sugar, beating well after each addition. Beat in the brandy, and continue adding the remaining sugar until the desired consistency is obtained.

Allow the coffee cream to stand for 10 minutes for the flavors to blend. Fill and cover the cake, and allow to set before cutting.

Vienna Butter Cream

Yield: Cream to cover the top of a 7- to 8-inch cake

½ stick butter or margarine, softened

½ teaspoon vanilla extract

1 tablespoon milk

1¼ cups confectioners' sugar

Beat the butter and vanilla in a bowl until creamy. Add the milk, and beat to blend in. Gradually add the sifted sugar, beating well after each addition.

While still soft, spread onto the top of the cake. Swirl or rough-up into an attractive design. Allow to firm before cutting.

As a Filling:

This soft cream may be used as a filling for cakes if made to a moister consistency. Use a little extra liquid or add such ingredients as crushed pineapple, apricot jam (apricot jelly), chopped canned fruits, fruit mince, etc.

Variations:

Citrus: Add 1 teaspoon of grated orange rind or lemon rind to the creamy butter, and substitute fruit juice for milk.

Chocolate Rum: Use rum extract with the butter, and add 1 to 2 tablespoons of chocolate-drink powder to the sugar.

Coffee: Blend 1 to 2 teaspoons of instant coffee with the milk, before adding it to the mixture.

Mocha: Add 1 tablespoon of cocoa and 1 teaspoon of instant coffee powder to the sugar.

Honey Spice: Add 1 tablespoon of honey to the creamy butter, use lemon juice instead of the milk, and add ¼ teaspoon of ground cinnamon with the sugar.

Nut Crunch: Fold ½ cup finely chopped nuts (walnuts, hazelnuts, pecans, etc.) into the creamy mixture.

Sherry: Omit the vanilla extract. Add 1 tablespoon of sweet sherry with 1 egg yolk to the creamy butter.

Lemon Butter Cream

Yield: 1 to 1¼ cups

3 egg yolks

½ stick butter or margarine, chopped

2 teaspoons cornstarch

⅓ cup sugar

2 teaspoons grated lemon rind

½ cup lemon juice

1½ cups whipped cream

Combine the egg yolks, butter, cornstarch, sugar, lemon rind, and lemon juice in the top half of a double boiler; blend well. Place over simmering water and cook, stirring frequently, until the mixture is of a thick custard consistency. Remove from the heat and allow to cool.

Fold in the whipped cream. (For a perfectly smooth Lemon Butter Cream, press the mixture through a fine sieve to remove any tiny pieces of lemon rind remaining.) Use as a filling for sponge cakes or meringues.

Variation:

Orange: Use orange rind and juice instead of lemon rind and juice, and omit 2 teaspoons of the sugar.

Lemon Ginger Cream

Yield: Cream to cover or fill a 9-inch-square cake

4 eggs, separated

1¼ cups sugar

4 tablespoons lemon juice

1 to 2 teaspoons grated lemon rind

⅓ cup chopped crystallized ginger

Combine the egg whites, sugar, lemon juice, and lemon rind in a heatproof glass bowl. Beat well. Place the bowl over a saucepan containing boiling water, and cook, beating with a rotary or electric hand beater until thickened—approximately 5 minutes.

Beat the egg yolks in a small bowl until lemon-colored; quickly add about 3 tablespoons of the hot mixture and beat briskly to combine. Turn the egg-yolk mixture into the hot mixture over the boiling water, and continue beating slowly for another 5 minutes. Remove from the heat and allow to cool.

Fold in the chopped ginger; chill slightly. Stir again before use.

Variations

Orange Jaffa: Substitute orange juice and rind for the lemon juice and rind; and substitute coarsely chopped chocolate for the ginger.

Pine Ginger: Use pineapple juice instead of the lemon juice and rind; add ½ cup of crushed well-drained pineapple with the ginger.

Coco-Pine: Omit the ginger, and substitute ¼ cup of crushed well-drained pineapple and ¼ cup of flaked coconut.

Lemallow: Omit the ginger, and fold 8 to 10 marshmallows, quartered, into the cooled mixture.

Almond Pastry Cream

Yield: 2 cups

½ cup Vanilla Pastry Cream (see recipe below)
¾ stick soft unsalted butter
⅔ cup ground almonds
¾ cup confectioners' sugar
1 egg
1 tablespoon cornstarch
2 teaspoons rum

Make and chill the vanilla pastry cream according to the recipe.

Cream the butter until soft, then add the ground almonds and powdered sugar and beat well, using either a wooden spoon or an electric mixer. Add the egg, and beat well. Add the cornstarch and rum, and beat at medium speed until evenly combined.

Add the vanilla pastry cream, a tablespoon at a time, beating at medium speed, until it is all combined. Cover and store in the refrigerator until required. May be prepared and stored in the refrigerator for up to a week.

Vanilla Pastry Cream

Yield: 1 cup

1 cup milk
1 vanilla bean, split lengthwise
3 large egg yolks
⅓ cup sugar
2 tablespoons flour or cornstarch

Place the milk and vanilla bean in a saucepan and bring to a boil; cover, and keep hot. Beat the egg yolks and sugar together with an electric mixer or a wire balloon whisk, until the mixture is thick enough to fall as a ribbon when the beater is lifted. Stir in the flour with a whisk.

Strain the hot milk into the mixture, beating continuously with the whisk. Return the mixture to the saucepan and bring to a boil, stirring continuously with a wooden spoon. Boil for 1 minute to thicken, stirring vigorously, then pour into a bowl and rub the surface with a lump of butter to prevent a skim forming while cooling. Use when cold, or cover and store in the refrigerator for up to a week.

Crème Pâtissière

Yield: 1½ to 2 cups filling

1¼ cups milk
2 egg yolks
¼ cup sugar
2 tablespoons cornstarch
¼ teaspoon salt
extra ¼ cup milk
1 teaspoon vanilla extract
½ stick unsalted butter (optional)

The second and subsequent stages in preparing this mixture require a double boiler with preheated water in the bottom half.

Heat the 1¼ cups of milk in a small saucepan until scalding; set aside.

Combine the egg yolks, sugar, cornstarch, and salt in the top half of a double boiler; gradually blend in the extra ¼ cup of milk. Add one-quarter of the scalded milk and stir quickly; gradually beat in the remaining milk.

Heat, beating constantly, over hot water until the mixture thickens. Simmer a few minutes, then remove from the heat and flavor with vanilla.

For a particularly rich cream, add the chopped butter and beat until smooth.

Pour into a small bowl and allow to cool. Chill before use.

Right: **Rich Fruit Cake (see p. 84), iced and decorated with Frangipani, Hyacinth, and Lily of the Valley (see p. 114 for instructions).**

Hazelnut Custard Cream

Yield: Cream to fill and cover the top of a 7- to 8-inch double-layer cake

3 egg yolks

⅓ cup sugar

1 teaspoon cornstarch

⅓ cup cream or evaporated milk

1 tablespoon sweet sherry

1½ sticks unsalted butter, softened

2 ounces hazelnuts, grated or ground coarsely

In the top half of a double boiler, place the egg yolks and sugar. Beat until thick and lemon colored—a small electric hand beater is ideal.

Scatter the cornstarch over the surface, and beat again; gradually add the cream. Place over hot—not boiling—water and cook, stirring constantly with a wooden spoon, until thickened to custard consistency.

Remove from the heat and stir in the sweet sherry. Allow to cool, and chill.

Beat the butter in a bowl, again with the electric hand beater, until white and creamy; add the hazelnuts and mix.

Gradually add spoonfuls of the chilled custard, beating gently with each addition. Remove the beater, place the bowl over a large basin containing iced water, and beat with a wooden spoon until the mixture is firm enough to spread onto the cake.

After spreading, chill the cake until the cream is firm before cutting.

Chocolate Almond Cream

Yield: Cream to cover or fill a 9-inch cake

½ cup slivered, blanched almonds

½ stick butter or margarine

½ cup semisweet chocolate pieces

1 cup thickened or heavy cream, chilled

1 tablespoon confectioners' sugar

Sauté the almonds in heated butter in a small pan until golden brown. Drain off (and discard) any excess butter, and set the almonds aside.

Melt the chocolate pieces over hot—not boiling—water; cool to just warm.

Beat the cream and sugar until thickened and standing in soft peaks. Gradually fold in the warm chocolate, allowing the chocolate to break off into hardened flecks. Fold the almonds through. Use to fill or cover light sponge cakes or chocolate cakes.

To Melt Chocolate: Mold a "bowl" to fit over a small saucepan, using heavy or double-thickness aluminum foil. Quarter-fill the saucepan with hot water, place the foil bowl over and crimp the edges to secure. Place the chocolate on the foil and allow to melt.

Lift the foil bowl off the saucepan, spread open slightly and scrape out the melted chocolate with a pliable spatula. Discard the foil.

Brazilian Butter Cream

Yield: Cream to fill or cover the top of a 9-inch cake

1½ sticks butter, softened

1 cup sugar

6 ounces unsweetened baking chocolate, melted and cooled

2 tablespoons rum

1 tablespoon coffee-rum liqueur

5 eggs, beaten

Cream the butter and sugar in a bowl; add the chocolate and beat well. Beat in the rum and coffee liqueur. Add the beaten eggs and whisk thoroughly until the mixture thickens.

Chill for about 1 hour, then whisk again before using to fill the cake. Chill the cake thoroughly to set the filling before cutting.

GLAZES

Brandied Apricot Glaze

Yield: Glaze to cover the top of an 8-inch sponge cake

1½ cups apricot jam (jelly)

¾ cup water

2 to 3 thin strips lemon peel

2 tablespoons brandy or brandy liqueur

Chop or mash the apricot jam to break up any pieces; push through a coarse sieve if necessary. Place in a nonstick saucepan with the water and lemon peel, and heat slowly until just beginning to boil; reduce the heat and simmer for 5 minutes.

Add the brandy, simmer for another 5 minutes; remove the lemon peel and allow to cool.

Spoon over the cake, allowing the glaze to be partially absorbed into the surface. Chill.

Variations:
Apple or redcurrant jelly and port wine.
Raspberry jam (jelly) and sweet vermouth.
Marmalade and orange brandy liqueur.
Cherry jam (jelly) and kirsch liqueur.

Chocolate Glaze

Yield: Glaze to cover the top of an 8-inch cake

4 ounces semisweet chocolate

½ stick butter, chopped

1 tablespoon light corn syrup

Grate the chocolate coarsely and place in a heatproof bowl with the butter and corn syrup; place over hot—not boiling—water and stir occasionally until the chocolate and butter are melted and blended.

Remove from the heat and stir until the mixture cools slightly and thickens to the desired consistency. Pour over the cake, and, when almost set, mark into cutting sections. Allow to set before cutting.

Notes: Heat over hot—not boiling—water so that the cocoa fats will not separate in the chocolate and cause a dull finish to the glaze.

Stir—do not beat—while the mixture cools slightly; beating will incorporate air that will form bubbles in the glaze.

Mark the glaze into sections before fully set, as this will help to prevent unsightly cracks forming on the top when final cutting is performed.

If the cake is chilled before covering with the glaze, setting time will be shortened considerably.

Cherry-Liqueur Glaze

Yield: Glaze to cover the top of an 8-inch cake

1 can (15 ounces) red cherries—approximate amount

water or lemon juice

1 tablespoon arrowroot

1 tablespoon cherry brandy liqueur

Drain the canned cherries well and set them aside; measure the syrup, and add water or lemon juice to make ¾ cup.

Blend the arrowroot with a little of the cherry syrup. Place the remaining syrup in a small saucepan; heat slowly until boiling.

Meanwhile arrange the pitted cherries over the top of a sponge or light butter cake in a single layer.

Stir the blended arrowroot into the boiling syrup and cook, stirring constantly, for 1 minute. Add the cherry brandy liqueur, quickly blend through, and drizzle immediately over the cherries on the cake. Allow to set and chill before cutting.

Variations:
Canned strawberries and orange brandy liqueur.
Canned apricots and apricot brandy liqueur.
Canned sliced pears and crème de menthe liqueur with green food coloring.

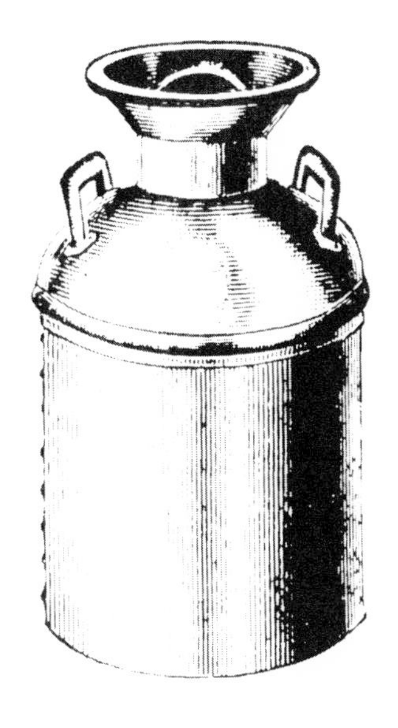

Snacks & Cookies

Handy hints

The amount of liquid required in a recipe to make a dough will vary, depending on the size of the eggs, the moisture in the flour, and the general humidity and weather prevailing. Measure the flour before sifting.

All ingredients, especially eggs, must be at room temperature before making a cookie dough. Eggs enrich a dough and make a crumblier cookie.

Approximately double the amount of flour to butter and sugar is used for cookies spooned directly onto baking sheets or for rolled-out and stamped-out cookies.

Minimize kneading the dough after addition of flour—otherwise the cookies will toughen. Only lightly flour the work surface on which dough is to be rolled.

Keep the dough chilled and covered before use, and dust the cutters with flour.

If greasing cookie sheets, use polyunsaturated oil only, as butter causes cookies to stick. Butter in the mixture, however, gives the best flavor.

Always use a shallow cookie sheet or one with a raised edge only on one side (except for bars and slices) so that they cook evenly. Make sure it is cold before use so that cookies won't lose their shape. Leave space between cookies for spreading (especially with drop cookies).

Always preheat your oven and, if cooking more than one pan of cookies, space them well apart. Rotate the cookie sheets as well as reversing the top and bottom shelves toward the end of the cooking time, for even browning.

After removing the cookie sheet from the oven, immediately lift off the cookies with a spatula (to prevent further cooking) and place onto a rack to cool. Do not pile them on top of one another.

Do not store soft and crisp cookies together. To keep soft cookies moist, store in a cool place, preferably in a stoneware jar fitted with a tight lid, and even place a clove-studded lemon or a piece of bread in with them. If crisp cookies are stored in a jar or tin with a loose-fitting cover, they should not soften. If necessary, restore crispness by giving them 5 minutes in a slow oven, 300°F.

The number of cookies made depends on the thickness of the dough, the cutter or spoon size, and whether or not you use the leftover pastry. The amount of flour used is also a guide. Generally 15 cookies, 1½ inches in diameter, are made for each cup of flour used.

SNACKS

Cheese Straws

Yield: about 30 sticks

2 cups self-rising flour
1 teaspoon salt
¼ to ½ teaspoon cayenne pepper (to taste)
4 ounces cheddar cheese, finely grated
3 ounces vegetable shortening, melted and cooled
2 tablespoons cold water

Preheat the oven to 450°F. Lightly grease the baking sheets with polyunsaturated oil.

Sift together the flour, salt, and cayenne pepper, and thoroughly mix in the grated cheese.

Add the water to the melted shortening and pour it over the flour–cheese mixture, mixing to form a firm dough. Roll it thinly, cut into strips ¼ inch × 4 inches, and twist each strip slightly.

Bake for 10 minutes. Turn onto wire racks to cool.

Sesame-Seed Cheese Buttons

Yield: about 30 little biscuits

1½ cups flour
1 teaspoon salt
1 teaspoon ground paprika
pinch of chili powder
1½ cups finely grated cheddar cheese
½ cup finely grated Parmesan cheese
1½ sticks butter, cut into ½-inch cubes
2 tablespoons freshly toasted white sesame seeds

Preheat the oven to 350°F. Grease the baking sheets.

Sift together the flour, salt, paprika, and chili powder.

Cream together the cheeses, butter, and sesame seeds. Combine both mixtures to make a dough, and roll it into four logs 1 to 1¼ inches in diameter. Wrap each log in aluminum foil and chill in the refrigerator until firm. Then slice into ¼-inch-thick rounds.

Bake for 10 minutes. Turn onto wire racks to cool.

Sri Lankan Curry Crisps

Yield: about 24 rounds

2 ounces finely grated cheddar cheese
½ stick butter
1¼ cups self-rising flour, sifted
1 teaspoon onion salt
1 teaspoon curry powder
3 tablespoons milk
milk for brushing rounds
¼ cup cornflake crumbs
1 tablespoon flaked coconut
1 teaspoon garam masala (ground spices)

Preheat the oven to 400°F. Grease the baking sheets.

Cream the cheese and butter together. Add alternate batches of sifted flour/onion salt/curry powder, and the milk, until a firm dough is formed. Turn out onto a floured board and knead lightly; roll out to a thickness of ¼ inch and cut into small rounds. Brush rounds with milk. Top with a mixture of cornflake and coconut crumbs; sprinkle the garam masala over the topping.

Bake for 10 to 12 minutes or until they are crisp and brown. These crisps may be served hot or cold.

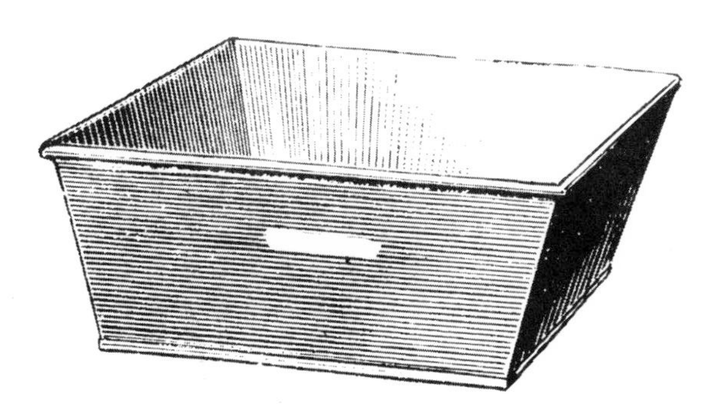

Hungarian Onion Ham Slice

Yield: 28 pieces

1 pound salted crackers
4 ounces ham, finely chopped
1 large onion, finely grated
½ green capsicum (pepper), finely chopped
1 clove garlic, minced
1 teaspoon dry English mustard powder
2 large eggs, lightly beaten
⅓ cup milk
¼ teaspoon salt
⅛ teaspoon ground black pepper
½ cup finely grated cheddar cheese
dried ground paprika, for garnish

Preheat the oven to 400°F. Thoroughly grease a shallow-sided 11 × 7-inch pan.

Crush the crackers finely with a rolling pin, or make fine crumbs in a food processor. Combine with the ham, onion, capsicum, garlic, and mustard, mixing well.

In a separate bowl, beat together the eggs, milk, and salt and pepper, then pour this into the crumb mixture and mix thoroughly. Turn into the pan and press in well. Sprinkle the cheese evenly over the top, and dust with paprika, to taste.

Bake for 15 to 20 minutes or until golden. Cut into 1 × 4-inch fingers and serve hot.

Bizcochos (Spanish Sherry Twists)

Yield: about 36 twists

6 egg yolks, unbeaten
3 teaspoons finely grated orange zest
1 teaspoon finely grated lemon zest
1 tablespoon Amontillado sherry
1 teaspoon salt
1 stick butter, softened
3 cups flour, sifted
beaten egg wash (1 egg, beaten with 1 tablespoon water)

Preheat the oven to 375°F. Grease the baking sheets.

Cream together the egg yolks, zest, sherry, salt, and butter, Gradually add the flour, kneading to make a smooth dough. Mold into twists and brush each twist with lightly beaten egg wash.

Bake for about 10 minutes or until golden brown. Turn onto wire racks to cool.

Russian Caraway Triangles

Yield: about 50 triangles

3 eggs, separated
½ cup sugar
¼ teaspoon salt
1 teaspoon vanilla extract
¾ cup flour
½ tablespoon caraway seeds

Preheat the oven to 425°F. Grease a jelly-roll pan.

Beat the egg whites until stiff.

In a separate bowl, beat the egg yolks until lemon-colored; combine with the sugar, salt, and vanilla extract.

Sift the flour three times, then mix in the caraway seeds. Combine the flour with the egg-yolk mixture, mixing well. Gradually fold in the stiffly beaten egg whites, then pour the mixture into the cake pan.

Bake for 10 minutes, remove from the oven and cut into triangles then into half, horizontally; return to the oven and reduce the temperature to 300°F, for 5 minutes to dry out. Turn out onto wire racks to cool.

Right: **Clockwise from bottom right: Russian Caraway Triangles (see above); Sri Lankan Curry Crisps (see p. 125); Bizcochos (see left); Cheese Straws (see p. 125).**

TULLOCH
1978

COOKIES

Coconut Macaroons

Yield: 20 to 24 cookies

2 cups flaked coconut
1 teaspoon cream of tartar
3 teaspoons cornstarch
4 egg whites, at room temperature
1⅓ cups powdered sugar
1 teaspoon vanilla extract

Preheat the oven to 250°F. Grease baking sheets and lightly dust with cornstarch.

Combine the coconut, cream of tartar, and cornstarch in a bowl; toss lightly to mix.

Whisk the egg whites in a clean glass bowl until frothy and soft peaks form; gradually add the sugar, beating well after each addition.

Add the vanilla, then quickly but lightly fold in the coconut mixture—do not overmix. Place in rough teaspoonfuls onto prepared baking sheets.

Bake for 40 to 45 minutes, until dry and crisp.

Open the oven door and allow to cool in the oven for 30 minutes. Remove and, when cold, lift into airtight containers to store.

German Aniseed Cookies

Yield: about 15 cookies

3 eggs
1 cup sugar
1 cup flour, sifted
1½ tablespoons anise seeds

Beat the eggs and sugar together for 10 minutes with an electric mixer (for 30 minutes by hand). Then gradually add flour and anise seeds and mix well. Drop spoonfuls onto greased baking sheets, allowing room for spreading. Allow to stand overnight. A hard crust will form on each. (The crust will puff up to resemble icing when they are baked.)

Preheat the oven to 350°F. Grease the baking sheets. Bake for 10 minutes.

Banana-Bender's Cookies

Yield: about 25 cookies

½ stick butter
1 cup sugar
1½ cups flour, sifted
1 teaspoon baking soda
½ teaspoon salt
2 eggs, well beaten
2 cups mashed ripe banana
1½ cups chopped pecans

Preheat the oven to 300°F. Grease the baking sheets.

Cream together the butter and sugar. Sift the flour, baking soda, and salt together and fold into the butter–sugar mixture. Mix in the beaten eggs, banana, and nuts. Spoon drops of the mixture onto the baking sheets, allowing space around each cookie.

Bake for 20 to 25 minutes. Turn onto wire racks to cool. Being rich and moist, they do not keep for very long.

Queensland Crunchies

Yield: about 25 cookies

½ cup flour, sifted
¼ teaspoon salt
1 teaspoon baking powder
⅓ cup sugar
¼ cup fine cake crumbs
1 egg, lightly beaten
¼ cup finely chopped macadamia nuts
¼ cup crushed pineapple, well drained and dried
powdered sugar, for dusting

Preheat the oven to 350°F. Thoroughly grease and flour the baking sheets.

Sift together the flour, salt, and baking powder, then mix with the sugar and cake crumbs. Mix in the egg, nuts, and pineapple to make a thick batter. Drop spoonfuls onto the baking sheets, allowing space between each.

Bake for 10 minutes. Dust with powdered sugar and allow to cool on the sheets.

Coconut Butterscotch Cookies

Yield: about 30 cookies

1 cup brown sugar
1½ sticks butter, softened
4 egg yolks, lightly beaten
2 cups flour, sifted
2 teaspoons baking powder
¼ cup milk
½ cup flaked coconut

Preheat the oven to 350°F. Grease the baking sheets thoroughly.

Cream the sugar and butter together. Beat in the egg yolks. Sift the flour and baking powder together and add to the mixture in alternate batches with the milk. Add the coconut. Drop teaspoonfuls onto the baking sheets, allowing space for spreading.

Bake for 10 to 12 minutes. Turn onto wire racks to cool.

Sweet Shrewsbury Coriander Cakes

Yield: about 60 little cakes

1½ sticks butter, softened
1 cup sugar
3 eggs, unbeaten
4 cups flour, sifted
¼ teaspoon baking soda
2 teaspoons ground coriander seeds
½ cup milk

Preheat the oven to 450°F. Grease the baking sheets.

Cream the butter and sugar together. Add the eggs, mixing well. Sift the flour, baking soda, and coriander seeds together. Add alternate batches of the flour mixture and the milk to the butter–egg–sugar mixture, about a third of each at a time, and mix well until a dough is made. Knead it until smooth. Roll it out, then cut into 2-inch circles.

Bake for about 15 minutes or until light brown. Turn onto wire racks and allow to cool.

Lemon Honey Cookies

Yield: about 25 cookies

2 cups flour, sifted
pinch of salt
1 teaspoon baking soda
½ teaspoon dried ground thyme
2 eggs, lightly beaten
finely grated rind of ½ lemon
2 tablespoons honey

Preheat the oven to 350°F. Grease the baking sheets.

Sift the dry ingredients together; then beat in the eggs, lemon rind, and honey, mixing well. Roll out thinly and cut into rounds or fancy shapes.

Bake for 15 minutes. Turn onto wire racks to cool.

Hazelnut–Popcorn Macaroons

Yield: about 15 macaroons

1 large egg white
pinch of salt
⅓ cup powdered sugar
½ teaspoon vanilla extract
1 cup popped corn
⅓ cup finely chopped hazelnuts

Preheat the oven to 300°F. Thoroughly grease the baking sheets.

Beat the egg white and salt until it holds stiff peaks. Gradually beat in the sugar, making sure it is beaten for long enough to dissolve the sugar. Add the vanilla, then fold in the popcorn and hazelnuts. Drop teaspoonfuls onto the baking sheet, allowing room for spreading.

Bake for about 15 minutes or until brown.

Variations: Cornflakes or puffed wheat can be used instead of popcorn. Other nuts can replace the hazelnuts.

Almond Macaroons

Yield: about 40 macaroons

7 egg whites

1 pound powdered sugar, sifted

2 tablespoons rose water or orange water

1 pound finely ground blanched almonds, sifted

Preheat the oven to 250°F. Thoroughly grease the baking sheets.

Beat the egg whites until dry, then gradually add sugar until it is all incorporated. Add the rose water to the ground almonds, mixing well. Gradually incorporate this into the egg-white–sugar mixture. Drop spoonfuls onto the baking sheets, allowing room for spreading.

Bake for 30 minutes. Allow to cool on the sheet.

Note: If making your own almond powder, thoroughly chill the almonds (to reduce oiliness) before chopping in a food processor. Sieve and re-crush coarser fragments.

Scottish Shortbread

Yield: 8 shortbread wedges

1½ cups all-purpose white flour, sifted

¼ cup powdered sugar

1 stick butter

¼ teaspoon vanilla extract

powdered sugar, for dusting

Preheat the oven to 300°F. Grease a baking sheet.

Combine all the shortbread ingredients in the bowl of a food processor and mix until it forms a ball of dough. (Or cream the butter and sugar together before adding the sifted flour to make a smooth dough.) Turn it onto the baking sheet and press it into a round flat cake less than ½ inch thick. Crimp the edges with the fingertips, and prick all over with a fork. If desired, shallow cuts may be made to make it into eight wedges.

Bake for about 1 hour, until firm and pale golden. Slide onto a wire rack to cool, and dust the top with powdered sugar. When cold, cut into wedges.

Swedish Christmas Cookies

Yield: about 36 cookies

2 yolks from hard-boiled eggs

¾ stick butter

⅓ cup powdered sugar

⅓ cup thick sour cream

zest from ½ lemon

zest from ½ orange

1 raw egg yolk

1 cup flour (more if required), sifted

⅛ teaspoon baking soda

⅛ teaspoon salt

Topping:
1 egg white, well beaten

1 tablespoon powdered sugar

1 tablespoon ground almonds

Preheat the oven to 325°F. Grease the baking sheets.

Mash the hard-boiled egg yolks with the butter until a smooth paste is formed. Blend in the sugar, mixing well. Add the sour cream, lemon and orange zest, and raw egg yolk.

Sift the flour, baking soda, and salt together and add to the other ingredients, mixing well and adding more flour (if necessary) to obtain a firm, rollable dough. Roll out to ¼ inch thickness and press out fancy shapes, such as stars or the shapes of animals. Brush with beaten egg white, and sprinkle with sugar–nut mixture.

Bake for 15 to 20 minutes. Turn onto wire racks to cool.

Right: **Clockwise from top: Scottish Shortbread (see left); Fruit and Nut Drops (see p. 133); Swedish Christmas Cookies (see above); Almond Macaroons (see above left).**

Wishes
Janice

Apple Surprises

Yield: about 40 cookies

2½ cups flour, sifted
1 teaspoon baking soda
½ teaspoon salt
1 teaspoon ground cinnamon
1 teaspoon ground cloves
1½ cups brown sugar
1 stick butter, softened
1 large egg, lightly beaten
¼ cup apple juice
½ cup finely chopped walnuts
1 cup peeled, cored, coarsely grated apple
1 cup raisins, finely chopped

Preheat the oven to 400°F. Thoroughly grease the baking sheets.

Sift the flour, baking soda, salt, cinnamon, and cloves together. In a large bowl, cream the sugar and butter together. Beat in the egg. Gradually fold in alternate batches of the flour mixture and the apple juice. Then add the walnuts, grated apple, and raisins. Drop teaspoonfuls onto the baking sheet.

Bake for 8 to 10 minutes. Turn onto wire racks to cool.

Anzac Cookies

Yield: about 30 cookies

1 cup rolled oats
1 cup brown sugar, firmly packed
1 cup flaked coconut
1 cup flour, sifted
2 teaspoons dried ground ginger
¼ teaspoon salt
1 stick butter
1 tablespoon light corn syrup
1 teaspoon baking soda
2 tablespoons boiling water

Preheat the oven to 350°F. Grease the baking sheets.

Place the oats, sugar, and coconut into a bowl; sift the flour, ginger, and salt over, and mix thoroughly.

Melt the butter in a saucepan; remove from the heat and add the corn syrup. Dissolve the baking soda in the boiling water and add to the saucepan, stirring well. Pour over the flour mixture and blend well. Drop spoonfuls onto the greased sheets, allowing room for spreading.

Bake for 10 to 12 minutes. Remove from the oven and allow to cool on the baking sheets.

Pecan Buttons

Yield: about 20 cookies

2 eggs, lightly beaten
½ cup powdered sugar
¾ cup self-rising flour, sifted
1 cup finely chopped pecans

Preheat the oven to 350°F. Grease and flour the baking sheets.

Beat the eggs and sugar together until light and creamy. Fold in the flour and the pecans. Form the mixture into small balls and place on the sheets; slightly flatten with a fork.

Bake for 12 to 15 minutes. Allow to cool on wire racks.

Date Pillows

Yield: about 20 cookies

8 ounces cream cheese, softened
1 stick butter
1 teaspoon vanilla extract
2 cups flour
Filling:
1 tablespoon sugar
¼ cup hot water
1 teaspoon lemon juice
½ cup finely chopped dates

Cream together the cheese and butter until smooth. Add the vanilla and flour, and mix well to form a dough. Cover, and chill for several hours.

To prepare the filling, dissolve the sugar in the hot water in a saucepan. Add the lemon juice and dates, and simmer until thickened, stirring often. Allow to cool.

Preheat the oven to 425°F. Grease a baking sheet.

Roll the dough out thinly and cut into 3-inch squares. Spoon a little filling along the center of each square, and fold over each side to seal, pressing with a floured fork. Prick the top and place on the baking sheet.

Bake for 12 to 15 minutes. Turn onto a wire rack to cool.

Fruit and Nut Drops

Yield: about 50 cookies

2 sticks butter
1½ cups brown sugar, firmly packed
½ cup currants
1 cup chopped dates
1 cup chopped blanched almonds
3 cups flour
1 teaspoon baking soda
½ teaspoon salt
1 teaspoon ground cloves
1 teaspoon ground cinnamon
1 teaspoon ground nutmeg
3 eggs, well beaten
3 tablespoons maple syrup
1 teaspoon grated lemon zest

Preheat the oven to 350°F. Grease the baking sheets.

Cream together the butter and sugar, then mix in the currants, dates, and almonds.

Sift the flour, baking soda, salt, and spices together, then incorporate this into the first-made mixture. Add the beaten eggs, maple syrup, and lemon zest, blending well. Drop spoonfuls onto the sheet, allowing room for spreading.

Bake for 15 to 20 minutes. Turn onto wire racks to cool.

Honey Strips

Yield: about 50 cookies

3¾ cups flour, sifted
2 teaspoons baking powder
¼ teaspoon salt
⅓ cup sugar
1 stick butter
1 large egg
2 tablespoons lemon juice, strained
1 cup clear aromatic honey, warmed
⅔ cup blanched chopped almonds

Preheat the oven to 350°F. Grease the baking sheets.

Sift the flour, baking powder, and salt together into a bowl. In a separate bowl, cream the sugar and butter together; then add the egg, and beat in well. Mix in the lemon juice and honey. Thoroughly blend in the flour mixture and the nuts, to make a dough. Roll out on a lightly floured board to ¼ inch thick and cut into strips.

Bake for 10 to 12 minutes, or until brown. Turn onto wire racks to cool.

Coffee Nut Cookies

Yield: about 30 cookies

2 cups flour
1 teaspoon baking powder
⅛ teaspoon salt
1 stick butter
1 cup sugar
1 tablespoon instant coffee powder
1 tablespoon hot water
1 large egg
½ cup finely chopped walnuts

Sift the flour, baking powder, and salt together into a bowl.

In a separate bowl, cream the butter and sugar together. Dissolve the coffee powder in the hot water and allow to cool.

Beat the egg and coffee together with the butter and sugar, combine this with the flour mixture, and add the walnuts to make a dough. Divide the mixture in half and roll into two cylinders, 2 inches in diameter. Wrap in foil and chill.

Preheat the oven to 375°F. Grease the baking sheets.

Cut the chilled rolls into ¼-inch rounds.

Bake for 8 to 10 minutes. Turn onto wire racks to cool.

Buttermilk Cookies

Yield: about 35 cookies

2 cups sugar

2 cups lard

1 egg, lightly beaten

1 teaspoon grated nutmeg

¼ teaspoon salt

2 cups buttermilk

1 teaspoon baking soda

enough flour for rolling dough

Preheat the oven to 350°F. Grease the baking sheets.

Cream the sugar and lard together. Beat in the egg, nutmeg, and salt.

Combine the buttermilk with the baking soda, and add this to the mixture. Add sufficient flour to make the mixture into a rollable dough. Roll out to ¼ inch thick, and cut into shapes.

Bake for 10 to 12 minutes. Allow to cool on wire racks.

Cinnamon Shapes

Yield: about 30 cookies

6 egg whites

pinch of salt

2½ cups powdered sugar

finely grated rind of 1 lemon

1 teaspoon ground cinnamon

1 pound ground almonds

Preheat the oven to 350°F. Grease the baking sheets thoroughly.

Beat the egg whites and salt until stiff. Gradually add the sugar, and continue beating until stiff peaks are formed. Beat in the lemon rind, then reserve a quarter of the mixture for covering the shapes.

To the larger quantity of mixture, add the cinnamon and ground almonds, mixing well. Sprinkle the work surface with a little additional powdered sugar to minimize sticking, and roll the mixture out thinly. Cut into shapes with cookie cutters and spread a small amount of the reserved mixture on the top of each shape.

Bake for about 20 minutes or until light brown. Turn onto wire racks to cool.

Coconut Chocolate-Drop Cookies

Yield: about 40 cookies

4 ounces dark cooking chocolate

2 cups flaked coconut

1 teaspoon vanilla extract

pinch of salt

3 tablespoons flour

1⅓ cups condensed milk

Melt the chocolate in a double boiler. Mix in the other ingredients, and chill the mixture.

Preheat the oven to 350°F.

Drop teaspoonfuls of the mixture onto a greased and floured baking sheet.

Bake for about 15 minutes, or until just browned. Allow to cool on wire racks.

Brazil-Nut Stars

Yield: about 40 cookies

2 large eggs, well beaten

2 cups brown sugar, firmly packed

1½ teaspoons vanilla extract

1¾ cups flour

½ teaspoon baking powder

1 pound Brazil nuts, finely chopped

powdered sugar, for dusting

To the well-beaten eggs, add the sugar and vanilla and beat until light and foamy.

In a separate bowl, sift the flour and baking powder together, then mix in the nuts. Combine the two mixtures, mixing well to form a dough. Cover the bowl and refrigerate for several hours.

Preheat the oven to 350°F. Grease the baking sheets.

Roll out the dough between two sheets of greaseproof paper. Remove paper and stamp out fancy shapes such as stars.

Bake for 12 to 15 minutes until they are lightly browned. Turn onto wire racks to cool and then dust with powdered sugar.

Right: **Brazil-Nut Stars (see above); Cinnamon Shapes (see left).**

Low-Calorie Energy Cookies

Yield: 36 squares

- ***1¼ sticks margarine***
- ***2 tablespoons honey***
- ***1 cup dried apricots***
- ***1 cup dried dates***
- ***1 cup finely chopped mixed nuts***
- ***2½ cups whole-wheat flour***
- ***1 teaspoon baking powder***
- ***3 tablespoons skim-milk powder***
- ***1½ cups water***

Preheat the oven to 350°F. Thoroughly grease a jelly-roll pan.

Melt the margarine in a saucepan; remove from the heat and add the honey. Transfer the mixture to a bowl, and mix in the fruits and nuts.

Sift the flour with the baking powder, then add any residue left in the sieve; combine with the fruit and nut mixture. Dissolve the milk powder in the water and combine with all the other ingredients, mixing well. Press into the jelly-roll pan.

Bake for 30 minutes, allow to cool in the pan, cut into squares, and serve cold.

Scandinavian Sour-Cream Cookies

Yield: about 25 cookies

- ***2 cups powdered sugar***
- ***1 cup thick sour cream***
- ***2 sticks butter, softened***
- ***2 large eggs, well beaten***
- ***1 teaspoon baking soda***
- ***1½ teaspoons vanilla extract***

Preheat the oven to 325°F. Thoroughly grease the baking sheets.

Mix together all the ingredients in the order listed, to make a dough. Roll the dough out to ¼ inch thick, then cut into fancy shapes with a cookie cutter.

Bake for 10 to 12 minutes. Turn onto wire racks to cool.

Honey Fig Cookies

Yield: about 50 cookies

- ***¾ cup powdered sugar***
- ***1 stick butter***
- ***2 large eggs, well beaten***
- ***1 teaspoon lemon extract***
- ***½ cup honey, warmed***
- ***2⅔ cups flour, sifted***
- ***1½ teaspoons baking powder***
- ***3 tablespoons milk***
- ***1 cup finely chopped dried figs***
- ***2 tablespoons finely chopped orange zest***
- ***½ cup flaked coconut***

Preheat the oven to 350°F. Grease the baking sheets.

Cream the sugar and butter together. Add the beaten eggs, lemon extract, and honey, mixing well. Sift in the flour and baking powder together; then add the milk. Mix in the figs, orange zest, and coconut. Drop spoonfuls onto the baking sheet, allowing room for spreading.

Bake for 10 to 15 minutes. Remove from the oven and allow to cool on the sheet.

Citrus Cookies

Yield: about 30 cookies

- ***1 cup sugar***
- ***1 stick butter, softened***
- ***1 egg, well beaten***
- ***1 tablespoon lemon juice***
- ***½ teaspoon finely grated lemon rind***
- ***1 teaspoon orange rind***
- ***2 cups flour, sifted***
- ***1 teaspoon baking powder***
- ***pinch of salt***

Cream the sugar and butter together. Beat in the egg, lemon juice, and lemon and orange rinds. Sift together the dry ingredients, and carefully mix together with the other ingredients to form a dough. Work into a cylindrical shape and chill thoroughly.

Preheat the oven to 425°F. Thoroughly grease baking sheets.

Slice off thin rounds of dough and place them on baking sheets.

Bake for 10 minutes. Turn onto wire racks to cool.

Orange Almond Cookies

Yield: about 30 cookies

1 stick butter, melted
½ cup sugar
1 tablespoon finely grated orange rind
1 tablespoon finely grated lemon rind
2 teaspoons lemon juice
2 teaspoons orange juice
1 large egg, separated
2 cups flour
1 teaspoon baking powder
pinch of salt
1 cup finely chopped almonds
candied peel or candied cherry, for garnish

Preheat the oven to 350°F. Thoroughly grease the baking sheets.

Cream the butter and sugar together. Add the citrus rinds and juices, plus the egg yolk, and mix well. Sift the flour, baking powder, and salt together and add this to the mixture. Mix well to form a stiff dough. Make small balls, dip into the beaten egg white, and roll in the chopped almonds. Place on the baking sheets and flatten with a fork. Decorate with candied peel or cherry.

Bake for 12 to 15 minutes. Allow to cool on wire racks.

Peanut–Peach Cookies

Yield: about 25 cookies

4 ounces dried peaches
1 pound shelled peanuts
2 tablespoons lemon juice
1½ cups condensed milk

Soak the dried peaches in hot water for at least 30 minutes. Very finely chop the peanuts in a food processor (or grind them in a mill) and set aside.

Preheat the oven to 350°F. Grease the baking sheets.

Drain the peaches, then mince or finely chop in a food processor. Add the ground peanuts, lemon juice, and condensed milk, and blend well. Drop spoonfuls onto baking sheets.

Bake for 20 minutes. Remove immediately from the baking sheet and cool on wire racks.

Apricot-Tang Slice

Yield: 28 pieces

4 ounces dried apricots, soaked
½ cup powdered sugar
1 stick butter, softened
1 egg, lightly beaten
¼ teaspoon ground cinnamon
2 tablespoons finely chopped preserved ginger
½ cup finely chopped blanched almonds
1¼ cups self-rising flour, sifted
½ cup cornstarch, sifted
pinch of salt
1 teaspoon cocoa
¼ to ½ cup milk
2 ounces dark cooking chocolate, finely grated

Preheat the oven to 400°F. Thoroughly grease a shallow 11 × 9-inch baking pan.

Chop the soaked apricots and set aside. Cream the sugar and butter together, then beat in the egg and cinnamon. Stir in the reserved apricots, and the ginger and almonds. Sift the flour, cornstarch, salt, and cocoa together; blend this into the butter–sugar–fruit mixture in alternate batches with the milk and chocolate, about a third of each at a time. Spread into the pan, pressing down firmly.

Bake for 25 to 30 minutes. Remove from the oven and allow to cool in the pan, then cut into bars, 1 × 4 inches.

Chocolate-Mint Fingers

Yield: 28 pieces

2 sticks butter, melted
2 cups cornflakes, crushed
2 cups flaked coconut
1 cup self-rising flour, sifted
3 tablespoons cocoa
1 teaspoon vanilla extract
1 teaspoon peppermint extract
1 cup powdered sugar

Preheat the oven to 350°F. Thoroughly grease a shallow pan.

Combine all ingredients in a bowl, mixing well. Turn the mixture into the pan and press it in firmly.

Bake for 25 to 30 minutes. With a sharp knife, mark into fingers while hot, then cool in refrigerator.

Poppy-Seed Tricorns

Yield: about 60 cookies

Dough: ***2½ cups flour, sifted***
½ teaspoon salt
3 teaspoons baking powder
½ cup sugar
¼ cup milk
1 egg, lightly beaten
½ cup melted butter
Filling: ***1 tablespoon sugar***
1 tablespoon poppy seeds
1 egg, lightly beaten

Preheat the oven to 350°F. Grease the baking sheets.

Make a dough by mixing together all the ingredients and kneading well. Roll the dough out thinly and cut into 2-inch rounds.

Make the filling by mixing together all the ingredients—you will not need all the egg. Place a spoonful of filling in the center of each round and fold up the edges so that it forms a tricorn. Pinch them together to seal.

Bake for 20 minutes. Cool on wire racks.

Coffee Lace Wafers

Yield: about 20 wafers

¾ stick butter
⅓ cup sugar
1 tablespoon flour
2 tablespoons milk
2 teaspoons instant coffee powder
½ cup ground almonds

Preheat the oven to 325°F. Grease and flour the baking sheets.

Combine all the ingredients in a saucepan and heat slowly until the mixture is well mixed. Drop spoonfuls onto the baking sheets, allowing about 4 inches around each, for spreading.

Bake for 5 to 10 minutes, until lightly browned. Remove from the oven, allow to stand for 30 seconds, then roll each wafer very carefully around the handle of a wooden spoon. Allow to cool on wire racks.

Basic Petits Fours

Yield: about 30 petits fours

2 cups flour, sifted
½ teaspoon baking powder
½ cup sugar
1 stick butter
½ teaspoon vanilla extract
2 eggs, lightly beaten
Decoration: ***colored sugar, halved or ground nuts, candied fruit, coconut, etc., or Glacé Icing (see recipe, page 102)***

Sift the flour and baking powder together. In a separate bowl, combine sugar, butter, vanilla, and eggs until well mixed, then add the flour to make a dough. Cover, and chill for several hours in the refrigerator.

Preheat the oven to 350°F. Grease the baking sheets.

Roll the dough out thinly and cut into small fancy shapes. Decorate with colored sugar, nuts, candied fruit, coconut, etc.

Bake for 15 minutes. Cool on a wire rack, and decorate with icing if baked plain.

Right: **Clockwise from bottom right: Chocolate-Mint Fingers (see above left); Petits Fours (see above); Coffee Lace Wafers (see above).**

Chocolate-Marshmallow Cookies

Yield: about 25 cookies

½ cup sugar

1 stick butter, softened

1 egg, lightly beaten

2 cups self-rising flour, sifted

Marshmallow Topping:
1 tablespoon gelatin

1 cup water

1 cup sugar

2 tablespoons chocolate topping (sauce)

Preheat the oven to 425°F. Grease the baking sheets.

Cream the sugar and butter together. Then beat in the egg. Add the flour, and mix well to make a stiff dough. Form into balls about 1 inch in diameter and place on the baking sheets. Flatten with a fork.

Bake for 12 to 15 minutes. Turn onto wire racks to cool.

Marshmallow Topping

Soak the gelatin in 2 tablespoons of the water. Heat the rest of the water with the sugar, and boil for 20 minutes. Remove from the heat, add the softened gelatin, place the saucepan in a bowl of ice, and whisk continuously until thick and white. Add the chocolate topping, blending well.

Spoon the topping onto cooled cookies, and allow to set. Cookies may be decorated with nuts or Glacé Icing (see recipe p. 102).

Cognac Drops

Yield: about 20 cookies

2 egg yolks

3 tablespoons sugar

1 tablespoon fresh white bread crumbs

1 tablespoon cognac

1 cup ground hazelnuts

1 egg white, lightly beaten

Preheat the oven to 350°F. Grease the baking sheet.

Beat together the egg yolks and sugar until creamy. Moisten the bread crumbs with cognac and add to the egg yolk–sugar mixture along with the nuts. Fold in the beaten egg white. Drop teaspoonfuls onto the baking sheet.

Bake for 15 minutes. Allow to cool on a wire rack.

Raspberry Meringue Twirls

Yield: about 20 cookies

1½ cups self-rising flour, sifted

pinch of salt

¼ cup sugar

½ cup ground almonds

1 stick butter

2 egg yolks, lightly beaten

a little milk, if necessary

Meringue Topping:
2 egg whites

½ cup powdered sugar

raspberry jam (jelly), heated

Sift the flour and salt together into a bowl; add the sugar and ground almonds. Rub in the butter until the mixture resembles fine bread crumbs. Add the egg yolks to bind the mixture into a firm dough—if necessary, adding a little milk. Cover, and chill thoroughly.

Preheat the oven to 375°F. Grease the baking sheets.

Roll the dough out thinly and cut into rounds, about 2 inches in diameter.

To make the meringue, beat the egg whites until stiff and gradually incorporate the sugar; beat until the mixture holds its shape. Pipe a spiral topping of meringue onto each round.

Bake for 20 to 25 minutes. Allow to cool on wire racks. When cold, trickle the heated and thinned raspberry jam over the top.

Mixed-Nut Bars

Yield: about 18 bars

1 stick butter, softened

2 tablespoons confectioners' sugar

2 teaspoons vanilla extract

½ cup cornstarch, sifted

½ cup flour

1 ounce ground almonds

Topping:
1 ounce very finely chopped hazelnuts

1 ounce very finely chopped unsalted peanuts

1 ounce dark chocolate

Preheat the oven to 350°F. Grease the baking sheets.

Beat the butter, sugar, and vanilla together until fluffy and light-textured. Sift the cornstarch, flour, and ground almonds together, then fold into the butter–sugar mixture and mix well. Spoon the mixture into a piping bag fitted with a ½-inch serrated nozzle. Pipe sticks of the mixture 3 inches long, allowing room between them for spreading, on the baking sheets. Carefully top with a light layer of hazelnut–peanut mixture.

Bake for 15 minutes. Cool on wire racks. Melt the chocolate in a double boiler and carefully coat half of each stick; allow to set.

Basic Filled Cookies

Yield: about 20 filled cookies

1 stick butter

1 cup sugar

1 teaspoon vanilla extract

1 egg

2¾ cups flour, sifted

1½ teaspoons baking powder

¼ teaspoon baking soda

½ cup milk

Cream together the butter and sugar with the vanilla. Add the egg, beating the mixture well. Sift together the dry ingredients and add alternately with the milk, beating well, to make a dough. Cover and chill the dough.

Preheat the oven to 350°F. Grease a baking sheet.

Roll the dough out thinly and cut into rounds. Fill the rounds, seal the edges, and prick their tops.

Bake for 10 minutes. Turn onto a wire rack to cool.

Note: A filled cookie can be made by sticking together two cooked cookies with a filling such as Jelly Cream or Butter Cream (see following Cream recipes).

Another method of filling is by placing a spoonful of the filling near one edge of a large round uncooked cookie and folding the other edge over, then sealing the two edges; or by placing the filling in the center and crimping up the edges around the filling. Square cookies can be folded up over the filling to make tricorns.

Two shapes (uncooked) could be stuck together with a filling and their edges sealed all the way around.

Butter-Cream Filling

Yield: Filling for 20 two-layer cookies

- ***1 cup confectioners' sugar, sifted***
- ***2 tablespoons softened butter***
- ***½ teaspoon vanilla extract***
- ***2 tablespoons condensed milk***

Beat together half of the sugar and the softened butter. Add the vanilla and then the condensed milk. Beat in the remaining sugar.

Chocolate Butter Cream

Add 2 teaspoons of cocoa powder to the first batch of sugar, and leave out 1 tablespoon of butter in the above recipe.

Brandy Cottage-Cheese Filling

Yield: Filling for 20 uncooked cookies

- ***1 cup cottage cheese***
- ***2 tablespoons finely chopped nuts***
- ***3 tablespoons currants***
- ***4 tablespoons sugar***
- ***¼ teaspoon finely grated lemon rind***
- ***¼ teaspoon ground nutmeg***
- ***¼ teaspoon ground cinnamon***
- ***2 tablespoons brandy or fruit juice***
- ***1 egg***

Combine all the ingredients into a spreadable filling.

Jelly-Cream Filling

Yield: Filling for 20 two-layer cookies

- ***1 tablespoon jelly—such as raspberry jam (jelly)***
- ***4 tablespoons confectioners' sugar***
- ***2 teaspoons softened butter***

Combine ingredients together to make a smooth, spreadable filling.

Dried-Fruit Filling

Yield: Filling for 20 uncooked cookies

- ***1 cup chopped dried fruit (raisins, apricots, prunes, dates, or figs)***
- ***½ cup chopped nuts, candied peel, or flaked coconut***
- ***½ cup sugar***
- ***½ cup water***
- ***1 teaspoon lemon juice***
- ***1 tablespoon flour***

Combine the ingredients in a saucepan and simmer until thickened, stirring often. Cool before use.

Right: **Clockwise from top left: Butter-Cream Filling (see above left); Brandy Cottage-Cheese Filling (see above); Jelly-Cream Filling (see above left); Dried-Fruit Filling (see above).**

Oatmeal Carrot Cookies

Yield: about 24 cookies

1½ sticks butter

¾ cup sugar

1 cup grated raw carrot

1 egg

2 teaspoons lemon rind

1¼ cups flour

½ teaspoon salt

2 teaspoons baking powder

1 cup rolled oats

Preheat the oven to 375°F. Butter a baking sheet.

Cream the butter, cream in the sugar, beat in the carrot and egg, and blend well. Mix in the lemon rind and the flour, salt, and baking powder sifted together. Stir in the rolled oats. Place teaspoons of dough onto a buttered baking sheet.

Bake for 10 to 12 minutes or until the cookies are a delicate brown around the edges. Loosen from the pan while still warm, cool on a rack, and store in airtight containers. They freeze well.

Sugar Cookies

Yield: about 36 cookies

1 stick butter

¾ cup sugar

1 egg

1½ teaspoons vanilla extract

2¼ cups flour

1½ teaspoons baking powder

pinch of salt

extra sugar

Cream the butter, sugar, egg, and vanilla until the mixture is light and fluffy. Add the sifted flour, baking powder, and salt gradually, mixing well. Chill the mixture for 1 hour.

Preheat the oven to 375°F. Grease the baking sheets.

Roll out small portions of the dough on a floured board to ⅛ inch thick. Cut into shapes, place on baking sheets, and sprinkle thickly with extra sugar.

Bake for 12 to 15 minutes or until golden.

Chocolate-Chip Cookies

Yield: about 30 cookies

1 stick butter

⅔ cup brown and white sugar mixed

1 egg

¾ cup flour

½ teaspoon baking soda

salt

1 tablespoon water

1 teaspoon vanilla extract

1½ cups quick-cooking oats

1¼ cups chocolate chips

Preheat the oven to 375°F. Grease the baking sheets.

Cream the butter and sugar until light. Mix in the egg and add half the flour, the baking soda, the salt, water, and vanilla. Beat well. Stir in the remaining flour, the oats, and the chocolate chips. Drop teaspoons of the mixture on baking sheets.

Bake for 10 minutes. Cool on wire racks.

Brownies

Yield: 16 brownies

2 ounces bitter chocolate

1 stick butter

1 cup sugar

2 eggs, well beaten

1 cup flour, sifted

2 teaspoons vanilla extract

1 cup finely chopped pecans

Preheat the oven to 350°F. Grease and flour a shallow square cake pan.

In a double boiler, melt the chocolate and butter with the sugar. Pour this gradually onto the well-beaten eggs, beating after each addition. Add the flour and vanilla, mixing well. Spread into the pan and sprinkle the top with the nuts.

Bake for 20 to 25 minutes. Cut into squares, and allow to cool on wire racks.

Old-Fashioned Chocolate Cookies

Yield: about 30 cookies

2 cups flour

½ teaspoon baking soda

pinch of salt

1 stick butter

2 ounces unsweetened chocolate

1 cup dark brown sugar, firmly packed

1 egg

1 teaspoon vanilla extract

½ cup milk

Chocolate Glaze:
1 ounce unsweetened chocolate

1 tablespoon butter

1½ tablespoons hot water

2 tablespoons cream

1 cup confectioners' sugar

pecans

Preheat the oven to 350°F. Grease the baking sheets.

Sift together the flour, baking soda, and salt and set aside. Cut the butter into pieces and place in a heavy saucepan. Add the chocolate and cook over low heat until melted. Remove from the heat and stir in the sugar. Add the egg and the vanilla to the warm chocolate mixture and stir until smooth. Stir in half of the sifted dry ingredients. Then, very gradually, just a few drops at a time at first, stir in the milk. Add the remaining dry ingredients and stir briskly until completely smooth.

Use a dessertspoon of dough for each cookie. Place them in even mounds 2 inches apart on greased baking sheets.

Bake for 12 to 15 minutes, turning the sheets around to ensure even baking. The cookies are done when the tops spring back firmly if lightly touched with a fingertip.

Let stand for a moment then turn out onto a wire rack to cool.

To make the glaze, melt the chocolate with the butter in the top of a small double boiler over hot water. Remove the saucepan from the heat and stir in the hot water and cream. Add the sugar and stir until smooth. If necessary, adjust with a bit more water or sugar to make the consistency similar to a heavy cream sauce.

With a small metal spatula, smooth the glaze over the tops of the cookies, staying about ½ inch away from the edges.

Let stand for a few hours to dry. Top each cookie with a pecan.

Peanut-Butter Cookies

Yield: about 40 cookies

2¼ cups flour, sifted

2 teaspoons baking soda

¼ teaspoon salt

2 sticks butter

1 cup peanut butter

1 cup brown sugar, firmly packed

½ cup powdered sugar

2 large eggs, lightly beaten

1 cup unsalted peanuts, coarsely chopped

Preheat the oven to 350°F.

Sift the flour, baking soda, and salt together into a bowl. In a separate bowl, cream together the butter, peanut butter, and sugars. Beat in the eggs until well combined, then gradually incorporate the flour mixture to make a dough. Fold in the peanuts. Form into balls about ¾ inch in diameter and place on an ungreased baking sheet; flatten them with a fork.

Bake for 12 to 15 minutes, or until their edges are brown. Remove from the oven and allow to cool on the sheet.

Pastries

Pastry-making

- Work in a cool kitchen in cool weather for best results. Pastry is difficult to handle in hot, humid conditions. However, air-conditioning, an electric fan, or cross-ventilation help create better conditions in hot weather.
- Use cool equipment. Chill bowls and rolling pins in the refrigerator in hot weather.
- The ingredients should also be cold. Chill fat in the refrigerator if using a mixer or food processor, but stand at room temperature for 30 minutes if rubbing in by hand. Use iced water.
- If rubbing fat in by hand, dip it into the flour, then cut it into small pieces with a round-bladed knife. Rub it in by lifting the mixture from the bottom of the bowl with both hands, palms up, and rub the thumbs forward over the fingertips, two or three times, before returning the hands to the bowl for more mixture.
- Keep the hands cold by holding them under cold running water for a few seconds.
- Test that the fat has been completely rubbed into the flour by shaking the bowl; the law of gravity means that any lumps rise to the surface. Squeeze any lumps and, if they are greasy, continue rubbing in or mixing, but, if they are dry, it is ready for the next stage.
- Add the liquid gradually—too much makes the dough sticky to handle and tough when baked; too little makes the pastry crumbly and difficult to roll out. Mix the liquid in with a cold, round-bladed knife when making pastry by hand, using a cutting rather than a stirring movement.
- Toss the completed dough lightly in flour, then knead very lightly but firmly to compress the dough, just until it is smooth underneath. Only 6 to 10 kneading actions should be required; over-kneading will result in a tough, hard pastry when baked. Turn the compressed dough over and pat it into a round cake ½ to 1 inch thick, then wrap securely in greaseproof paper and chill before rolling out. Clear plastic wrap should be avoided since it makes the dough sweat.
- Chill the dough for 15 minutes in cold weather, and for 30 minutes in hot weather, before rolling out. If dough has been chilled for a long time, stand it at room temperature until it is soft enough to roll out without cracking. A well-chilled hard dough may be softened quickly in a microwave, set at defrost, testing the texture after each single revolution, or after every 8 seconds, until it is soft enough for rolling out.
- Roll out on a marble slab preferably, as it is cold, smooth, and hygienic. Otherwise roll out on a clear, cold, dry laminated or formica-topped kitchen counter. Pastry boards are good in cold climates but tend to sweat in hot climates.
- Use a traditional long, smooth wooden rolling pin, sprinkled lightly with flour, and rub the flour into the wood with a cool hand to prevent sticking.
- Before rolling out, press across the round cake of dough 3 times with the rolling pin, then turn dough around and press 3 times more at right angles, to give a thinner round of dough.
- Roll the pastry dough out on a lightly floured surface with the rolling pin "drill" action of down, forward, back, and up, thus giving firm, quick, and even pressure.
- When rolling, move the pastry around constantly, not the direction of rolling, to achieve evenly thinner dough, i.e. never roll sideways.
- If the pastry starts to stick to the surface or the rolling pin, sprinkle on more flour. If the pastry sticks to the surface, loosen with a palette knife and sprinkle flour under it before continuing.
- Never turn pastry over during rolling. After rolling, since the rolled side is the best, turn it over if lining a flan tin, but do not turn over if topping a pie.
- It is preferable to bake pastry in an electric oven instead of a gas oven, because it has a dry radiant heat that gives a crisp pastry. Burning gas gives off water vapor as a by-product, so the pastry is not as crisp.

Storage of pastry

Pastry dough should be wrapped in greaseproof paper, then sealed in a plastic bag for storage overnight in the refrigerator. In an efficient refrigerator, it may be kept in this way for up to five days.

To freeze pastry dough, wrap it in greaseproof paper, then place in a freezer bag, extract the air, then seal well and store in the freezer. It will keep frozen successfully for up to three months.

Flour and fats

Always use plain household white flour for pastry unless otherwise stated in recipe. Self-rising flour results in a spongy rather than a short, crisp pastry. Flours vary, so select a well-known national brand, avoiding both light cake flours, for they absorb less liquid, and high-gluten flours, for they absorb more liquid.

Fats vary in type and proportion from pastry to pastry, but, in general, butter is used for its color and flavor; lard is used for its shortening qualities; firm margarine for its color, shortening properties, and economy; polyunsaturated margarine is used for its health advantages; suet is used for its flavor and texture in traditional suet-crust pastry.

Liquids

The liquid usually used to bind pasty together is cold or iced water. Sometimes egg yolk or eggs are used to enrich. Milk may be used to achieve a softer-textured pastry. An approximate measurement only can be given for the liquid used in most pastry recipes, for it varies according to the softness or hardness of the wheat grain used to make the flour. It also varies according to the temperature of the surroundings and to the amount of humidity in the atmosphere.

Shortcrust Pastry

Yield: 8 ounces pastry

2 cups flour

pinch of salt, optional

½ stick chilled butter or firm margarine

4 tablespoons lard or shortening

about 4 tablespoons cold water, to mix

Sift the flour and salt into a cold mixing bowl. Cut the butter and lard into the flour with a round-bladed knife and coat the small pieces of fat with the flour. Rub the fat into the flour with the cool fingertips of both hands, lifting the mixture up and rubbing from a height, moving the thumbs from the little fingertips to the fore-fingertips, palms uppermost, to lighten and aerate the pastry.

Continue rubbing in until the mixture resembles bread crumbs. To test for complete rubbing in, shake the bowl gently and the lumps will rise to the surface. Squeeze them—if they are dry, the fat is rubbed in sufficiently. If the lumps feel greasy, you must continue rubbing in until you get a positive result to this test.

Sprinkle the cold water over gradually and mix in with a round-bladed knife or a palette knife, until the mixture begins to form lumps that leave the sides of the bowl cleanly. Knead the dough together lightly with a clean, cool hand.

Using an electric mixer: Sift the flour and salt into the bowl of the electric mixer, then add butter and lard, cut into small cubes. Using a K-beater or pastry mixers, turn the machine on at minimum speed and increase gradually to Speed 2 as the fats break up, then continue mixing at Speed 2 until the mixture resembles fine bread crumbs (about 2 minutes). Add cold water gradually, and mix at Speed 2 until the mixture forms a dough that leaves the sides of the bowl clean; switch off immediately.

Using a food processor: Mix the flour, salt, butter, and lard together in the food processor, fitted with a steel blade, for 30 seconds or until the mixture resembles bread crumbs. Add the cold water gradually, and process until the mixture forms a dough that leaves the sides of the bowl cleanly.

Turn the dough onto a lightly floured pastry board or marble slab and knead very lightly with clean, cool hands until smooth underneath. Then turn it over and pat into a round cake shape ½ to 1 inch thick. Wrap in greaseproof paper, and chill in the refrigerator for at least 30 minutes before use.

Note: This pastry dough freezes well. It can also be stored for a few days in greaseproof paper inside a plastic freezer bag in the refrigerator.

Rich Shortcrust Pastry

Yield: 8 ounces, or pastry to line or cover and decorate a 9-inch-round pie dish

2 cups flour

1 stick unsalted butter, chilled

1 tablespoon powdered sugar

pinch of salt, optional

1 egg yolk

2 teaspoons lemon juice

1 to 2 tablespoons cold water

Sift the flour into a cold mixing bowl. Cut the butter into the flour with a round-bladed knife, then rub the butter into the flour with the fingertips until the mixture resembles bread crumbs. Stir in the sugar and salt if used, with a round-bladed knife. Stir the egg yolk and lemon juice together and sprinkle over the mixture, then mix together with the knife. Gradually mix in sufficient cold water until the mixture forms lumps that leave the sides of the bowl clean. Knead the dough together lightly with a clean, cool hand.

Using an electric mixer: Sift the flour into the bowl of the electric mixer. Add the butter, cut into small cubes, and the sugar and salt. Switch to minimum speed and gradually increase the speed to 2 as the butter mixture breaks up. Mix until the mixture resembles fine bread crumbs (about 1½ minutes). Stir the egg yolk, lemon juice, and water together; add this to the mixture and mix at Speed 1 for about 30 to 50 seconds, until the mixture leaves the sides of the bowl. Switch off as soon as the ingredients are mixed.

Using a food processor: Mix the flour, butter, sugar, and salt together in the food processor for 30 seconds or until the mixture resembles bread crumbs. Add the egg yolk, lemon juice, and sufficient water gradually, and process until the mixture forms a dough that leaves the sides of the bowl cleanly.

Turn the dough onto a lightly floured board or marble slab and knead until smooth underneath. Turn over and pat into a round cake shape ½ to 1 inch thick. Wrap in greaseproof paper and chill for 30 minutes in the refrigerator before use.

Note: This can be refrigerated or frozen as for Shortcrust Pastry.

Sweet Shortcrust Pastry

Yield: 8 ounces

2 cups flour
pinch of salt, optional
½ stick chilled butter or firm margarine
4 tablespoons lard or shortening
1 tablespoon powdered sugar
about 4 tablespoons cold water

Make as for Shortcrust Pastry, and add sugar at the "bread crumb" stage.

Low-Cholesterol Shortcrust Pastry

Yield: 8 ounces pastry

11 tablespoons (5½ ounces) polyunsaturated margarine, chilled
5 teaspoons cold water
2 cups flour, sifted

Make as for One-Stage Shortcrust Pastry.

Wrap in greaseproof paper, and chill in the refrigerator for at least 30 minutes before use.

Note: Its characteristic short texture can make it difficult to handle; if so, roll it out between two sheets of greaseproof paper.

One-Stage Shortcrust Pastry

Yield: 8 ounces pastry

1½ sticks soft margarine, chilled
5 teaspoons cold water
2 cups flour, sifted

Place the soft margarine, water, and 2 tablespoons of the measured flour into a mixing bowl and mix to a smooth paste using a fork. Add the remaining flour, and continue mixing with the fork until the mixture forms a stiff dough and leaves the sides of the bowl cleanly. Press the dough together in the bowl with a clean cool hand, then turn it onto a lightly floured marble slab and knead very lightly until smooth underneath. Turn over, pat into a thin, round cake shape, wrap in greaseproof paper and chill in the refrigerator for at least 30 minutes before use. If difficult to handle, roll out between two sheets of greaseproof paper.

Note: This pastry may also be made in a food processor fitted with a steel blade, by placing all ingredients in together and mixing until a dough is formed that leaves the sides of the bowl clean. Knead, shape, and chill as above, before use.

Shortcrust Pastry

1. Sift flour and salt into bowl.

2. Rub in fat, using fingertips until mixture resembles fine bread crumbs.

3. Stir in water and draw dough together using a knife.

4. Knead dough lightly until smooth.

5. Roll out on a lightly floured marble slab or pastry board.

6. Use to line tart tins or as required.

2

4

6

Cheese Pastry

Yield: 6 ounces pastry

4 ounces mature cheddar cheese, finely grated

2 tablespoons finely grated Parmesan cheese, fresh or vacuum packed

1 stick butter or firm margarine

1½ cups flour

pinch of salt

pinch of ground white pepper

pinch of cayenne pepper

2 egg yolks

Place the finely grated cheeses and the butter in a mixing bowl and beat with the back of a wooden spoon until it is soft and creamy. Add the flour, salt, white pepper, cayenne pepper, and beaten egg yolks and mix together with a round-bladed knife until the mixture forms lumps that leave the sides of the bowl clean. Knead lightly to form a dough, with clean, cool hands.

Using an electric mixer: Place the finely grated cheeses and the butter in the bowl of the electric mixer and mix with a K-beater or pastry mixers at Speed 2 until creamy. Sift the flour and seasonings onto a square of greaseproof paper. Add the sifted flour and the egg yolks to the creamed mixture, and mix at Speed 2 until the mixture forms a stiff dough (about 2 minutes).

Using a food processor: Mix the finely grated cheeses with the butter in the food processor, fitted with a steel blade, until creamy. Add all the remaining ingredients and process until the mixture forms a dough that leaves the sides of the bowl cleanly.

Turn the dough onto a lightly floured pastry board or marble slab and knead lightly until smooth. Then turn over and shape into a round cake shape ⅜ inch thick. Wrap it in greaseproof paper and chill for 30 minutes before use.

Note: This pastry is ideal for cheese straws or cheese pastry canapés. If used for pies or flans, when it is necessary to roll it out thinly, it may be rolled out between two sheets of greaseproof paper to prevent crumbling.

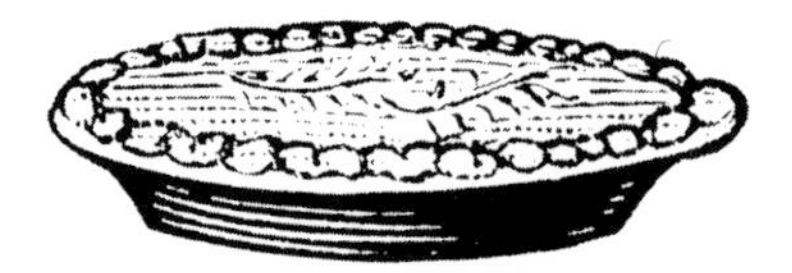

Cream-Cheese Pastry

Yield: 8 ounces pastry

2 sticks butter or margarine

8 ounces cream cheese, softened

½ teaspoon salt

2 cups flour

Using an electric mixer: Place the butter, cream cheese, and salt into the bowl of the electric mixer and beat with a K-beater or pastry mixers until smooth and evenly combined. Sift the flour onto a square of greaseproof paper, then add it to the bowl and mix at Speed 2 until the dough leaves the sides of the bowl cleanly.

Using a food processor: Cut the butter and cream cheese into ⅜-inch cubes. Place all the ingredients together into the food processor, fitted with a steel blade, and process until the mixture forms a dough that leaves the sides of the bowl clean.

Turn the dough onto a lightly floured marble slab and knead lightly until smooth underneath. Then turn over and pat into a round cake shape ½ to 1 inch thick. Wrap in greaseproof paper and chill in the refrigerator for 30 minutes before rolling out.

Fruit-Pie Pastry

Yield: 8 ounces pastry

10 tablespoons (5 ounces) lard

3 tablespoons cold water

2 cups self-rising flour

Using an electric mixer: Place the lard and water in the bowl of the electric mixer, and mix at Speed 2 until soft and creamy. Add the sifted flour, then mix at minimum speed, gradually increasing to Speed 2 until the mixture resembles bread crumbs (about 1½ to 2 minutes). Continue mixing until the mixture forms a dough.

Using a food processor: Place all the ingredients together in the food processor and mix until a dough forms that leaves the sides of the bowl clean.

Turn the dough onto a lightly floured board, and knead lightly. Pat into a round cake shape, then wrap securely in greaseproof paper and chill in the refrigerator for at least 30 minutes.

Suet-Crust Pastry

Yield: 8 ounces pastry

2 cups self-rising flour or 2 cups white all-purpose flour and 1 teaspoon baking powder

pinch of salt

4 ounces suet, finely chopped

cold water to mix

Sift the flour and salt into a mixing bowl. Remove the tissues from the suet and chop the suet finely in a food processor or blender. Add the suet to the flour and mix well, then mix in sufficient cold water to form a soft, light dough, cutting it in with a round-bladed knife. Knead the dough on a lightly floured surface until it is smooth. Use it immediately.

Note: One cup fresh white bread crumbs can be substituted for ½ cup flour to give a lighter crust.

Whole-Wheat Pastry

Yield: 8 ounces pastry

1¾ cups whole-wheat flour, medium or coarse ground

1 teaspoon salt

1 stick butter or firm margarine

cold water, to mix

Place the whole-wheat flour and salt into a mixing bowl, and continue as for Shortcrust Pastry (page 149).

Note: The pastry dough stores well in greaseproof paper in a plastic bag in the refrigerator for a few days. It also freezes well.

Sour-Cream Pastry

Yield: 8 ounces pastry

2 cups flour

1 stick chilled butter or firm margarine

¾ cup sour cream

Sift the flour into a cold mixing bowl. Cut the butter into the flour with a round-bladed knife. Rub the butter into the flour with the fingertips until the mixture resembles bread crumbs. Add the sour cream and mix with the knife until the mixture begins to form lumps that leave the sides of the bowl. Knead the dough together lightly with a clean, cool hand.

Using an electric mixer: Sift the flour into the bowl of an electric mixer. Cut the butter into small cubes and add it to the flour. Beat with a K-beater or pastry mixers at Speed 2 for 1 minute and 30 seconds. Increase the speed to 4 for another 15 seconds or until the mixture resembles coarse bread crumbs. Add the sour cream and beat at Speed 1 for 25 seconds or until the dough leaves the sides of the bowl clean.

Using a food processor: Place the flour and cubes of butter into the food processor, fitted with a steel blade, and mix for 30 seconds. Add the sour cream and mix until the dough leaves the sides of the bowl clean.

Turn the dough onto a lightly floured pastry board or a marble slab, and knead it very lightly into a smooth, round cake shape. Wrap in greaseproof paper and chill for at least 30 minutes before use.

Low-Cholesterol Whole-Wheat Pastry

Yield: 8 ounces pastry

1 stick polyunsaturated margarine

2 tablespoons cold water

1¾ cups whole-wheat flour, fine or medium ground

Make as for One-Stage Shortcrust Pastry (page 150).

Puff Pastry

Yield: 8 ounces pastry

2 sticks unsalted butter

2 cups flour

pinch of salt, optional

1 teaspoon lemon juice

cold water, to mix

Shape the butter into a flat square pat ¼ inch thick, and press it between two pieces of muslin to absorb excess moisture. Place it in the refrigerator until cool and firm.

Sift the flour (and salt, if used) into a large mixing bowl or the bowl of an electric mixer. Using a round-bladed knife or a K-beater or pastry mixers, mix in the lemon juice and sufficient cold water, on minimum speed, to form an elastic dough.

Alternatively, mix the flour, lemon juice, and sufficient cold water together in a food processor to form a dough.

Turn the dough onto a floured pastry board or marble slab, and knead lightly until the paste is smooth and elastic and not sticky.

Roll the dough out on a lightly floured surface to a rectangle twice as big as the butter pat. Place the butter on the top half of the dough, and fold the bottom half over. Roll it out evenly to a long strip, taking care that the butter does not break through. Fold the strip of pastry into thirds—folding the bottom third up and top third down. Allow to cool in the refrigerator for 10 to 15 minutes.

Place the pastry on the rolling surface, with the folded edge to the right. Roll and fold into thirds twice, placing the folded edge alternately to the left. Then return to the refrigerator to cool.

Repeat the rolling and folding processes until the pastry has had seven rolls and folds, chilling whenever necessary. Wrap the dough in greaseproof paper and chill well before use.

Note: The pastry dough stores overnight in greaseproof paper inside a plastic bag in the refrigerator. It also freezes well.

Rough Puff Pastry

Yield: pastry to cover a 1-quart oval pie dish

¾ stick butter or firm margarine

6 tablespoons lard

2 cups flour

pinch of salt

3 tablespoons cold water

Mix the butter and lard together on an enamel plate with a round-bladed knife until well blended, then chill until firm.

Sift the flour and salt into a large mixing bowl or into the large bowl of an electric mixer. Cut the fat into even-sized pieces the size of a walnut and drop them into the flour, tossing each piece well to coat it. Add the cold water and, using a round-bladed knife or the K-beater or pastry mixers, mix at minimum speed for 15 seconds, or until a dough forms.

Turn the dough onto a lightly floured board and roll out to an oblong about 10×6 inches. Fold into thirds and make a half turn so that an open end faces you. Repeat rolling, folding, and turning twice more, turning alternately to the right, then to the left. Refrigerate the dough at any stage when it becomes too soft and greasy to handle. Wrap in greaseproof paper and refrigerate for at least 30 minutes before use.

Note: The pastry dough stores well for a few days in greaseproof paper inside a plastic bag in the refrigerator. It also freezes well.

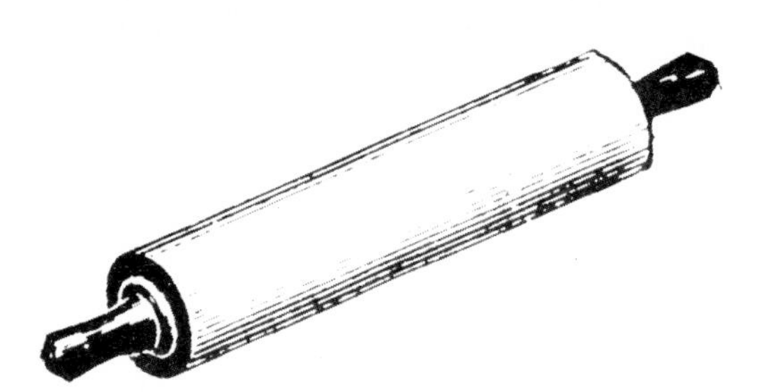

Puff Pastry

1. Beat the butter into a flat rectangle between sheets of greaseproof paper.

2. Knead dough lightly until smooth and elastic.

3. Roll out dough on a lightly floured surface. Place chilled butter on the top half of dough, fold bottom half over.

4. Roll dough out evenly into a long strip.

5. Fold pastry into thirds.

6. Between folding, press dough firmly with rolling pin to distribute the butter evenly, then roll, fold, and repeat (see recipe, left).

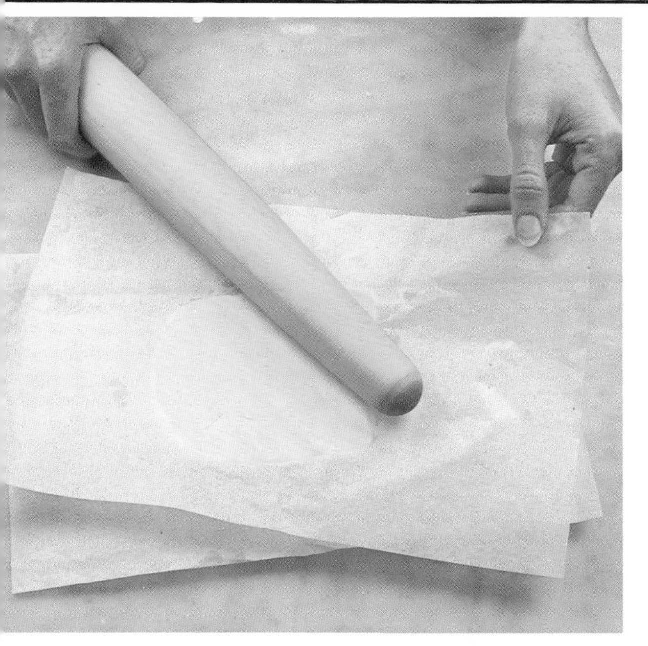

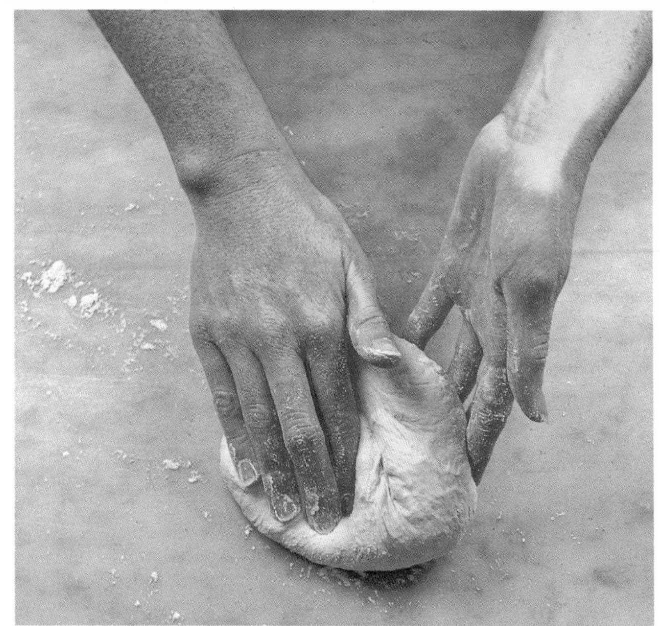

2

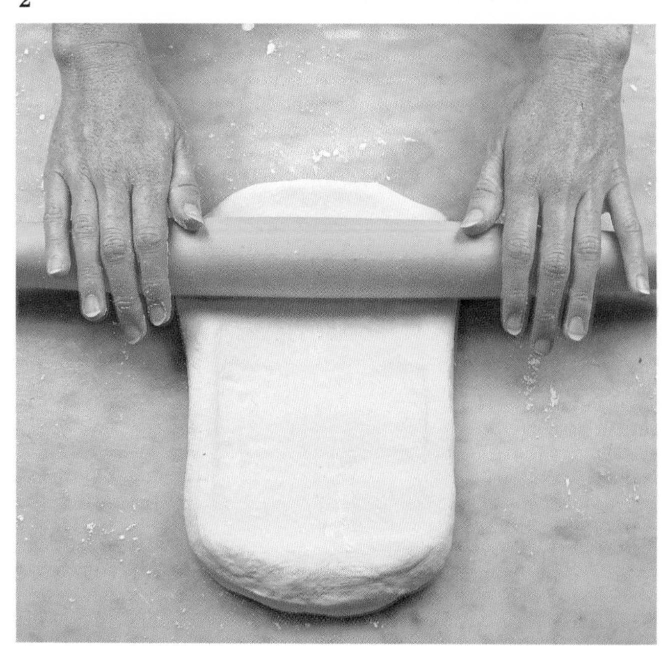

4

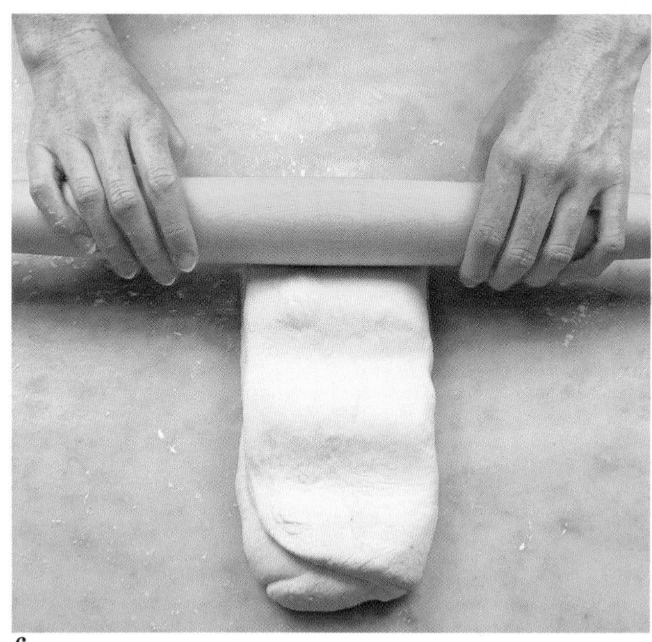

6

Flaky Pastry

Yield: 8 ounces pastry

2 cups flour

pinch of salt

¾ stick butter or firm margarine

6 tablespoons lard

½ cup cold water

Sift the flour and salt into a mixing bowl. Mix the fats together on an enamel plate with a round-bladed knife and shape into a square block. Place a quarter of the mixed fat into the flour, coating it well, then cut it into small pieces with the round-bladed knife. Rub the fat into the flour with cool fingertips until the mixture resembles bread crumbs. Sprinkle the cold water over and mix with a knife to form a dough that leaves the sides of the bowl cleanly.

Using an electric mixer: Sift the flour and salt into the bowl of an electric mixer. Mix the fats together on an enamel plate with a round-bladed knife and shape into a square block. Add a quarter of the mixed fat to the flour; mix at minimum speed, then increase to Speed 2 and mix until the mixture resembles fine bread crumbs (about 2 minutes). Stop the mixer, add the water, then mix at Speed 2 to a firm dough that leaves the sides of the bowl cleanly—adding more water if necessary.

Turn the dough onto a lightly floured board and knead it lightly until smooth. Roll out to an oblong shape about 10×6 inches. Put another quarter of the mixed fat, in flakes or small pieces, on the top two-thirds of the dough. Fold into thirds—folding the bottom third up and the top third over it. This gives you even layers of dough and fat. Half-turn the pastry (so that an open end faces you, and the top is now on the right side) and roll out again to an oblong shape.

Repeat flaking, folding, and rolling the dough twice more. Refrigerate the dough at any stage when it becomes too soft and greasy to handle. Fold pastry into thirds once more. Wrap in greaseproof paper and refrigerate until required.

Note: This pastry dough will keep well for a few days in the refrigerator, in greaseproof paper in a plastic bag. It also freezes well.

Chocolate Puff Pastry

Yield: 8 ounces pastry

2 cups flour

4 tablespoons cocoa

4 tablespoons confectioners' sugar

¼ teaspoon salt, optional

2 sticks unsalted butter

about ½ cup cold water

Sift the flour, cocoa, and sugar (and salt, if used) into the large bowl of an electric mixer. Add ½ stick of the butter, cut into ⅜-inch cubes. Mix at Speed 2 for 2 minutes or until the mixture resembles bread crumbs. Sprinkle the water in, then mix at Speed 2 until the mixture forms a dough that leaves the sides of the bowl cleanly.

Place the dough on a lightly floured marble slab or cold surface, and knead lightly until smooth underneath. Then turn over and pat into a square shape ⅜ inch thick. Wrap in greaseproof paper and chill in the refrigerator for 10 to 15 minutes.

Knead and squeeze the remaining 1½ sticks butter into a square, ¼ inch thick, between two pieces of muslin, in order to absorb excess moisture. Chill well until firm but not hard.

Roll the dough out on a floured marble slab or cold surface to a rectangle twice as big as the square of butter. Place the butter on the top half of the dough, and fold the bottom half over. Roll it out evenly to a long strip, taking care that the butter does not break through. Fold the strip of pastry into thirds, folding the bottom third up and the top third down. Cool in the refrigerator for 10 to 15 minutes.

Roll and fold seven times (as for Puff Pastry), then chill well before use.

Whole-Wheat Wheat-germ Pastry

Yield: 8 ounces pastry

1¼ cups whole-wheat flour, fine or medium ground

2½ ounces wheat-germ

1 stick butter or polyunsaturated margarine

4 tablespoons iced water

Place the whole-wheat flour in a large, cold mixing bowl and add the wheat germ. Cut the butter into the flour and the wheat germ with a round-bladed knife, coating each piece well. Rub the butter into the flour and wheat germ with the fingertips until the mixture resembles bread crumbs.

Sprinkle iced water over gradually and mix in with the round-bladed knife until the mixture begins to form lumps that leave the sides of the bowl cleanly. Knead the dough with a cold, clean hand to compress together lightly.

Using an electric mixer: Mix the flour and wheat germ together in the bowl of the electric mixer. Add the butter or margarine and mix at Speed 2 for about 1 minute or until the mixture resembles fine bread crumbs. Add the iced water, 1 tablespoon at a time, still mixing at Speed 2 for about 45 to 60 seconds or until the mixture leaves the sides of the bowl clean and forms a ball around the beater.

Using a food processor: Place the flour, wheat-germ, and butter or margarine in the food processor and mix for 30 seconds. Add the iced water and mix until a dough forms that leaves the sides of the bowl clean.

Turn the pastry onto a lightly floured board or marble slab, and knead until smooth. Then turn over and shape into a round cake shape. Wrap in greaseproof paper and chill in the refrigerator for at least 30 minutes.

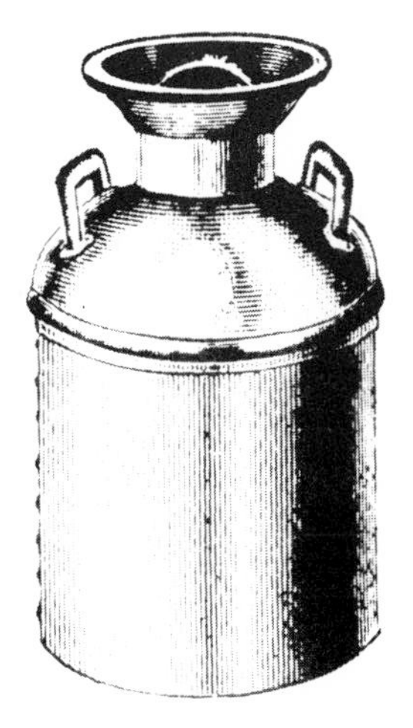

Hot-Water-Crust Pastry

Yield: 12 ounces pastry

3 cups flour

1 teaspoon salt

8 tablespoons lard

1 cup water

1 egg yolk

Sift the flour and salt into a large, warm mixing bowl or the warm bowl of an electric mixer. Heat the lard and water together in a saucepan, then bring rapidly to a boil. Quickly pour the boiling lard and water mixture onto the flour. Using a wooden spoon or a K-beater or pastry mixers, mix gently or at minimum speed for 15 seconds. Add the egg yolk and continue to beat for another 15 seconds. Beat quicker with the wooden spoon or increase to Speed 2 and beat for another 30 seconds or until the mixture leaves the sides of the bowl clean and forms a smooth ball around the beater.

Knead very lightly, then wrap in greaseproof paper and allow to rest at room temperature for 20 to 30 minutes before use.

Note: This pastry must be kept warm at all times, not cold.

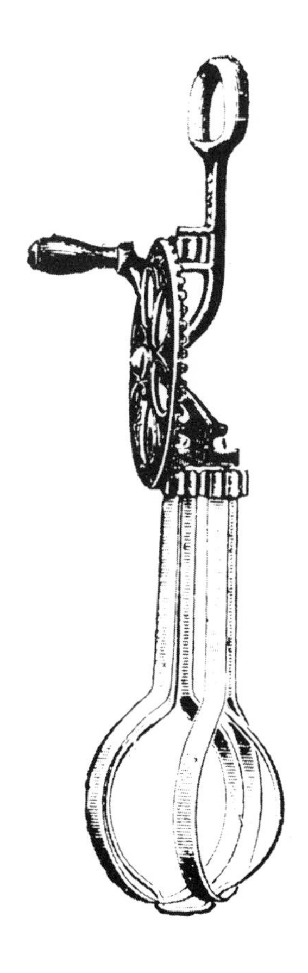

Pâte Brisée

Yield: 8 ounces pastry

1½ sticks chilled butter

2 cups flour

¼ teaspoon salt, optional

about 4 to 6 tablespoons iced water

Cut the butter into the sifted flour in a cold mixing bowl. Rub the butter into the flour with cold fingertips until the mixture resembles fine bread crumbs. Add the salt, if used. Sprinkle iced water over, a tablespoon at a time, and mix with a round-bladed knife or a palette knife until the dough forms small lumps that leave the sides of the bowl cleanly. Knead the dough together lightly with a clean, cold hand.

Using an electric mixer: Cut the butter into ⅜-inch cubes and place in the bowl of the electric mixer. Sift flour and salt together onto a square of greaseproof paper. Add a little flour to the butter and mix with a K-beater or pastry mixers at minimum speed until mixture begins to break up. Then gradually add the remaining flour, increase the speed to 2, and mix for 2 minutes. Increase the speed to 3 for ½ to 1 minute more, or until the mixture resembles fine bread crumbs. Add 4 tablespoons of the iced water all at once, and mix at Speed 3 for 10 seconds. If the dough has not come together, add the remaining water gradually on minimum speed until the mixture leaves the sides of the bowl clean.

Using a food processor: Place the butter, flour, and salt into the food processor, fitted with a steel blade, and mix for 30 seconds or until the mixture resembles bread crumbs. Then add 3 tablespoons of the iced water and mix for 5 seconds. If the dough does not leave the sides of the bowl cleanly, add 1 tablespoon of iced water and mix for another 5 seconds; repeat until the dough leaves the sides of the bowl cleanly.

Turn the dough onto a lightly floured marble slab or board and knead lightly with the fingertips until smooth. Turn over and pat into a round cake shape ½ to 1 inch thick, then wrap in greaseproof paper and chill in the refrigerator for 30 minutes or until firm.

Note: This pastry dough freezes well. It also stores well in greaseproof paper inside a plastic bag in the refrigerator for a few days.

Pâte Sucrée

Yield: 8 ounces pastry

2 cups flour

½ cup confectioners' sugar

1 stick unsalted butter, chilled

2 egg yolks or 1 egg

1 teaspoon iced water, only if necessary

Sift flour onto marble slab. Using the cushion of your hand, sweep a large ring. Sift sugar into center of ring and make a well. Place butter and egg yolks in the well, then, using a pecking motion with your fingertips, combine butter and egg yolks.

Gather in flour and sugar to combine dough. Knead very lightly until a smooth ball. Chill if necessary.

Using an electric mixer: Cut the butter into ⅜-inch cubes, and place in the bowl of the electric mixer. Sift the flour and sugar together onto a square of greaseproof paper. Add a little flour to the butter and mix with a K-beater or pastry mixers at minimum speed until the butter begins to break up. Gradually add the remaining flour. Increase the speed to 2 for 2 minutes, then increase the speed to 3 for another 30 seconds or until the mixture resembles fine bread crumbs. Reduce the speed to 1, add the egg, and mix until the dough comes together. If the dough is too dry and will not come together, add water and mix to bind.

Using a food processor: Place the butter, flour, and sugar into the food processor, fitted with a steel blade, and mix for 30 seconds or until the mixture resembles bread crumbs. Add egg yolks or beaten egg, and process until the mixture forms a dough that leaves the sides of the bowl cleanly. It is normally unnecessary to add the water when mixing in a food processor.

Turn the dough onto a lightly floured marble slab or pastry board, and knead lightly just until smooth. Turn over and pat into a round cake shape ½ to 1 inch thick, then wrap in greaseproof paper and chill in the refrigerator for 30 minutes or until firm.

Pâte Sucrée

1. Place butter and sugar into a well in flour/sugar mixture.

2. Using a pecking motion with your fingertips, combine butter and egg yolks.

3. Gather in flour and sugar to combine dough.

4. Knead very lightly until smooth. Chill if necessary.

5. Roll out dough and carefully lift onto pie pan.

6. Roll away excess dough.

2

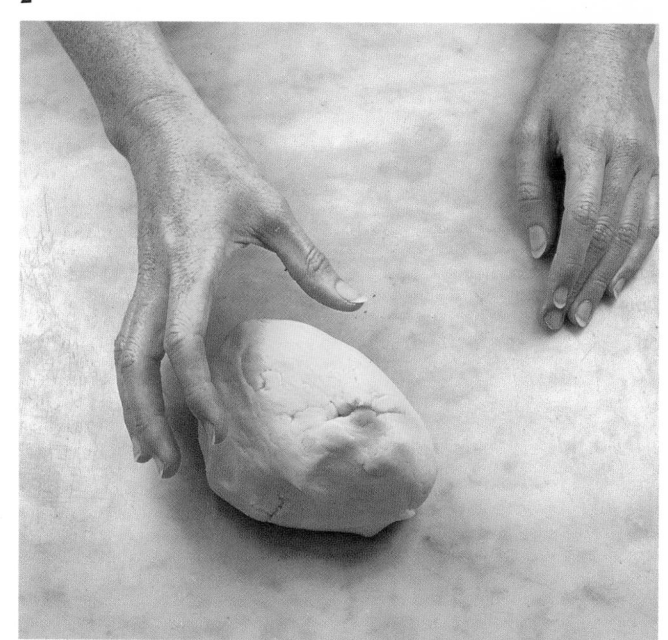

4

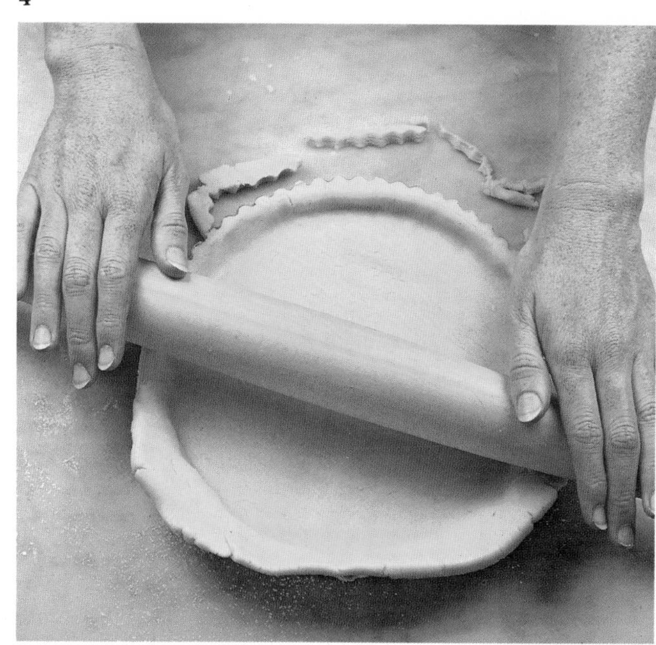

6

Biscuit Pastry

Yield: 12 ounces pastry

1 stick butter

⅓ cup sugar

1 egg

½ teaspoon vanilla extract

3 cups self-rising flour

¼ teaspoon salt

In a mixing bowl, cream the butter and sugar until light and fluffy. Add the egg and vanilla and mix well. Stir in the sifted flour and salt, form the dough into a ball, and knead lightly. Wrap the dough in greaseproof paper until you are ready to use it.

Almond Crust

Yield: pastry for a 10-inch pie

2 egg whites

pinch of cream of tartar

pinch of salt

¼ teaspoon vanilla extract

½ cup sugar

1½ cups finely chopped blanched almonds

Preheat the oven to 375°F.

Beat the egg whites until foamy. Add cream of tartar, salt, and vanilla. Gradually add the sugar and continue beating until the mixture is stiff and glossy. Fold in the almonds.

Spread the mixture over the bottom and sides of an oiled pie dish.

Bake for 15 to 20 minutes or until lightly browned. Cool.

Oil Pastry

Yield: 8 ounces pastry

2 cups flour

1 teaspoon salt

⅔ cup vegetable oil

3 tablespoons water or milk

Sift the flour into a mixing bowl with the salt. Mix together the oil and water or milk and stir it into the flour. Form the dough into a ball, then pat it into a round cake shape ½ to 1 inch thick. Wrap in greaseproof paper and chill in the refrigerator for at least 30 minutes before use.

Pastry

Yield: 8 ounces pastry

½ stick butter

¼ cup powdered sugar

¼ cup milk

1 egg

2 cups self-rising flour

Put the butter, sugar, and milk into a saucepan; heat until the butter has melted and the sugar has dissolved. Beat the egg in a bowl and stir in the butter–sugar mixture. Sift in the flour and beat with a wooden spoon until the mixture forms a soft dough. Use while still warm.

Orange Pastry

Yield: 5 ounces pastry

1¼ cups flour

¼ teaspoon salt

5 tablespoons butter

juice and grated rind of ½ cold orange

Sift the flour and salt into a bowl. Cut the butter into small pieces and rub them into the flour with your fingertips until the mixture resembles coarse bread crumbs. Add the orange rind and mix well.

Gradually add the orange juice until the mixture begins to stick together. Gather into a ball, flatten lightly with the palm of your hand, wrap in greaseproof paper, and chill for 30 minutes before use.

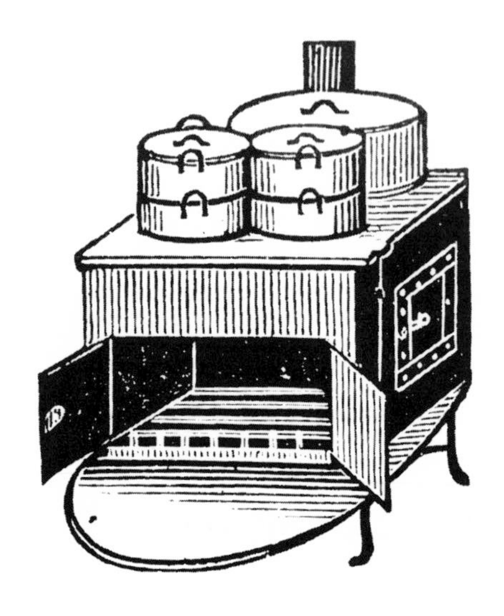

Pecan or Walnut Pastry

Yield: 10 ounces pastry

2½ cups flour

½ teaspoon salt

¾ stick butter, cut into small pieces

2 ounces vegetable fat

½ cup powdered sugar

¼ cup finely chopped pecans or walnuts

2 egg yolks, lightly beaten

3 tablespoons iced water

Sift the flour and salt into a large mixing bowl. Add the butter and vegetable fat and cut them into small pieces in the flour. Rub the fats into the flour with your fingertips until the mixture resembles coarse bread crumbs. Add the sugar and pecans or walnuts and mix well.

Add the egg yolks and half the water and mix together with a round-bladed knife until the mixture forms lumps that leave the sides of the bowl clean. Add more water if the dough is too dry. Knead the dough lightly until it is smooth, then form it into a ball, flatten it slightly, and wrap in greaseproof paper. Chill for 30 minutes before use.

Turnover Pastry

Yield: 10 ounces pastry

2½ cups flour

½ teaspoon salt

pinch of cream of tartar

1 stick butter

3 tablespoons pure lard, cut into pieces

½ cup iced water

Sift the flour, salt, and cream of tartar into a bowl. Cut the butter into small pieces. Rub the butter and lard into the flour with your fingertips until the mixture resembles coarse bread crumbs. Add the iced water. Toss until the mixture is blended and form it into a ball.

Knead lightly with the heel of your hand and add the lard, blending it evenly through the dough.

Form into a ball and roll out on a lightly floured board into a rectangle 10 × 5 inches. Fold into thirds with the open side facing you. Roll out and repeat the process three more times. Chill the dough for at least 1 hour.

Apricots in Nightdress

Yield: 6 pastries

1 pound Puff Pastry
(see recipe, page 154)

3 medium-size apricots

2 tablespoons sugar

1 egg white, lightly beaten

confectioners' sugar, for dusting

Preheat the oven to 450°F. Thoroughly grease a baking sheet.

Divide the pastry into six portions; roll out to about ⅛ inch thick. Cut into squares.

Peel, halve, and remove the pits from the apricots. Place an apricot half in the center of one square of pastry and sprinkle with a little of the sugar. Brush the edges of the pastry with egg white and wrap tightly to encase the apricot half firmly in the pastry. Place on the baking sheet, pastry seams down, and brush the top of the pastry with egg white.

Bake for 40 minutes or until golden brown in color. Dust with the sugar while hot, then allow to cool on a wire rack. Serve warm as a dessert or cold with afternoon tea or coffee.

Apple Rings in Pastry

Yield: 8 pastries

2 tablespoons butter

2 tablespoons sugar

2 tablespoons currants

2 medium-size cooking apples

1 pound Puff Pastry
(see recipe, page 154)

1 egg white, lightly beaten

Cream the butter and sugar together until pale and fluffy; add the currants and mix thoroughly.

Roll out the pastry to a thickness of about ⅛ inch.

Peel and core the apples. Slice them crosswise into rings about ½ inch thick.

Preheat the oven to 450°F. Grease a baking sheet.

Place one of the apple slices onto a 10×5-inch strip of pastry, toward one end of the strip. Fill the apple-core cavity with a spoonful of the butter–currant mixture. Wrap the pastry around the apple slice, folding the edges in and sealing with the egg white as it is rolled end-over-end. Make three slashes in the top of the rolled pastry and brush the top and sides with egg white. Repeat until all ingredients are used. Place on the baking sheet.

Bake for 40 minutes or until rich golden brown in color. Serve warm with cream or custard.

Choux Pastry

Yield: 2 ounces pastry

½ cup flour
⅛ teaspoon salt
½ cup water
½ stick butter
2 large eggs
drops of vanilla extract

Sift the flour and salt together onto a square of greaseproof paper.

Place the water and butter into a ceramic-lined, cast-iron saucepan and bring to boiling point over medium heat. Remove immediately from the heat to prevent evaporation. Quickly stir in the sifted flour and salt all at once, using a wooden spoon. Beat the mixture until it forms a smooth paste that leaves the sides of the saucepan clean. Cool.

Beat the eggs, then beat them into the mixture in four stages, beating well after each addition, until no trace of egg remains. Finally beat in a few drops of vanilla.

Use the pastry according to a given recipe, and bake immediately.

Cheese Choux Pastry

Yield: 4 ounces pastry

1 cup flour
pinch of salt
1 cup water
¾ stick butter
3 large eggs
3 tablespoons grated Parmesan cheese
salt and pepper
mustard powder

Prepare as for Choux Pastry, but beat the beaten eggs into the mixture in six stages, beating well after each addition, until no trace of egg remains and the mixture is smooth and shiny.

Finally beat in the Parmesan cheese and season to taste with salt, pepper, and mustard powder. Use and bake immediately for best results.

Chocolate Choux Pastry

Yield: 2½ ounces pastry

⅔ cup water
½ stick butter or firm margarine
½ cup flour
1 tablespoon cocoa
2 large eggs

Place the water and butter into a ceramic-lined cast-iron saucepan and bring to boiling point over medium heat. Meanwhile, sift the flour and cocoa together onto a square of greaseproof paper. Remove the saucepan from the heat as soon as the mixture boils, and stir in the sifted flour and cocoa all at once, using a wooden spoon. Return the saucepan to a low heat and beat for 1 minute, or until the mixture is shiny and leaves the sides of the saucepan clean. Remove from the heat and allow to cool slightly.

Beat the eggs well with a fork, then beat them into the mixture in four parts, beating well after each addition, until the mixture is smooth and shiny.

Use according to a particular recipe, and bake immediately for best results.

Choux Pastry

1. Tip sifted flour all at once into butter–water mixture.

2. Stir with wooden spoon.

3. Stir until mixture leaves the sides of the pan, then cool.

4. Add eggs gradually.

5. Beat well until mixture is smooth and shiny.

6. Spoon or pipe onto greased baking sheets.

2

4

6

Bakewell Squares

Yield: 12 to 16 squares

Pastry:
1 stick butter

1¾ cups flour

pinch of baking powder

1 tablespoon + 1 teaspoon cold water

½ egg yolk

¼ cup powdered sugar

Filling:
½ stick butter

¼ cup powdered sugar

1½ eggs

almond extract

½ cup ground almonds

½ cup sponge or white bread crumbs

raspberry jam (jelly)

confectioners' sugar

Pastry: Blend the butter and 1 cup of flour. Mix the water, egg yolk, and sugar together; add to the flour and butter. Work in the remaining flour and baking powder, turn out onto a floured surface, and work the mixture together. Refrigerate for 10 to 20 minutes.
Filling: Cream the butter and sugar together thoroughly. Continue mixing and add the beaten eggs gradually. Flavor with the almond extract. Lightly mix in the almonds and crumbs.
To Assemble: Preheat the oven to 350°F.

Roll out the pastry to ¼ inch thick and line a small cake pan. Spread the pastry with the raspberry jam. Place the almond mixture on top and spread evenly.

Bake for 15 to 20 minutes. Dredge with sugar, or brush lightly with Lemon Glacé Icing (see recipe, page 102). Portion into serving slices. Serve cold.

Peanut-Crunch Pastry Slices

Yield: 16 pieces

4 ounces Sweet Shortcrust Pastry (see recipe, page 150)

1 stick butter

⅓ cup honey

⅓ cup raw sugar

5 cups puffed rice

⅔ cup flaked coconut

⅓ cup roasted peanuts

Preheat the oven to 325°F.

Roll the pastry out thinly and fit it into the bottom of a 9-inch-square cake pan. Prick all over with a fork.

Bake for about 20 minutes. Leave it in the pan to cool.

Peanut Crunch

Melt the butter in a large saucepan. Add the honey and sugar, bring to a boil, then reduce the heat a little, and cook for 3 minutes. Mix in the puffed rice, coconut, and peanuts, coating them thoroughly.

Spread the mixture over the cool pastry, pressing firmly in place. Allow it to set, then cut into fingers. When slices are cold, store in an airtight container.

Apricot Delights

Yield: 24 pastries

1 quantity Sweet Shortcrust Pastry (see recipe, page 150)

Filling:
½ stick butter

⅓ cup sugar

1 egg

1 cup finely chopped apricots

Preheat the oven to 375°F.

Roll out the pastry thinly, cut out rounds, and press these into muffin tins. Reserve small strips of pastry.

Cream the butter and sugar together, then beat in the egg. Mix in the chopped apricots.

Place a small spoonful of the filling into each pastry-lined muffin cup. Place a cross of pastry on the top of each.

Bake for 20 to 25 minutes. Serve warm or cold.

Coconut Apple Slices

Yield: 16 fingers

Pastry Base:
1 stick butter or margarine
½ cup brown sugar
1 cup flour
1 teaspoon mixed spice
Topping:
2 eggs
1 cup brown sugar
1 cup roughly chopped walnuts
½ cup flaked coconut
1 tablespoon flour
1 teaspoon vanilla extract
1 to 1½ cups dried apples, lightly cooked in water and drained

Preheat the oven to 350°F. Thoroughly grease a baking pan 11 × 7 inches.

To make the pastry, cream the butter and sugar together; stir in the flour and spice. Spread the mixture into the prepared baking pan.

Bake for 20 minutes. Remove from the oven and allow to cool for 10 minutes.

In the meantime, prepare the topping. Beat together the eggs and sugar; stir in the walnuts, coconut, flour, and vanilla.

Spoon the cooked and drained apples in an even layer onto the semi-cooked pastry base. Spread the topping mixture over the apples.

Bake in the preheated oven for about 25 minutes or until the topping is brown. May be cut into fingers or large squares and served warm, with cream or custard, as a dessert.

Black-Cherry Strudel

Yield: 6 to 8 servings

1 quantity Strudel (see recipe, page 168)
1½ pounds black cherries, pitted and drained
4 ounces soft bread crumbs, fried in butter
2 ounces currants
½ cup sugar
½ teaspoon ground cinnamon
grated rind of ½ lemon
1 stick butter, melted

Make up the Strudel Dough.

Preheat the oven to 425°F. Butter a large baking sheet.

While the dough is "resting" prepare the filling. Dice the cherries, and gently mix them with all the other ingredients except the butter. When the pastry is ready, trim off any hard or thick outside edges and spread with the cherry filling, leaving approximately ¾ inch uncovered all around the outer edges. Roll the dough, filling very gently and carefully, and pinch the edges together. Carefully place onto a large, buttered baking sheet. Brush lavishly with the melted butter.

Bake the strudel for 20 minutes, then reduce the oven temperature to moderate, 325°, and bake for another 30 minutes. Brush with melted butter several times during baking.

Serve hot or cold with whipped, slightly sweetened cream.

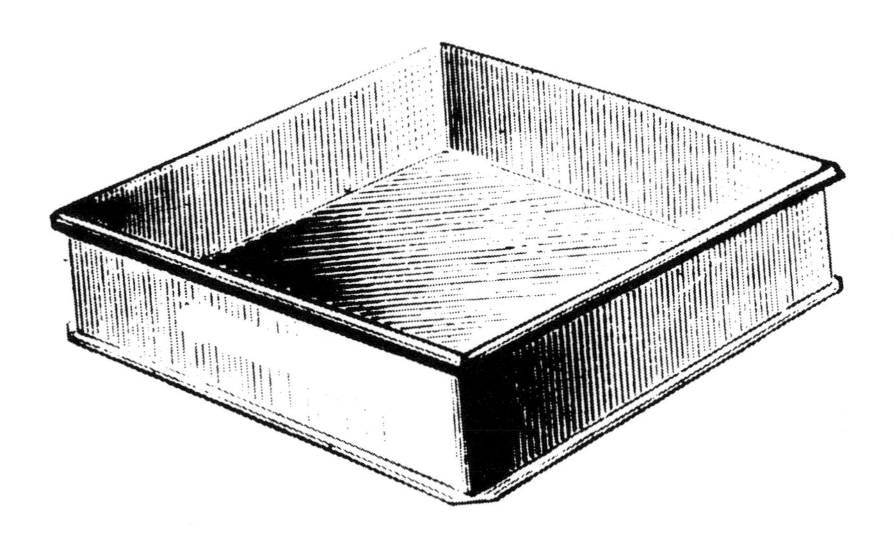

Raspberry Crescents

Yield: 24 crescents

1 cup flour

3 ounces cream cheese, softened

½ stick butter or margarine

¼ cup raspberry preserve

confectioners' sugar, for sprinkling

Sift the flour into a bowl; add the cream cheese and butter, and knead to form a manageable dough. Divide the dough in half, and form into two balls. Wrap and chill overnight.

Next day: Preheat the oven to 400°F. Lightly grease a baking sheet.

On a lightly floured board, roll out each ball into a circle about 9 inches in diameter. Cut each into 12 wedges. Place ½ teaspoon of raspberry preserve on the wide end of each wedge. Roll toward pointed end and shape into a crescent. Arrange crescents on the baking sheet.

Bake for 10 to 15 minutes or until golden brown. Cool on wire racks; sprinkle with sugar. Store in an airtight container (may be frozen for up to 6 months).

Maids of Honor

Yield: 24 little cakes

1 quantity Shortcrust Pastry (see recipe, page 150)

raspberry jam (jelly)

½ cup ground almonds or flaked coconut

⅓ cup powdered sugar

2 ounces ground rice

2 tablespoons self-rising flour

1 large egg

4 tablespoons milk

2 teaspoons honey

¼ teaspoon vanilla extract

Preheat the oven to 325°F. Grease the muffin tins.

Roll the pastry out to a thickness of ¼ inch and cut to line each muffin cup. Place a little jam in each.

Blend together the ground almonds, sugar, ground rice, and flour. Beat together the egg, milk, honey, and vanilla, and combine this with the dry ingredients to form a soft mixture. Spoon the mixture into the pastry-lined muffin tins.

Bake for 15 to 20 minutes. Turn out onto wire racks to cool.

Bohemian Pastry Roll

Yield: 12 to 16 servings

Pastry:
8 ounces cottage cheese

3 ounces brown sugar

6 tablespoons oil

6 tablespoons milk

1 teaspoon vanilla extract

3 cups self-rising flour

pinch of salt

½ stick butter, melted

Filling:
3 ounces raisins

2 ounces currants

2 ounces blanched, slivered almonds

Glacé Icing (optional) (see recipe, page 102)

To make the pastry, beat the cheese with the sugar, oil, milk, and vanilla. Add half the flour and the salt, stir in, then knead in the remainder of the flour. If the dough is sticky, add a little more flour. Roll out into a rectangle about 20 × 12 inches and brush lavishly with the melted butter.

Preheat the oven to 400°F. Grease a couple of baking sheets.

Combine the raisins, currants, and almonds, and sprinkle over the pastry; roll the pastry up. Cut into slices about ¾ inch thick. Slightly flatten each slice and place onto the greased baking sheet.

Bake for about 15 minutes. Turn onto a wire rack and allow to cool before icing the slices (if desired).

Right: **Clockwise from top left: Bohemian Pastry Roll (see above); Raspberry Crescents (see above left); Hazelnut Yeast Pastry Roll (see p. 181); Bread Cheesecakes (see p. 169).**

Traditional Apple Strudel

Yield: 8 to 10 servings

Strudel Pastry: ***2 cups flour***
pinch of salt
1 tablespoon melted butter
1 egg
⅔ cup warm water
1 teaspoon lemon juice
additional 3 tablespoons melted butter
confectioners' sugar, for sprinkling
Filling: ***1 tablespoon butter***
2 tablespoons fresh white bread crumbs
1 pound cooking apples
¼ cup sugar
½ cup raisins
1 level teaspoon ground cinnamon
finely grated rind of ½ lemon

To make the dough, sift the flour and salt into a bowl, and make a well in the center. Mix 1 tablespoon of melted butter with the egg, warm water, and lemon juice, and pour into the dry ingredients. Stir with a wooden spoon, gradually drawing the flour into the well. When well blended, turn the dough onto a lightly floured board. The dough will be sticky, but flour both hands liberally and knead until it is smooth and elastic. From time to time, slap the dough sharply onto the board. Sprinkle the dough with a little flour and cover it with a large warmed inverted bowl for 30 minutes (do not allow the bowl to touch the dough).

Prepare the Filling: Melt the butter in a pan, stir in the bread crumbs and fry until golden; set aside. Peel, core, and thinly slice the apples; mix with the sugar, raisins, cinnamon, and lemon rind; set aside.

After 30 minutes the dough will be stretchable. Place a clean cloth on the work surface and sprinkle with flour. Place the dough, floured side down, in the center of the cloth and carefully roll out thinly. Brush with a little melted butter, then gently slip both hands under the dough and carefully pull it outward, being very careful not to tear it (always work from the center outward). When the dough is paper-thin, brush with a little more melted butter and leave for 10 minutes.

Preheat the oven to 375°F. Grease a baking sheet.

To fill the strudel, sprinkle buttered bread crumbs onto the pastry and arrange the apple mixture evenly on top. Brush the edges with water, and roll it up like a jelly roll, using the cloth to support it. Very carefully lift it onto the baking sheet and gently form into a horseshoe shape. Brush with melted butter.

Bake for about 50 minutes. When cold, or at least warm, dredge with powdered sugar and cut into slices.

Cherry Rolls

Yield: 8 rolls

8 ounces Puff Pastry (see recipe, page 154)
egg white
1 can (15 ounces) red cherries, pits removed, drained
1 tablespoon sugar
confectioners' sugar, for dusting

Preheat the oven to 450°F. Grease a baking sheet.

Roll out the Puff Pastry to about ⅛ inch thick. Cut into squares 5 × 5 inches, and brush all four edges of each square with egg white.

Place a single row of cherries in the center of each pastry square. Sprinkle each with sugar. Roll the pastry to cover the cherries, and secure the side edges by folding in and pressing firmly. Continue to roll until the pastry forms neat tight rolls. Brush the tops and edges generously with egg white.

Bake for about 20 minutes. When golden brown, remove from the oven and dust with powdered sugar. Serve warm or cold. Cherry Rolls are best when eaten the day they are baked.

Bread Cheesecakes

Yield: 12 little cakes

4 ounces Short or Rough Puff Pastry (see recipes, pages 149 and 154)

4 ounces white bread crumbs

¼ cup sugar

pinch of grated nutmeg

⅔ cup milk

2 tablespoons butter

2 ounces currants

grated lemon rind

2 eggs

2 tablespoons jam (jelly)

Roll out the pastry. Cut into rounds large enough to line the cups in a small muffin tin. Line each cup.

Preheat the oven to 400°F.

Combine the bread crumbs, sugar, and nutmeg. Heat the milk and butter in a small saucepan until boiling, then add to the bread crumb mixture. Add the currants and a little lemon rind, and mix thoroughly.

Separate the yolks from the whites of the egg. Lightly whisk the yolks and add to the bread crumb–currant mixture.

Put a little jam in the bottom of each pastry case.

Beat the egg whites to a firm peak; fold into the mixture using a metal spoon. Put a generous teaspoonful of the prepared mixture into each pastry case.

Bake for 20 minutes or until the center is firm and golden in color. Remove the cakes from the oven, then carefully turn onto a wire rack to cool completely. Serve cold.

Baked Jelly Roll

Yield: 6 servings

8 ounces Sweet Shortcrust Pastry (see recipe, page 150)

6 tablespoons jelly

1 tablespoon powdered sugar, for sprinkling

pure cream

Sweet Glaze:
2 tablespoon water

2 tablespoon sugar

Roll the pastry into a rectangle about 12×8 inches. Spread with the jelly, leaving a ½-inch rim all around. Brush the edges lightly with water, roll up like a jelly roll. Place onto a lightly greased oven tray, joined edges underneath.

Preheat the oven to 400°F.

To make the glaze: Combine the sugar and water in a small saucepan, bring to a boil, then cook until it has a syrupy consistency. Brush the glaze over the unbaked jelly roll.

Bake for 15 to 20 minutes, or until golden and crisp. Sprinkle with a little powdered sugar, if desired, and serve each portion with a spoonful of pure cream.

Cream Horns

Yield: 12 pastries

8 ounces Rough Puff Pastry (see recipe, page 154)

1 egg white, beaten

¾ cup cream

2 teaspoons powdered sugar

vanilla extract

strawberry jam (jelly)

pistachio nuts, finely chopped

Preheat the oven to 475°F.

Lightly grease 12 cream horn molds and a baking sheet.

Roll out the pastry to ¼ inch thick, cut into strips 1 inch long; brush these lightly with beaten egg white. Wind the pastry around the cream-horn molds, starting at the point and overlapping each round. Trim the tops, brush again with the egg white, and set onto the baking sheet.

Bake for 7 to 8 minutes, until crisp and golden brown. Remove the horns.

Whip the cream with the sugar and drops of vanilla. When the horns are cold, place ½ teaspoon of jam at the bottom of each horn and fill with the whipped cream. Decorate each horn with a sprinkle of pistachio nuts.

Million-Leaves Cakes (Matchsticks)

Yield: 8 cakes

3 sheets puff pastry, each about 10×5 inches

2 tablespoons raspberry jam (jelly)

1 cup fresh cream

drops of vanilla extract

water, to mix

1 cup confectioners' sugar

Preheat the oven to 350°F.

Prick each sheet of puff pastry thoroughly with a fork.

Bake the three sheets of pastry on separate baking sheets in the middle of the oven until a rich brown color (20 to 30 minutes). Allow to cool on wire cake racks.

Spread one sheet of pastry with the raspberry jam and place a second sheet on top.

Flavor the fresh cream with a few drops of vanilla and whip until stiff. Spread the cream down the length of the pastry. Place the third sheet of pastry on top and press lightly, to spread the encased cream to the edges.

Prepare a spreadable but not over-soft water icing by combining a little water with the confectioners' sugar. (Color as required). Spread over the top layer of pastry and allow to set. Using a serrated knife, slice into serving portions.

Cream Puffs

Yield: 16 puffs

½ cup self-rising flour

¼ teaspoon salt

½ stick butter

½ cup water

½ teaspoon sugar

2 eggs

⅔ cup cream

powdered sugar, for dusting

Sift the flour and salt onto a square of paper and leave in a warm dry place until required.

Preheat the oven to 425°F. Lightly grease a baking sheet.

Cut up the butter and place into a saucepan with the water and sugar; bring quickly to a boil. Tip the flour in all at once while the pan is still on the heat. Stir to mix and remove the pan from the heat. Beat the mixture thoroughly until it leaves the sides of the saucepan, then allow it to cool until the hand can be held comfortably against the side of the pot.

Lightly mix the eggs and beat in gradually. When the eggs have been added, the choux paste should appear thick and glossy and just stiff enough to hold its shape when piped. Place the mixture into a piping bag fitted with a ½-inch tube and pipe 16 small mounds onto the baking sheet, allowing 3 inches between mounds.

Bake for 20 minutes, then reduce the oven temperature to 350°F and cook for another 10 minutes, until golden brown and crisp. Remove from the oven and pierce the bottoms of the puffs. Allow to cool on a wire rack.

While the puffs are cooling, make the filling. Whip the cream until almost stiff. Do not overbeat.

When the puffs are cold and just before serving, make a slit in each puff, fill with the cream, and dust with powdered sugar.

***Right:* Cream Horns (see above left); Matchsticks (see left).**

Coconut Cheesecakes

Yield: 12 little cakes

4 ounces Rough Puff Pastry (see recipe, page 154)
½ stick butter
¼ cup powdered sugar
1 egg
1 ounce rice flour
⅔ cup flaked coconut
½ teaspoon baking powder
jam (jelly)

Preheat the oven to 400°F. Butter 12 muffin tins.

Roll out the pastry very thinly and cut rounds to line the muffin tins.

Cream the butter and sugar together. Add the egg and rice flour; beat well. Finally add the coconut and baking powder. Put a little jam onto the pastry in each cup and half fill the cups with the mixture.

Bake for 20 minutes or until the center of each little cake is firm and golden in color.

Cream-Cheese and Jelly Puffs

Yield: 12 puffs

1 cup flour
1 stick butter
4 ounces cream cheese
⅓ cup jam or fruit jelly
a little chopped fresh mint
powdered sugar, for sprinkling

Preheat the oven to 425°F. Grease a couple of baking sheets.

Sift the flour onto a pastry board (a marble slab is best, if you have one). Cut the butter into small cubes; then lightly crumble the cream cheese and butter cubes into the flour, handling as lightly and as little as possible. Press lightly into a ball, using fingertips only.

Roll the dough out to ¼ inch thick and cut into about 12 squares. Spoon a portion of the jam or fruit jelly into the center of each; sprinkle with a little chopped mint. Gather up the four corners of the pastry, twist on top, and press the edges firmly together. Place on the lightly greased baking sheets.

Bake for 15 minutes. Serve hot, sprinkled with powdered sugar.

Currant Fingers

Yield: 18 pieces

Pastry:
2½ cups flour
pinch of salt
1½ sticks butter
about ½ cup iced water
1 egg white, for glazing
powdered sugar, for sprinkling

Filling:
¾ stick butter
⅓ cup brown sugar, firmly packed
1 tablespoon light corn syrup
1 tablespoon marmalade
1 tablespoon flour
1 teaspoon powdered cinnamon
2½ cups currants

Pastry: Sift the flour and salt into a bowl. Grate the butter over the flour; stir in with a knife. Stir in enough iced water with a knife to give a firm, pliable dough. Refrigerate for 30 minutes.

Filling: Combine all the filling ingredients in a saucepan; stir over low heat until the butter is melted and the ingredients are combined. Allow the mixture to become cold.

To Assemble: Preheat the oven to 375°F. Grease an 11 × 7-inch shallow pan.

Roll out two-thirds of the pastry to line the base and sides of the greased pan. Spread this evenly with the cold filling; top with the remaining pastry. Glaze the surface lightly with beaten egg white and sprinkle with powdered sugar.

Bake for 25 minutes or until golden brown. When cold, remove from the pan and cut into fingers.

Golden Cheesecake Pastry Squares

Yield: 8 servings

Pastry:
2 cups self-rising flour (all whole-wheat, all white, or half and half)

pinch of salt

1 stick butter, melted

¾ cup milk

½ cup sugar

2 eggs

grated peel of ½ lemon

Topping:
12 ounces cream cheese

2 egg yolks

1 teaspoon vanilla extract

½ cup brown sugar

¾ cup raisins, chopped

grated peel of 1 lemon

2 egg whites

1 cup slivered almonds

1 teaspoon ground cinnamon

2 tablespoons honey, slightly warmed

To make the pastry base, place the flour and salt into a large bowl. In a separate bowl, blend together the melted butter, milk, sugar, and eggs; stir this into the flour. Blend in the lemon peel. Press the pastry into a greased pan 11 × 7 inches.

Preheat the oven to 350°F.

Topping: Beat the cream cheese, and add the egg yolks, vanilla, and sugar. Beat until smooth. Stir in the raisins and lemon peel. Beat the egg whites until stiff; fold into the cream-cheese mixture. Spread carefully onto the pastry base. Combine the almonds and cinnamon, and sprinkle over the surface of the cheese mixture; drizzle with the warm honey.

Bake on a low shelf in the oven for about 30 minutes. Reduce the oven temperature to 300°F and bake for another 10 minutes. Topping should be set and golden brown.

Allow to cool slightly, then cut into squares. Serve each slice with a little whipped cream into which a teaspoon of freshly grated orange peel has been folded.

Date Oatmeal Pastry Slices

Yield: 36 slices

Filling:
2¾ cups chopped dates

⅔ cup water

2 tablespoons lemon juice

grated peel of 1 lemon

grated peel of ½ orange

Pastry:
1¼ sticks butter or margarine

1 cup raw sugar

2 cups whole-wheat flour

1 heaped teaspoon baking soda

pinch of salt

2½ cups rolled oats

Filling: Mix all the ingredients. Cook for 5 minutes over low heat, stirring constantly until the mixture is smooth and thick. Allow to cool before putting onto pastry.

Preheat the oven to 350°F. Thoroughly grease a baking pan.

To Make the Pastry

Work the butter (or margarine), sugar, flour, soda, and salt into a crumbly mixture. Add the rolled oats, and mix well. Press half of the mixture into the baking pan and pat lightly into place.

Spread the cooled date filling onto the pastry. Top with a layer of the rest of the pastry mixture, pressing gently into place.

Bake for about 35 minutes. Allow to cool, then cut into 3 × 1-inch bars.

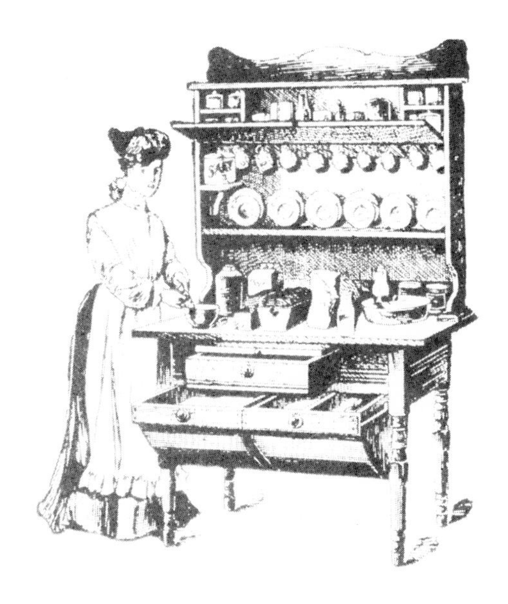

Danish Pastry I

Yield: 12 crescents

pinch of ground cardamom

2½ cups flour

1 tablespoon butter

pinch of salt

⅔ cup milk

6 teaspoons sugar

½ lightly beaten egg

1 cake fresh yeast or 1 package dried yeast

1¾ sticks margarine

egg white, for glazing

powdered sugar, for sprinkling

Rub the cardamom-scented flour and butter together. In a separate bowl, mix the salt, milk, sugar, egg, and yeast together. Combine the dry mixture and the liquid mixture, being careful not to overmix.

Soften the margarine slightly, and encase the margarine with the dough. Roll out and fold into thirds. Roll out again, and fold in half. Place the two halves together and roll again. Fold into thirds. Allow to rest for 15 minutes.

Danish Pastry Crescents

Preheat the oven to 400°F.

Roll the pastry out thinly and cut into triangle shapes. Moisten the edges with water, and roll each pastry piece, starting from the long edge on the bottom of the triangle, toward the point at the top. Curve into a crescent shape. Brush the surface with egg white and dust with powdered sugar. Place on ungreased baking sheets.

Bake for 15 to 20 minutes. Serve warm or allow to cool on wire racks.

Danish Pastry II

Yield: 15 small pastries

3 cups flour

pinch of salt

1 cake fresh yeast or 1 package dried yeast

2 tablespoons powdered sugar

1 egg, beaten

¾ cup lukewarm milk

2 sticks butter: ½ stick melted, and the remainder chilled

Sift the flour and salt into a large bowl. In a smaller bowl, cream together the yeast and 1 teaspoon of the sugar; add the beaten egg, milk, and ½ stick of melted butter. (Chill the rest of the butter.) Make a well in the center of the flour and add the liquid ingredients slowly. Mix to a smooth dough and knead lightly. Cover and leave at room temperature for 1 hour or until doubled in bulk.

Punch down the dough and turn onto a floured board; knead lightly. Roll out to an oblong shape. Cut one-third of the chilled butter into small pieces and spread these over two-thirds of the dough.

Fold into thirds, folding the bottom third up and the top third over it. Half turn the dough (so that an open end faces you and the top is now on the right side) and roll out again to an oblong shape. Spread with the second quantity of butter, fold, and leave for 15 minutes. Repeat with the last portion of the butter, roll out, and fold in half. Cover with pastic wrap and refrigerate for several hours or overnight.

Fillings and cooking methods are included in the recipes that follow.

Right: **Danish Pastries, Top basket left: Danish Cockscombs (see p. 177); Danish Crème Buns (see p. 176); Top basket right: Danish Cartwheels (see p. 176); Danish Crescent Moons (see p. 176); Bottom Basket: Danish Whirligigs (see p. 177).**

DANISH-PASTRY FILLINGS

Almond Filling

2 ounces ground almonds

3 tablespoons powdered sugar

½ lightly beaten egg

2 drops almond extract

Mix all the ingredients in a bowl. It is ready for use.

Apple Marmalade

1 pound cooking apples

strip of lemon peel

good squeeze of lemon juice

½ cup brown sugar

Cut cored but unpeeled apples into very thick wedges, and place into a well-buttered saucepan. Add lemon rind and juice. Cover the saucepan with a lid and cook over very low heat, stirring often, until the apples are soft. Put through a sieve or blender.

Rinse out the saucepan, return the apple mixture to it, add the sugar, and cook over a moderate heat, stirring often, until thick. Spoon into a bowl and chill before use.

Danish Crescent Moons

Yield: 12 pastries

1 quantity Danish Pastry (see recipe, page 174)

1 quantity Apple Marmalade (see recipe, above)

beaten egg, for glazing

Roll the pastry into a large circle about ½ inch thick. Cut into wedge shapes, about 3 inches at the outer edge. Place a teaspoon of Apple Marmalade filling at the base of each wedge; roll up from the base toward the tip. Gently bend into crescents and arrange on a greased baking sheet. Allow to stand at room temperature for about 15 minutes.

Preheat the oven to 425°F.

Glaze the pastries with the beaten egg.

Bake for 20 to 25 minutes. Turn onto wire racks to cool.

Danish Crème Buns

Yield: 12 buns

1 quantity Danish Pastry (see recipe, page 174)

⅔ quantity Crème Pâtissière (see recipe, page 177)

beaten egg, for glazing

Glacé Icing:
1½ cups confectioners' sugar

about 2 tablespoons warm water or orange juice

flavoring and coloring to taste

Roll the pastry out into a rectangle, and cut into 6-inch squares. Place a generous teaspoonful of Crème Pâtissière into the center of each. Fold four corners around the filling, ensuring it is completely covered. Place on a greased baking sheet, with folds underneath. Allow to stand at room temperature for 15 minutes.

Preheat the oven to 425°F.

Glaze the pastry with the beaten egg.

Bake for 15 to 20 minutes.

To prepare the Glacé Icing: Sift the confectioners' sugar. Mix with warm liquid, adding sufficient liquid to make the icing coat the back of spoon without slipping off too easily. Beat well. Add flavoring and coloring to taste.

Note: 1 tablespoon of butter or margarine may be added, if desired.

Ice the buns while they are still warm.

Danish Cartwheels

Yield: 12 pastries

1 quantity Danish Pastry (see recipe, page 174)

1 quantity Almond Filling (see recipe, above left)

⅓ cup raisins, chopped

beaten egg, for glazing

1 ounce flaked almonds, for sprinkling

Roll the pastry out to a large rectangle 14×9 inches. Spread with the Almond Filling and sprinkle with the chopped raisins. Roll the pastry up (like a jelly roll) and cut into slices 1 inch thick. Place cut-side down onto a greased baking sheet. Allow to stand at room temperature for 15 to 20 minutes.

Preheat the oven to 425°F.

Glaze the cartwheels with beaten egg, and sprinkle with almonds.

Bake for 20 to 25 minutes. Turn onto wire racks to cool.

Danish Cockscombs

Yield: 12 pastries

1 quantity Danish Pastry (see recipe, page 174)

(1 quantity Apple Marmalade or Almond Filling (see recipes, page 176)

beaten egg, for glazing

2 tablespoons powdered sugar, for sprinkling

Roll out the pastry and cut into rectangles 5 × 3½ inches. With the long side facing you, spoon the filling along the lower edge. Brush the top edge with the beaten egg and fold over. Make about 6 incisions along the uncut edge and form the rectangles into crescent shapes. Place onto a greased baking sheet and allow to stand at room temperature for 15 minutes.

Preheat the oven to 425°F.

Glaze the pastries with the beaten egg and sprinkle with the powdered sugar.

Bake for 20 to 25 minutes. Turn onto wire racks to cool.

Danish Whirligigs

Yield: 12 pastries

1 quantity Danish Pastry (see recipe, page 174)

⅔ quantity Almond Filling (see recipe, page 176)

beaten egg, for glazing

confectioners' sugar, for sprinkling

Preheat the oven to 425°F. Grease the baking sheets.

Roll the pastry into a large rectangle. Cut into 5-inch squares. Snip from each corner to within ⅜ inch of the center of each square. Place a spoonful of Almond Filling in the middle, then take alternate points to the center. Place on the prepared sheets and allow to stand at room temperature for about 15 minutes. Brush the pastry with the beaten egg.

Bake for 20 to 25 minutes. Turn onto wire racks to cool. To serve, dust with powdered sugar.

Palmiers

Yield: 8 pastries

8 ounces Puff Pastry (see recipe, page 154)

1 egg, beaten

¼ cup powdered sugar

⅔ cup cream, whipped

Roll out the pastry to a thickness of ⅛ inch and a rectangle 12 inches long. Brush with some of the beaten egg and sprinkle with some powdered sugar. Fold over the pastry 2 inches at each end, and then fold again so that the folds meet in the middle. Fold again to make a roll 6 folds thick.

Preheat the oven to 400°F. Grease a baking sheet.

Cut the pastry roll into ⅜-inch-wide slices. Dip each side into the remaining beaten egg and then dust with powdered sugar.

Place the slices on a greased baking sheet and pinch the end of each to make a heart shape.

Bake for 15 minutes. Allow to cool, and serve with the whipped cream.

Crème Pâtissière

1 egg, separated

1 extra egg yolk

¼ cup powdered sugar

1½ tablespoons flour

1 flat tablespoon cornstarch

1½ cups milk

2 to 3 drops vanilla extract

In a bowl, blend the two egg yolks with the sugar, flour, and cornstarch to make a smooth paste. (If necessary, add a tablespoon of cold milk). In a saucepan, bring the 1½ cups of milk to a boil; add to the egg-yolk mixture, whisking constantly. Add the vanilla and pour the mixture back into the saucepan. Cook gently, stirring constantly, until the mixture thickens.

Whisk the egg white until stiff; fold into the custard mixture.

Healthy Baklavas

Yield: 20 pieces

1 cup chopped walnuts

1 cup chopped almonds or hazelnuts

2 ounces lecithin meal

2¼ tablespoons brown sugar

2 tablespoons toasted wheat germ

1 teaspoon ground cinnamon

pinch of ground cloves

about 17 to 18 sheets filo pastry

1½ sticks unsalted butter, melted

Honey Syrup:
1 cup water

¾ cup honey

1 to 2 tablespoons lemon juice

piece of cinnamon stick

3 whole cloves

Mix together the walnuts, almonds, lecithin meal, sugar, wheat germ, cinnamon, and cloves.

Preheat the oven to 325°F. Lightly butter the base of a large shallow oven dish or baking pan.

Place a sheet of filo pastry into the dish, brush with melted butter, and repeat with seven more sheets, brushing each with butter. Spread half the nut mixture over this.

Cover with two more sheets of pastry, brushing each with butter. Spread the remainder of the nut mixture onto the pastry. Place seven or eight more sheets of pastry on top, brushing each with butter, including the top layer.

Using a very sharp knife, neatly trim away any pastry overlapping the edges of the dish. Mark diamond patterns in the surface, cutting through the top couple of layers of pastry. Sprinkle with a little cold water (this creates a crispy, delicious surface).

Bake on a low shelf in the oven for about 30 minutes, then move the dish up to a higher shelf and bake for another 30 minutes. Remove from the oven and cut the baklava into diamond shapes. While still hot, spoon the honey syrup over the top.

Honey Syrup

In a saucepan mix together all the ingredients, bring to a boil, then simmer for another 10 minutes.

Strain, and pour over the baklava. Allow to stand for at least 4 hours before serving with coffee or as a dessert.

Honey Nut Pastry Rolls

Yield: 20 rolls

1 quantity Shortcrust Pastry (see recipe, page 150) to which ½ teaspoon cinnamon has been added

2 tablespoons honey

¼ cup chopped walnuts or almonds

⅓ cup raisins

⅓ cup white raisins

2 tablespoons mixed peel

½ teaspoon mixed spice

beaten egg, or milk, for glazing

Preheat the oven to 375°F. Grease a baking sheet.

Roll the pastry out thinly into an oblong shape. Spread with the honey. Sprinkle with the nuts, fruits, peel, and spice. Roll up; cut into slices 1½ inch thick. Place on the baking sheet and glaze with the egg or milk.

Bake for 15 to 20 minutes.

Fruit Cream Puffs

Yield: 24 puffs

1 quantity Choux Pastry (see recipe, page 162)

⅔ cup cream, whipped

sliced bananas, strawberries, or blackberries

confectioners' sugar, for dusting

Preheat the oven to 375°F. Grease a baking sheet.

Place small mounds of Choux Pastry onto the baking sheet.

Bake for 10 minutes, then reduce the oven temperature and continue baking until dry and crisp (about 30 minutes).

Split each puff as soon as it is cooked, in order to allow the steam to escape.

When cold, fill with the whipped cream blended with the sliced bananas, strawberries, or blackberries. Dust the surface with powdered sugar; or, alternatively, pour a thin soft icing over the puffs and decorate with a piece of fruit rolled in powdered sugar.

Right: **Healthy Baklavas (see above left).**

Poppy-Seed Yeast Pastry Rolls

Yield 2 rolls (plus sufficient pastry for the Hazelnut Yeast Pastry Roll)

Filling:
6 ounces poppy seeds
½ cup sugar
⅔ cup milk
3 tablespoons chopped prunes
finely grated rind of ½ orange
finely grated rind of ½ lemon
2 tablespoons black-currant jelly
Sweet Yeast Pastry:
1 cake compressed yeast
1 teaspoon sugar
3 tablespoons barely warm milk
4 cups flour
½ cup sugar
2 sticks butter
1 egg yolk
¼ cup sour cream
a little milk (at room temperature), for glazing
confectioners' sugar, for sprinkling

Filling: Grind the poppy seeds in a blender. Combine all the ingredients for the filling in a saucepan; bring to a boil, stirring constantly, then simmer for 15 minutes or until the mixture becomes thick and smooth. Allow to cool.

Sweet Yeast Pastry

Cream the yeast with the sugar and milk in a small bowl; blend until the yeast liquifies. Sift the flour into a large bowl, and add the sugar. Chop the butter into small pieces, add to the flour, and rub in; mix until the mixture is the consistency of coarse bread crumbs. Blend together the egg yolk and sour cream, add to the flour, and mix to form a soft, pliable dough. Allow to stand for 30 minutes.

Preheat the oven to 450°F. Grease a baking sheet.

Knead the dough gently on a lightly floured board. Leave to stand for another 30 minutes; divide the dough into three portions. (Retain one portion for Hazelnut Yeast Pastry Roll). Roll out the two remaining dough portions into squares about 13 × 13 inches.

On one square, spread half the filling mixture. Roll the dough very carefully, like a jelly roll, starting at one wide edge. Transfer gently to the baking sheet, with the seam on the underside. Repeat with the second portion of the pastry and the remainder of the filling. Brush the surface with a little milk, for glazing.

Bake for 10 minutes, then reduce the oven temperature to 350°F and bake for another 20 minutes or until golden. Allow to cool on the baking sheet before removing to a wire rack. Before serving, sprinkle generously with powdered sugar. Serve with coffee.

Honey-Sweet Fried Pastries

Yield: 45 pastries

⅔ cup oil
⅓ cup dry white wine
⅓ cup sweet white wine
3 tablespoons Grand Marnier (or preferred orange liqueur)
juice of 1 orange (approximately 3 tablespoons)
1 tablespoon toasted sesame seeds
2 teaspoons caraway seeds (optional)
3½ to 4 cups flour
oil, for frying
1 cup honey
¼ cup water
confectioners' sugar, for sprinkling
ground cinnamon, for sprinkling

Combine the oil, sweet and dry wines, Grand Marnier, orange juice, sesame seeds, and (if using) caraway seeds in a large bowl. Sift the flour, and gradually work the mixture into the flour until a soft, sticky dough forms. Knead on a lightly floured board until pliable; cover, and allow to stand for 30 minutes.

Divide the mixture into about 45 walnut-sized balls. Flatten each between fingers and thumb to rectangles about 3 × 1½ inches.

Heat ⅜ inch of oil in a deep frying pan. Add three or four pastries at a time. Cook each for about 1½ minutes, turning over with tongs. Drain on kitchen paper.

Combine the honey and water in a saucepan; simmer until the honey melts. Using tongs, dip each pastry into the honey mixture, coating both sides; place onto a wire rack over a bowl, so that excess honey drips through. Before serving, sprinkle with powdered sugar and cinnamon.

These pastries actually improve if made two or three days before they are to be used. To store, allow to become cold, then place into an airtight container lined with greaseproof paper. Sprinkle with sugar and cinnamon just before serving. Delicious served with black coffee.

Hazelnut Yeast Pastry Roll

Yield: 1 roll

Filling:
4 ounces ground roasted hazelnuts

1 teaspoon sugar

a little ground cinnamon

⅓ cup brown sugar

½ cup milk

2 tablespoons chopped raisins

1 teaspoon finely grated lemon rind

Pastry:
portion reserved from Poppy-Seed Yeast Pastry Rolls
(see recipe, page 180)

Filling: Combine all the filling ingredients in a small saucepan, bring to a boil, then simmer, stirring constantly, for 15 minutes. Allow to cool.

Preheat the oven to 450°F.

Spread the filling onto the rolled-out pastry and make up as in the recipe for Poppy-Seed Yeast Pastry Roll.

Bake for 10 minutes, then reduce the oven temperature to 350°F and bake for another 20 minutes or until golden.

Bay St.
398 2455

Pies & Tarts

Tips for Better Pie-Making

It is not always necessary to chill the pastry if it is handling well. Tests show that there is little difference in the shrinkage and shortness of the pastry if it has not been chilled. But if the weather is warm and the pastry is soft and oily looking, chill the pastry for at least 15 minutes before rolling and baking.

Rolling Pastry to Fit a Pie Dish

Place the ball of dough on a lightly floured surface. Pound it lightly with a rolling pin to flatten it, then roll it out, working from the center to the edge in a quick stroke away from you.

Using a large spatula, slide under the dough to release it from the working surface, and give the dough a half-turn clockwise.

Roll the dough out in the same manner as before, keeping in mind the required end shape. Even the edges with the palms of your hands, pushing the dough back toward the center.

Roll out the pastry to about ⅛ inch thick and about 2 inches larger than the dish to be lined.

To line the pie plate: Slide the spatula under the dough to release it. Gently roll the dough over the rolling pin and lay the pastry over the center of the dish. Ease the dough into the dish and press the dough against the base and sides.

Trim off surplus edges of the dough, using a sharp knife and drawing the knife against the rim in a downward action in short swift strokes. Or, roll the surplus pastry back under itself to form a thicker rim. Pinch or crimp the edges as desired.

If a double crust is desired, do not trim any overhang. Brush the bottom and sides well with beaten egg white if the filling is extra juicy, and let it dry for a few minutes. Add the filling to the pie shell, mounding it up in the center. Roll out the top crust, making it slightly thinner if you like. Brush the pastry rim with a little water or egg, and fit the top crust over the filling. Trim both crusts evenly, press to seal the edges, and crimp. Decorate the top with pastry shapes, if you desire, and cut decorative steam vents in the top crust.

Baking Blind

Here is a little advice to aspiring bakers of pâtisserie on the lining of pie pans and the mystery of baking "blind." When lining a pie pan, roll the pastry out to a round, large enough to line the base and sides of the pan and allow at least ¼ inch extra. The rolled side of the pastry is the best side, so lift the pastry over the rolling pin, then unroll the pastry into the pan, turning it over. In doing so, the rolled side of the pastry will be on the outside of the pie (or tart). Working quickly, press the pastry from the center of the pan into the sides with the back of the fingers, then ease the edges of pastry down to counteract shrinkage, and, finally, with the rolling pin, roll over the top edge of the pie pan, trimming off the excess pastry. Prick the bottom of the pastry well, but not all the way through, with the tines of a fork. Take a square of greaseproof paper, large enough to line the bottom and sides of the pie pan and crumple it in the hands (this prevents pulling a skin of pastry off when removing the blind filling), then spread it smoothly into the pastry crust. Pour some dried beans, dried peas, or rice into the paper, making a single layer over the bottom. Pile up the beans around the edges to prevent the edges of the pastry from falling in. Finally, trim off excess greaseproof paper to prevent scorching.

To bake blind, the pastry crust is put into a hot oven for 10 minutes, then the greaseproof paper and baking beans or the "blind filling" is removed and the pastry crust is returned to the oven for 10 minutes, or until set, sometimes at a reduced temperature. This is known as baking "blind."

If the pastry crust rises in a bubble at this stage, prick it with a toothpick while it is still soft, and allow the air bubble to escape.

The filling is then put in, or the empty pastry crust is cooked completely according to the particular recipe.

About Baking Pies

Always preheat the oven before baking, so that the pastry starts to cook as soon as it is placed in the oven.

Baking the pie on a baking sheet that has been heated through in the oven gives the bottom crust instant and even heat. It sets the bottom crust, so that the filling does not seep through the pastry and make the base crust soggy.

When baking more than one pie at a time, stagger the pie pans on the oven racks, leaving plenty of room between them for heat to circulate.

If the crust is browning too fast, cover it with a piece of aluminum foil. Crimped edges, in particular, brown faster than the rest; these may be covered with strips of aluminum foil to protect them.

If the pie is juicy and you wish to have a crisp base crust, dry out the base over a very low heat on a heat-dispersing ring or mat for 15 minutes or so. (This can be done only if the pie plate is metal.)

Cutting Pies

Most pies should be cooled for a few minutes on a wire rack before being cut.

Divide the pie mentally into the number of pieces required, before making the first cut. Use a very sharp thin-bladed knife. After cutting, lift the segment out of the pan with the flat of the knife or with a pie slicer.

Meringue pies: Use a sharp knife dipped into hot water after each cut, to stop the meringue from sticking to the knife.

PIES

Black-Cherry Pie

Yield: 6 to 8 servings

¾ quantity (6 ounces) Pâte Sucrée or Pâte Brisée *(see recipes, page 158)*
***Filling:* 4 egg yolks**
⅓ cup powdered sugar
2 cups cream
½ teaspoon vanilla extract
1 can (about 14 ounces) black cherries
3 teaspoons arrowroot
1 tablespoon cold water
2 tablespoons kirsch
whipped cream, for decoration (optional)

Preheat the oven to 425°F.

Roll out the pastry thinly and line a deep-sided 8-inch pie pan. Prick the base of the pastry with a fork (and line with greaseproof paper and baking beans).

Bake blind near the top of the oven for 10 minutes. Remove the blind filling and bake for another 10 minutes or until golden. Allow to cool on a wire rack.

Filling: Beat the egg yolks with sugar, then stir in the cream and vanilla.

Drain the cherries, remove their pits, and reserve ¼ cup of syrup. Blend the arrowroot smoothly with water, add the reserved syrup, then bring to a boil in a saucepan, stirring continuously, and simmer for 2 minutes. Remove from the heat, stir in the kirsch, and allow to cool to room temperature.

To finish the pie: Reduce the oven to 375°F.

Pour the custard mixture into the pie crust.

Bake in the middle of the oven for 30 minutes, then cover the pie lightly with foil and bake for another 20 to 30 minutes or until the custard is set. Allow to cool on a wire rack.

When cold, spread the cherries on top of the custard and cover with thickened syrup. Chill until set. Serve at room temperature, decorated with whipped cream.

French Cherry Pie

Yield: 6 to 8 servings

¾ quantity (6 ounces) Pâte Sucrée ***(see recipe, page 158)***
***Filling:* 1 pound fresh cherries or 2 14-ounce cans cherries, drained**
¼ cup sugar
2 tablespoons kirsch
1 large egg
2 tablespoons powdered sugar
1 teaspoon vanilla extract
3 tablespoons cream
confectioners' sugar, for decoration

Roll out the pastry thinly and line a 9-inch pie pan. Prick the base and chill for ½ to 1 hour.

Filling: Pit the cherries (with a cherry pitter or pointed knife), place in a bowl, sprinkle with the sugar and kirsch, and let them stand for 1 to 2 hours. (If using canned cherries, sprinkle with kirsch only and let stand for 30 minutes.

Beat the egg with the powdered sugar, vanilla, and cream.

To finish the pie: Preheat the oven to 400°F.

If using fresh cherries, transfer them with a slotted spoon to the pie crust.

Bake in the middle of the oven for 25 minutes. Remove the pie from the oven, pour the egg mixture over, then bake in the bottom half of the oven for another 20 minutes or until the custard is set. (If using canned cherries, place them in the pie crust, pour the egg mixture over immediately, and bake in the bottom of the oven for 20 minutes or until the custard is set.) Remove the pie from the oven, stand on a wire rack, and sift sugar over while still warm. Serve warm or chilled with whipped cream.

Tarte Tatin

Yield: 8 servings

3/4 quantity (6 ounces) Flaky Pastry (see recipe, page 156)
Topping: ***4 large green cooking apples***
1 stick unsalted butter
1 cup sugar

Roll the pastry out thinly on a lightly floured surface to a 10-inch round. Place on a plate or board, prick well with a fine fork, and chill in the refrigerator.

Topping: Preheat the oven to 400°F.

Peel, core, and halve the apples. Use a round cast-iron enamel-lined ovenproof casserole 19 inches in diameter and at least 2 inches deep. In this melt the butter and sugar over a low heat. Place the apple halves in, very close together, and cook very slowly until the sugar just begins to caramelize (about 20 minutes). Place the casserole in the preheated oven for 5 minutes. Remove from the oven.

To finish the pie: Increase the oven temperature to 450°F, cover the apple mixture with the round of pastry, then return to the oven and bake for 20 minutes or until the pastry is cooked.

To turn out of the casserole, loosen the pastry around the edge with a round-bladed knife, place a serving dish on top of the casserole and, holding firmly, turn both over to turn out the tart. Serve warm, with whipped cream.

Prune Pie

Yield: 8 servings

3/4 quantity (6 ounces) Pâte Brisée or Pâte Sucrée (see recipes, page 158)
Filling: ***1 cup pitted prunes***
2 large egg yolks
1/4 cup sugar
1 tablespoon flour
1/2 cup milk or cream
2 tablespoons kirsch
1 tablespoon orange-flower water

Roll the pastry out thinly and line a 9-inch pie pan. Prick the base of the pastry and chill for 10 minutes.

Preheat the oven to 425°F.

Bake blind near the top of the oven for 10 minutes, then remove the blind filling and bake for another 10 minutes. Let it stand on a wire rack.

Filling: Cut the prunes into quarters. Mix all the remaining ingredients together in a bowl with a balloon-shaped whisk.

To finish the pie: Reduce the oven to 375°F.

Arrange the prunes evenly in the pie crust; pour the egg mixture over.

Bake in the middle of the oven for 20 to 30 minutes or until the filling is firm and golden. Cool the pie on a wire rack. Serve warm or cold accompanied by whipped cream.

Fig Pie

Fresh figs can be used in this delicious pie instead of the prunes. Use 8 ripe figs and cut them into quarters or smaller segments.

Bakewell Pie

Yield: 6 servings

3/4 quantity (6 ounces) Sweet Shortcrust Pastry (see recipe, page 150)
Filling: ***3/4 stick soft butter or margarine***
1/3 cup powdered sugar
2 large eggs
1/2 cup ground almonds
1/2 cup self-rising flour, sifted
drops of almond extract
3 tablespoons raspberry jam (jelly)
6 split almonds, for decoration
confectioners' sugar, for sprinkling

Prepare the pastry according to the recipe, and chill well.

Roll the pastry out thinly to a round, and line a deep-sided 8-inch pie pan. Reserve the pastry trimmings. Prick the base of the pastry crust.

Filling: Place all the ingredients except the jam and split almonds into a mixing bowl and beat well with an electric mixer or in a food processor until well mixed (about 1 to 2 minutes).

To finish the pie: Preheat the oven to 350°F.

Spread the jam over the base of the pie crust, then spread with the filling mixture. Roll the pastry trimmings into a long strip and cut strips 3/8 inch wide; place on the pie in a lattice pattern, and trim neatly. Decorate the top of the pie with split almonds.

Bake in the middle of the oven for 45 to 50 minutes, until cooked. Allow to cool on a wire rack. Serve warm sprinkled with confectioners' sugar for a dessert, accompanied by custard or pouring cream.

Right: **Clockwise from left: Bakewell Pie (see above); Tarte Tatin (see above left); Prune Pie (see left).**

Banana and Pineapple Pie

Yield: 8 to 10 servings

1 quantity (8 ounces) Pâte Sucrée or Sweet Shortcrust Pastry (see recipes, pages 158 and 150)

Filling:
⅔ cup sugar

⅔ cup water

½ cup rum

5 ripe bananas

1½ pounds fresh pineapple or 1 can (1¾ pounds) unsweetened pineapple, drained

¼ to ½ cup powdered sugar

1 quantity Vanilla Pastry Cream (see recipe, page 118)

Preheat the oven to 425°F.

Roll the pastry out thinly and line a 10-inch pie pan.

Bake blind near the top of the oven for 10 minutes, then remove the blind filling and bake for another 10 minutes or until cooked and golden. Cool on a wire rack, remove from pan when firm, and allow to cool completely.

Filling: Place the sugar, water, and rum into a large, heavy-based frying pan and bring to a boil, stirring occasionally. Peel the bananas and cut into slices ⅜ inch thick; add to the rum syrup and simmer for 10 minutes. Peel the pineapple, remove the core, and chop the fruit coarsely; mix to a puree in a blender or food processor. Add ¼ to ½ cup powdered sugar, to taste.

To finish the pie: Spread the Vanilla Pastry Cream into the pie crust. Cover neatly with the drained banana slices. Spoon some pineapple puree over the bananas until well coated, using a pastry brush, if necessary to coat evenly.

Serve immediately, accompanied by the remaining pineapple puree served in a pitcher.

Normandy Apple Pie

Yield: 6 to 8 servings

¾ quantity (6 ounces) Pâte Sucrée (see recipe, page 158)

Filling:
4 large green cooking apples

2 tablespoons sugar

2 tablepoons cold water

2 red apples

juice of 2 lemons

2 tablespoons butter, melted

3 tablespoons apricot jam (jelly)

Make the pastry, and chill well.

Peel, core, and slice the cooking apples into a heavy-based saucepan. Add the sugar and water, cover the pan, and stew gently until tender and thick. Allow to cool, then mix the apples to a puree in an electric blender or food processor.

Roll the pastry out on a lightly floured board to a round shape and line an 8-inch deep-sided or a 9-inch shallow-sided pie pan. Prick the base of the pastry with a fork, and chill for 30 minutes.

Preheat the oven to 425°F.

Bake blind toward the top of the oven for 10 to 15 minutes or until the base is firm. Remove the blind filling.

Core and slice the red apples very thinly and dip into lemon juice.

Spread apple puree into the pie crust, and cover neatly with circles of overlapping slices of red apple. Brush the apples with the melted butter, and return to the oven for another 15 to 20 minutes or until the apple is golden. Allow to cool on a wire rack for 5 to 10 minutes, then remove the pan when the pastry is firm.

Warm the apricot jam, and brush it on top to coat the apples completely. Serve cold, with whipped cream.

Shortcut Mille-Feuille with Strawberries

Yield: 6 servings

¼ cup water

⅔ cup granulated sugar

1 quart ripe strawberries, sliced (reserve 6 whole berries)

2 tablespoons Grand Marnier or Framboise

6 sheets filo pastry

2 tablespoons unsalted butter, melted

1⅓ cups whipping cream

2 to 3 teaspoons powdered sugar

½ teaspoon vanilla extract

confectioners' sugar, for sprinkling

In a medium-sized saucepan, combine the water and sugar. Stir until the sugar dissolves, then bring to a boil, and cook for 3 to 4 minutes. Remove from heat, cool, and stir in the sliced strawberries and the Grand Marnier or Framboise. Cover and refrigerate for 1 to 2 hours.

Preheat the oven to 400°F. Lightly grease a baking sheet.

Cut each filo sheet into six 4-inch circles. Place the pastry circles onto the baking sheet. Brush each lightly with a little melted butter.

Bake only until golden, probably about 2 minutes. Using a spatula, remove the filo circles onto kitchen paper; allow to cool.

Lightly whip the cream until soft peaks form, then gradually beat in the powdered sugar and vanilla. Beat until the cream is stiff.

To serve, set aside six of the filo circles. Spread each of the remainder with about 1½ tablespoons of whipped cream. Place one creamed pastry circle on each of six small serving plates; spoon 1 tablespoon of the strawberry mixture (without juice) over each. Continue layering with the remaining creamed circles, then a spoonful of the strawberry mixture. Top each serving with the reserved uncreamed pastry circles. Sprinkle each with confectioners' sugar. Spoon the remaining strawberry mixture and juice onto each serving plate. Garnish each with a whole berry, and serve.

Strawberry Shortcake

Yield: 4 to 6 servings

Pastry:
2 cups flour

⅓ to ½ cup powdered sugar

pinch of salt

7 tablespoons butter

3 egg yolks

½ teaspoon grated orange peel

Filling:
3 egg yolks

½ cup sugar

½ cup flour

2 drops almond extract

1½ cups milk

1½ cups hulled strawberries, lightly sweetened

¼ cup apple jelly or red-currant jelly

Pastry: Sift the flour, sugar, and salt together onto a pastry board; make a well in the center of the flour. Cut the butter into small cubes and add to the flour with the egg yolks and orange peel. Knead lightly with the fingertips. Do not overwork—knead only until smooth and manageable. Chill for 30 minutes.

Preheat the oven to 350°F. Lightly grease a 9-inch pie pan.

Roll the pastry out lightly into a circle. Place over the pie pan and press into the pan. Prick the base of the pastry several times with a fork.

Bake for about 20 minutes. Allow the pastry to cool, and then remove it carefully from the pan.

Filling: In a saucepan, beat together the egg yolks, sugar, flour, and almond extract until well blended. Heat the milk, and add to the mixture in the saucepan in small quantities, beating constantly over low heat until the mixture thickens. Do not allow to boil.

To finish the pie: Spread this creamy mixture onto the cooked pastry. Arrange the strawberries over the entire surface. Melt the jelly over low heat, and brush generously over the strawberries.

Apricot and Almond Pie

Yield: 6 to 8 servings

3/4 quantity (6 ounces) Rich Shortcrust Pastry or Pâte Sucrée (see recipes, pages 149 and 158)

4 tablespoons ground almonds

Filling:
1 1/4 cups cream

1 can (1 3/4 pounds) apricot halves

6 tablespoons apricot jam (jelly)

2 teaspoons arrowroot or cornstarch

blanched toasted almonds, for decoration

Make the pastry according to the recipe, but add ground almonds with the sugar. Chill well.

Preheat the oven to 425°F.

Roll the pastry out thinly and line an 8-inch deep-sided or a 9-inch shallow-sided pie pan.

Bake blind in the top of the oven for 10 to 15 minutes or until the pastry is set in shape. Remove the blind filling, reduce the oven temperature to 375°F, and bake for another 10 to 15 minutes or until the pastry is cooked. Cool on a wire rack. After a few minutes remove the pastry from the pan, then leave until cold.

Filling: Whip the cream until thick. Drain the canned apricots well and reserve 1/2 cup of juice. Place the apricot juice and the jam in a saucepan and dissolve the jam over a medium heat. Strain the juice and jam mixture and return to the saucepan. Blend the arrowroot (or cornstarch) smoothly with a little extra apricot juice, add to the saucepan, and bring to a boil, stirring continuously until the glaze clears and thickens. Cool, but do not allow to set.

To finish the pie: Spread whipped cream over the bottom of the pie crust, then top it neatly with apricot halves. Decorate with toasted almonds placed between apricot halves. Brush the glaze over the fruit, and allow to set before serving.

Note: Canned peaches can be used instead of apricots.

Basic Fruit Pie

Yield: 6 to 8 servings

3/4 quantity (6 ounces) Pâte Sucrée (see recipe, page 158)

Filling:
1 quantity Vanilla Pastry Cream (see recipe, page 118)

1 pound fresh fruit such as sliced ripe apricots, blackberries, black currants, blueberries, pitted cherries, pitted chopped dates, peeled seedless grapes, peeled sliced kiwi fruit, melon balls, mandarin or orange segments, sliced peeled peaches, peeled sliced pineapple, sliced pitted plums, raspberries, red currants, sliced strawberries

allow 8 ounces extra if fruit has pits or thick skin

1/2 cup strained apricot jam (jelly) to glaze yellow fruits or 1/2 cup red-currant jelly to glaze red fruits

1 tablespoon water, strained orange juice, sweet sherry, or liqueur

Preheat the oven to 425°F.

Roll the pastry out thinly and line a deep-sided 8-inch or shallow-sided 9-inch pie pan. Prick the base of the pastry and line with greaseproof paper and baking beans, for baking blind.

Bake near the top of the oven for 10 minutes, then remove the blind filling and bake for another 10 minutes or until golden and cooked. Cool on a wire rack until firm, then remove the pan and leave the pie crust to cool completely.

Prepare the Vanilla Pastry Cream and leave to cool. Prepare the fresh fruit accordingly (peeling, slicing, pitting, chopping).

Melt the jam or jelly with water, orange juice, sherry, or liqueur in a small pan. Bring to a boil, stirring, and simmer for 1 minute. Allow to cool to room temperature.

Spread the Vanilla Pastry Cream carefully into the pie crust and cover neatly with an attractive but simple arrangement of fresh fruit. Spoon the glaze over and brush over all the fruit and custard to seal well, using a pastry brush. Allow the glaze to set. Serve with whipped cream.

Almond Pie

Yield: 8 servings

¾ quantity (6 ounces) Pâte Sucrée (see recipe, page 158)

Filling:
1 cup sliced (flaked) blanched almonds

¾ cup powdered sugar

¾ cup cream

1 teaspoon orange-flavored liqueur

¼ teaspoon almond extract

pinch of salt

Preheat the oven to 425°F.

Roll the pastry out thinly and line a 9-inch pie pan.

Bake blind near the top of the oven for 10 minutes.

Filling: Place all the ingredients together in a mixing bowl, stir until evenly mixed, then let stand for 15 minutes.

To finish the pie: Spoon the filling into the pie crust and bake in the lower half of a preheated oven at 400°F for 30 to 40 minutes or until the top is caramelized and golden brown. It is advisable to protect the edge of the pie crust with foil after 15 minutes to prevent over-browning. Allow the pie to cool on a wire rack. Serve with vanilla ice cream or whipped cream.

Strawberry Pie

Yield: 6 to 8 servings

¾ quantity (6 ounces) Rich Shortcrust Pastry or Pâte Sucrée (see recipes, pages 149 and 158)

Filling:
1 to 1½ pounds strawberries, depending on size of berries

1¼ cups cream

6 tablespoons red-currant jelly

2 teaspoons arrowroot or cornstarch

1 tablespoon cold water

about 3 tablespoons orange juice

Prepare the pastry according to the recipe, and chill well.

Preheat the oven to 425°F.

Roll the pastry out thinly and line a 9-inch pie pan.

Bake blind in the top of the oven for 10 to 15 minutes or until the pastry is set in shape. Remove the blind filling, reduce the oven temperature to 375°F, and bake for another 10 to 15 minutes or until the pastry is cooked. Cool on a wire rack. After a few minutes remove the pastry from the pan and allow to cool.

Filling: Hull the strawberries and check them to make sure they are clean; slice or halve large berries. Whip the cream until thick.

Heat the red-currant jelly in a saucepan until melted and smooth. Blend the arrowroot or cornstarch with cold water until smooth; stir this into the red-currant jelly and bring to a boil, stirring continuously until the mixture is thick, clear, and smooth. Stir in sufficient orange juice to give a smooth consistency.

To finish the pie: Spread the cream evenly over the bottom of the pie crust. Arrange the strawberries attractively on top of the cream, then spread or brush the red-currant glaze over and allow to set. Serve the pie slightly chilled.

Variations: The whipped cream may be replaced with Vanilla Pastry Cream (see page 118). Try substituting raspberries for strawberries.

Pineapple Hazelnut Pie

Yield: 12 servings

1 quantity (8 ounces) Pâte Sucrée (see recipe, page 158)

¼ cup ground hazelnuts

Filling:
2 quantities (2 cups) Vanilla Pastry Cream (see recipe, page 118)

½ cup ground toasted hazelnuts

1 tablespoon rum

1 large pineapple

½ cup sieved apricot jam (jelly)

1 tablespoon water

hazelnuts for decoration

Make the pastry according to the recipe, but add ground hazelnuts with the egg. Chill well.

Preheat the oven to 425°F.

Roll the pastry out thinly and line a 12-inch pie pan. Prick the base with a fork.

Bake blind near the top of the oven for 10 minutes. Remove the blind filling, and bake for another 10 minutes or until cooked. Allow to cool on a wire rack.

Filling: Mix the Vanilla Pastry Cream with the ground, toasted hazelnuts and rum. Peel and core the pineapple and cut into slices ⅜ inch thick.

To finish the pie: Spread the Vanilla Pastry Cream in the bottom of the cold pastry case. Cover neatly with slices of pineapple. Heat the apricot jam with water, then spoon it over the pineapple, brushing the entire surface of the pie to seal. Decorate with the hazelnuts, and chill until firm. Serve with whipped cream.

French Pear Pie

Yield: 6 to 8 servings

¾ quantity (6 ounces) Rich Shortcrust Pastry or Pâte Sucrée (see recipes, pages 149 and 158)

Filling:
3 ripe dessert pears
1 large egg
2 tablespoons powdered sugar
¼ teaspoon salt
⅛ teaspoon ground ginger
⅛ teaspoon ground nutmeg
finely grated rind of 1 lemon
1 cup sour cream

Topping:
2 tablespoons flour
3 tablespoons brown sugar
½ stick chilled butter
¼ teaspoon ground nutmeg

Roll the pastry out thinly and line a 9-inch pie pan. Trim and decorate the edge, and prick the base. Chill the pastry while preparing the filling.

Filling: Peel the pears, cut in half lengthwise, and remove the core. Beat the egg, sugar, salt, spices, lemon rind, and sour cream together.

Topping: Mix all the ingredients together in a food processor or blender until the mixture resembles coarse bread crumbs.

To finish the pie: Preheat the oven to 400°F.

Place the pears neatly into the pie crust, narrow tops toward the center. Pour the egg and sour cream mixture over, and sprinkle with the topping.

Bake in the center of the oven for 25 minutes or until the filling is set. Allow to cool on a wire rack until firm, then remove from the pan. Serve warm with whipped cream.

Black-Bottom Pie

Yield: 8 servings

¾ quantity (6 ounces) Pâte Sucrée (see recipe, page 158)

Filling:
2 ounces dark baking chocolate
1¾ cups milk
3 large eggs, separated
½ cup sugar
1 tablespoon cornstarch
1 tablespoon gelatin
¼ cup cold water
1 tablespoon rum
pinch of cream of tartar
¼ cup powdered sugar
grated chocolate, for decoration

Preheat the oven to 425°F.

Roll the pastry out thinly and line a 10-inch pie pan.

Bake blind near the top of the oven for 10 minutes. Remove the blind filling and bake for another 10 minutes or until cooked. Allow to cool on a wire rack.

Filling: Melt the chocolate over gently simmering water in the top of a double boiler. Scald the milk. Mix the egg yolks with ½ cup sugar and the cornstarch. Stir in the hot milk, then transfer to a saucepan and bring to a boil, stirring continuously. Remove from the heat. Measure out 1 cup of this custard and stir into the melted chocolate.

Soak the gelatin in ¼ cup cold water, then add this to the remaining custard to dissolve. Add the rum and allow to cool.

Whisk the egg whites with cream of tartar until soft peaks form; add the powdered sugar gradually, whisking continuously. Fold the egg whites into the remaining custard.

To finish the pie: Pour the chocolate custard into the pie crust and chill until set. When firm, swirl the rum-flavored custard mixture on top, then chill again until firm. Serve decorated with grated chocolate sprinkled on top.

Plum Pie Moulin de Mougins

Yield: 12 servings

1 quantity (8 ounces) Pâte Sucrée (see recipe, page 158)

Filling:
2 pounds ripe plums

¼ cup ground almonds

4 tablespoons vanilla sugar

2 large eggs

5 tablespoons cream

4 tablespoons brandy

1 tablespoon orange-flower water

2 tablespoons unsalted butter, melted

Prepare the pastry according to the recipe and chill well.

Roll the pastry out thinly and line a 12-inch pie pan. Trim and decorate the edge; prick the base of the pastry case. Chill until the filling is ready.

Filling: Cut the plums in half and remove the pits. Mix the ground almonds, vanilla sugar, eggs, cream, brandy, and orange-flower water together with an electric mixer or a whisk. Add the melted butter and mix well.

To finish the pie: Preheat the oven to 425°F.

Arrange the plums, overlapping, in circles in the pie crust, starting around the edge and finishing in the center. Pour the egg mixture over the plums. Bake near the top of the oven for 25 minutes or until the fruit is cooked and the filling is set. Serve warm or cold, with whipped cream.

Note: Fresh apricots could be used instead of the plums.

Vanilla sugar is made by placing one vanilla bean in 1 pound of sugar and allowing it to infuse for at least 5 days before use.

Daiquiri Pie

Yield: 8 servings

¾ quantity (6 ounces) Pâte Brisée or Pâte Sucrée (see page 158)

Filling:
1 tablespoon gelatin

1 cup powdered sugar

½ teaspoon salt

3 large eggs, separated

¼ cup water

½ cup juice of fresh limes

1 teaspoon finely grated lime rind

2 or 3 drops green food coloring

4 tablespoons white rum

whipped cream, for decoration

grated chocolate, for decoration

Prepare the pastry according to the recipe, and chill well.

Preheat the oven to 425°F.

Roll the pastry out thinly and line a 9- or 10-inch pie pan. Prick the base and chill well.

Bake blind near the top of the oven for 10 minutes. Remove the blind filling and bake for another 10 minutes or until golden. Allow to cool on a wire rack.

Filling: Place the gelatin, two-thirds of the sugar, salt, egg yolks, and water in the top of a double boiler. Cook over boiling water, stirring constantly, for about 20 minutes or until the mixture has thickened slightly. Remove from the heat, and stir in the lime juice, lime rind, food coloring, and rum. Pour into a bowl and chill until just beginning to set, stirring occasionally.

In a clean, dry bowl, whisk the egg whites until stiff, then gradually whisk in the remaining sugar. Fold into the rum mixture.

To finish the pie: Pour the filling into the pie crust and refrigerate for 2 to 3 hours. Serve decorated with whipped cream and grated chocolate.

English Custard Pie

Yield: 6 to 8 servings

¾ quantity (6 ounces) Rich Shortcrust Pastry (see recipe, page 149)
Filling: 3 large eggs
1 tablespoon powdered sugar
1¼ cups milk
½ teaspoon vanilla extract
egg white, for sealing
freshly grated nutmeg

Make the pastry according to the recipe, and chill well.

Roll the pastry out thinly and line a deep-sided 8-inch pie pan. Press the base of the pastry case down firmly, then chill while preparing the filling.

Break the eggs into a mixing bowl and beat with a whisk until the eggs run smoothly through the wires of the whisk. Add the sugar, milk, and vanilla, and stir well.

Preheat the oven to 400°F. Place the pie pan on a baking sheet.

Bake blind for 10 to 15 minutes, until set in shape.

Leave the oven on at 400°F. Brush the base of the pie crust with lightly whisked egg white, then strain the filling into it. Sprinkle grated nutmeg on top. Place the pie in the top of the oven for 7 minutes, then reduce the temperature to 350°F and bake for another 7 to 12 minutes or until the custard is set.

Allow the custard to cool before removing the pie from the pan. Serve cold.

Mince Pie

Yield: 8 servings

¾ quantity (6 ounces) Sweet Shortcrust Pastry (see recipe, page 150)
Filling: 2 cups Homemade Mincemeat (see recipe page 222)
1 cup stewed apple
beaten egg and powdered sugar, for glazing
confectioners' sugar, for decoration

Make the pastry according to the recipe, and chill well.

Roll three-quarters of the pastry out thinly to a round, and line a 9- or 10-inch pie pan, trim and neaten the edge, prick the base, and chill for 30 minutes.

Preheat the oven to 425°F.

Mix the fruit mincemeat with the stewed apple.

Bake the pastry case blind, near the top of the oven for 10 minutes. Remove the blind filling, and spread the fruit-mince filling in the pie crust. Roll the remaining pastry out thinly to a rectangle then cut into strips ⅜ inch wide; place these on the pie in a lattice pattern and trim the edges. Glaze the pastry with the beaten egg and sprinkle with sugar. Bake near the top of a moderate oven at 350°F for 25 minutes or until cooked. Serve warm or cold sifted generously with confectioners' sugar, accompanied by whipped cream or ice cream.

Lemon Pie René Verdon

Yield: 12 servings

1 quantity (8 ounces) Pâte Sucrée (see recipe, page 158)
Filling: 4 large eggs
1¼ cups sugar
1 cup lemon juice
⅔ cup orange juice
finely grated rind of 3 lemons
½ cup cream
2 tablespoons unsalted butter
whipped cream and chocolate curls or slices of kiwi fruit for decoration

Preheat the oven to 425°F.

Roll the pastry out thinly and line a shallow-sided 12-inch pie pan; press the pastry into the pan, then roll off the excess and neaten the edges. Prick the base of the pastry case with a fine fork.

Bake blind near the top of the oven for 10 minutes. Remove the blind filling, and bake for another 10 minutes or until golden.

Filling: Beat the eggs lightly; place in a saucepan, add the sugar, lemon juice, orange juice, and lemon rind. Stir the mixture continuously over low to medium heat until thick, but do not allow to boil. Remove from the heat and stir in the cream and butter until absorbed. Transfer the lemon mixture to a mixing bowl set in a larger bowl of iced water and leave to cool, stirring occasionally.

Preheat the oven to 325°F.

Pour the now-cold lemon mixture into the pie crust.

Bake in the top of the oven for 25 minutes or until a skin forms on top. Allow to cool on a wire rack.

***Right:* Clockwise from top: English Custard Pie (see above left); Mince Pie (see left); Lemon Pie René Verdon (see above).**

Wet-Bottom Shoofly Pie

Yield: 8 servings

¾ quantity (6 ounces) Pâte Brisée or Pâte Sucrée (see recipe, page 158)

Filling:
¾ cup unsulfured molasses

¾ cup boiling water

½ teaspoon baking soda

2 cups all-purpose white flour

¾ cup dark brown sugar

1 stick unsalted butter

confectioners' sugar, for decoration

Roll the pastry out thinly and line 10-inch pie pan. Chill, while preparing the filling.

Preheat the oven to 350°F.

Place the molasses, boiling water, and baking soda together in a mixing bowl, stir together, and allow to foam.

Place the flour, brown sugar, and butter, previously cut into ⅜-inch cubes, into a food processor or electric mixer, and mix until mixture resembles bread crumbs.

To finish the pie: Pour the molasses mixture into the pie crust, then sprinkle the flour mixture evenly over the top.

Bake in the middle of the preheated oven for 30 to 40 minutes or until the filling is firm. Allow to cool on a wire rack. Sift confectioners' sugar generously over the top before serving. Serve with thick soured cream or ice cream.

Brown-Sugar Pie

Yield: 8 servings

¾ quantity (6 ounces) Pâte Sucrée (see recipe, page 158)

Filling:
2½ cups brown sugar

1 cup cream

2 teaspoons unsalted butter

½ teaspoon vanilla extract

2 eggs, beaten

Preheat the oven to 425°F.

Roll the pastry out thinly and line a 9-inch pie pan; reserve and chill the trimmings for decoration. Prick the base of the pastry case.

Bake blind for 10 minutes, then cool on a wire rack until the filling is ready.

Filling: Place the sugar and cream in a heavy-based saucepan, bring to a boil, and simmer for 15 minutes, stirring frequently. Remove from the heat, stir in the butter and vanilla, then allow to cool until lukewarm. Beat the eggs into the warm mixture until well mixed.

To finish the pie: Reduce the oven to 400°F. Pour the filling into the pastry case. Roll the remaining pastry out to a long thin shape and cut into strips ⅜ inch wide. Arrange the strips lattice-fashion on the pie, pressing the ends into the pastry case to seal. Bake in the lower half of the oven for 20 to 25 minutes or until the filling is set. Serve warm or cold, accompanied by a dollop of Mascarpone (Italian cream cheese) or plain yogurt.

Kiwi Pie

Yield: 12 servings

1 quantity (8 ounces) Pâte Sucrée (see recipe, page 158)

Filling:
10 large kiwi fruits

1 cup cream

1 cup confectioners' sugar, sifted

2 large eggs

¼ cup brandy or Cointreau

additional ¼ cup confectioners' sugar, for dusting

Make the pastry according to the recipe and chill well.

Preheat the oven to 425°F.

Roll the pastry out thinly and line a 12-inch pie pan.

Bake blind near the top of the oven for 10 minutes or until the pastry is set in shape. Remove the blind filling, reduce the oven temperature to 375°F and bake for another 10 to 15 minutes or until the pastry is golden. Stand the pan on a wire rack to cool.

Filling: Peel the kiwi and cut into slices ¼ inch thick. In a bowl, combine the cream, sugar, eggs, and brandy, and beat until well mixed.

To finish the pie: Reduce the oven to 375°F. Arrange the slices of kiwi to overlap in circles in the pie crust. Pour the egg mixture over, then brush over all the fruit. Bake for 40 minutes.

Preheat the broiler. Cover the pastry edge with foil, sieve extra confectioners' sugar over, and place under the broiler for 3 to 5 minutes or until the top is lightly caramelized. Remove the foil and remove the pie from the pan. Serve hot or at room temperature with whipped cream.

Apple and Rum Custard Pie

Yield: 8 to 10 servings

¾ quantity (6 ounces) Pâte Brisée (see recipe, page 158)

Filling:
⅓ cup currants

3 tablespoons rum

3 small cooking apples

¼ cup fresh white bread crumbs

2 tablespoons butter, melted

Custard:
2 large eggs

2 egg yolks

⅓ cup sugar

2 cups cream

Topping:
1 tablespoon sugar, mixed with 1 tablespoon melted butter

Make the pastry according to the recipe and chill for ½ to 1 hour or until firm. Place the currants in a small bowl, pour the rum over and let soak for at least 20 minutes.

Preheat the oven to 400°F.

Roll the pastry out thinly to a round, and line an 8-inch springform cake pan. Peel and core the apples, and cut into ¼-inch-thick slices.

Mix the bread crumbs with the melted butter, and sprinkle this over the base of the pastry case. Cover with the sliced apples. Drain the currants (reserve the rum) and sprinkle the currants over the apples.

Bake in the center of the oven for 15 minutes.

Prepare the custard mixture during this first baking. Beat the eggs, egg yolks, and sugar together with a rotary beater until they are thick and lemon-colored. Beat in the reserved rum and the cream.

Remove the pie from the oven and, working quickly, pour half of the custard mixture evenly over the apples in the partly baked pastry case. Reduce the oven temperature to 375°F, and cook the pie for 20 to 30 minutes or until the custard is set.

Then pour the rest of the liquid custard in, and bake for another 30 minutes or until set.

Sprinkle the top of the pie with the sugar mixed with melted butter. Bake in the top third of the oven for about 15 to 20 minutes, or until the top of the pie browns lightly.

Remove the pie from the oven and allow to cool completely before removing the outer frame of the pan. Slide the pie onto a cake plate, and serve accompanied by whipped cream.

Raspberry and Apple Pie

Yield: 12 servings

1 quantity (8 ounces) Pâte Sucrée (see recipe, page 158)

1 egg white

Filling:
1½ pounds green cooking apples

8 ounces raspberries

¼ cup sugar

2 tablespoons quick-cooking tapioca

2 small oranges

4 tablespoons red-currant jelly

whipped cream, for decoration

Roll the pastry out thinly to a round, and line a 12-inch pie pan. Prick the base with a fine fork and chill for 10 minutes.

Preheat the oven to 425°F.

Bake blind near the top of the oven for 10 minutes, then remove the blind filling and brush the base of the pastry case with lightly beaten egg white. Bake for another 10 minutes or until pastry is cooked. Allow to cool on a wire rack.

Filling: Reduce the oven to 400°F. Peel the apples, cut each into sixteen segments, and remove the core. Into an enamel-lined casserole, place the apples, raspberries, sugar, tapioca, and finely grated orange rind. (Reserve the oranges themselves.) Cover the casserole and cook in the preheated oven for 20 minutes. Allow to cool slightly.

To finish the pie: Leave the oven on at 400°F. Spread the filling into the pastry case, return to the oven, and bake for another 20 minutes. Allow to cool on a wire rack.

Peel the oranges neatly and cut them into segments; arrange neatly on top of the filling. Warm the red-currant jelly, brush it over the pie, and let set. Serve decorated with rosettes of cream.

Raspberry and Rhubarb Pie

Instead of the apples, try using rhubarb. Use 1½ pounds rhubarb. Wash and trim the stems and cut them into 1-inch lengths. Place in the enamel-lined casserole with the raspberries, sugar, tapioca, and orange rind, and cook as in the recipe above.

Orange Almond Pie

Yield: 6 to 8 servings

¾ quantity (6 ounces) Pâte Sucrée (see recipe, page 158)

4 tablespoons ground almonds (optional)

Filling:
1 stick unsalted butter

⅓ cup powdered sugar

2 large eggs

1 cup blanched almonds, ground in a blender or food processor

2 tablespoons flour

5 large navel oranges

1 tablespoon Cointreau or Grand Marnier

2 tablespoons confectioners' sugar

½ cup sieved orange marmalade

1 tablespoon toasted sliced almonds, for decoration (optional)

Make the pastry according to the recipe, but if using ground almonds, add them with the egg. Chill well.

Preheat the oven to 425°F.

Roll the pastry out thinly and line a 9-inch pie pan. Prick the base of the pie crust.

Bake blind near the top of the oven for 10 minutes. Remove the blind filling and bake for another 10 minutes, until golden, then allow to cool on a wire rack.

Cream the butter and sugar together with an electric mixer. Add the eggs one at a time and beat well. Stir in the ground almonds and flour until evenly mixed.

Peel the oranges, working on a plate, with a small serrated knife; remove all the white pith and discard the rind. Cut the orange segments away from the membrane, then squeeze juice from the membrane over the orange segments. Sprinkle the liqueur and sugar over them; cover and soak for 30 minutes.

Reduce the oven to 350°F. Spread the almond mixture into the pie crust and bake in the middle of the oven for 20 to 25 minutes or until golden and a skewer comes out fairly dry. Allow to cool on a wire rack. Transfer the orange segments to a plate with a slotted spoon and pat dry with kitchen paper towels; reserve the liquor.

Place the sieved marmalade and 2 tablespoons of reserved liquor into a saucepan; bring to a boil, stirring continuously. Simmer for 1 minute, then cool for 1 minute. Brush the marmalade glaze over the top of the pie, arrange the orange segments in circles on it, then brush with more glaze. Decorate the pie with toasted sliced almonds, if desired. Serve immediately, or store in the refrigerator and serve chilled, plain or with whipped cream.

Peach Pie with Almond Cream

Yield: 8 to 10 servings

1 quantity (8 ounces) Pâte Sucrée (see recipe, page 158)

1 quantity (2 cups) Almond Cream (see recipe, page 118)

4 large fresh peaches (or 8 canned peach halves)

½ cup sieved apricot jam (jelly)

1 tablespoon water

Make the pastry according to the recipe and chill well.

Preheat the oven to 425°F.

Roll the pastry out thinly and line a 10-inch pie pan. Prick the base of the pastry case.

Bake blind near the top of the oven for 10 minutes. Cool for 10 minutes on a wire rack.

Filling: Prepare the Almond Cream according to the recipe. Halve the fresh peaches, then remove their pits and peel. (If using canned peaches, drain well.) Cut each peach half into thin slices crosswise.

To finish the pie: Spread the Almond Cream in the pastry case. Place one sliced peach half in the center, then arrange the other sliced peach halves radiating in a star shape from the center peach. Bake near the top of the preheated oven for 30 minutes or until the cream is set. Allow to cool on a wire rack.

When cold, brush the top with the apricot jam that has been warmed with 1 tablespoon of water. Serve with whipped cream.

The Almond Cream can be made in advance and stored in the refrigerator for up to a week.

Right: **Orange Almond Pie (see left).**

Chocolate Walnut Pie

Yield: 8 servings

¾ quantity (8 ounces) Pâte Sucrée (see recipe, page 158)

Filling:
½ cup sugar

3 tablespoons water

pinch of cream of tartar

1 cup coarsely chopped walnuts

½ cup honey

1 cup cream

2 large eggs, lightly beaten

4 ounces fresh or dessert dates, seeded and chopped

3 tablespoons dry sherry

Chocolate Icing:
6 ounces dark baking chocolate

½ cup sour cream

raspberry or blackberry puree, for serving

Make the pastry according to the recipe, and chill well.

Preheat the oven to 425°F.

Roll the pastry out thinly to a round, and line a 9-inch pie pan.

Bake blind near the top of the oven for 10 minutes. Remove the blind filling, reduce the oven temperature to 375°F, and bake for another 10 to 15 minutes or until the pastry is light golden and cooked. Allow to cool on a wire rack.

Filling: Place the sugar, water, and cream of tartar into a heavy-based saucepan. Bring slowly to a boil over a low heat, stirring and washing down any sugar crystals clinging to the sides of the pan with a brush dipped in cold water, until the sugar is dissolved. Increase the heat to medium, and cook the syrup until it is a deep caramel color. Add the chopped walnuts, honey, and cream, and cook over a high heat for 2 to 3 minutes or until slightly thickened. Reduce the heat to low, stir in the eggs and dates and cook gently for 2 minutes.

Chocolate Icing

Melt the chocolate over simmering water in the top of a double boiler, then stir in the sour cream.

To finish the pie: Pour the filling into the pie crust, and allow to set. Then cover with chocolate icing, and chill for another 1 to 2 hours. Allow the pie to return to room temperature before serving, and accompany it with raspberry or blackberry puree.

Linzertorte

Yield: 6 to 8 servings

Pastry:
1 cup flour

¼ cup powdered sugar

½ teaspoon baking powder

½ teaspoon ground cinnamon

pinch of ground cloves

1 cup ground almonds

finely grated rind of 1 lemon

1 stick butter

milk or kirsch

Filling:
1½ cups jam (jelly) (raspberry, red-currant, or strawberry)

beaten egg, for glazing

fresh raspberries, to decorate (optional)

Sift the flour, sugar, baking powder, and spices into a mixing bowl. Mix in the almonds and lemon rind. Rub in the butter with the fingertips, or use an electric mixer or food processor. Add the milk or kirsch, if required, to form a dry dough. Knead only until combined. Wrap in greaseproof paper and chill in the refrigerator for 30 minutes.

Roll out two-thirds of the pastry and press onto the base of an 8-inch greased springform pan. Spread the jam on top. Roll out the remaining pastry, cut it into ⅜-inch strips, and arrange crosswise on top, using the last strip as an edging around the side of the pie. Press down lightly. Chill the pie well.

Preheat the oven to 375°F.

With beaten egg, brush the pastry only.

Bake for 35 to 40 minutes. Allow to cool in the pan, then remove it carefully. Serve decorated with fresh raspberries, if available, and accompany with whipped cream.

Coffee and Bran Pie

Yield: 6 servings

¾ quantity (6 ounces) Rich Shortcrust Pastry (see recipe, page 149)

Filling:
¾ stick soft butter or margarine

⅓ cup powdered sugar

1 large egg

1 cup bran cereal

¼ cup chopped hazelnuts

1 cup self-rising flour, sifted

2 teaspoons instant coffee dissolved in 3 teaspoons hot water

¼ cup milk

4 tablespoons apricot or raspberry jam (jelly)

1 cup sour cream or plain yogurt

Make the pastry according to the recipe, and chill well.

Roll the pastry out thinly on a lightly floured board to a round, and line a deep-sided 8-inch pie pan. Prick the base of the pastry case. Chill while preparing the filling.

Filling: Cream the butter and sugar together in a mixing bowl with an electric mixer until light and fluffy. Add the egg gradually, beating well after each addition. Stir in the bran cereal and hazelnuts, then fold in the sifted flour alternately with the dissolved coffee and milk.

To finish the pie: Preheat the oven to 400°F.

Spread the jam over the base of the pastry case, then spread the coffee mixture over the jam.

Bake in the middle of the oven for 10 minutes, then reduce the temperature to 325°F and bake for another 20 minutes. Remove the pie from the oven, quickly spread the sour cream (or yogurt) over the top, and return to the oven for 2 minutes. Serve warm.

Cuba Libre Pie

Yield: 8 servings

¾ quantity (6 ounces) Pâte Brisée or Sucrée (see recipe, page 158)

Filling:
1 tablespoon gelatin

1 cup Coca-Cola, heated

½ cup rum

¼ cup brown sugar

½ cup undrained, crushed, unsweetened pineapple (fresh or canned)

½ cup seedless raisins

½ cup pecans, roughly chopped

1¼ cups cream, whipped

¼ cup confectioners' sugar

2 teaspoons cocoa

grated chocolate, for decoration

Roll the pastry out thinly and line a 10-inch pie pan.

Prick the base and chill well.

Preheat the oven to 425°F.

Bake the pastry case blind near the top of the oven for 10 minutes. Remove the blind filling and bake for another 10 minutes or until cooked. Cool on a wire rack until firm, then remove from the pan and cool completely.

Filling: Dissolve the gelatin in hot Coca-Cola. Allow to cool. Add the rum, brown sugar, pineapple, raisins, and pecans; mix well and refrigerate until it begins to set.

To finish the pie: Pour the filling mixture into the pie crust and refrigerate until well set. Decorate with whipped cream mixed with the confectioners' sugar and cocoa. Sprinkle with grated chocolate.

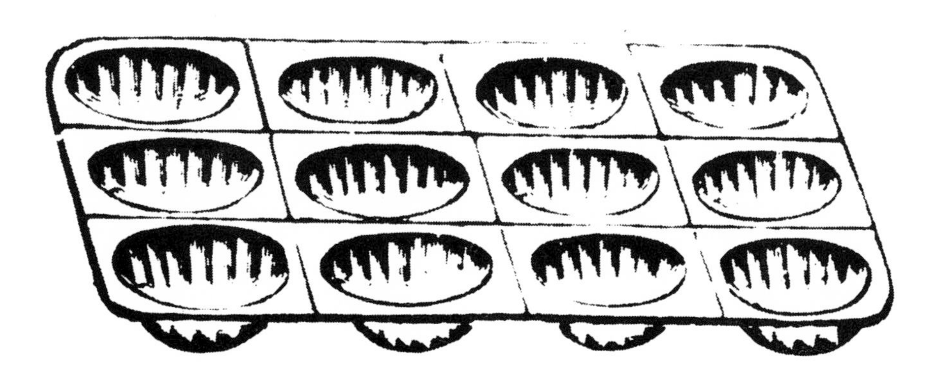

Pecan Pie

Yield: 6 servings

6 ounces Rich Shortcrust Pastry (see recipe, page 149)

Filling:
¾ stick butter
1 cup corn syrup
½ teaspoon salt
1 cup sugar
4 eggs
2 cups pecan halves
1 teaspoon vanilla extract

Roll out the pastry on a lightly floured surface and use to line a 9-inch pie plate. Chill while making the filling.

Preheat the oven to 375°F.

Filling: Melt the butter and stir in the corn syrup, salt, sugar, and eggs. Mix well to combine. Add the nuts and vanilla. Pour the filling into the prepared pie crust, arranging the pecans face up.

Bake for 35 to 40 minutes or until the filling is cooked and the pastry golden brown. Serve warm or cold, with pouring cream.

Shortbread Pie

Yield: 6 servings

1½ cups flour
pinch of salt
1¾ sticks butter
⅓ cup confectioners' sugar
2 egg yolks
drops of vanilla extract
1⅓ cups ground almonds
¾ cup raspberry or blackberry jam (jelly), slightly warmed
¼ cup flaked almonds
sugar, for sprinkling

Sift the flour and salt onto a board. Make a well in the center, and put in the butter, confectioners' sugar, egg yolks, and vanilla. Sprinkle the ground almonds onto the flour. Work the ingredients in the center with the fingertips until thoroughly blended. Using a metal spatula, quickly draw in the flour and ground almonds. Knead the dough lightly, then chill for at least 1 hour.

Preheat the oven to 325°F.

Grate the dough on a coarse grater into a greased 8-inch springform pan or pie dish, using about two-thirds of the quantity to cover the base thickly with dough. Spread with the slightly warmed jam, then grate the remaining dough over the jam. Press lightly into the pan, and sprinkle with the flaked almonds.

Bake for 1¼ hours. Allow to cool.

When cold, sprinkle the top thickly with confectioners' sugar. If using a springform pan, turn the pie out of the pan; if using a pie dish, serve straight from the dish. Serve with whipped cream.

Orange and Pine-Nut Pie

Yield: 4 servings

6 ounces Pâte Sucrée (see recipe, page 158)

Filling:
1 stick unsalted butter
⅓ cup powdered sugar
3 tablespoons cream
¾ cup pine nuts
⅓ cup Candied Orange Peel
rind from 1 orange
3 tablespoons sugar
½ cup water

Make the pastry according to the recipe, and chill.

Roll out the pastry on a lightly floured surface and use to line an 8-inch pie plate.

Preheat the oven to 375°F.

Filling: Melt the butter and sugar in a small heavy pan. Bring to a boil and add the cream, pine nuts, and candied orange peel. Return to a boil, then remove the pan from the heat.

To finish the pie: Bake the prepared pie shell blind in a moderately hot oven for 10 minutes. Remove the baking beans and paper, and spoon the warm filling into the pastry shell. Return the pie to the oven and bake for another 20 to 25 minutes or until the pastry is golden and the filling is lightly caramelized.

Candied Orange Peel

Cut the orange rind into strips. Place into a saucepan with the sugar and water. Bring to a boil and cook over a moderate heat until the water has evaporated and the orange zest is slightly candied but still moist. Remove from the saucepan and set aside on wax paper or on a rack.

Right: **Pecan Pie (above left).**

Pecan Caramel Pie

Yield: 12 servings

1 quantity (8 ounces) Pâte Sucrée (see recipe, page 158)
Filling: ***1 stick unsalted butter***
2 cups light brown sugar
⅓ cup corn syrup
4 cups pecan halves
½ cup cream
¼ teaspoon mixed spice
2 tablespoons brandy or rum

Roll the pastry out thinly and line a 12-inch pie pan, prick the base of the pastry case, and chill for 10 minutes.

Preheat the oven to 425°F.

Bake blind near the top of the oven for 10 minutes. Remove the blind filling and bake for another 5 to 10 minutes or until golden. Allow to cool on a wire rack.

Melt the butter in a heavy-based saucepan. Add the sugar and corn syrup, and cook over a medium-low heat, stirring continuously with a wooden spoon, for 8 to 10 minutes or until a sugar (candy) thermometer registers 260°F.

Remove from the heat and stir in the pecans, cream, and mixed spice. Stir over a low heat for 5 minutes or until a thermometer registers 200°F. Cool for 5 minutes, then stir in the brandy. Spread the mixture in the pie crust, and chill for at least 2 hours before serving.

Treacle Pie

Yield: 6 servings

1 quantity (6 ounces) Sweet Shortcrust Pastry (see recipe, page 150)
Filling: ***8 tablespoons light corn syrup***
6 tablespoons fresh white bread crumbs (or crushed cornflakes)
finely grated rind of 1 lemon
1 tablespoon lemon juice
1 grated apple (optional)

Prepare the pastry according to the recipe, and chill well.

Roll the pastry out to a round, and line an 8-inch ovenproof (enamel is best) plate. Trim off excess pastry.

Filling: Mix all the ingredients together. Dip the measuring spoon into very hot water before measuring the corn syrup, or soften the syrup in a microwave oven.

To finish the pie: Preheat the oven to 425°F.

Spread the filling to within 1 inch of the edge of the pastry case. Roll the remaining scraps of pastry out and cut into thin strips. Twist the strips and place in a lattice pattern over the filling, sealing the ends with water.

Bake toward the top of the oven for 20 to 30 minutes or until the pastry is cooked. Serve warm with custard or cream.

Pear and Hazelnut Pie

Yield: 4 to 6 servings

Pastry:
2 cups flour

pinch of salt

½ cup ground hazelnuts

2 teaspoons ground cinnamon

1¼ sticks butter

½ cup powdered sugar

1 egg

2 or 3 drops vanilla extract

1 tablespoon water

Filling:
3 or 4 ripe dessert pears

about 1 tablespoon powdered sugar

whipped cream, for serving

Pastry: Sift the flour and salt onto a working surface. Make a large well in the center. Sprinkle the ground hazelnuts and cinnamon into the center, and make another well, using the cushion of your hand. Place the butter in the center of the well and make a depression in the slab. Sprinkle over the sugar and break the egg on top; add the vanilla. Pinch the butter, sugar, and egg together, using the tips of your fingers only, until combined. Draw the ground hazelnuts and flour into the center, using a spatula. Add the tablespoon of water to the dough if needed. Gather the dough together and wrap in a sheet of greaseproof paper. Chill for 15 minutes.

Preheat the oven to 375°F.

Filling: Peel and quarter the pears, and remove the cores.

To finish the pie: Roll out two-thirds of the pastry on a lightly floured surface and use to line a shallow 8-inch pie plate. Arrange the pear quarters over the base and sprinkle with some powdered sugar. Roll the remaining pastry into a round, large enough to cover the pie, and cut a 2½-inch circle out of the center. Lay the pastry over the pears, and trim the edges. Press the edges together using the back of a fork or knife.

Bake for 35 minutes or until evenly golden brown. Sprinkle with a little more powdered sugar, and return to the oven for a few minutes. Cook on a rack. Serve warm, with lightly whipped cream.

Cherry Pie

Yield: 6 to 8 servings

Pastry:
2 cups self-rising flour

pinch of salt

4 ounces lard

5 tablespoons water

Filling:
2½ cups pitted, stewed, drained cherries

1 cup cherry juice

½ cup sugar

½ teaspoon salt

2 drops almond extract

1 tablespoon fine tapioca

1 tablespoon melted butter

egg white, for glazing

powdered sugar, for glazing

Pastry: Sift the flour and salt into a bowl and cut in the lard; rub in until the mixture resembles fine bread crumbs. Add the water, and mix in with a knife until a rough dough forms. Refrigerate the dough for 30 minutes.

Filling: Combine all the ingredients for the filling, and allow to stand for 15 minutes.

Preheat the oven to 375°F. Line a deep 8-inch pie dish with two-thirds of the pastry.

Fill the pie dish with the cherry mixture. Roll out the remaining pastry and use to cover the pie. Pinch the edges, and make four slits on the top of the pastry. Glaze the pastry with egg white, and sprinkle powdered sugar over the top.

Bake for 35 minutes.

Apple Amber

Yield: 6 to 8 servings

6 ounces Rich Shortcrust Pastry (see recipe, page 149)

Filling:
1 pound green cooking apples

3 tablespoons brown sugar

rind and juice of 1 lemon

1 tablespoon water

3 tablespoons butter

2 eggs, separated

2 tablespoons powdered sugar for meringue

extra powdered sugar, for sprinkling

Make the pastry according to the recipe, and chill.

Preheat the oven to 350°F.

Filling: Peel, core, and slice the apples. Place the apples, brown sugar, strips of lemon rind, and water into a saucepan; cover, and cook gently until the apple is very soft. Remove the lemon-rind strips, and puree the apple in a food processor. Cut the butter into small pieces and add with the egg yolks and lemon juice to the hot puree. Blend well.

To finish the pie: Roll out the pastry and use to line a deep 9-inch pie dish. Crimp the edges or, using the cut-off scraps of pastry, decorate the edges with small circles of pastry placed overlapping all around the rim of the pie. Brush the pastry shell with a little lightly beaten egg white. Pour in the apple mixture.

Bake for 30 minutes or until the pastry is crisp and golden.

Prepare the meringue topping in the meantime. Whisk the egg whites until stiff, then fold in the powdered sugar gently, using a large metal spoon. When the pastry is cooked and golden, remove the pie from the oven, and increase the oven temperature to 375°F. Pile the meringue on top of the apple, taking the meringue to the edges of the pastry. Sprinkle with a little extra powdered sugar.

Bake for 15 minutes or until the meringue is golden. Serve warm or cold.

Apple Pie

Yield: 6 to 8 servings

Pastry:
1 cup flour

1 cup self-rising flour

pinch of salt

1¼ sticks margarine

1 egg

3 tablespoons powdered sugar

Filling:
6 or 7 large apples

3 tablespoons sugar

1 tablespoon butter

Pastry: Sift the flours and salt into a large mixing bowl. Rub in the margarine until the mixture resembles coarse bread crumbs. Beat the egg with the sugar and add to the flour, mixing quickly into a dough. Wrap and chill for 30 minutes.

Preheat the oven to 375°F.

Filling: Peel, quarter, and core the apples. Cut into slices, and toss them in the sugar.

To finish the pie: Roll out two-thirds of the pastry on a lightly floured surface to line a 1½- to 2-inch-deep 8-inch pie pan (use a metal one for a crispy undercrust). Fill with the apple slices and dot with the butter. Brush around the rim of the pastry with a little water. Roll out the remaining pastry and use it to cover the pie. Trim the excess pastry, and seal the edges by pressing them down with a fork. Make a few slits to allow the steam to escape, brush over with water, and sprinkle with a little extra sugar.

Bake in the preheated oven for about 1 hour. Serve warm, with whipped cream or ice cream.

Right: **From top: Apple Amber (see left); Dutch Apple and Mincemeat Pie (see page 212); Apple Pie (see above).**

Coffee-Cream Pie

Yield: 6 servings

6 ounces Pâte Sucrée (see recipe, page 158)

Filling:
2 cups milk
1 vanilla pod
1½ tablespoons instant coffee powder
3 egg yolks
¼ cup powdered sugar
1 tablespoon + 1 teaspoon gelatin
¼ cup hot water
⅔ cup thickened cream
chocolate coffee beans or grated chocolate, to decorate

Make the pastry according to the recipe, and chill. Preheat the oven to 375°F.

Roll out the pastry on a lightly floured surface and use to line a 9-inch pie plate.

Bake blind for 10 to 15 minutes. Remove the blind filling and paper, and bake for another 10 minutes or until the pastry is evenly golden and crisp. Allow to cool.

Scald the milk with the vanilla pod (split open). Leave to infuse for 10 minutes. Stir in the instant coffee. Remove the vanilla pod (store it in sugar).

Beat the egg yolks and sugar together until pale. Pour the hot milk over them, then return the liquid to the saucepan. Cook, stirring, without boiling, until thickened.

Dissolve the gelatin in the hot water, and stir it through the custard mixture. Pour the mixture into a bowl set over crushed ice, and stir it until just thickening.

Whip the cream, and fold half of the cream into the custard. Spoon the custard filling into the prepared pie shell, and chill until ready to serve.

Cover the top of the pie with the remaining cream, and decorate with the chocolate coffee beans or grated chocolate.

Chocolate-Cream Pie

Yield: 6 servings

6 ounces Pâte Sucrée (see recipe, page 158)

Filling:
2 cups milk
¼ cup powdered sugar
3 ounces dark sweet chocolate
4 egg yolks
1 cup thickened cream
1 teaspoon vanilla extract
2 tablespoons brandy
2 tablespoons broken walnut pieces
whipped cream, for decoration
chopped walnuts, for decoration

Make the pastry according to the recipe, and chill. Preheat the oven to 375°F.

Roll out the pastry on a lightly floured surface and use to line an 8-inch pie plate.

Bake blind for 15 minutes. Remove the blind filling and paper and continue baking until evenly golden brown and crisp (about 10 minutes).

Filling: Place the milk and powdered sugar into a heavy saucepan, bring to a boil, and stir until the sugar has dissolved. Grate the chocolate and stir into the hot milk, stirring until dissolved. Beat the egg yolks in a bowl and pour in a little of the hot milk. Return this liquid to the saucepan and heat over very low heat, stirring until thickened. Pour into a bowl as soon as the mixture coats the back of a spoon. Chill.

Beat the cream until it holds its shape, and fold in the vanilla and brandy. Fold the cream and the broken walnut pieces through the cold custard. Spoon the filling into the prepared pie shell and chill until set.

When ready to serve, decorate with extra whipped cream and walnuts.

French Mint Pie

Yield: 6 to 8 servings

1 Cookie-Crumb Crust (see recipe, page 216)

Filling:
2 ounces dark chocolate

¾ stick unsalted butter

1½ cups confectioners' sugar

2 large eggs

2½ cups cream

drops of peppermint extract

chopped walnuts, to decorate

Preheat the oven to 375°F.

Make the Crumb Crust according to the recipe, and use to line an 8-inch pie plate.

Bake for 10 minutes. Allow to cool.

Filling: Melt the chocolate on a plate over a pan of simmering water. Allow to cool.

Beat the butter and confectioners' sugar together until light and creamy. Beat the cooled chocolate into the butter mixture with the eggs until the mixture is light and fluffy.

Whip the cream until it holds its shape; fold half into the chocolate mixture. Stir through a couple of drops of peppermint extract to taste, and spoon the mixture into the prepared pie shell. Chill until the filling is firm.

When ready to serve, decorate with remaining cream and the chopped walnuts.

Coconut-Cream Pie

Yield: 4 to 6 servings

4 ounces Shortcrust Pastry (see recipe, page 149)

Filling:
½ cup powdered sugar

1 tablespoon arrowroot

pinch of salt

¾ cup water

drops of almond extract

drops of vanilla extract

2 egg whites

¾ cup cream

¾ cup flaked coconut

Make the pastry according to the recipe, and chill.
Preheat the oven to 375°F.

Roll out the pastry and use to line a 7-inch pie plate. Crimp the edges.

Bake blind for 7 minutes. Remove the blind filling and paper, and bake for 15 minutes or until the pastry is evenly golden and crisp. Allow to cool on a wire rack.

Filling: Place 5 tablespoons of the powdered sugar, and the arrowroot, salt, and water into a small saucepan; cook over low heat until smooth and clear. Add 1 drop of almond extract and 2 drops of vanilla extract to flavor. Allow to cool.

Beat the egg whites stiffly and stir into the sugar mixture. Pour into the cooled pie shell.

Whip the cream and sweeten it with the remaining 1¼ tablespoons of powdered sugar and add a drop each of almond extract and vanilla extract. Fold in half of the coconut, and spread over the pie. Sprinkle the top with the remaining coconut.

Set in the freezer for 30 minutes, then remove to the refrigerator. Serve chilled.

Gravel Pie

Yield: 6 servings

6 ounces Rich Shortcrust Pastry (see recipe, page 149)

Filling:
1 cup sugar or honey

⅓ cup water

3 eggs, lightly beaten

½ cup seedless raisins

1 cup cake crumbs

⅓ cup flour

1 teaspoon cinnamon

pinch of ground nutmeg

pinch of ground ginger

¾ stick butter

Make the pastry according to the recipe, and chill.

Filling: Place the sugar (or honey), water, and eggs into a bowl over a pan of simmering water. Stir until the sugar has dissolved and the mixture thickens. Allow to cool.

When cool, stir the raisins into the mixture.

Mix the cake crumbs, flour, and spices together. Rub in the butter as you would for pastry.

To finish the pie: Preheat the oven to 350°F.

Roll out the pastry on a lightly floured surface and use it to line an 8- to 9-inch pie dish. Crimp or decorate the edges. Pour in the raisin mixture, sprinkle the cake-crumb mixture over the top, then sprinkle with the nutmeg and ginger.

Bake for 30 minutes or until the topping is golden brown and the pastry is crisp.

Allow to cool. Serve with ice cream or whipped cream.

Chocolate Praline Pie

Yield: 4 to 6 servings

6 ounces Pâte Sucrée (see recipe, page 158)

Filling:
3 tablespoons cocoa
⅓ cup sugar
2 cups water
1 tablespoon flour
4 tablespoons cornstarch
½ cup milk
2 egg yolks, lightly beaten
½ stick butter

Topping:
½ cup cream
1 teaspoon powdered sugar
drops of vanilla extract

Praline:
⅓ cup whole unblanched almonds
¼ cup sugar

Make the pastry according to the recipe, and chill.

Preheat the oven to 375°F.

Roll out the pastry on a lightly floured surface and use to line an 8-inch pie plate.

Bake blind for 7 minutes. Remove the blind filling, and bake for another 15 minutes or until the pastry is crisp and evenly golden. (Do not bake the pastry too dark or it will be bitter).

Filling: Place the cocoa and sugar into a saucepan and mix in the water; bring to a boil, and simmer for 10 minutes. Mix the flour and cornstarch with the milk until it forms a smooth paste, and add to the chocolate mixture, stirring over the heat until the mixture boils. Pour a little of the hot mixture over the egg yolks, mix in, and then pour this into the saucepan. Stirring constantly, add the butter a small piece at a time, until the butter is melted and the mixture is smooth. Allow it to cool a little, and pour into the prepared pie shell. Chill.

Topping: Whip the cream with the sugar until it holds its shape, flavoring with a couple drops of vanilla. Spread over the chilled pie top, and sprinkle with 3 tablespoons of ground praline.

Praline

Place the almonds and sugar into a small heavy saucepan. Cook over a very low heat until the sugar begins to caramelize and the nuts begin to toast. Tip the pan from side to side to coat the nuts in the liquid caramel; or use a metal spoon just to prod the nuts into the caramel. Do not stir. When a good deep caramel, turn the mixture out into a greased baking pan to set.

When it is set, crush with a rolling pin or in a food processor. Store immediately in an airtight jar until ready to use.

Lemon Meringue Pie

Yield: 4 to 6 servings

6 ounces Rich Shortcrust Pastry (see recipe, page 149)
1 egg white

Filling:
4 tablespoons cornstarch
¾ cup sugar
1½ cups water
4 tablespoons lemon juice
grated rind and juice of 1 lemon
2 eggs, separated
½ stick butter
4 tablespoons powdered sugar, for meringue

Make the pastry according to the recipe, and chill.

Preheat the oven to 375°F.

Roll out the pastry thinly and use to line an 8-inch pie plate. Crimp the edges well, bringing the pastry up quite high on the rim. Prick the base of the pastry with a fork and brush with beaten egg white.

Bake for 20 minutes.

Leave the oven on, at 375°F.

Filling: Place the cornstarch, sugar, and water into a saucepan. Blend well and bring to a boil, stirring until the mixture thickens. Lower the heat, and cook for a few minutes longer. Stir in the lemon juice, lemon rind, egg yolks, and butter. Beat well until smooth and shiny, then pour immediately into the prepared pie shell.

Whip the egg whites with a pinch of salt until stiff. Add the sugar gradually, making a stiff meringue. Spread the meringue over the lemon filling, sealing to the edges of the pastry, and swirling peaks into the meringue.

Bake in the preheated oven for 15 minutes. Allow to cool before cutting.

Right: **Chocolate Praline Pie (see left).**

Apple Streusel Pie

Yield: 8 servings

Pastry: ***1½ cups flour***
pinch of salt
1 stick butter
½ cup rolled oats
2 tablespoons sugar
finely grated rind of 1 lemon
1 egg yolk
2 to 3 tablespoons water
Filling: ***2 pounds cooking apples***
1 tablespoon lemon juice
½ cup raisins
½ cup brown sugar
½ teaspoon ground cinnamon
Topping: ***2 tablespoons butter***
2 tablespoons brown sugar
2 tablespoons flour
½ cup rolled oats
egg white, for glazing

Pastry: Sift the flour and salt into a bowl. Rub in the butter until the mixture resembles fine bread crumbs. Stir in the rolled oats, sugar, and grated lemon rind. Mix the egg yolk with water, then stir it into the flour mixture to form a smooth dough. Knead lightly and wrap in greaseproof paper. Chill for 15 minutes.

Preheat the oven to 400°F.

Filling: Peel, core, and slice the apples. Place in a bowl and sprinkle with the lemon juice. Add the raisins, brown sugar and cinnamon; mix gently.

Topping: Place all the ingredients into a food processor and blend briefly, just until crumbly.

To finish the pie: On a lightly floured surface, roll out the pastry to a thin round and line a 9-inch pie plate. Decorate the edges by crimping or with the back of a knife or fork. Prick the base of the pastry with a fork, and brush all over with the lightly beaten egg white. Place the filling carefully into the pastry shell, shaping it into a dome in the center. Sprinkle the topping over the filling.

Bake in the preheated oven for 10 minutes, then reduce the oven temperature to 350°F and continue baking for another 40 minutes or until the apples are just tender and the topping is crisp. Serve hot or cold, with whipped cream or ice cream.

Dutch Apple and Mincemeat Pie

Yield: 6 to 8 servings

6 ounces Pâte Sucrée   ***(see recipe, page 158)***
Filling: ***5 green cooking apples***
rind from 1 lemon
pinch of ground cinnamon
pinch of ground cloves
1 tablespoon powdered sugar
1 tablespoon water
4 tablespoons Homemade Mincemeat   ***(see recipe, page 222)***
2 tablespoons soft brown sugar

Make the pastry according to the recipe, and chill. Preheat the oven to 375°F.

Roll the pastry out thinly and use to line a 9-inch pie dish. Trim off excess pastry and crimp the edges.

Bake blind for 10 to 12 minutes or until the pastry is a golden brown. Remove the blind filling, and set the pie aside while making the filling.

Reset the oven temperature at 350°F.

Filling: Peel and core three of the apples and slice them into a small saucepan. Add the lemon rind, spices, powdered sugar, and water, and stew until soft.

Spread the base of the prepared pie shell with the mincemeat, then spoon the stewed apples on top. Peel and core the two uncooked apples, slice them very thinly, and arrange them over the stewed apples in concentric circles. Sprinkle with the soft brown sugar.

Bake for 25 minutes. Serve warm, with whipped cream or ice cream.

Berry Pie

Yield: 6 to 8 servings

Pastry:
1 cup all-purpose white flour
1 cup self-rising flour
pinch of salt
1¼ sticks butter
2 tablespoons powdered sugar
1 egg, lightly beaten
1 tablespoon water
Filling:
4 cups fresh berries
¼ to 1½ cups sugar, depending on the fruit
¼ cup flour (see note on thickening), depending on the fruit
pinch of salt
1½ tablespoons lemon juice
grated lemon rind
egg white, for glazing

Pastry: Sift the flours and salt into a bowl. Rub in the butter until the mixture resembles fine bread crumbs. Mix in the sugar until combined. Stir in the egg using a knife, and add the water to make a smooth dough. Chill for about 10 minutes.

Preheat the oven to 400°F. Set a baking sheet on a shelf ready for baking.

Roll out two-thirds of the pastry on a lightly floured surface and use to line a 9-inch pie dish or shallow cake pan.

Filling: Pick over the berries and hull or remove any stems. Rinse, and dry well on absorbent kitchen paper. Combine the berries with the sugar, flour, salt, lemon juice, and lemon rind. (See the note if using tapioca or cornstarch for thickening.) Spoon into the prepared pie dish.

Roll out the remaining pastry and cover the pie. Press the edges to seal and crimp the edges. Cut two vents in the pie. Brush with lightly beaten egg white, and sprinkle with sugar.

Bake for 10 minutes on the baking sheet set on the shelf. Reduce the oven temperature to 350°F and bake for another 35 to 40 minutes or until the pastry is golden brown and the berries are cooked.

Note: About 4 cups of fresh fruit (3 cups of cooked fruit) will fill a 9-inch pie. Sweetening is a matter of taste, but for this amount ½ cup of sugar will usually be sufficient for the sweeter fruits and 1 to 1½ cups of sugar for the tarter fruits such as gooseberries.

Thickening, too, depends on the fruit. For this quantity, ¼ cup of flour is about right. However, if the fruit is acid, use 2 tablespoons of tapioca mixed with the sugar or 2 tablespoons of cornstarch blended with ¼ cup of juice or water; let stand with the fruit for 15 minutes.

Use strawberries, raspberries, blueberries, mulberries, loganberries, blackberries, or gooseberries.

Mulberry Pie

Yield: 6 servings

8 ounces Rich Shortcrust Pastry (see recipe, page 149)
Filling:
3 cups fresh mulberries
1 cup sugar
1 tablespoon flour
1 tablespoon lemon juice
pinch of salt
1 tablespoon butter
egg white, for glazing
powdered sugar, for glazing

Make the pastry according to the recipe, and chill.

Preheat the oven to 400°F. Place a baking sheet on a shelf ready for baking.

Roll out two-thirds of the pastry and line an 8-inch pie dish.

Filling: Pick over the mulberries and remove the stems. Combine the berries with the sugar, flour, lemon juice, and salt. Spoon the berry mixture into the pastry shell and dot with butter.

Roll out the remaining pastry and use to cover the pie. Trim off surplus pastry, using a sharp knife. Crimp the edges and cut vents in top. Brush with the egg white, and sprinkle with the powdered sugar. Place the pie dish on the baking sheet.

Bake for 10 minutes, then reduce the oven temperature to 350°F and bake for another 40 minutes or until the berries and pastry are cooked.

Buttermilk Chess Pie

Yield 6 to 8 servings

5 ounces Shortcrust Pastry (see recipe, page 149)

Filling:
½ stick butter

1 cup powdered sugar

3 large eggs, beaten

¼ cup flour

pinch of salt

1 cup buttermilk

1 teaspoon vanilla extract

ground nutmeg, for sprinkling

Make the pastry according to the recipe, and chill. Preheat the oven to 400°F.

Filling: Cream the butter and sugar until light and creamy. Add the beaten eggs gradually, beating well after each addition. Fold in the sifted flour with the salt, beating well. Add the buttermilk and vanilla.

To finish the pie: Roll out the pastry on a lightly floured surface and use to line a 9-inch pie plate.

Bake blind in the preheated oven for 10 minutes. Remove the blind filling and paper, reduce the oven temperature to 375°F, and continue baking for 10 minutes. Remove from the oven, carefully spoon in the filling mixture, then return to the oven and bake for 30 minutes or until the filling is set.

Serve warm or cold, sprinkled with grated nutmeg and with a bowl of whipped cream.

Custard Pie

Yield: 6 servings

6 ounces Rich Shortcrust Pastry (see recipe, page 149)

Filling:
2½ cups milk, or half-and-half

vanilla pod

3 eggs

1 egg yolk

2 tablespoons powdered sugar

nutmeg

Make the pastry according to the recipe, and chill. Use to line a 9-inch pie plate.

Preheat the oven to 400°F.

Filling: Heat the milk with the vanilla pod (slit open to release the black seeds) until scalding. Beat the eggs and egg yolk and powdered sugar together, and pour over the scalded milk. Strain into a pitcher and allow to cool. (Dry out the vanilla pod and store it in sugar.)

To finish the pie: Bake the pastry blind in the preheated oven for 10 minutes. Remove the blind filling (the baking beans and paper). Pour the now-cool custard over, and sprinkle with freshly grated nutmeg. Reduce the oven temperature to 350°F, return the pie to the oven, and continue baking for 25 minutes or until the custard is set and the pastry is golden. Allow to cool on a wire rack.

Note: Be careful not to overbake, as this makes the custard watery. If the custard begins to rise, remove from the oven at once.

Eggnog Pie

Yield: 6 to 8 servings

8 ounces Rich Shortcrust Pastry (see recipe, page 149)

Filling:
1¼ cups milk

½ cup sugar

4 large eggs, separated

1 tablespoon gelatin

¼ cup hot water

¾ cup cream

1 tablespoon brandy

1 tablespoon powdered sugar

dark chocolate, for decoration

Make the pastry according to the recipe, and chill. Preheat the oven to 375°F.

Roll out the pastry and use to line a 9-inch pie plate. Decorate the edge.

Bake blind for 10 minutes. Remove the blind filling and paper, and bake for another 15 minutes or until the pastry is evenly golden brown and crisp. Allow to cool.

Filling: Heat the milk until lukewarm. Lightly beat the sugar and egg yolks together, and pour over the milk. Return the milk–egg mixture to the top of a double boiler and cook, stirring, until the custard coats the back of a spoon. Let cool, with a piece of wet greaseproof paper on top to prevent a skin forming.

Dissolve the gelatin in the hot water, and stir through the custard. Leave until just beginning to set.

Whip the cream until it holds its shape, and then fold it into the custard with the brandy. Whisk the egg whites until stiff and beat in 1 tablespoon of powdered sugar. Fold in the custard mixture. Pour the filling into the prepared pastry shell, and chill.

When ready to serve, decorate with rosettes of whipped cream and grated curls of chocolate.

Christmas Cottage Cheese Pie

Yield: 8 servings

8 ounces Shortcrust Pastry (see recipe, page 149)

Filling:
1 cup cottage cheese

2 large eggs

¼ cup powdered sugar

1 teaspoon vanilla extract

1 cup fruit mince

confectioners' sugar, for dusting

Make the pastry according to the recipe, and chill.
Preheat the oven to 400°F.

Filling: Beat the cottage cheese, eggs, sugar, and vanilla together.

To finish the pie: Roll out the pastry on a lightly floured surface and use to line a 9-inch pie plate. Bake blind for 10 minutes. Remove the blind filling and paper, and allow to cool.

Preheat the oven to 375°F.

Spread the fruit mince over the base of the pastry shell, and spoon the cottage-cheese mixture over.

Bake for 25 minutes. Allow to cool. Serve dusted with confectioners' sugar and a sprig of holly.

Cream-Cheese Peach Pie

Yield: 6 servings

Filling:
1 pound fresh peaches (or canned peaches, drained)

½ cup sugar

1 tablespoon apricot jam (jelly)

1 tablespoon lemon juice

4 ounces cream cheese

grated rind of 1 lemon

sour cream

Pastry:
6 ounces filo pastry

1 stick butter, melted

confectioners' sugar, for sprinkling

Filling: Peel the peaches and remove their pits; chop roughly. Place into a heavy saucepan, and add the sugar, apricot jam, and lemon juice. Simmer over a low heat until the mixture is quite thick (about 20 minutes). Allow to cool.

Preheat the oven 350°F.

Beat the cream cheese with the grated lemon rind and 1 tablespoon of sour cream.

To finish the pie: Brush a sheet of filo pastry with the melted butter; lay butter-side-down into a 9-inch pie plate. Brush with melted butter, and lay over another sheet of filo pastry. Brush with melted butter, and repeat with about three more layers of pastry.

Spoon the cream-cheese mixture over, and smooth the top. Spoon the cooled peach filling over, and smooth the top. Top the filling with about five sheets of pastry, brushing each one (as before) with the melted butter. Trim off the edges of the pastry with a sharp knife.

Bake for 30 to 40 minutes or until crisp and golden. Sprinkle with confectioners' sugar. Serve warm with sour cream.

Ricotta Pie

Yield: 8 servings

6 ounces Pâte Brisée (see recipe, page 158)

Filling:
3 tablespoons pine nuts

2 tablespoons slivered almonds

2 tablespoons chopped mixed peel

2 tablespoons currants

1 tablespoon flour

4 eggs

¾ cup sugar

1½ pounds ricotta cheese

1 teaspoon vanilla extract

Make the pastry according to the recipe, and chill.
Preheat the oven to 375°F.

Roll out the pastry on a lightly floured surface and use to line a deep 9-inch pie dish; crimp the edges.

Bake blind for about 10 minutes. Remove the blind filling and paper, and allow to cool while preparing the filling.

Reset the oven temperature to 350°F.

Filling: Toast the pine nuts in a dry frying pan until just beginning to brown.Remove, and mix with the almonds, mixed peel, currants, and flour.

Beat the eggs until light and fluffy, and gradually add the sugar. Beat the ricotta cheese with the vanilla until creamy, then beat in the egg mixture. Stir in the nut and fruit mixture.

Pour the filling into the prepared pie shell.

Bake for about 40 minutes. Allow to cool.

Peach-Cream Pie

Yield: 6 servings

Crumb Crust:
1¼ cups crushed cookies

1 tablespoon sugar

5 tablespoons butter, melted

Filling:
3 egg yolks

⅓ cup powdered sugar

1 lemon

1¼ cups cream

3 to 4 peaches, depending on their size

Crumb Crust

Preheat the oven to 375°F.

Mix together the crumbs and sugar. Blend in the butter, and press into a greased 9-inch pie plate, taking the crumbs up the sides to form a small rim.

Bake for 8 to 10 minutes. Allow to cool.

Filling: Beat the egg yolks and sugar together in a small bowl until pale. Blend in the finely grated rind and the juice of the lemon. Place the bowl over a saucepan of simmering water, and cook, stirring until the mixture forms a smooth thick cream. Allow to cool.

Beat the cream until it holds its shape, and fold most of it into the cold lemon mixture.

Skin the peaches by plunging them into boiling water for a minute or so, then slipping off the skins. Slice the peaches and fold them into the cream mixture, reserving a few slices for decoration. Pile the cream and peach mixture into the prepared pie crust, and chill. Decorate with the reserved cream and sliced peaches.

Rhubarb Pie

Yield: 6 servings

6 ounces Rich Shortcrust Pastry or Flaky Pastry
(see recipes, pages 149 and 156)

Filling:
¾ cup sugar

4 to 5 cups fresh rhubarb

grated rind and a little juice from 1 lemon

2 tablespoons tapioca

egg white, for glazing

powdered sugar, for glazing

Make the pastry according to the recipe, and chill.

Filling: Combine the sugar, rhubarb, grated rind and juice from the lemon, and the tapioca in the base of a deep pie dish or ovenproof dish; dome the fruit in the center. Leave for 15 minutes.

To finish the pie: Preheat the oven to 400°F.

Roll out the pastry on a lightly floured surface slightly larger than the top of the pie dish. Trim off ⅜ inch of the pastry and press this strip onto the rim of the pie dish. Dampen the pastry rim with a little water. Lay the pastry cover over the filling and rim, and press edges together with the back of a fork or knife. Cut a few slits to allow the steam to escape during baking. Brush the pastry with the egg white, and sprinkle with powdered sugar.

Bake in the preheated oven for 10 minutes, then reduce the oven temperature to 350°F and cook for 25 minutes or until the pastry is golden and the rhubarb is cooked. Serve warm, with custard or pouring cream.

Variation: Use half apple and half rhubarb.

Raspberry-Cream Pie

Yield: 6 servings

1 quantity Cookie-Crumb Crust made with chocolate cookies
(see recipe, above left)

Filling:
3 eggs

2 egg yolks

¼ cup powdered sugar

1 tablespoon gelatin

¼ cup hot water

juice of ½ lemon

⅔ cup raspberry puree

⅔ cup cream

extra cream, for decoration

grated chocolate, to decorate

Preheat the oven to 375°F.

Make the Cookie Crumb Crust according to the recipe, and use to line an 8-inch pie dish.

Bake for 10 minutes. Allow to cool.

Filling: Combine the eggs, egg yolks, and sugar in a bowl over a pan of simmering water, and whisk until thickened. Remove from the heat, and continue whisking until cool. Dissolve the gelatin in the hot water, and stir it through the egg mixture with the lemon juice and raspberry puree. Chill until just about to set.

Whip the cream until it holds its shape, and fold it into the raspberry mixture. Spoon into the prepared pie shell and chill until set. Serve decorated with extra whipped ceam and grated chocolate.

Note: Raspberry puree can be made by processing fresh, frozen, or canned raspberries in a food processor or blender until smooth.

Peach Pie

Yield: 4 to 6 servings

6 ounces Whole-Wheat Pastry or Rich Shortcrust Pastry (see recipes, pages 153 and 149)

Filling:
8 fresh peaches, peeled and sliced, or 1 pound 10 ounces canned sliced peaches

2 tablespoons tapioca

egg white, for glazing

powdered sugar, for glazing

Prepare the pastry according to the recipe, and chill.

Preheat the oven to 400°F.

Filling: If using canned peaches, drain the peaches and reserve the juice. Layer the sliced peaches with the tapioca in a 4-cup oval pie dish and pour over a little of the reserved juice.

To finish the pie: Roll the pastry out to an oval shape 1 inch larger than the top of the dish. Cut a ⅜-inch rim off the pastry. Brush the rim of the pie dish with cold water, place the ⅜-inch pastry strip around the rim of the dish, and press it down; trim the ends of the pastry strip where they meet, so that they meet without overlapping. Brush this pastry rim with cold water. Place the oval pastry top over the peach filling, easing it in carefully to avoid shrinkage during baking. Press around the rim to seal the pastry, and trim away any overhanging pastry with a sharp knife. Scallop or flute the edges, and make a few slits to allow the steam to escape during baking. Brush the pastry with the egg white, and sprinkle with the powdered sugar.

Stand the pie dish on a baking sheet.

Bake for 20 to 30 minutes or until the pastry is cooked. Serve hot or cold, with whipped cream, custard, or ice cream.

Pineapple Meringue Pie

Yield: 6 servings

6 ounces Rich Shortcrust Pastry (see recipe, page 149)

Filling:
1 medium-sized fresh pineapple

3 tablespoons cornstarch

pinch of salt

½ cup sugar

2 tablespoons water

juice of ½ lemon

2 egg yolks

Meringue:
2 egg whites

4 tablespoons powdered sugar

Make the pastry according to the recipe, and chill.

Preheat the oven to 375°F.

Roll out the pastry on a lightly floured surface and use to line an 8-inch pie dish.

Bake blind for 10 minutes. Remove the blind filling and paper, and return to the oven for another 10 minutes. Allow to cool while making the filling.

Reset the oven temperature at 325°F.

Filling: Peel the pineapple and cut the flesh into chunks. Use a food processor or blender to puree the pineapple. Place the pureed pineapple into a heavy-based saucepan. Blend the cornstarch, salt, sugar, and water together, and stir into the pineapple. Bring to a boil and, stirring constantly, simmer for 10 minutes. Add the lemon juice and egg yolks, and stir until the mixture is thickened without boiling. Pour into the prepared pie shell.

Meringue: Whisk the egg whites until stiff, then gradually add the sugar until it is the texture of a smooth stiff meringue.

Pile the meringue on top of the filling, taking it to the edges of the pastry.

Bake for 15 minutes or until the meringue is golden. Serve warm or cold.

Gâteau de Pithiviers Feuilleté

Yield: 6 to 8 servings

12 ounces Puff Pastry (see recipe, page 154)

Filling:
1 stick butter

1/3 cup powdered sugar

1 egg

1 egg yolk

1 1/4 cups ground almonds

2 teaspoons flour

1 teaspoon vanilla extract

beaten egg, for glazing

extra sugar, for glazing

Make the pastry according to the recipe, and chill.
Filling: Cream the butter and sugar until pale and creamy. Beat in the egg and egg yolk. Stir in the ground almonds, flour, and vanilla.
To finish the pie: Preheat the oven to 425°F.

Roll out half of the pastry on a lightly floured surface, into a round 11 inches across. Using a saucepan lid, cut a circle 10 inches across, angling the knife away from the lid slightly. Roll out the remaining pastry slightly thicker than for the first, and cut into a 10-inch round. Place the thinner of the circles onto a baking sheet, and mound the filling in the center, leaving a 1-inch border. Brush the edge with water and place the second pastry round over the filling. Press the edges together firmly. Scallop the edge of the pie with the back of a knife, pulling it in at intervals. Brush the pie with beaten-egg glaze and, working from the center, score the top in curves like the petals of a flower. Chill for 15 minutes.

Bake for 30 to 35 minutes or until firm and puffed. Sprinkle the top with powdered sugar and place the pie under a hot broiler until the sugar has caramelized and the surface is shiny. Allow to cool on a wire rack.

Variation: Mound 4 or 5 dessert pears, peeled, cored, and sliced, in the center of the pastry circle. Sprinkle with a little sugar and cinnamon or ground cardamom, and continue as above. Serve warm with whipped cream.

Almond and Poppy-Seed Pie

Yield: 4 to 6 servings

Filling:
1 apple

3/4 cup ground almonds

3/4 cup ground poppy seeds

1/2 cup milk

1/4 cup cream

1/4 cup currants

1/4 cup sugar

1 tablespoon honey

2 tablespoons butter

1 teaspoon ground cinnamon

grated rind of 1/2 lemon

grated rind of 1/2 orange

Pastry:
6 ounces filo pastry

1 stick butter, melted

confectioners' sugar, for sprinkling

Filling: Peel and grate the apple into a bowl. Add the remaining ingredients for the filling, and place the bowl over a pan of simmering water. Cook, stirring continuously, over simmering water until very thick (about 20 minutes). Remove from the heat and allow to cool.
To finish the pie: Preheat the oven to 350°F.

Brush a sheet of filo pastry with the melted butter. Lay butter side down in a pie plate. Brush with melted butter and lay another sheet of filo pastry over it. Brush with melted butter and repeat with three more layers of pastry. Spoon the filling into the prepared pie base, and smooth the surface. Top the filling with about five more sheets of pastry, brushing each one (as before) with the melted butter. Trim off the edges of the pastry with a sharp knife.

Bake in the preheated oven for 30 to 40 minutes or until crisp and golden. Sprinkle with confectioners' sugar, and slice with a serrated knife. Serve warm or at room temperature.

***Right:* Almond and Poppy-Seed Pie (see above); Gâteau de Pithiviers Feuilleté (see left).**

Key Lime Pie

Yield: 4 to 6 servings

6 ounces Shortcrust Pastry
(see recipe, page 149)

Filling:
2 cups sweetened condensed milk

1 tablespoon grated lime rind

½ cup lime juice

pinch of salt

2 egg yolks

Meringue:
2 egg whites

2 tablespoons sugar

Make the pastry according to the recipe, and chill.
Preheat the oven to 375°F.
Roll out the pastry on a lightly floured surface and use to line a 9-inch pie plate.
Bake blind for 10 minutes. Remove the blind filling and paper, and bake for another 20 minutes or until the pastry is crisp and golden. Allow to cool.
Set the oven temperature at 350°F.
Filling: Beat the sweetened condensed milk, lime rind, lime juice, and salt together until thickened. Beat in the egg yolks. Pour into the prepared pie shell and smooth the top.

Meringue
Whisk the egg whites until stiff, and beat in the sugar until stiff.
Spoon the meringue over the top of the lime filling.
Bake for 10 minutes or until golden. Allow to cool.

Lemon-Curd Pie

Yield: 6 to 8 servings

6 ounces Pâte Brisée
(see recipe, page 158)

Filling:
6 egg yolks

1 cup powdered sugar

grated rind and juice of 4 lemons

1½ sticks butter

2 teaspoons cornstarch

cream

Make the pastry according to the recipe, and chill.
Filling: Place the egg yolks and sugar into a bowl over a pan of simmering water. Add the lemon rind and lemon juice. Beat with a wooden spoon until smooth and the sugar is dissolved. Gradually add the butter in small pieces, slipping it through your fingers to soften it; stir until melted before adding the next lot of butter. Mix the cornstarch with a little cream, and add to the lemon-curd mixture. Cook over simmering water until thick and smooth. Then allow to cool.
To finish the pie: Preheat the oven to 375°F.
Roll out the pastry on a lightly floured surface and use to line a 9-inch pie plate.
Bake blind for 10 minutes. Remove the blind filling and paper, pour the cooled lemon-curd filling in, and return to the oven for another 25 to 30 minutes. Serve warm or cold, with pouring cream.

Crème Brûlée Pie

Yield: 6 servings

6 ounces Pâte Sucrée
(see recipe, page 158)

Filling:
2 cups cream

6 tablespoons soft brown sugar

5 egg yolks

Make the pastry according to the recipe, and chill.
Preheat the oven to 375°F.
Roll out the pastry and use to line a shallow 9-inch pie dish.
Bake blind for 15 minutes. Remove the blind filling and paper, and bake for another 10 to 15 minutes or until evenly golden brown. Remove from the oven and allow to cool.
Filling: Scald the cream and 3 tablespoons of the brown sugar. Leave this mixture to cool a little.
Beat the egg yolks in a heatproof bowl until pale, then pour in the cream mixture, stirring constantly. Place the bowl over a pan of simmering water and cook until the mixture thickens, stirring constantly. When the custard coats the back of the spoon, remove from the heat and allow to cool slightly.
Pour the custard into the pie shell and chill in the refrigerator.
To finish the pie: Half an hour before serving, sprinkle the top of the pie with the remaining 3 tablespoons of brown sugar. Place strips of aluminum foil over the edge of the pie crust. Preheat the broiler and place the pie under the hot broiler to caramelize the brown sugar. Allow to cool before serving.

Note: The filling can be varied by adding half a cup of chopped walnuts, almonds, or pistachio nuts to the cream before pouring it into the shell. Or it can be used to fill a meringue shell and served with poached fresh fruit.

Pointers for chiffon pies:

- Beat the egg yolks with the sugar over simmering water, not boiling.
- Do not let the gelatin and egg mixture go beyond "just beginning to set" before adding the whipped cream and egg whites, otherwise they will not combine smoothly and the filling will be lumpy. If the gelatin mixture does set before adding the egg whites, gently warm the gelatin mixture to soften it and allow it to cool once again before adding the beaten egg whites or cream.
- "Just beginning set" is when the mixture will stay apart for a few seconds when the spoon is pulled through it.
- Beat the egg whites until stiff but not dry. They lose their elasticity and therefore hold less air when beaten until dry.
- Whip the cream until it will hold its shape—but not too stiffly or it will be difficult to fold into the gelatin mixture.
- Make sure the pastry shell or crumb crust is cold before spooning in the chiffon mixture.

Prune Chiffon Pie

Yield: 6 to 8 servings

6 ounces Rich Shortcrust Pastry (see recipe, page 149)

Filling:
1 cup pitted stewed prunes

¾ cup prune juice

½ cup sugar

pinch of salt

finely grated rind and juice of 1 lemon

1½ tablespoons gelatin

3 tablespoons hot water

2 egg whites

Make the pastry according to the recipe, and chill.

Preheat the oven to 425°F.

Roll out the pastry on a lightly floured surface and use to line a 9-inch pie plate.

Bake blind for 10 minutes. Remove the blind filling, and bake for another 10 minutes or until the pastry is golden and crisp. Allow to cool on a wire rack.

Filling: Place the stewed prunes and prune juice into a blender or food processor and blend until smooth. Add the sugar, salt, lemon rind, and lemon juice; blend again. Pour into a small saucepan and stir over moderate heat to dissolve the sugar. Allow to cool.

Dissolve the gelatin in the 3 tablespoons of hot water, and add to the prune mixture. Chill until just beginning to set.

Whisk the egg whites until stiff, and fold them into the prune mixture. Spoon the filling into the prepared pie shell, and chill until ready to serve.

Serve with whipped cream or fresh yogurt.

Macadamia Rum Chiffon Pie

Yield: 12 servings

6 ounces Rich Shortcrust Pastry (see recipe, page 149)

Filling:
2 teaspoons gelatin

4 eggs, separated

2 tablespoons powdered sugar

½ cup boiling water

3 tablespoons rum

finely grated rind of 1 lemon

additional 2 tablespoons powdered sugar

½ cup chopped macadamia nuts

1¼ cups thickened cream

Prepare the pastry according to the recipe, and chill.

Preheat the oven to 425°F.

Roll out the pastry on a lightly floured surface and use to line a 9-inch pie plate.

Bake blind for 10 minutes. Remove the blind filling and return to the oven for another 10 minutes or until golden and crisp. Allow to cool.

Filling: Dissolve the gelatin in a little hot water. Place the egg yolks and sugar into a mixing bowl over a pan of simmering water, and beat until thick and pale. Pour in the boiling water and beat until thick. Add the dissolved gelatin, and allow to cool.

When just beginning to set, stir in the rum and lemon rind.

Whisk the egg whites until stiff and gradually add the 2 tablespoons of powdered sugar, whisking until it is the texture of a smooth meringue. Carefully fold in the rum mixture and the macadamia nuts. Pour into the cold pastry shell and refrigerate until set.

Whip the cream, with an extra tablespoon of rum if liked, and pipe rosettes of cream to decorate the top of the pie. Sprinkle with extra macadamia nuts. Serve lightly chilled.

Homemade Mincemeat

Yield: 14 cups

4 ounces blanched almonds

1 pound dried raisins

1 pound dried currants

1 pound dried white raisins

6 ounces candied fruit, such as apricot, pineapple, or fig

4 ounces candied cherries

8 ounces candied peel

2 cooking apples

12 ounces brown sugar

½ teaspoon each cinnamon, allspice, nutmeg, and cardamom

10 ounces fresh suet, grated

grated rind and juice of 2 oranges

¾ cup brandy or rum

Chop the nuts and the dried and candied fruit roughly. Mix in candied peel. Peel and grate the apples and mix into the dried-fruit and nut mixture with the sugar, spices, suet, and orange rind. Pour over the orange juice and brandy or rum. Mix thoroughly and pack into clean sterilized jars. Cover with a circle of waxed paper and seal with a lid.

Note: Mincemeat can be made well in advance and stored in airtight jars. Preferably leave the mincemeat to mature for about a month before using. The suet can be replaced with 2 sticks of butter if a lighter mincemeat is preferred. Keeps well for about 6 months. Once jars are opened, keep in the refrigerator.

Mincemeat Pies

Yield: 12 little pies

8 ounces Rich Shortcrust Pastry (see recipe, page 149)

1 cup Homemade Mincemeat (see recipe, above)

1 egg

beaten egg, for glazing

powdered sugar, for sprinkling

Make the pastry according to the recipe, and chill.

Preheat the oven to 375°F. Assemble twelve small (individual-serving), deep pie pans, and line six of them at a time.

Roll out half of the pastry into a rectangle. Gently lift it and lay it over six pie pans. Press the pastry into the pans lightly, and roll the rolling pin over to cut the edges; gather pastry off-cuts into a ball and set aside for the pie tops. Roll out the second half of the pastry and line the other six pans. (Alternatively, cut the pastry into rounds using a cutter, and line the pie pans.)

Spoon about 2 teaspoons of mincemeat, mixed with the egg, into each pie.

Roll out the ball of off-cuts and, using a tiny star cutter, cut twelve pastry stars for each pie top. Lay a top over each pie and brush with beaten egg. Sprinkle with powdered sugar and place the pie pans onto a baking sheet.

Bake in the preheated oven for 25 minutes or until pale golden brown. Serve warm or cold.

Apricot Pie

Yield: 8 servings

12 ounces Rich Shortcrust Pastry (see recipe, page 149)

Filling:
2 pounds fresh apricots, halved and pitted, or a 1-pound 10-ounce can apricot halves

1 cup apricot jam (jelly)

rind and juice of 1 lemon

egg white, for glazing

powdered sugar, for glazing

Make the pastry according to the recipe, and chill.

Preheat the oven to 425°F. Place a baking sheet on a shelf ready for baking.

Roll out half of the pastry on a lightly floured surface and use to line a 9-inch pie plate.

Filling: Drain the apricots if using canned fruit. Place the apricot halves into the pastry shell, cover with the apricot jam, then grate the lemon rind over the top. Sprinkle with the lemon juice.

To finish the pie: Roll out the remaining pastry to a round, and cover the pie. Pinch the edges. Brush with the lightly beaten egg white, and sprinkle with the powdered sugar.

Place the pie plate on the baking sheet.

Bake for 20 to 30 minutes or until the pastry is cooked and golden brown. Serve warm, with whipped cream, custard, or ice cream.

Chocolate-Crunch Pie

Yield: 6 servings

Cookie Crust:
6 ounces cookies

½ stick butter

2 tablespoons powdered sugar

Filling:
2 tablespoons butter

3 tablespoons cornstarch

1 tablespoon powdered sugar

1½ cups milk

3 ounces dark cooking chocolate

cream, for decoration

extra chocolate for decoration

Cookie Crust
Preheat the oven to 350°F.
Crush the cookies, but not too finely (this would make the crust rather dense). Melt the butter and stir it into the crushed cookies with the sugar. Press the mixture into an 8-inch pie plate.
Bake for 10 minutes. Allow to cool.

Filling: Melt the butter in a saucepan. Blend in the cornstarch and sugar, and gradually add the milk, stirring continuously while bringing it to a boil; cook for a few minutes, then remove the saucepan from the heat.
Break the chocolate into pieces and stir into the hot milk sauce until melted. Cool a little, then pour into the prepared pie crust. Leave until set.
Whip the cream and decorate the pie top with swirls of whipped cream and grated chocolate.

Honey Yogurt Pie

Yield: 4 to 6 servings

6 ounces Shortcrust Pastry
(see recipe, page 149)

Filling:
1 cup plain yogurt

1 cup cottage cheese or farm cheese

1 teaspoon vanilla extract

1 tablespoon honey

ground cinnamon, for sprinkling

Preheat the oven to 375°F.
Make the pastry according to the recipe and use to line an 8-inch pie dish.
Bake blind for 10 minutes. Remove the blind filling and paper, and bake for another 20 minutes or until evenly golden brown. Remove from the oven and allow to cool.
Filling: Blend the yogurt, cottage cheese (or farm cheese), and vanilla in a food processor until smooth. Warm the honey by placing its jar in hot water to allow easier mixing; add 1 teaspoon of the yogurt mixture, and blend. Spoon into the prepared pie shell and refrigerate for 2 to 3 hours.
Dust with cinnamon. Serve with poached fruit, if desired.

Variations: Fold whole strawberries or sliced banana or ½ cup broken walnuts into the filling. Mix before spooning it into the pie shell.

Latticed Pumpkin Pie

Yield: 6 to 8 servings

8 ounces Rich Shortcrust Pastry
(see recipe, page 149)

Filling:
1 pound pumpkin

pinch of salt

¾ cup brown sugar

½ cup raisins

1 teaspoon ground cinnamon

½ teaspoon grated nutmeg

1 tablespoon flour

grated rind and juice of 1 lemon

2 tablespoons butter

egg white, for glazing

powdered sugar, for glazing

Make the pastry according to the recipe, and chill.
Preheat the oven to 400°F.
Filling: Peel the pumpkin and remove its seeds. Cut into small cubes and place into a saucepan with water and salt. Bring to a boil and simmer for 5 minutes or until just tender. Drain well. Combine the sugar, raisins, cinnamon, nutmeg, flour, lemon rind, and lemon juice with the drained pumpkin.
To finish the pie: Roll out two-thirds of the pastry on a lightly floured surface and use to line a deep 9-inch pie plate. Spoon in the filling, and dot with the butter.
Roll the remaining pastry into a round, large enough to cover the pie; cut into strips and use to form a lattice pattern on the pie.
Brush the lattice with a little egg white and dust with powdered sugar.
Bake for 10 minutes, then reduce the heat to 350°F and bake for another 30 minutes or until the pastry is crisp and the pumpkin is cooked. Serve warm or cold, with whipped cream.

Butterscotch Meringue Pie

Yield: 6 to 8 servings

6 ounces Rich Shortcrust Pastry (see recipe, page 149)

Filling:
¾ cup soft brown sugar

¼ cup sugar

3 tablespoons cornstarch

pinch of salt

2½ cups milk

3 egg yolks, beaten

2 tablespoons butter

1 teaspoon vanilla extract

Meringue:
3 egg whites

pinch of cream of tartar

½ cup powdered sugar

Make the pastry according to the recipe, and chill.

Preheat the oven to 400°F.

Roll out the pastry on a lightly floured surface and use to line a 9-inch pie plate.

Bake blind for 10 minutes. Remove the blind filling and paper, and bake for another 10 minutes.

Set the oven temperature at 375°F.

Filling: Combine the sugars, cornstarch, and salt together in a saucepan. Gradually stir in the milk and mix until smooth. Bring to a boil, stirring constantly, and allow to simmer for 1 minute. Pour half of the mixture onto the beaten egg yolks, mix, and then pour this into the saucepan. Cook, while stirring, for a few minutes longer. Add the butter and vanilla, mix well, and pour into the pie shell.

Meringue

Beat the egg whites with a pinch of cream of tartar until stiff but not dry. Gradually add the sugar, beating well after each addition; beat until stiff peaks form.

Spread the meringue over the pie top, taking it right to the edge of the pastry.

Bake for 7 to 10 minutes or until the meringue is golden. Allow to cool before serving.

Pumpkin Pie

Yield: 6 to 8 servings

6 ounces Rich Shortcrust Pastry or Whole-Wheat Pastry (see recipes, pages 149 and 153)

Filling:
2 cups cooked or canned pumpkin

1½ cups evaporated milk or cream

¾ cup brown sugar

pinch of salt

1 teaspoon ground cinnamon

½ teaspoon ground ginger

pinch of ground nutmeg

pinch of cloves

2 eggs

Make the pastry according to the recipe, and chill.

Place all the filling ingredients into the container of a food processor and blend until smooth. Or blend together in a bowl until smooth.

Preheat the oven to 400°F.

Roll out the pastry on a lightly floured surface and use to line a 9-inch pie plate; crimp the edges. Pour the filling into the pie shell.

Bake for 10 minutes. Reduce the oven temperature to 350°F, and bake for 40 minutes or until the filling is set and the pastry is a golden color. Allow to cool. Serve with extra whipped cream and a sprinkling of nutmeg.

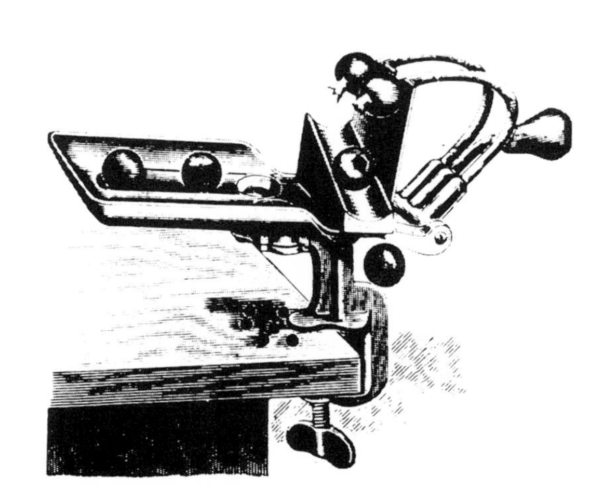

TARTS

Almond Frangipane Tarts

Yield: 12 tarts

1 quantity (8 ounces) Pâte Sucrée (see recipe, page 158)

Filling:
½ stick butter

¼ cup powdered sugar

1 large egg

½ cup ground almonds

1½ tablespoons flour, sifted

lemon juice (or vanilla extract), to flavor

½ cup flaked almonds

sieved apricot jam (jelly), to glaze

Make the pastry and chill as directed. Roll the pastry out thinly and line twelve 3-inch-round tart tins. Prick the base of each pastry case with a fine fork.

Preheat the oven to 375°F.

Cream the butter and sugar together until light and fluffy. Beat the egg in well. Stir in the ground almonds and flour, then flavor to taste with either lemon juice or vanilla.

Divide the filling between the pastry cases and spread smooth. Sprinkle the flaked almonds on top. Stand the tart tins on a baking sheet.

Bake near the top of the preheated oven for 10 to 15 minutes or until firm and golden.

Have the apricot-jam glaze ready and hot, and, as soon as the tarts come out of the oven, remove them from the tins and brush the tops generously with the apricot glaze.

Strawberry-Cream Tarts

Yield: 12 tarts

¾ quantity (6 ounces) Rich Shortcrust Pastry (see recipe, page 149)

Filling:
6 ounces packaged cream cheese

¼ cup powdered sugar

1 teaspoon kirsch

8 ounces small strawberries

½ cup red-currant jelly

Make the pastry according to the recipe, and chill well.

Preheat the oven to 400°F.

Roll the dough out thinly and line twelve 2½-inch tart tins. Prick the base of each pastry case; place the tins on a baking sheet.

Bake near the top of the oven for 10 to 12 minutes or until cooked. Allow to cool on wire racks.

Filling: Mix the cream cheese, sugar, and kirsch with an electric mixer or in a food processor. Hull the strawberries, and halve or quarter them if large.

To finish the tarts: Place 1 heaped teaspoon of filling in each cold tart case, then top neatly with strawberries.

Heat the red-currant jelly until melted in a saucepan or microwave oven; brush it over the berries and filling, then allow to set.

Strawberry Rhubarb Tarts

Yield: 12 tarts

1 quantity (8 ounces) Pâte Sucrée or Brisée (see recipe, page 158)

Filling:
1 pound ripe pink rhubarb

½ cup sugar

2 tablespoons cold water

1 cup red-currant jelly

1 tablespoon kirsch

1 pound strawberries

confectioners' sugar, for decoration

Roll the pastry out thinly and line twelve boat-shaped tart tins arranged close together. Prick the base of each pastry case and chill for 20 to 30 minutes.

Preheat the oven to 400°F.

Bake blind near the top of the oven for 10 minutes. Remove the blind filling and bake for another 5 minutes or until golden and cooked. Allow to cool on wire racks.

Trim and wash the rhubarb stems, and cut them into ⅜-inch pieces. Place the rhubarb, sugar, and water into a stainless-steel or enamel-lined pan, bring to a boil, then simmer uncovered for 30 minutes, stirring occasionally, to form a thick puree. Cool, then chill until required.

Melt the red-currant jelly with the kirsch, then bring to a boil and simmer for 1 minute.

Hull and slice the strawberries.

To finish the tarts: Brush the pastry cases with red-currant glaze. Spread 2 tablespoons of rhubarb puree into each tart, top neatly with strawberry slices, then brush with more red-currant glaze. Sift with powdered sugar before serving. Serve with whipped cream.

Ricotta Tarts

Yield: 12 tarts

¾ quantity (6 ounces) Sweet Shortcrust Pastry or Pâte Sucrée (see recipes, pages 150 and 158)

Filling:
1 pound fresh ricotta cheese

1 tablespoon cream

½ cup powdered sugar

¼ cup mixed peel or chopped crystallized fruit

2 ounces dark baking chocolate, grated

1 tablespoon Grand Marnier

Roll the pastry out thinly and line twelve tart tins. Prick the base of each pastry case, then chill for 10 to 15 minutes.

Preheat the oven to 425°F.

Bake the tart cases in the middle of the oven for 8 to 10 minutes or until golden and cooked. Allow to cool on wire racks.

Filling: Mix the ricotta cheese with the cream and sugar until well combined, then fold in the mixed peel or crystallized fruit, grated chocolate, and Grand Marnier. Spoon the filling mixture into the pastry cases just before serving.

Lemon Chess Tarts

Yield: 4 tarts

¾ quantity (6 ounces) Pâte Sucrée (see recipe, page 158)

Filling:
2 large eggs

4 tablespoons melted unsalted butter

¾ cup powdered sugar

2 tablespoons lemon juice

2 tablespoons cornmeal

2 teaspoons finely grated lemon rind

Roll the pastry out thinly and line four 3-inch tart tins. Prick the base of each pastry case, and chill while preparing the filling.

Filling: Beat the eggs lightly in a bowl. Add the remaining ingredients, and mix until well combined.

To finish the tarts: Preheat the oven to 300°F.

Divide the filling between the pastry cases and spread smooth.

Bake in the middle of the oven for 20 to 30 minutes, until the filling is bubbling and the pastry is cooked. Allow to cool on wire racks (the filling will firm on cooling). Serve with whipped cream and strawberry puree.

Fruit Tarts

Yield: 12 tarts

1 quantity (8 ounces) Pâte Sucrée or Brisée (see recipes, page 158)

Filling:
1 cup Vanilla Pastry Cream (see recipe, page 118)

2 teaspoons brandy or liqueur (optional)

assorted fresh fruit, such as sliced apricots, sliced banana dipped in lemon juice, blueberries, black currants, blackberries, pitted cherries, sliced kiwi fruit, seedless skinned grapes, ripe gooseberries, melon balls, mandarin and orange segments, sliced plums or peaches, raspberries, red currants, sliced strawberries

½ cup apricot jam (jelly)

1 tablespoon water, brandy, liqueur, or orange juice

Roll the pastry out thinly on a lightly floured surface to a rectangle. Arrange twelve 3-inch tart tins close together in rows, three by four. Drape the pastry loosely over the tins, allowing it to fall generously into each one, and press in with the fingers if necessary. Then roll over the top edge of the tins with the rolling pin to cut off the excess pastry. Press the pastry firmly into each tin with the tops of bent fingers, shaping to an even thickness around the sides. Prick the base of each pastry case with a fine fork, then chill for 20 to 30 minutes.

Preheat the oven to 400°F.

Line the pastry cases with greaseproof paper and baking beans or identical tins.

Bake blind near the top of the oven for 10 minutes. Then remove the paper and beans or tins, and bake for another 5 minutes or until golden and cooked. Allow to cool on wire racks.

Filling: Mix the Vanilla Pastry Cream with the brandy. Prepare the fruit accordingly. Heat the jam; then strain, and stir in the water.

To finish the tarts: Brush each pastry case with apricot glaze. Place 1 tablespoon of the Vanilla Pastry Cream mixture into each pastry case, and top neatly with an attractive arrangement of prepared fresh fruit. Brush the fruit carefully with apricot glaze, making sure that the glaze seals to the edge of the pastry. Serve for afternoon tea or with whipped cream for dessert.

Right: **Fruit Tarts (see above).**

Savory
Pies

The History of the Pie

Throughout history, foods have been encased in pastry of a kind. There is written evidence to suggest that this practice existed in Roman times. Pastries then were very crude and probably were meant to be discarded, rather than eaten. Presumably this was a refinement of the previously employed method of encasing food in a clay and water "dough" that retained the juices during cooking. This shell was then broken open and discarded when the food was cooked.

It is thought that Australian aborigines used this technique to cook small animals such as echidnas and lizards; so, though the cooking medium was new to the Romans, the technique itself probably goes back into the culinary history of primitive cultures.

If one believes the history books—both culinary and academic—it was England that turned the baking of pies into an art form. From the king's banquet table to the humblest cottage, the pie has its place in history.

And think how many expressions relating to pies have crept into our language—"a finger in every pie," "promises like pie crusts," "pie in the sky," "eating humble pie" to name just a few. Incidentally, the "humble pie" expression actually refers to Umble Pie, a pie made from the offal and entrails of game meat and birds. The superior flesh of the game was used in the pies served at the nobleman's table and the rejected portions in the pies eaten by his servants.

To define a pie is not easy. How about a Shepherd's Pie? There is not a scrap of pastry in sight. And what about the Italian pizza? That's another version of a pie!

Nowadays we include a great diversity of pastries under the generic term "pie." Flans, savory tarts, and quiche are all accepted in this category. Fortunately, we no longer refer to "coffins," an early term for pie shells.

In this chapter we will explore the realms of both prosaic and exotic pies. We will encounter the Cornish pastie—originally developed as a convenient lunchtime meal for a miner to carry to work in his pocket. We will also meet the Greek spinach pie, layered in its wafer-thin leaves of filo pastry.

Chicken and Asparagus Pie

Yield: 4 to 6 servings

1 quantity Rich Shortcrust Pastry (see recipe, page 149)

2 chicken breasts

salt and peppercorns

sprig of thyme

sprig of parsley

small can of green asparagus, drained

1½ cups sour cream

2 eggs

Roll out the pastry to line a 9-inch pie pan. Trim the edges, and refrigerate until ready to use.

Place the chicken breasts into a small saucepan with a little salt, a few peppercorns, and sprigs of thyme and parsley; add sufficient water to cover. Cover the saucepan and cook gently until the chicken is tender.

Preheat the oven to 375°F.

Finely chop the chicken meat. (Reserve the stock for soups, etc.) Sprinkle the diced chicken over the base of the pie crust. Cover with the well-drained asparagus pieces.

Lightly beat together the sour cream, eggs, and (if necessary) salt and pepper. Pour very carefully into the pie crust.

Bake in the preheated oven for 10 minutes, then reduce the oven temperature to 325°F and continue baking for another 25 to 30 minutes or until the custard is set. Serve warm.

Chicken and Parsley Pie

Yield: 6 servings

6 chicken breasts, skinned and trimmed

salt and peppercorns

sprig of thyme

sprig of parsley

2 tablespoons butter

6 shallots (or spring onions), finely chopped

4 ounces button mushrooms, sliced

1 cup finely chopped parsley

salt and pepper

2 tablespoons whole-wheat flour

3 hard-boiled eggs, sliced

1 quantity Puff Pastry (see recipe, page 154)

egg white, for glazing

Place the chicken breasts into a saucepan with a little salt, a few peppercorns, and sprigs of thyme and parsley; add sufficient water to cover. Cover the saucepan and cook gently for about 30 minutes.

Preheat the oven to 400°F.

Strain off and reserve the chicken stock. Dice the chicken meat.

Heat the butter in a frying pan, add the shallots, mushrooms, parsley, and salt and pepper, and sauté for 5 minutes. Stir in the flour and cook for a few minutes. Pour in ½ cup of chicken stock and continue whisking until the mixture has thickened. Mix in the chicken meat and adjust the seasonings.

Place half of the mixture in the base of a deep pie dish. Arrange the sliced eggs on top, then cover with the remainder of the chicken mixture. Cover with the rolled Puff Pastry. Crimp around the edges and cut three or four vents in the pastry. Cut remnants of pastry into leaf shapes and arrange on top. Brush lightly with a little beaten egg white.

Bake in the preheated oven for 15 minutes, then reduce the oven temperature to 325°F and continue baking for about 30 minutes. Serve hot.

If desired, 2 strips of fried bacon can be crumbled and added to the filling.

Carrot Pie

Yield: 4 to 5 servings

1 quantity Whole-Wheat Pastry (see recipe, page 153)

Filling:
1 pound young carrots, cooked and mashed

2 egg yolks

⅓ cup table cream

4 tablespoons grated sharp cheese

3 tablespoons finely chopped chives (or onion greens)

½ teaspoon finely chopped fresh rosemary

salt and pepper

Preheat the oven to 300°F.

Make the pastry according to the recipe. Roll it out and use it to line an 8-inch pie pan.

Bake blind for 20 minutes.

Turn the oven up to 350°F.

Filling: When the carrots have been cooked and mashed, beat in the egg yolks, cream, cheese, chives, rosemary, salt, and pepper. Spoon the mixture into the pie crust.

Bake for about 30 minutes or until the filling is firm. Serve warm, with a green salad.

Quiche with Olives

Yield: 6 servings

9-inch shortcrust pie shell, partially cooked and cooled

Filling:
1½ cups light cream

½ cup buttermilk

4 eggs, lightly beaten

4 ounces bacon, grilled and crumbled

4 ounces Edam cheese, grated

8 spring onions, finely chopped

4 ounces black or green olives, pitted and slivered

Partially bake the pastry shell.

Preheat the oven to 375°F.

Filling: Beat together the cream, buttermilk, and eggs. Fold in the bacon, cheese, onions, and olives, and pour into the partially baked pastry shell.

Bake for about 35 minutes or until the custard is golden and lightly set. Serve warm or cold.

Whole-Wheat Pizza

Yield: 6 servings

Dough:
1 cake fresh yeast or 1 package active dry yeast
2 teaspoons molasses or honey
1 cup lukewarm water
2 cups all-purpose white flour
2 cups whole-wheat flour
pinch of salt
1 tablespoon soft margarine
Topping:
1 can (1 pound 14 ounces) tomatoes
2 white onions, finely chopped
½ clove garlic, crushed
1 teaspoon brown sugar
½ teaspoon dried basil or 1 teaspoon fresh chopped basil
½ teaspoon oregano or 1 teaspoon fresh chopped oregano
salt and pepper
½ cup cooked soy beans
1 tablespoon oil, for brushing
6 ounces sharp cheese, grated
4 ounces mushrooms, sliced
6 green or black olives, pitted and slivered
4 ounces mozzarella cheese, sliced

In a medium-sized bowl, blend together the yeast and molasses or honey. Stir in the warm water, and leave in a warm place until the mixture froths.

In a large bowl, combine the flours and salt. Rub in the margarine. Make a well in the center, and pour in the yeast liquid, stirring until mixed. Tip the dough onto a lightly floured board and knead for 5 minutes. Return it to the bowl, cover with a tea towel, and leave it to rise until it doubles in size.

Preheat the oven to 400°F.

While the dough is rising, prepare the filling. Chop the tomatoes and spoon them into a saucepan with the liquid from the can. Add the onions, garlic, sugar, herbs, salt, and pepper, and simmer gently until the mixture thickens. Stir in the soy beans.

Punch the dough down with your fist, and roll it to fit a lightly greased pizza pan. Prick the surface in several places, then brush with the oil. Sprinkle the pizza dough with the grated cheese, then spoon the tomato mixture over it, spreading evenly. Arrange the mushroom slices and slivered olives, then arrange the sliced mozzarella cheese in a circle on top.

Bake for about 30 minutes.

Hearty Whole-Wheat Vegetarian Pie

Yield: 6 to 8 servings

Double quantity Whole-Wheat Pastry (see recipe, page 153)
First Layer:
½ cup cooked brown rice
4 spring onions or shallots, chopped
2 tablespoons plain yogurt
2 tablespoons grated Parmesan cheese
2 tablespoons chopped parsley
freshly ground pepper
Second Layer:
8 ounces ricotta cheese
1 cup cooked and chopped spinach
3 tablespoons grated Parmesan cheese
salt and pepper

Preheat the oven to 350°F. Roll out two-thirds of the pastry and line a 9 × 8-inch pie dish.

Mix together all the ingredients for the first layer, and spoon into the pastry shell.

Cream the ricotta cheese. Stir in the spinach, Parmesan cheese, salt, and pepper. Spread over the rice layer. (A little grated cheddar cheese may be added for extra flavor and nutrition.)

Roll out the remainder of the pastry and place it on top of the filling. Pinch the pastry edges together and cut a few vents in the top crust. (If desired, brush the surface with a little milk and add a sprinkle of Parmesan cheese.)

Bake for about 50 minutes. Remove from the oven and cut into squares for serving. This is a delicious "pie" to serve as part of a buffet and, provided it is not overcooked initially, it reheats quite well.

Right: **From top: Whole-Wheat Pizza (see left); Hearty Whole-Wheat Vegetarian Pie (see above); Whole-Wheat Onion Pie (see p. 236).**

Cheese and Mushroom Potato Pie

Yield: 6 servings

Pastry:
½ stick butter, softened

1 cup flour

1 cup warm mashed potatoes

2 tablespoons finely chopped parsley

salt and pepper

Filling:
3 eggs

½ cup reduced cream or evaporated milk

3 ounces sharp cheese, grated

1 teaspoon dried mixed herbs or 3 teaspoons fresh chopped herbs

salt and pepper

3 ounces button mushrooms, sliced

2 tomatoes, sliced

Preheat the oven to 375°F.

To make the pastry, rub the butter into the flour, then work in the mashed potatoes, parsley, salt, and pepper. Roll out thinly and line an 8-inch pie pan. Reserve any pastry scraps.

Filling: Beat the eggs and cream together, then stir in the cheese, herbs, salt, and pepper. Pour or spoon the mixture into the pie crust. Arrange the sliced mushrooms and tomatoes over the egg–cream mixture.

Roll out the reserved pastry scraps, cut into thin strips, and arrange decoratively over the top of the filling.

Bake on a lower shelf in the oven for 35 to 45 minutes or until the filling has set and the pastry is a golden brown. Serve warm or cold.

Corn and Cheese Pie

Yield: 6 servings

1 quantity Shortcrust Pastry (see recipe, page 149)

Filling:
1 cup sweet corn (fresh, frozen, or canned)

1 cup table cream

¾ cup milk

2 eggs

4 ounces sharp cheese, grated

2 strips bacon, crumbled

½ teaspoon Dijon mustard

2 tablespoons finely chopped parsley

salt and pepper

Make the pastry according to the recipe. Roll it out and use it to line a deep 8-inch pie pan.

If using fresh corn, cook it lightly and then drain. Allow frozen corn to thaw. Or, if using canned corn, drain it well.

Filling: Preheat the oven to 350°F.

Place the cup of corn into a large bowl. Lightly mix together the cream, milk, and eggs, and add to the corn. Add the cheese, bacon, mustard, parsley, salt, and pepper, and mix in. Spoon the mixture into the pie crust.

Bake for about 45 minutes.

(If preferred, use ½ cup of cream, 1¼ cups of milk and an extra egg.)

Whole-Wheat Onion Pie

Yield: 6 servings

1 quantity Whole-Wheat Pastry (see recipe, page 153)

Filling:
½ stick butter

8 ounces white onions, sliced

½ cup milk

½ cup cream

3 eggs

3 ounces sharp cheese, grated

salt and pepper

6 ounces mozzarella cheese

Make the pastry according to the recipe. Roll it out thinly and line an 8- or 9-inch pie pan.

Preheat the oven to 350°F.

Filling: Melt the butter and sauté the onions until soft and golden. Beat together the milk, cream, and eggs; stir in the grated cheese, salt, and pepper. Combine with the onions, then spoon the mixture into the pie crust. Thinly slice the mozzarella cheese, and arrange it gently on top of the onion filling.

Bake for about 45 minutes. If the filling is firm and golden after this time, remove the pie from the oven; otherwise continue cooking for a little longer. Serve hot or cold.

Potato Galette with Savory Layer

Yield: 6 servings

1½ pounds potatoes

4 tablespoons grated sharp cheese

2 tablespoons butter

2 tablespoons milk

1 teaspoon English mustard powder

salt and pepper

Savory Layer:

8 ounces small mushrooms, sliced

1 tablespoon butter

4 lean strips of bacon, fried

2 stalks celery, chopped

1 medium-sized onion, chopped

2 tablespoons chopped parsley

1 teaspoon chopped fresh herbs or ½ teaspoon dried herbs

2 tablespoons melted butter

parsley sprigs, for garnish

Preheat the oven to 400°F.

Peel and cube the potatoes, and cook them in salted water until tender. Mash while still hot, and beat in the cheese, butter, milk, mustard, salt, and pepper.

Savory layer: While the potatoes are cooking, prepare the savory layer. Sauté the mushrooms in butter; add the bacon, celery, onion, parsley, and herbs. Sauté until the vegetables are tender.

To finish the pie: Line a greased pie dish or cake pan with half of the hot mashed potatoes. Spoon the savory-layer mixture over the top. Then cover with the remainder of the potatoes. Roughen the surface with a fork, and brush generously with the melted butter.

Bake for about 35 minutes or until the top is golden brown. Serve hot, garnished with sprigs of parsley.

Cheese and Spinach Pie

Yield: 6 to 8 servings

8-ounce bunch of spinach

1 tablespoon butter

2 medium onions, chopped

½ clove garlic, crushed

6 ounces cream cheese

6 ounces feta cheese

4 ounces sharp cheese

1 tablespoon chopped parsley

2 tablespoons chopped fresh dill or ¾ teaspoon dried dill

3 eggs, lightly beaten

good pinch of ground nutmeg

salt and pepper

16 sheets filo pastry

1¼ sticks butter, melted

Wash the spinach well, remove coarse stems, shred or coarsely chop the green leaves, and drain well in a colander.

Preheat the oven to 325°F.

Melt 1 tablespoon butter in a frying pan, and sauté the onions and garlic until golden. Combine the onions–garlic and chopped spinach in a large bowl.

In another bowl, mash the cream cheese, grate the feta cheese and sharp cheese, and mix in the parsley and dill. Stir this cheese mixture into the spinach and onion. Add the lightly beaten eggs, nutmeg, salt, and pepper, and blend thoroughly.

Place a sheet of filo pastry into a greased baking dish; brush with melted butter. Repeat with another seven sheets of the pastry, brushing each one with the butter. Spread the spinach and cheese mixture evenly onto the top layer of pastry. Cover with another eight layers of pastry, brushing between each with the melted butter. Using a sharp knife, trim off excess pastry around the edges of the baking dish, and slightly score the top layer of the pastry—this ensures a crisp and flaky topping.

Bake for about 50 minutes, or until golden brown.

Pumpkin Pasties

Yield: 6 servings

1 quantity Shortcrust Pastry (see recipe, page 149)

egg wash (1 egg with 2 tablespoons cream), for glazing

2 tablespoons sesame seeds, for sprinkling

Filling:

2 tablespoons butter or margarine

1 white onion, grated or finely chopped

1 cup finely shredded cabbage

1 cup frozen peas

½ teaspoon mixed dried herbs or thyme

4 ounces pumpkin, grated

4 ounces sharp cheese, grated

1 tablespoon finely chopped parsley

salt and pepper

Preheat the oven to 400°F.

Make the pastry, roll it out thinly, and cut into six saucer-sized rounds.

Filling: Melt the butter or margarine in a saucepan, add the onion, cabbage, peas, and herbs, and sauté for 5 minutes. Remove from the heat and stir in the pumpkin, cheese, parsley, salt, and pepper.

Place equal portions of the filling onto the center of each pastry round. Dampen the outside edges of the pastry and bring them together over the filling, crimping the joined edges into a frill. Place onto a greased baking sheet, brush over each pastie with the egg glaze, and sprinkle with a few sesame seeds.

Bake in the preheated oven for 8 to 10 minutes, then reduce the oven temperature to 350°F and continue baking for another 25 to 30 minutes. Serve hot or cold.

Savory Pumpkin Pie

Yield: 6 to 8 servings

Pastry:

1 stick butter or margarine, softened

2 tablespoons hot water

2 cups whole-wheat self-rising flour

pinch of salt

3 tablespoons crushed nuts

Filling:

1½ cups cooked dry pumpkin

2 eggs, separated

⅔ cup sour cream

⅔ cup milk

½ teaspoon ground ginger

salt and pepper

3 ounces sharp cheese, grated

6 spring onions, finely chopped

2 teaspoons finely grated lemon peel

2 teaspoons Worcestershire sauce

½ teaspoon dried mustard

1 tablespoon finely chopped parsley

Preheat the oven to 325°F.

Place the butter in a bowl, pour on the hot water, and mash well with a fork. Add the flour and salt, add the nuts, and work together until it is a soft dough. Allow to firm up in the refrigerator if necessary. Roll out and line (or press into) a 9-inch pie dish. Prick the base of the pastry well with a fork.

Bake blind for 10 to 15 minutes. Remove the blind filling and allow to cool.

Preheat the oven to 425°F.

Filling: Mash the pumpkin, and beat in the egg yolks, cream, milk, ginger, salt, and pepper. Stir in the cheese, chopped spring onions, lemon peel, Worcestershire sauce, dried mustard, and parsley. Beat the egg whites and fold into the mixture. Pour into the cold pie crust.

Bake for 15 minutes, then reduce the temperature to 325°F and continue baking for another 35 minutes. Serve warm, with a crisp green salad.

Right: **Savory Pumpkin Pie (see above).**

Onion and Edam-Cheese Pie

Yield: 6 servings

1 quantity Shortcrust Pastry (see recipe, page 149)

Filling:
8 ounces Edam cheese, grated

2 tablespoons flour

1 tablespoon butter

1 large onion, finely sliced

4 eggs

1 cup cream

1 cup milk

¼ teaspoon grated nutmeg

drops of Tabasco sauce

salt and freshly ground pepper

Preheat the oven to 300°F.

Make the pastry and use it to line a 9-inch pie pan. Bake blind for 20 minutes. Remove the blind filling.

Set the oven temperature at 400°F.

Filling: Mix the cheese and flour together, and sprinkle into the pie crust. Heat the butter in a pan and sauté the onion until it is transparent; arrange over the cheese–flour. Beat the eggs lightly and add the cream, milk, nutmeg, Tabasco sauce, and salt and pepper to taste; pour the mixture carefully over the onion.

Bake for 30 to 35 minutes or until the filling is set and the top is golden brown. Serve hot or cold.

Vegetable Pie

Yield: 6 to 8 servings

1 pound potatoes

1 small cauliflower

1 small bunch of celery, finely sliced

1 small parsnip, chopped

1 white onion, sliced

1 carrot, chopped

3 tablespoons finely chopped parsley

freshly ground pepper

Sauce:
2 tablespoons butter

1 tablespoon flour

1¼ cups milk

3 tablespoons grated cheese

salt and pepper

Prepare the potatoes and boil them in lightly salted water until tender. Break the cauliflower into small florets and boil in lightly salted water until tender. Combine the celery, parsnip, onion, and carrot in a saucepan, cover with salted water, and simmer until tender.

Preheat the oven to 350°F.

Drain the potatoes and mash them with a little milk until quite smooth. Line a buttered casserole with two-thirds of the potato mixture.

Drain the cauliflower well. Drain the other vegetables (save the stock to use in soups). Combine the vegetables with the parsley and pepper, and spoon half of the quantity into the potato-lined casserole.

Sauce: Melt the butter in a small saucepan, add the flour, and cook for 3 minutes, stirring with a wooden spoon. Add the milk, and whisk constantly until the sauce thickens. Remove from the heat, stir in the cheese, and add salt and pepper to taste.

Pour half of the sauce over the vegetables in the potato case, add the remainder of the vegetables, and top with the rest of the sauce. Cover with the remaining potatoes.

Bake for 40 minutes or until golden brown.

Economical Steak and Kidney Pie

Yield: 6 servings

2 pounds chuck steak
2 sheep kidneys
1 tablespoon flour
salt and pepper
2 tablespoons oil
1 medium-sized onion, chopped
½ cup stock
2 teaspoons flour
2 teaspoons butter
1 quantity Puff Pastry (see recipe, page 154)
beaten egg, for glazing

Cut the meat into small cubes. Discard the skin and tubes from the kidney and dice it. Toss the meat and kidney in the flour mixed with the salt and pepper. Heat the oil and sauté the onion until golden. Add the meat and kidney, and cook until browned. Transfer the onions and meats to a small saucepan, add the stock, cover the saucepan and simmer gently for 1½ hours or until the meat is tender.

Preheat the oven to 475°F.

Blend together 2 teaspoons of flour and 2 teaspoons of butter, and drop this into the simmering liquid in tiny pieces, stirring constantly until the liquid thickens. Spoon the meat and liquid into a pie dish.

Roll out the pastry and use it to cover the pie dish. Trim the edges to the shape of the dish. Cut several steam vents in the pastry surface and garnish with shapes cut from pastry scraps. Brush with the beaten egg.

Bake in the preheated oven for 20 minutes, then reduce the oven temperature to 350°F and bake for another 40 minutes or until the crust is crisp and golden.

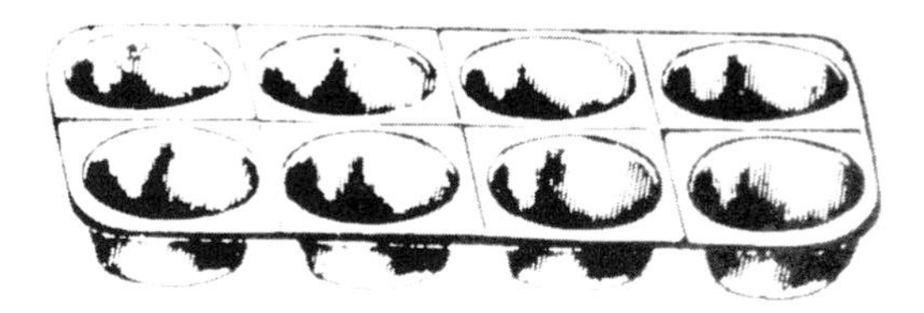

Tarte à l'Ancienne

Yield: 6 servings

Filling:
8 ounces veal steak
8 ounces pork fillet
2 beef kidneys
1 ounce pork fat, finely chopped
½ teaspoon mixed dried herbs
generous pinch of ground nutmeg
salt and freshly ground black pepper
1 marrow bone, about 4 inches long
1 egg
1 egg yolk
½ cup dry white wine
1 pound Puff Pastry (see recipe, page 154)
egg white or water, for sealing
egg white or milk, for glazing
Béchamel Sauce (see below)
3 tablespoons butter
¼ cup flour
½ cup milk

Preheat the oven to 325°F.

Filling: Mince (grind) the veal, pork, and kidneys together, and combine with the pork fat, herbs, nutmeg, salt, and pepper. Scoop out the marrow from the bone, and add to the meat mixture. Beat the egg and egg yolk together, and add to the meat mixture, together with the wine and Béchamel Sauce. Blend thoroughly.

Roll out the pastry into two rounds, one about 12 inches in diameter, and the other about 10 inches. Place the smaller round on a greased baking sheet. Pile the filling in a dome shape on it, leaving a 1-inch border of pastry uncovered. Brush the border with a little egg white or water. Place the second pastry round over the filling and press the edges firmly together. Pinch into a frill around the edges. Using a sharp knife, lightly cut a crisscross pattern into the pastry. Make a small hole in the center of the dome and insert a small foil cylinder (made by rolling a piece of foil around a wooden spoon handle). Brush the pie with the beaten egg white or milk.

Bake for about 1 hour.

Béchamel Sauce

Melt the butter in a saucepan, add the flour, and cook for several minutes, stirring constantly. Remove from the heat, and add the milk. Return to the heat and stir constantly until the mixture boils and thickens.

Pizza Siciliano

Yield: 4 to 6 servings

Dough:
¾ cup all-purpose white flour
¾ cup self-rising flour
½ teaspoon dry mustard
salt and cayenne pepper
½ stick butter or margarine
1 egg
3 tablespoons milk
1 tablespoon oil
Topping:
1 tablespoon oil
8 ounces ground steak or ham
1 white onion, chopped
½ clove garlic, crushed
3 medium-sized tomatoes, peeled and chopped
4 ounces sharp cheese, grated
1 tablespoon chopped parsley

Preheat the oven to 375°F.

To make the dough: Sift together the flours, mustard, salt, and cayenne. Rub in the butter or margarine. Beat together the egg and milk, add to the dry ingredients, and stir in. Mix to a firm dough. Knead lightly only until the dough is smooth. Roll it out to ⅛ inch thick and place onto a greased pizza tray. Brush liberally with the oil.

Topping: Heat the oil in a large pan, add the minced steak, onion, and garlic. Sauté until the meat changes color and the onion is tender. Spoon the mixture into a bowl and allow to cool.

Add the remaining ingredients to the mixture, mix well, and spread onto the pizza crust.

Bake for about 30 minutes. Cut into wedges. Serve hot.

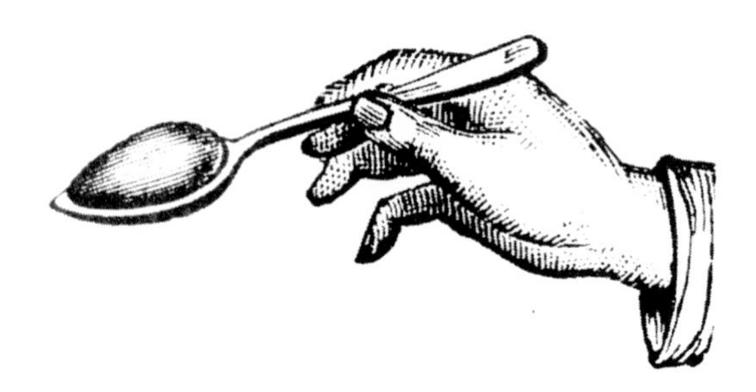

Pissaladière

Yield: 6 to 8 servings

Pastry:
1½ cups flour
pinch of salt
¾ stick butter
about 2 tablespoons water
Topping:
2 tablespoons olive oil
2 medium-sized white onions, thinly sliced
freshly ground pepper
3 tablespoons freshly grated Parmesan cheese
5 large tomatoes, peeled and chopped
1 tablespoon tomato paste
8 anchovy fillets
8 black olives, pitted and halved

Pastry: Sift the flour and salt into a bowl and rub in the butter. Add enough water to make a firm dough; knead lightly. Roll on a lightly floured board and place onto a greased pizza tray. Pinch the edges to form a decorative border and prick the base all over with a fork. Refrigerate for 1 hour.

Preheat the oven to 350°F. Bake for 15 minutes, then remove the pastry from the oven but leave the oven on.

Topping: Heat the olive oil in a frying pan, and sauté the onions for about 10 minutes or until tender. Remove from the pan, allow to cool slightly, then arrange them on the pastry. Sprinkle with the pepper and grated Parmesan cheese.

Place the chopped tomatoes and tomato paste into the frying pan; cook for about 10 minutes or until the moisture has evaporated. Spoon the tomato over the cheese and sprinkle with a little more pepper. Arrange the anchovies in a lattice design on top of the tomatoes and place half an olive in each diamond.

Bake in the preheated oven for 10 minutes. Serve hot, with a green salad.

Note: If the anchovies are very salty, soak them for an hour or so in milk. Pat dry before using. (Your cat will be in a state of ecstasy if you give it the anchovy-flavored milk.)

Right: **Pizza Siciliano (see above left); Pissaladière (see above).**

Traditional Cornish Pasties

Yield: 6 pasties

1 pound Shortcrust Pastry (see recipe, page 149)

1 pound steak, finely chopped

4 ounces kidney, finely chopped

8 ounces mixed, diced potatoes, turnips, onions, and carrot

salt and pepper

beaten egg, for glazing

Prepare the pastry according to the recipe, and chill.

Preheat the oven to 375°F. Grease a baking sheet.

Chop the meats and vegetables, and mix with the salt and pepper. Roll out the pastry and cut six saucer-sized circles. Place a portion of the filling mixture onto the center of each round. Dampen the outside edges of the pastry and bring them together over the filling, crimping the joined edges into a decorative frill. Place onto the baking sheet. Prick each pastie several times with a fork and glaze with the beaten egg.

Bake in the preheated oven for about 15 minutes, then reduce the oven temperature to 325°F and continue baking for another 40 minutes. Serve hot or cold.

Homestead Pasties

Yield: 8 pasties

1½ pounds Shortcrust Pastry (see recipe, page 149)

1½ pounds ripe tomatoes

1½ pounds sausage meat

salt and pepper

1 tablespoon chopped parsley

½ teaspoon mixed dried herbs or 1½ teaspoons fresh chopped herbs

Prepare the pastry according to the recipe, and chill.

Preheat the oven to 400°F.

Pour boiling water over the tomatoes, remove their skins, and cut into slices. Roll out the pastry and cut into eight rounds. Spread a portion of the sausage meat onto half of each pastry round, then place a slice of tomato on each. Sprinkle with salt, pepper, and herbs. Fold the pastry over the filling, moisten the edges, and press together. Place the pasties on a baking sheet.

Bake for about 25 minutes.

The pasties can be glazed with a little milk (at room temperature) before cooking.

Sausages in Cream-Cheese Pastry

Yield: 10 servings

2½ cups flour

8 ounces cream cheese

2 sticks butter, softened

¼ cup cream

salt

10 pork sausages

1 cup dry white wine

1 cup water

2 teaspoons Dijon mustard

egg yolk beaten with water, or milk, for glazing

Place the flour in a bowl, add the chopped cream cheese, butter, cream, and salt. Using the fingertips, lightly work into a paste by blending the cream cheese, cream, and butter into the flour. When the dough is smooth, wrap it in plastic and refrigerate.

Place the sausages in a heavy saucepan with the wine and water, and simmer gently for approximately 20 minutes or until the sausages are cooked. Drain the sausages and remove their skins; allow to cool.

Preheat the oven to 450°F.

On a lightly floured board, roll out the dough to ¼ inch thick, and cut into 10 rectangles, each large enough to encase a sausage. Place a sausage on each pastry portion; spread each with mustard. Wrap the pastry around each sausage and press the pastry edges together. Brush with egg glaze or milk, and prick the pastry with a fork. Arrange the sausage rolls on a lightly buttered baking sheet.

Bake in the preheated oven for 10 minutes, then reduce the oven temperature to 350°F and cook for another 20 minutes or until the pastry is golden brown.

Cheesy Tuna Puffs

Yield: 12 puffs

Choux Pastry:
½ cup self-rising flour

pinch of salt

½ cup water

½ stick butter

2 eggs

Filling:
1 15-ounce can tuna, drained

1½ ounces sharp cheese, grated

1 cup chopped celery

2 spring onions, finely chopped

½ small red pepper, finely chopped

½ cup mayonnaise

2 tablespoons finely chopped parsley

salt and pepper

Preheat the oven to 425°F. Lightly grease a baking sheet.

Choux Pastry: To make the pastry, sift the flour and salt onto a piece of paper. Combine the water and butter in a saucepan, bring to a rapid boil, and pour all the flour into the boiling liquid. Cook for a couple of minutes, stirring constantly until the mixture leaves the sides of the saucepan. Transfer the mixture to a bowl and allow to cool to lukewarm, then beat in the eggs.

Beat the eggs into the mixture, one at a time; beat until it is smooth and shiny. Spoon twelve rounds onto the baking sheet.

Bake for 20 minutes, then reduce the oven temperature to 375°F, and bake for another 10 minutes. Remove from the oven and prick the bottom of each puff so that steam can escape. Allow to cool on wire racks.

Filling: Drain and flake the tuna, and combine with all the other ingredients. Split the puffs when cool, fill with the tuna mixture, and serve. (If preferred, heat the pastry shells; gently heat the filling in a small saucepan and spoon into the split heated shells.)

Salmon and Mushroom Pie

Yield: 4 to 6 servings

Filling:
8 ounces mushrooms, sliced

⅔ cup milk

2 tablespoons butter

¼ cup flour

1½ cups table cream

salt and black pepper

½ teaspoon dried dill tips or 1½ teaspoons fresh chopped dill

grated rind of ½ lemon

1 15-ounce can salmon (or tuna), drained and flaked

1 quantity Shortcrust Pastry (see recipe, page 149)

Preheat the oven to 400°F.

Simmer the mushrooms in the milk, then drain, and retain the milk.

Filling: Melt the butter in a heavy saucepan, add the flour, and cook over moderate heat for 3 to 4 minutes, stirring with a wooden spoon. Pour in the milk from the mushrooms. Add the cream, salt, pepper, and dill, and whisk until the sauce is smooth and thick. Add the lemon rind.

Combine the mushrooms and salmon in a large bowl, blend in the white sauce, and spoon the mixture into a pie dish. Roll out the pastry and place it over the filling. Press the pastry firmly onto the edges of the pie dish and cut several vents in the pastry top.

Bake for about 40 minutes. Garnish with lemon wedges. Serve with a green salad.

Potato-Topped Fish Pie

Yield: 4 servings

8 ounces whitefish fillets
2 cups milk
6 scallops
3 tablespoons butter
1 heaped tablespoon flour
6 ounces mushrooms, sliced
6 ounces shelled cooked shrimp, chopped
6 oysters, chopped
salt and pepper
Topping:
1 pound potatoes, cooked and still hot
2 tablespoons finely chopped parsley
salt and pepper
small amount of melted butter

Preheat the oven to 425°F. Butter a pie dish.

Cut the fish fillets into chunks, and poach in the milk until tender enough to flake. Add the scallops for the last 3 to 4 minutes while the fish is cooking. Drain, and reserve the liquid; place the fish into a bowl.

Melt 2 tablespoons of the butter in a saucepan, blend in the flour, and cook for 3 minutes. Gradually whisk in the poaching liquid, stirring constantly until the mixture thickens.

Melt the remaining tablespoon of butter and sauté the mushrooms until just tender. Fold them into the fish mixture; add the chopped shrimp and oysters and the salt and pepper.

Spoon a layer of the fish and mushroom mixture into the pie dish. Cover with a layer of sauce, then the remainder of the fish mixture, then the remaining sauce.

Topping: Mash the hot potatoes; stir in the parsley, salt, and pepper. Spread evenly over the mixture in the pie dish. Pour the melted butter over, and roughen the surface.

Bake for 15 to 20 minutes.

Smoked-Cod Pie

Yield: 4 servings

8 ounces Shortcrust Pastry (see recipe, page 149)
Filling:
8 ounces smoked cod, cooked, well drained, and flaked
2 hard-boiled eggs, sliced
4 ounces cooked rice
2 spring onions, finely chopped
grated peel of ½ lemon
2 tablespoons chopped parsley
salt and pepper
egg wash (1 egg with 2 tablespoons cream)

Preheat the oven to 450°F. Roll out the pastry to about a 10-inch square and place onto a greased baking sheet.

Filling: In a large bowl, mix together the flaked smoked cod, sliced eggs, rice, onion, lemon peel, parsley, salt, and pepper.

Spoon the mixture along the center of the pastry shape. Brush the edges with water and fold over the two flaps to overlap. Brush the pastry surface with the egg wash.

Bake for about 30 minutes.

Emergency Pie

Yield: 4 to 5 servings

1 5-ounce can tuna
1½ cups cream of celery soup
½ cup chopped celery
½ cup frozen peas
1 tablespoon chopped parsley
salt and pepper
12 ounces potatoes, boiled and mashed

Preheat the oven to 325°F.

Combine the drained tuna with the soup, chopped celery, frozen peas, parsley, salt, and pepper. Spoon into a pie dish, and cover with a layer of mashed potatoes.

Bake for 30 minutes or until heated through.

Right: **Potato-Topped Fish Pie (see above left); Smoked Cod Pie (see above).**

Asparagus Pie

Yield: 4 to 6 servings

1 quantity Shortcrust Pastry (see recipe, page 149)

Filling:
1 tablespoon butter
1 onion, finely chopped or grated
2 eggs, lightly beaten
½ cup cream
4 ounces sharp cheese, grated
½ teaspoon Dijon mustard
salt and black pepper
12 canned or cooked asparagus spears, drained

Make the pastry according to the recipe. Roll it out and use it to line an 8-inch pie pan.

Preheat the oven to 400°F.

Filling: Heat the butter and sauté the onion until soft. Beat the eggs and cream together, stir in the cheese, mustard, salt, and pepper, then the cooled onion. Pour into the pastry shell, and arrange the asparagus spears on top.

Bake in the preheated oven for 10 minutes, then reduce the oven temperature to 375°F and continue baking for another 30 minutes or until set. Serve warm or cold.

Gourmet Seafood Pie

Yield: 6 servings

1 quantity Rich Shortcrust Pastry (see recipe, page 149)

Filling:
2 tablespoons butter
2 or 3 white onions, sliced
2 tablespoons flour
⅔ cup table cream or milk
2 eggs beaten
1 pound mixed cooked seafood meat (oysters, scallops, shrimp)
2 teaspoons dried green dill tips
salt and pepper
1½ ounces grated cheese

Roll out the prepared pastry and line a lightly greased 7-inch pie pan.

Preheat the oven to 375°F.

Filling: Melt the butter in a frying pan, add the onions, and sauté until softened. Add the flour and continue cooking, stirring constantly, for about 3 minutes. Pour the cream or milk into the pan, simmer, stirring for 3 minutes or until the mixture thickens. Cool to lukewarm.

Beat the eggs into the mixture. Add the chopped seafood, dill, salt, and pepper. Pour the filling into the pastry shell, and sprinkle with the cheese.

Bake for 30 minutes, or until set. Serve warm.

Herbed Vegetable Pie

Yield: 4 to 6 servings

1 quantity Whole-Wheat Pastry (see recipe, page 153)

Filling:
1 tablespoon butter
2 tablespoons whole-wheat flour
1 15-ounce can vegetable juice
2 small zucchini, thinly sliced
2 small carrots, grated
1 small onion, thinly sliced
1 clove garlic, crushed
1 teaspoon chopped fresh herbs
2 ounces mushrooms, sliced

Topping:
3 tablespoons butter
1 clove garlic, crushed
1 cup fresh whole-wheat bread crumbs
½ cup grated sharp cheese
2 tablespoons chopped parsley

Preheat the oven to 350°F.

Roll out the pastry thinly and line a 10-inch pie pan.

Bake blind until golden.

Filling: Melt the butter in a saucepan. Add the flour and cook for several minutes, stirring constantly. Gradually stir in the vegetable juice and whisk until smooth. Add the zucchini, carrots, onion, garlic, and herbs. Simmer over low heat until the vegetables are just tender and the mixture has thickened. Add the mushrooms and cook for another minute or two. Allow to cool.

Preheat the oven to 375°F. Spoon the now-cooled filling into the pastry.

Topping: Melt the butter, add the crushed garlic, and sauté for a minute or two. Add the bread crumbs and stir until the crumbs are coated with butter. Remove from the heat; stir in the cheese and parsley. Spread onto the vegetable filling.

Bake for 10 to 15 minutes or until the crumb topping is crisp and brown. Serve hot or warm.

Right: **Clockwise from top: Herbed Vegetable Pie (above); Gourmet Seafood Pie (left); Asparagus Pie (above left).**

Tarte Niçoise

Yield: 4 to 6 servings

Pastry: ***1¾ cups flour***
pinch of salt
1 teaspoon baking powder
1 stick butter
1 egg yolk
1 teaspoon lemon juice
1 tablespoon iced water
Filling: ***6 small tomatoes***
½ cup grated sharp cheese
¼ cup dried bread crumbs
1 tablespoon butter
salt
pinch of cayenne pepper
grated nutmeg
2 teaspoons chopped fresh basil or 1 teaspoon dried basil
2 eggs
1½ cups cream
salt and black pepper
6 black olives, pitted and halved

To make the pastry, sift the flour, salt, and baking powder into a bowl. Rub in the butter until the mixture resembles bread crumbs (a food processor may be used). Beat the egg yolk, lemon juice, and water, and stir into the flour. Mix lightly with a knife blade to form a smooth but rather dry dough. (If necessary add a little more water—but not unless essential.) Knead as little as possible. Allow to stand for 30 minutes.

Preheat the oven to 325°F.

Roll out the pastry and line a 9-inch pie pan. Line with greaseproof paper and baking beans.

Bake blind for 12 to 15 minutes, or until just set but not browned.

Reset the oven temperature at 375°F.

Filling: Cut the tomatoes in half and gently scrape out the seeds and juice. Combine the cheese, bread crumbs, butter, salt, cayenne pepper, nutmeg, and basil and stuff the mixture into the cavities of the tomatoes. Arrange them (cut side up) in the base of the pie crust.

Beat together the eggs, cream, salt, and black pepper, and pour into the pie crust around the tomatoes. Arrange the olives between the tomatoes.

Bake for about 35 minutes, reducing the heat slightly if the top is browning too quickly. Serve warm or cold.

Neapolitan Quiche

Yield: 4 to 6 servings

1 quantity Whole-Wheat Pastry (see recipe, page 153)
Filling: ***2 tablespoons butter***
1 white onion, chopped
½ clove garlic, crushed
2 tablespoons finely chopped red or green pepper
3 tomatoes, sliced
1 teaspoon fresh basil or ½ teaspoon dried basil
salt and pepper
3 ounces sharp cheese, grated
3 eggs
1 cup milk
2 slices green pepper
3 small tomatoes, quartered
8 black olives, pitted and slivered

Preheat the oven to 375°F. Line a 9-inch pie pan with the pastry.

Filling: Heat 1 tablespoon of the butter and sauté the onion, garlic, and chopped pepper until tender. Remove from the pan.

Add the second tablespoon of butter to the pan, and add the tomato slices; fry gently until just tender, then drain and arrange in the base of the pastry case. Sprinkle with the basil and salt and pepper. Spoon the sautéed onion–garlic–peppers into the pie shell. Then add the grated cheese. Beat the eggs lightly and add the milk; pour carefully into the pie shell. Arrange the green-pepper slices, quartered tomatoes, and slivered olives on top.

Bake for 35 to 40 minutes or until the filling is set and golden brown. Serve hot or cold.

Tyropita

Yield: 34 pieces

2 sheets pre-rolled puff pastry

Filling:
8 ounces cottage cheese

2 ounces blue cheese, crumbled

2 ounces cheddar cheese, grated

2 eggs

2 tablespoons dry bread crumbs

2 teaspoons chopped fresh mint or ½ teaspoon dried mint

salt

pinch of cayenne pepper

egg yolk beaten with a little water, for glazing

Preheat the oven to 375°F. Place 1 layer of pastry into a lightly greased baking pan.

Filling: Beat the cottage cheese; then add the blue cheese, cheddar cheese, and eggs, and beat until smooth. Stir in the bread crumbs, mint, salt, and cayenne pepper. Spread the mixture over the pastry, and top it with the remaining dough. Brush over with the egg yolk and water.

Bake for 35 to 40 minutes or until the pastry is golden. Cut into diamond shapes. Serve hot.

Savory Tarts

Yield: 12 small tarts

1 quantity Puff Pastry (see recipe, page 154)

Filling:
4 ounces sharp cheese, grated

1 egg yolk

½ teaspoon dry mustard

salt and pepper

1 tablespoon butter, softened

2 ounces finely chopped walnuts

2 egg whites, stiffly beaten

Preheat the oven to 325°F.

Prepare the pastry, roll it out thinly, and line twelve greased muffin tins.

Filling: Blend together the grated cheese and the egg yolk; season with the mustard, salt, and pepper. Stir in the soft butter and the walnuts, then lightly fold in the stiffly beaten egg whites. Place a generous portion into each pastry-lined muffin tin.

Bake for about 20 minutes or until the filling is puffed and the pastry is golden. Serve at once, as the soufflé-like texture of the filling will drop as it cools. A delicious appetizer with pre-dinner drinks.

Rich Bacon and Cheese Pie with Bran Crust

Yield: 6 servings

Pastry:
1 cup processed bran (such as All-Bran)

½ cup milk

1½ cups self-rising flour

salt

1 stick butter or margarine

Filling:
6 lean strips bacon, grilled and crumbled

8 ounces sharp cheese, grated

1¾ cups light cream

2 eggs, beaten

salt and pepper

1 spring onion, chopped

2 tablespoons chopped parsley

Preheat the oven to 375°F.

Soak the bran in the milk for about 5 minutes. Sift the flour and salt together, then rub in the butter. Combine the two mixtures and knead lightly until smooth. Roll the pastry out, and line a 9-inch pie pan.

Filling: Combine all the filling ingredients, and pour the mixture into the pastry shell.

Bake for about 40 minutes or until golden brown.

This nutritious but rich pie can be lightened by substituting evaporated milk for the cream.

Little Lamb Pies

Yield: 6 servings

Pastry:
1 stick butter or margarine

1½ cups water

4 cups flour

salt

Filling:
12 ounces lean lamb, finely diced or ground

1 small onion, chopped

salt and pepper

chopped parsley

1 to 2 tablespoons rich stock

milk or beaten egg, for glazing

Preheat the oven to 350°F.

Pastry: Place the butter and water in a saucepan and bring to a boil. Sift the flour and salt into a bowl; make a well in the center, and pour in the hot liquid. Mix to a soft dough with a knife blade, and then knead on a board until the dough is smooth.

Cut off a quarter of the dough and keep it warm. Line six small tart tins with the larger quantity of pastry.

Filling: Combine the chopped lamb with the onion, salt, pepper, and parsley; add a little stock to moisten. Fill the pastry shells with the meat mixture.

Roll out the remainder of the pastry and cut lids for the pies. Moisten the edges and press onto the filled pastry shells, pinching the edges together. Cut a small air vent in the top of each, then brush the pastry surfaces with a little milk or beaten egg.

Bake for 40 minutes. Serve hot.

If desired, make up a little rich gravy and spoon in through the vent holes before serving.

Bedfordshire Clanger

Yield: 3 pastries

1 pound Shortcrust Pastry
(see recipe, page 149)

Savory Filling:
2 tablespoons butter

1 small carrot, finely diced

2 to 3 tablespoons frozen peas

1 spring onion, chopped

6 ounces very finely diced or ground lamb or beef

1 teaspoon dried mixed herbs

2 teaspoons Worcestershire sauce

salt and pepper

Sweet Filling:
1 green cooking apple, peeled and diced

1 tablespoon powdered sugar

generous pinch of cinnamon or cloves

beaten egg, for glazing

Roll the pastry to ¼ inch thick and cut it into six saucer-sized rounds. Roll out the trimmings and cut three strips about 6 × ½ inches.

Savory Filling: Melt the butter in a pan and sauté the carrot, peas, and onion for several minutes. Add the meat, herbs, sauce, salt, and pepper. Cover the pan and cook very gently until the meat is tender. (If necessary, add 1 tablespoon of water or stock to prevent browning.) Allow to cool.

Preheat the oven to 350°F.

Sweet Filling: Mix together the diced apple, sugar, and spice.

To finish the pie: Brush the center of each pastry round with the beaten egg. Set aside three rounds. Place a pastry strip across each round, spoon a portion of the meat filling onto one end of each pastry round, then spoon a portion of the apple onto the other end (the pastry strip acts as a divider). Place the three reserved pastry rounds on top of the fillings; seal the outer edges and lightly press down the pastry over the strip. Prick the tops in several places and glaze with the beaten egg.

Bake for about 30 minutes.

Right: **Clockwise from top: Tarte a l'Ancienne (see p. 241); Carrot Pie (see p. 233); Bedfordshire Clanger (see above).**

WHITECHAPEL
BOW BUS. 25
(PASSES THE DOOR
HAM
RD
RD

Economical Shepherd's Pie

Yield: 4 servings

1 tablespoon butter or margarine

1 pound lean ground beef

6 spring onions, chopped

3 teaspoons flour

½ teaspoon mixed dried herbs or 1 teaspoon fresh herbs

1 tablespoon tomato sauce

2 teaspoons Worcestershire sauce

salt and pepper

Topping:
1 pound potatoes, cooked, and mashed with milk

2 tablespoons chopped parsley

salt and pepper

a little extra butter, melted

1 tomato, sliced

Melt the butter or margarine in a pan, add the meat, onions, and flour and cook gently, stirring occasionally, until the meat is lightly cooked. Remove from the heat, and stir in the herbs, tomato sauce, Worcestershire sauce, salt, and pepper. Spoon into a slightly greased deep enamel pie dish.

Preheat the oven to 425°F.

Topping: Prepare the mashed potatoes; add the parsley, salt, and pepper. Spread onto the meat mixture, roughen the surface, and brush with the butter. Arrange the tomato slices on top.

Bake for about 25 minutes or until the top is well browned.

Exotic Shepherd's Pie

Yield: 8 to 10 servings

2 tablespoons olive oil

2 tablespoons butter

3 large onions, chopped

2 pounds lean ground beef

¾ cup raisins

3 ounces green olives, pitted and sliced

¼ teaspoon ground cloves (more if preferred)

½ teaspoon ground cumin

1 clove garlic, crushed

salt and pepper

1 15-ounce can tomatoes, drained and chopped

4 hard-boiled eggs

3 pounds potatoes, boiled and mashed with milk

2 tablespoons butter, melted

Preheat the oven to 375°F.

Heat the oil and butter in a saucepan or deep frying pan, and sauté the onions until softened. Add the beef, raisins, olives, spices, garlic, and salt and pepper; simmer for 10 minutes, then add the chopped tomatoes. Simmer gently until most of the liquid has evaporated; adjust the seasoning, if necessary.

Turn the mixture into an ovenproof casserole. Cut the eggs into quarters and lightly fold into the meat mixture. Cover with the prepared mashed potatoes, roughen the surface, and pour melted butter over the top.

Bake for about 40 minutes or until golden brown. This pie can be successfully reheated.

Raised Veal and Ham Pie

Yield: 5 to 6 servings

Filling:
12 ounces veal steak

1¼ cups water

bouquet garni

¼ teaspoon dried thyme

4 ounces ham, diced

1 spring onion, chopped

salt and pepper

1 quantity Hot-Water Crust Pastry (see recipe, page 157)

2 hard-boiled eggs

beaten egg, for glazing

Jelly:
2½ teaspoons gelatin

1¼ cups veal stock

salt and pepper

Filling: Place the veal steak in a saucepan and add the water. Bring to a boil, skim, add the bouquet garni and thyme; simmer for 15 minutes. Remove the veal from the liquid and allow to cool. Strain the veal stock and place into a small saucepan. Boil the stock rapidly until it reduces to 1 tablespoon. Cool and reserve.

Preheat the oven to 400°F.

Cut the veal into ⅜-inch cubes; mix with the ham, onion, salt, and pepper.

To finish the pie: Make the pastry and press two-thirds of it into a greased raised-pie mold; reserve the remainder for a pastry lid. Fill the pastry shell with the meat mixture, and arrange the hard-boiled eggs in the center of the meat. Spoon the reserved veal stock over the meat.

Roll out the remaining pastry to fit the top of the pie. Place it over the filling and press the edges of the pastry together to seal. Brush the top of the pie with the beaten egg. Trim the surplus pastry edge with scissors. Roll out leftover scraps of pastry, cut out four decorative leaves, and mold a decorative flower bud. In the top of the pie, cut two slits crosswise in the center and fold back the four pieces of pastry. Brush the folded-back pastry with the egg. Arrange the pastry leaves on top and place the flower bud in the center of the leaves. Brush all over with the egg.

Bake in the preheated oven for 30 minutes, then reduce the oven temperature to 325°F, cover the pie with greaseproof paper if becoming overbrown, and bake for another 60 minutes. Remove the paper, unmold the pie, and allow to cool.

To make the jelly, dissolve the gelatin in the stock, and add the seasoning. When the pie is cool and the jelly has thickened, pour the jelly into the pie through the vent. Allow to set. Serve cold.

Desserts

Soufflé

Antonin Câréme is claimed as the originator of the baked soufflé, a dessert which for some reason or other has achieved the reputation of being difficult to make. This is not necessarily true. All that is needed is a light mixing hand and a consistent oven, plus the patience not to peek during the first three-quarters of the baking time. For further sure success, the soufflé must be eaten within minutes of being removed from the oven. Far from being a special guest-occasion masterpiece, soufflés are light, nutritious, and economical when compared with other sweet desserts—and can be quickly and easily prepared. (Recipes for soufflés are included in this chapter.)

Pavlova

Several people have claimed to be the originator of this meringue confection made to honor the famous Russian ballerina. However, if one looks at the basic method for making a Vacherin, a meringue torte, or several other European classics, they are remarkably similar to the Pavlova.

Included on the following pages are two recipes for Pavlova—which has become an Australian national dessert and an international classic. Traditionally, the dish is made with passion fruit and kiwi fruit. Where passion fruit is unavailable, the dessert can be made with just kiwis.

Baked Milk Custards

Baked milk custards and their variations are an invaluable standby in many households. The ingredients are almost always on hand, they are economical, and, also of importance, they are nutritious. Another great advantage is that they can be cooked while the main course roast is in the oven, or they can be baked ahead of time while the oven is in use for other baking, then refrigerated for a day or so until they are served.

Fruit Desserts

Fruit in all its forms—fresh, canned, dried, or preserved in other ways—is an integral part of the final food for a meal. Its versatility for use in almost any type of dessert, plus its multitude of delicious flavors, ensures that it is well represented in all sections of this chapter on baked desserts.

Rice, cereal, and pasta desserts, shortcakes, babas, cobblers, crumbles, crunches, and the currently popular cheesecake desserts are all featured in this chapter.

Wines

Wines, particularly sweet table and fortified wines, play an important role in the flavor of many desserts. They help to provide a subtle yet distinguished taste that transforms a simple dessert into a delightful finale to the meal. Should a wine be used in the preparation of a dessert, it is suggested that the same wine be served for the beverage. Otherwise, choose a wine that complements the tastes of the ingredients used for the dish.

Choosing A Dessert

Consider the number and type of preceding courses when choosing a dessert. Light and delicate sweet foods are more acceptable after a many-course or lavish dinner, whereas the more substantial or hearty pudding types may be best appreciated after a simple one- or two-course meal.

Color, texture, flavor, repetition, seasonal changes, the occasion, and (last but not least) the needs and tastes of those partaking of the meal must all be part of the final consideration. There are no hard and fast rules—simply cook what you feel your family, your guests, and you yourself most enjoy.

The qualities that go into making a memorable dessert are imagination, care in preparation, and attractive presentation.

Snow-Peak Peaches

Yield: 4 to 6 servings

12 large canned peach halves

1 cup crushed Macaroons (see recipe, page 130)

¼ cup chopped almonds or walnuts

¼ cup chopped candied cherries

2 eggs, separated

1 to 1¼ cups canned peach syrup

2 tablespoons brandy

2 teaspoons lemon juice

¼ cup sugar

slivered almonds, for decoration

Preheat the oven to 300°F.

Drain the peaches and place them in a single layer, hollow side uppermost, into a well-greased shallow casserole.

Combine the macaroon crumbs with the almonds, cherries, and egg yolks. Spoon the mixture into the hollow of each peach half.

Heat the peach syrup, brandy, and lemon juice with a little of the sugar in a small saucepan until boiling and pour it over and around the peaches.

Beat the egg whites until stiff and glossy; gradually add the remaining sugar. Roughly pile this meringue mixture over each peach and spike with the slivered almonds.

Bake for 20 to 25 minutes. Serve warm.

Spiced Orange Delight

Yield: 5 or 6 servings

5 or 6 large oranges—one for each serving

¾ stick butter or margarine, melted

¼ cup light corn syrup

½ cup brown sugar

2 to 3 tablespoons sweet sherry

½ cup raisins

1 teaspoon ground cinnamon

ice cream, for servings

Preheat the oven to 375°F.

Peel the oranges, removing as much of the white pith as possible; cut into rings and arrange over the base of a well-greased casserole.

Combine the melted butter, corn syrup, sugar, sweet sherry, raisins, and cinnamon, and spoon over the orange slices. Cover loosely with aluminum foil.

Bake for 15 to 20 minutes. Arrange scoops of ice cream on each serving plate and spoon the hot orange slices over. Serve at once.

Fruited Apple Charlotte

Yield: 5 or 6 servings

4 or 5 large cooking apples, peeled and cored

1 lemon

2 tablespoons light corn syrup or honey

¼ cup water

½ teaspoon ground cinnamon or cloves

1 cup raisins

8 to 10 slices white bread, crusts removed

1 stick butter or margarine, melted

additional 1 tablespoon corn syrup or honey

whipped cream, for serving

Thinly slice the apples and place into a small saucepan with 2 or 3 strips of lemon peel, the juice of the lemon, the syrup, and water; cover and cook over low heat until the apples are softened.

Allow to cool, remove the lemon peel, and beat until the apples form a pulp. Add the spice and raisins, and mix through.

Preheat the oven to 375°F.

Cut the bread into finger-sized pieces; brush each piece generously with melted butter all over and arrange over the base and sides of a casserole; press down firmly. Fill the center with the fruited apple pulp, and cover the top with the remaining bread slices (buttered). Drizzle the extra corn syrup over the surface.

Bake for 50 to 55 minutes. Remove from the oven and allow to stand for 25 to 30 minutes. Serve with whipped cream, if desired.

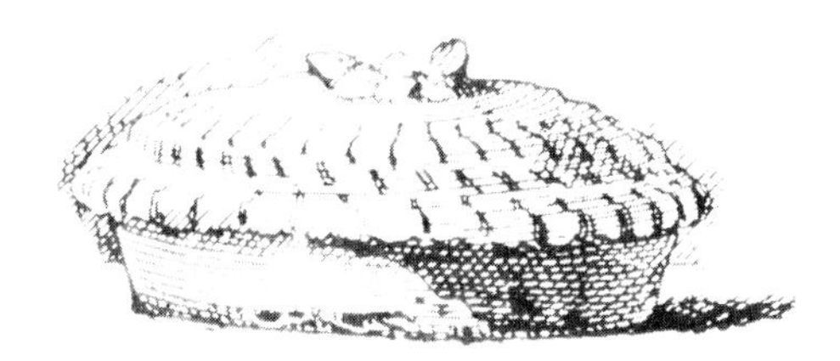

Apricot Yogurt Custard

Yield: 6 to 8 servings

2¼ cups unflavored yogurt

3 eggs, beaten

1 cup milk

¼ cup sugar

1 tablespoon cornstarch

1¼ cups cooked and drained riced (3 ounces uncooked)

6 canned apricot halves, coarsely chopped

grated nutmeg, for sprinkling

Preheat the oven to 350°F.

Combine the yogurt, eggs, and milk, beating well. Blend in the combined sugar and cornstarch.

Spread the rice over the base of a well-greased casserole, and arrange the apricot pieces over; sprinkle with nutmeg as desired. Carefully spoon the yogurt mixture over the top. Place the casserole into a baking pan containing 2 to 3 cups of hot water.

Bake for 55 to 60 minutes or until set. Serve warm or cold.

Sliced-Apple Pudding

Yield: 5 or 6 servings

4 large cooking apples

½ stick butter or margarine, melted

1 tablespoon cornstarch

¾ cup powdered sugar

1 to 2 teaspoons grated lemon rind

½ teaspoon cinnamon

¾ cup raisins, chopped

4 ounces cream cheese, softened

3 eggs, beaten

¾ cup evaporated milk

2 tablespoons confectioners' sugar

whipped cream, for serving

Preheat the oven to 350°F.

Peel and core the apples and cut into thick slices or rings. Brush each piece with the melted butter, and coat with the combined cornstarch, half of the powdered sugar, lemon rind, and cinnamon. Arrange the apple slices in a well-greased casserole; scatter the raisins over the surface.

Beat the cream cheese, remaining powdered sugar, eggs, and evaporated milk together, and pour over the apples and raisins.

Bake in the preheated oven for 15 to 20 minutes, then reduce the oven temperature to 300°F and cook until the apples are softened and the custard mixture is set (about 30 minutes). Remove from the oven, and dust the confectioners' sugar over the surface. Serve warm, with whipped cream.

Stuffed Apples

Yield: 4 or 5 servings

4 to 5 large cooking apples

lemon juice

Apple Stuffing—see the variations below

½ cup sugar

1½ cups sweet white wine

1½ cups water

whipped cream, for serving

Preheat the oven to 350°F.

Remove the core from each apple, and remove the peel from the top half of each. Brush the peeled section with the lemon juice to prevent browning.

Prepare the apple stuffing by combining all the ingredients. Fill the core cavity of each apple and pile the filling high over the top.

Place the apples into a small casserole or baking pan. Combine the sugar, wine, and water, and drizzle this around the apples in the casserole. Cover loosely with aluminum foil.

Bake for 30 to 40 minutes until the apples are just soft. Lift the apples onto serving plates, and reduce the liquid in the casserole by boiling briskly; spoon over the apples. Serve hot with whipped cream.

Apple Stuffings: The quantities of the ingredients are approximate only, as the amount required depends on the sizes of the apples and the core cavities.
Apricot: ½ cup apricot jam, ¼ cup brown sugar, ¼ cup chopped almonds, and 1 tablespoon rum or brandy.
Raisin: ½ cup chopped raisins, ¼ cup brown sugar, ¼ cup chopped walnuts, 1 teaspoon mixed spices, and 1 tablespoon sweet sherry.
Date: ½ cup chopped dates, ¼ cup brown sugar, ¼ cup chopped orange, and ¼ teaspoon cinnamon.
Fruitmince: ¾ cup prepared fruitmince and 1 tablespoon brandy or sweet sherry.
Banana: ¾ cup chopped banana, 2 tablespoons light corn syrup, and 1 tablespoon lemon juice.

Right: **Stuffed Apples (see above).**

Fruity Rice Custard

Yield: 5 or 6 servings

2 cups cooked rice (3/4 cup uncooked)
3/4 cup pitted and chopped dates
1/4 cup honey or light corn syrup
1/2 to 1 teaspoon ground nutmeg
2 eggs, beaten
1 1/4 cups milk
1/4 cup condensed sweetened milk
whipped cream, for serving

Preheat the oven to 325°F.

Arrange the rice, dates, and honey or syrup in layers in a well-greased casserole, beginning and ending with rice. Sprinkle nutmeg over the surface. Combine the beaten eggs with the fresh and condensed milks, and drizzle over the layered ingredients.

Bake for 40 to 50 minutes or until the custard is softly set. Remove from the oven. Serve warm, with whipped cream.

Note: Baking time can be reduced by 10 to 15 minutes if the rice is freshly cooked and hot when arranged in the casserole.

Apricot-Custard Cream

Yield: 5 or 6 servings

1/2 to 3/4 cup thick apricot preserve
2 1/2 cups milk
1 1/4 cups evaporated milk
3 whole eggs
1 egg yolk
1/4 cup sugar
1 teaspoon vanilla extract
1 cup heavy cream, chilled
2 to 3 tablespoons grated chocolate
1 to 2 tablespoons flaked toasted almonds

Preheat the oven to 300°F.

Spread the apricot preserve to a depth of about 1/4 to 1/2 inch over the base of a well-greased casserole.

Heat the milk and evaporated milk in a nonstick saucepan until scalding. Beat the whole eggs, egg yolk, sugar, and vanilla extract well. Gradually add about one-quarter of the milk to the egg mixture, whisking constantly; pour all back into the remaining milk, stirring well.

Strain carefully over the apricot preserve; cover the casserole loosely with aluminum foil.

Bake for 1 hour or until the custard is set. Remove, allow to cool, and chill.

Whip the cream until stiff, fold in the grated chocolate, and spoon it over the chilled custard. Scatter the toasted almonds over the surface, and serve.

Petits Pots de Crème

Yield: 5 or 6 servings

1 1/2 cups milk
1/2 cup cream
4 egg yolks
1 whole egg
1/4 cup sugar
1 to 1 1/2 teaspoons brandy extract or rum extract
2 ounces pure baking chocolate, grated
whipped cream, for decoration

Preheat the oven to 325°F.

Combine the milk and cream in a small nonstick saucepan and heat slowly until scalding. Strain into a bowl.

Beat the egg yolks, the egg, and sugar well. Gradually add about one-quarter of the milk, then pour all back into the remaining milk, stirring constantly. Flavor with the extract and add the grated chocolate; stir to dissolve.

Pour the chocolate mixture into five or six small custard cups and stand these in a baking pan containing 3 to 4 cups of hot water. Cover loosely with aluminum foil.

Bake for 50 to 60 minutes or until the custard is set. Remove, allow to cool, and then chill. Serve with a rosette of whipped cream on each little pot.

Cottage-Cheese Cocottes

Yield: 5 or 6 servings

2 eggs, firm-cooked and cooled
12 ounces cottage cheese
3 eggs, separated
1 cup powdered sugar
½ stick butter or margarine, melted
¼ cup self-rising flour
½ cup raisins
1 teaspoon grated lemon rind
whipped cream, for serving

Preheat the oven to 325°F. Grease five or six individual cocotte or custard cups.

Shell the firm-cooked eggs and press through a fine sieve with the cottage cheese; mix well.

Beat the egg yolks and sugar until thick, add the cooled butter, mix into the cottage cheese, and beat well. Fold in the sifted flour, raisins, and lemon rind.

Beat the egg whites until well foamed and lightly fold into the cottage-cheese mixture. Spoon the mixture into the prepared containers and arrange them on a cookie sheet.

Bake for 35 to 40 minutes, or until set. Remove, allow to stand for 2 to 3 minutes, then run a knife around the sides of each dish before carefully turning out onto a dessert plate. Serve warm, with whipped cream if desired.

Cottage Custard Cream

Yield: 6 servings

3 eggs
¼ cup cornstarch
½ cup sugar
12 ounces creamed cottage cheese
1¼ cups milk
1¼ cups cream, whipped
2 teaspoons grated orange rind (optional)
18 to 20 strawberries

Preheat the oven to 350°F.

Beat the eggs with the cornstarch and sugar until thick and fluffy. Gradually add the cottage cheese and milk, beating well. Fold in half of the whipped cream and the orange rind (or use other flavorings as desired). Pour into a greased casserole.

Place the casserole into a baking pan containing 2 to 3 cups of hot water.

Bake for 50 to 60 minutes or until just set. Remove from the oven, allow to cool, and chill. Serve with the sliced strawberries and remaining whipped cream.

Creamy Peach Roll

Yield: 6 to 8 servings

3 eggs
¾ cup powdered sugar
½ teaspoon almond extract
¾ cup packaged pancake mix
confectioners' sugar, for dusting
1 can (15 ounces) sliced peaches, drained well
½ cup flaked almonds
about 2 cups vanilla ice cream
1¼ cups heavy cream
2 teaspoons powdered sugar, for sweetening cream
flaked almonds, for decoration

Preheat the oven to 400°F. Prepare a 12 × 10-inch jelly-roll pan by lining it with greaseproof paper and greasing thoroughly.

Beat the eggs until thick and frothy; gradually add the sugar, beating well after each addition. Add the extract, then fold in the pancake mix. Spread the batter into the prepared pan.

Bake for 8 to 10 minutes.

Prepare a rolling surface with aluminum foil or greaseproof paper; dust generously with confectioners' sugar. When the roll is baked, carefully loosen the sides and turn it out onto the prepared foil or paper. Roll up, let stand for 20 minutes, then unroll.

Meanwhile, reserving 3 or 4 peach slices, chop the remainder, and combine with the almonds and ice cream. Quickly spread over the roll, reroll carefully, and wrap in the foil. Freeze for 2 to 3 hours.

Just before serving, remove the foil from the frozen roll and coat all over with the whipped sweetened cream. Place onto a serving plate, and decorate with the reserved peach slices and extra flaked almonds. Serve, cut into slices, while the roll is still partially frozen.

Pineapple Ginger Dessert

Yield: 5 or 6 servings

1-pound can crushed pineapple
water
¾ cup sugar
1¼ cups evaporated milk
2 teaspoons grated lemon rind
3 tablespoons cornstarch
2 eggs, separated
2 tablespoons butter or margarine, melted
⅓ cup candied ginger in syrup
6 or 7 macaroons, crushed
additional ½ cup sugar

Preheat the oven to 350°F.

Drain the canned pineapple, reserving the syrup. Arrange the pineapple in the base of a greased casserole dish. Measure the drained syrup, and make up the quantity to 1¼ cups with the water (set aside ¼ cup for later use).

Combine the sugar, 1 cup of pineapple water, evaporated milk, and lemon rind in a thick-based nonstick saucepan. Heat, beating slowly, until it begins to simmer. Beat the cornstarch, reserved pineapple water, egg yolks, and butter together; gradually add to the saucepan, stirring constantly. When thickened and starting to bubble, lower the heat and simmer for 1 to 2 minutes, stirring frequently. Remove from the heat and add the ginger. Allow to cool slightly.

Pour the cooled mixture over the crushed pineapple; scatter the macaroons over.

Beat the egg whites to meringue consistency; gradually beat in the sugar and pile roughly over the casserole contents.

Bake for 12 to 15 minutes. Serve warm.

Brazilian Bananas

Yield: 5 or 6 servings

6 large firm bananas
1 to 2 tablespoons rum or coffee liqueur
1 to 2 tablespoons lemon juice
½ stick butter or margarine, melted
2 tablespoons brown sugar
¾ cup chopped dates
½ cup sliced Brazil nuts
2 ounces marshmallows, halved
coffee-flavored ice cream, for serving

Preheat the oven to 350°F.

Peel the bananas and diagonally slice each into four pieces; brush all over with the combined rum and lemon juice.

Pour the melted butter into a casserole, and sprinkle the brown sugar over. Layer the banana slices, dates, Brazil nuts, and marshmallows over the top, finishing with marshmallows.

Bake for 20 to 25 minutes. Serve hot over scoops of coffee ice cream.

Flambé: For a special dramatic effect, slightly warm a little extra rum or coffee liqueur, set on fire, and carefully spoon over the banana dessert.

Honey-Rhubarb Crunch

Yield: 4 or 5 servings

4 to 5 cups diced rhubarb
½ cup honey, warmed
2 tablespoons lemon juice
½ cup chopped dates
½ cup chopped pecans or walnuts
6 to 8 Macaroons, coarsely crushed (see recipe, page 130)
whipped cream, chilled

Preheat the oven to 350°F.

Arrange the washed rhubarb pieces over the base of a well-greased nonmetal casserole. Drizzle the honey over the surface, then sprinkle with the lemon juice. Cover loosely with aluminum foil.

Bake for 25 to 30 minutes. Remove the foil, carefully fold in the dates and nuts, and continue cooking for another 5 minutes.

Remove from the oven, allow to cool, then chill. Just before serving, spoon into dessert glasses or bowls, sprinkle the macaroon crumbs over each serving, and top with a dollop of whipped cream.

Pear Crumble Cake

Yield: 5 or 6 servings

1 package yellow cake mix

1 or 2 eggs

water

5 or 6 cooked pear halves, drained well

Crumble Topping:
¾ cup self-rising flour, sifted

⅛ teaspoon salt

1 teaspoon mixed spices

2 tablespoons brown sugar

½ stick butter or margarine

custard, for serving

Preheat the oven to 350°F.

Make up the cake mix as directed on the package, using the egg or eggs, as specified, but use only half the amount of water, to make a firmer batter. Spread into a well-greased 8-inch springform pan.

Arrange the pear halves over the cake mixture, hollow side up in a cartwheel pattern.

Crumble Topping

Combine the flour, salt, spices, and brown sugar in a bowl; rub in the butter with the fingertips.

Crumble the topping over the top of each pear half.

Bake for 30 to 35 minutes. Remove from the oven, place on a cake rack, and loosen the springform ring. Allow to stand for 10 to 15 minutes, then lift the dessert onto a serving plate. Cut into slices. Serve with hot custard, if desired.

Cherry Mallow Pie

Yield: 6 to 8 servings

5 or 6 thin slices milk bread

melted butter or margarine

1½ pounds ripe tart cherries

¼ cup sugar

14 to 16 marshmallows, halved

¾ cup flaked almonds

confectioners' sugar, for topping

whipped cream, for serving.

Preheat the oven to 375°F.

Cut the crusts off the bread slices and cut each slice into halves or quarters. Brush both sides generously with melted butter, and arrange over the base and sides of a 9-inch pie dish to resemble a pastry crust.

Remove the stems and pits from the washed cherries, and mix with the sugar; scatter over the bread crust. Place the marshmallow halves on top and sprinkle with the flaked almonds. Cover loosely with aluminum foil.

Bake for 15 minutes; remove the foil and continue baking for another 15 to 20 minutes. Remove from the oven and dust the surface with a little confectioners' sugar. Allow to stand until just warm, then slice. Serve with whipped cream if desired.

Note: Cherry pitters can be purchased at most specialty kitchenware stores.

Fruit Pudding Cups

Yield: 8 to 10 servings

3 cups mixed dried fruits

½ cup chopped dates

2 to 3 teaspoons grated orange rind

1 stick butter or margarine

1 cup sugar

¾ cup water

2 eggs, beaten

½ cup sweet sherry

2 cups flour

1 teaspoon baking powder

1 teaspoon mixed spices

½ teaspoon baking soda

Combine the dried fruits (chopping, if required), dates, orange rind, butter, sugar, and water in a saucepan; bring slowly to a boil, stirring frequently, then simmer for 2 minutes. Remove from the heat and allow to cool.

Preheat the oven to 350°F.

Add the beaten eggs and sweet sherry to the fruit mixture, and mix. Sift the dry ingredients into a bowl; add the fruit mixture and mix well.

Spoon the mixture into 8 to 10 well-greased large custard cups, filling them two-thirds full. Cover each cup with greased aluminum foil, pressing the foil tightly around each cup. Place the cups into a large baking pan half-filled with boiling water, and carefully place the pan into the oven.

Steam-bake the cups for 1¼ to 1½ hours.

Remove from the oven and carefully lift the cups from the water; loosen and remove the aluminum foil covers, and unmold the puddings into bowls. Serve with custard, cream, or ice-cream, as desired.

Strawberry Crêpes Royale

Yield: 5 or 6 servings

Crêpes: Makes 10 to 12
1¼ cups flour
¼ teaspoon salt
½ teaspoon baking powder
2 teaspoons sugar
2 eggs
1 teaspoon vanilla, rum, or brandy extract
2 tablespoons light vegetable oil
2 cups milk
water, as required
butter or oil for frying
Filling:
2 tablespoons sweet sherry
8 ounces cream cheese, softened
2 tablespoons confectioners' sugar
1½ teaspoons grated orange rind
¼ cup orange juice
20 to 24 strawberries, hulled and sliced
¾ cup apricot preserve
additional 2 tablespoons sweet sherry
2 tablespoons butter or margarine, melted
½ cup flaked almonds
sour cream, for serving

Crêpes: Sift the flour, salt, baking powder, and sugar into a bowl; make a well in the center.

Beat the eggs with the extract, oil, and milk; add to the flour mixture gradually, whisking until the mixture is a smooth, creamy consistency.

Set aside for at least 30 minutes. Then, whisk in sufficient water to produce a thin cream consistency.

Heat a shallow crêpe or omelette pan and grease lightly with butter or oil; pour in 2 to 3 tablespoons of the batter and tilt the pan to coat the base—pour off any excess batter.

Place over medium-high heat and cook until the underside is lightly browned; carefully flip or turn over and cook another minute.

Lift out and place on a plate; make remaining crêpes in a similar way, placing a strip of greaseproof paper between each while stacking to complete the required number.

Preheat the oven to 350°F.

Filling: Lightly brush one side of each crêpe with the sweet sherry. Combine the cream cheese, confectioners' sugar, orange rind, and orange juice, and spoon about 2 tablespoons across each crêpe. Roll up loosely, and arrange in a single layer in a well-greased shallow casserole.

Spoon the sliced strawberries over the crêpes. Combine the apricot preserve, remaining sweet sherry, and melted butter, and spoon this over the top. Scatter with almonds, and loosely cover with aluminum foil.

Bake for 15 to 20 minutes. Serve at once, with a spoonful of sour cream on top.

Flambé Crêpes

Carefully pour a little flaming brandy over the crêpes just before serving.

Danish Apple Dessert

Yield: 5 or 6 servings

3 large cooking apples
water and lemon juice
¼ cup cherry brandy liqueur
¼ cup sugar
20 to 24 Macaroons
(see recipe, page 130)
½ teaspoon ground cinnamon or nutmeg
¾ stick butter or margarine
½ cup chopped candied cherries
whipped cream, for serving

Preheat the oven to 350°F.

Peel and core the apples, cut into thin slices, and place into the water and lemon juice to prevent discoloration. Drain, and place in a saucepan with the cherry liqueur and sugar. Cover tightly and place over low heat; cook slowly, stirring occasionally, until just softened.

Coarsely crush the macaroons and mix with the cinnamon. Heat the butter in a small pan, and sauté the macaroon crumbs, tossing constantly until lightly browned.

Place layers of apples, macaroons, and cherries into a well-greased casserole.

Bake for 20 to 25 minutes. Serve warm or cold, with whipped cream.

Rhubarb Apple Cobbler

Yield: 5 or 6 servings

2½ to 3 cups diced, fresh rhubarb
2 cooking apples, cored and thinly sliced
2 teaspoons grated orange rind
½ cup orange juice
2 cups flour
3 teaspoons baking powder
½ stick butter or margarine
¼ cup sugar
1 egg
¾ cup milk
1 tablespoon flaked coconut
extra sugar, for sprinkling

Preheat the oven to 375°F.

Arrange the rhubarb pieces in the base of a well-greased casserole and top with a layer of the apple slices; sprinkle the orange rind over and drizzle the juice over the surface. Cover loosely with aluminum foil.

Bake until the fruits are softened—15 to 20 minutes.

Meanwhile sift the flour and baking powder into a bowl; rub in the butter with the fingertips and sprinkle with the sugar.

Beat the egg with half the milk and stir into the mixture; add sufficient of the remaining milk to mix to a firm cake consistency.

Add the coconut and drop the mixture in rough spoonfuls over the hot fruit; sprinkle the surface with sugar and return to the oven for another 30 to 35 minutes. Serve hot, warm, or cold.

Rosy Apple Crumble

Yield: 6 or 7 servings

6 or 7 firm, red apples
lemon water, for soaking
¾ cup self-rising flour
½ cup quick-cooking oats
2 teaspoons grated lemon rind
1 tablespoon lemon juice
1 stick butter or margarine, chilled
½ cup brown sugar
Sauce: ***2 egg yolks***
1 tablespoon sugar
1 tablespoon brandy
½ teaspoon ground cinnamon
1 cup cream or evaporated milk

Preheat the oven to 325°F.

Halve the apples, remove the core, and cut each half into 6 or 7 wedges; drop into the lemon water to prevent discoloration.

Place the flour, quick-cooking oats, lemon rind, lemon juice, and chopped butter into a processor and cut until well combined (or rub the butter through with the fingertips). Add the sugar, and mix.

Drain the lemon water off the apples and, holding the skin edge, dip each wedge into the crumble mixture. Arrange in overlapping pieces in a generously greased round shallow casserole or quiche dish. Drizzle 1 to 2 tablespoons of the lemon water over, and scatter any remaining crumble over the top.

Bake for 30 to 35 minutes; if desired, cover loosely with aluminum foil to prevent drying out or over-browning the sauce.

Sauce: Combine the egg yolks, sugar, brandy, and cinnamon in the top half of a double saucepan; stir in the cream and cook over simmering water, stirring constantly until thickened to a custard consistency.

Serve the apple dessert warm with the sauce in a pitcher for individual use.

Pineapple Ginger Cheesecake

Yield: 8 to 12 servings

- ***8 ounces coconut-flavored cookies***
- ***2 ounces whole-wheat crackers***
- ***1 cup crushed, drained pineapple***
- ***⅓ cup chopped preserved ginger***
- ***2 eggs***
- ***½ cup sugar***
- ***1 to 2 teaspoons lemon juice***
- ***8 ounces cream cheese, softened***
- ***12 ounces cottage cheese***
- ***1 cup sour cream***
- ***½ teaspoon ground cinnamon***
- ***½ teaspoon ground ginger***

Crush the coconut and whole-wheat crackers, and scatter over the base of a well-greased 9-inch springform pan. Cover with the combined crushed pineapple and ginger, pressing firmly into the crumbs. Chill for 30 to 40 minutes.

Preheat the oven to 325°F.

Beat the eggs, sugar, and lemon juice together until thick and fluffy. Gradually beat in the cream cheese and cottage cheese. Pour into the springform pan on top of the crumb mixture.

Bake for 35 to 40 minutes. Carefully spread the combined sour cream and spices over the surface of the cheesecake, and return to the oven for another 7 to 10 minutes. Open the oven door and allow the cheesecake to cool in the oven for 15 to 20 minutes. Remove and set in a draft-free area until cold. Chill for several hours or overnight before slicing.

Marbled Chocolate Cheesecake

Yield: 10 to 12 servings

- ***8 ounces chocolate-flavored cookies, finely crushed***
- ***2 ounces coffee-flavored cookies, finely crushed***
- ***½ teaspoon ground cinnamon***
- ***1¼ sticks butter or margarine, melted***
- ***1½ pounds cream cheese, softened***
- ***1 cup powdered sugar***
- ***3 eggs, beaten***
- ***½ cup cream***
- ***1 teaspoon brandy extract or rum extract***
- ***6 ounces baking chocolate, melted***
- ***whipped cream, for decoration***

Combine the crushed cookies with the cinnamon and cooled butter; mix thoroughly and press onto the base and sides of a well-greased 9-inch springform pan. Chill for 30 minutes.

Preheat the oven to 300°F.

Beat the cream cheese until well blended in a bowl. Gradually add the sugar, then the beaten eggs, beating well after each addition. Mix in the cream and extract. Spoon all but about 1 cup of the mixture into the crumb crust.

Combine the remaining mixture with the just-warm melted chocolate, and drizzle this over the plain mixture; with a thin-bladed knife or skewer, swirl the chocolate mixture through the plain mixture to create a marbled effect.

Bake for 35 to 40 minutes. Open the oven door and leave the cheesecake in the oven until cold. Chill for several hours or overnight, then decorate with the whipped cream and cut into slices for serving.

Right: **From top: Mincemeat Cheesecake (see p. 273); Marbled Chocolate Cheesecake (see above); Pineapple Ginger Cheesecake (see above left).**

Layered Apricot Crumble

Yield: 4 or 5 servings

1 large can (1 pound 13 ounces) apricot halves
2 tablespoons lemon juice
1 teaspoon almond extract
10 to 12 macaroons or tiny meringues, crumbled
⅓ cup brown sugar
½ teaspoon ground cinnamon
½ stick butter or margarine, melted
whipped cream, for serving

Preheat the oven to 350°F.

Drain the apricots (reserve the syrup), and slice the halves into 4 or 5 pieces. Arrange half of the apricots over the base of a well-greased casserole. Combine the lemon juice, almond extract, and ½ cup of apricot syrup, and drizzle half of this liquid over the apricots. Combine the macaroon crumbs, brown sugar, and cinnamon, and scatter half of the mixture over the apricots. Repeat each of the layers, then drizzle the melted butter over the surface. Loosely cover with aluminum foil.

Bake for 15 to 20 minutes; remove the foil cover and continue baking for another 15 to 20 minutes or until the top is crusty. Serve warm, with whipped cream if desired.

Variation: Use canned peaches, pears, rhubarb, or berries in place of the apricots.

Rhubarb Apple Crunch

Yield: 5 or 6 servings

1 cup cooked sweetened apples, drained
2 cups cooked sweetened rhubarb, drained
1 to 2 tablespoons orange juice
½ teaspoon ground cinnamon
2 eggs, separated
2 tablespoons light corn syurp or honey
1½ tablespoons custard powder
2 cups milk
2 tablespoons brown sugar
2 tablespoons rolled oats
2 tablespoons flaked coconut
½ stick butter or margarine, melted

Preheat the oven to 325°F.

Layer the cooked apples and rhubarb in the base of a greased casserole. Drizzle the orange juice over, and sprinkle with the cinnamon.

Make a rich custard with the egg yolks, corn syrup, custard powder, and milk, stirring over low heat until thickened. Pour over the apples and rhubarb.

Beat the egg whites until stiff and glossy; add the brown sugar, and beat well. Fold in the oats, coconut, and cooled butter. Spoon this roughly over the custard.

Bake for 20 to 25 minutes. Serve warm.

Note: Extra baking time may be required if the apples, rhubarb, and custard are very cold before topping with the meringue crunch.

Crusted Peach Dessert

Yield: 4 or 5 servings

1 can (15 ounces) sliced peaches
water
1 tablespoon lemon juice
1½ tablespoons cornstarch
½ teaspoon almond extract
2 tablespoons butter or margarine
1 cup self-rising flour
¼ teaspoon salt
1 egg, beaten
additional ½ stick butter or margarine, melted
¼ cup sugar
½ teaspoon ground cinnamon
whipped cream, for serving

Preheat the oven to 350°F.

Drain the peaches and set ⅓ cup of the syrup aside for the topping; measure the remaining syrup and make up to 1 cup with water.

Blend the lemon juice and cornstarch together; combine this with the syrup water and almond extract in a saucepan. Heat, stirring constantly, until thickened and bubbling, then add the butter and stir.

Arrange the peach slices over the base of a well-greased casserole, and pour the thickened syrup mixture over the top.

Sift the flour and salt into a bowl. Combine the beaten egg, melted butter, reserved peach syrup, and half of the sugar; add this to the flour and mix to a firm batter. Drop in rough spoonfuls over the peaches. Sprinkle the remaining sugar and cinnamon over the surface.

Bake for 30 to 35 minutes. Serve warm, with whipped cream if desired.

Mincemeat Cheesecake

Yield: 8 to 10 servings

8 ounces gingersnap crumbs

1 stick butter or margarine, melted

1 egg, separated

1¾ cups prepared Mincemeat (see recipe, page 222)

2 teaspoons Angostura bitters

1 pound cream cheese

1¼ cups sour cream

4 eggs, beaten

1 cup powdered sugar

2 teaspoons grated orange rind

1 tablespoon orange juice

½ teaspoon ground nutmeg

whipped cream, for topping

Combine the cookie crumbs with the cooled, melted butter and the egg yolk. Press firmly over the base and sides of a well-greased 9-inch springform pan; brush lightly beaten egg white over the surface. Chill for 1 hour.

Preheat the oven to 350°F.

Mix the prepared mincemeat and bitters together, and spoon onto the crumb crust; press lightly.

Press the cream cheese and sour cream through a fine sieve into a bowl. Beat the eggs and sugar until thickened, then gradually add the cream-cheese mixture, beating well after each addition. Flavor with the orange rind and orange juice, and spoon the mixture over the mincemeat.

Bake for 15 minutes, then reduce the oven temperature to 300°F and continue baking for 20 to 25 minutes. Allow to stand in the oven with the door ajar for 15 minutes, then remove, allow to cool, and refrigerate (preferably overnight). Just before serving, dust the surface of the cheesecake with nutmeg and decorate with whipped cream.

Continental Raisin Squares

Yield: 9 to 12 dessert squares

Base:
1½ cups flour

½ cup cornstarch

1 teaspoon baking powder

¼ teaspoon salt

1 stick butter or margarine

2 tablespoons confectioners' sugar

1 egg

milk, as required

Topping:
8 ounces cream cheese

1 stick butter or margarine

3 eggs

¼ cup powdered sugar

2 teaspoons grated lemon rind

½ cup chopped raisins

1 teaspoon cinnamon or nutmeg

whipped cream, for serving

Preheat the oven to 350°F. Grease a 9- to 10-inch-square cake pan.

Base: Sift the flour, cornstarch, baking powder, and salt together. Beat the butter until creamy, stir in the confectioners' sugar, and gradually beat in the egg. Mix in the flour mixture and add sufficient milk to make a soft dough. Press over the base of the cake pan. Prick the dough generously with a fork.

Bake for 10 minutes only; lift out and set aside.

Topping: Beat the cream cheese and butter together until very creamy; beat the eggs and sugar together and add to the creamed mixture gradually. Add the lemon rind and fold the raisins into the mixture; spoon over the partly baked base and sprinkle the cinnamon over the top.

Place the cake pan on a cake sheet and return to the oven for 35 to 40 minutes; allow to stand in the oven with the door ajar for 10 minutes before removing. Serve cool or chilled, cut into squares; add a dot of whipped cream for decoration.

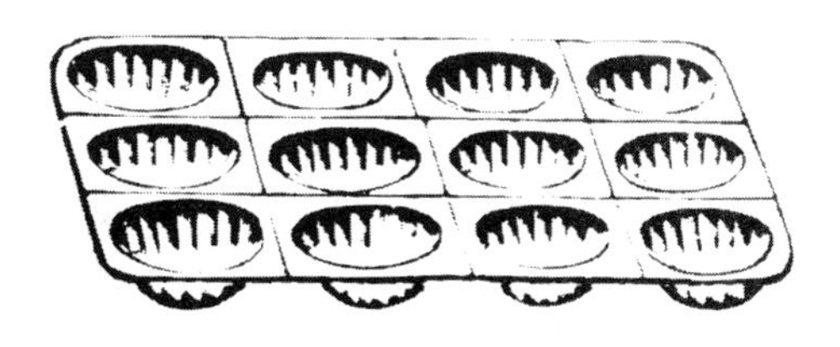

One-Dish Date Pudding

Yield: 5 or 6 servings

1 cup chopped dates
½ stick butter or margarine, chopped
1 cup boiling water
1 teaspoon grated lemon rind
1 egg
1½ cups self-rising flour, sifted
½ cup brown sugar
¼ teaspoon ground cinnamon
¼ cup chopped walnuts
additional 1 cup brown sugar
additional 1 cup boiling water

Preheat the oven to 375°F.

Scatter the dates over the base of a casserole 8 inches round. Add the butter, then the boiling water, stirring to soften the dates.

Add the lemon rind, egg, flour, brown sugar, and cinnamon. Beat lightly until well blended; scrape the base and sides of the casserole occasionally while mixing. Scatter the combined walnuts and additional brown sugar over the surface. Carefully pour the additional boiling water over all.

Bake for 40 to 45 minutes. Serve hot or warm.

Oven-Steamed Syrup Pudding

Yield: 5 or 6 servings

1 cup self-rising flour, sifted
1 cup soft white bread crumbs
⅓ cup brown sugar
1 teaspoon grated lemon rind
4 ounces grated chilled suet or margarine
1 egg, beaten
⅓ to ½ cup milk
¾ cup light corn syrup
warm custard, for serving

Preheat the oven to 375°F.

Combine the flour, bread crumbs, sugar, and lemon rind in a bowl. Add the grated suet, and mix to a fairly soft dough with the beaten egg and as much milk as required.

Spread a little corn syrup over the base of a well-greased ovenproof bowl. Add the dough and the remaining syrup in layers until the bowl is about two-thirds filled. Cover with greased aluminum foil and press to seal around the sides. Lower the bowl into a larger pan containing 2 to 3 cups of boiling water and place into the preheated oven.

Steam-bake for 30 minutes, then lower the oven temperature to 325°F and cook for 1 to 1¼ hours, replenishing the boiling water as required. Remove and allow to stand for 5 to 6 minutes before unmolding onto a serving plate; cut into slices. Serve with custard.

Steam-Baked Carrot Ring

Yield: 6 to 8 servings

½ stick butter or margarine, softened
½ cup sugar
2 eggs
1 teaspoon mixed spices
¼ teaspoon salt
¾ cup soft white bread crumbs
⅓ cup raisins
½ cup chopped walnuts
1 cup cooked, mashed carrots, cooled
2 tablespoons sweet sherry
2 tablespoons evaporated milk

Preheat the oven to 350°F.

Beat the butter and sugar until creamy. Add the eggs one at a time, and beat well before adding the spices, salt, and bread crumbs. Mix in the raisins, walnuts, mashed carrots, sherry, and evaporated milk.

Turn the mixture into a well-greased and crumb-coated fluted ring mold and cover securely with greased aluminum foil. Stand in a baking pan containing 1 to 1½ inches boiling water.

Steam-bake for 55 to 60 minutes. Serve hot with custard, cream, or ice cream.

Microwave Cooking: The pudding mixture can be placed into a nonmetal ring mold and cooked in a microwave oven for 8 to 10 minutes on medium heat. Allow to stand for 8 to 10 minutes before slicing and serving.

Right: **Steam-Baked Carrot Ring (see above).**

Golden Cheesecake Squares

Yield: 9 servings

2 cups self-rising flour

1½ teaspoons grated lemon rind

¼ teaspoon salt

1 stick butter or margarine, melted

½ cup powdered sugar

2 eggs, beaten

¾ cup milk

8 ounces thinly sliced canned peaches, drained

Topping:
3 eggs, separated

½ cup sugar

12 ounces cream cheese, sieved

½ cup cream

1½ tablespoons cornstarch

½ cup flaked almonds

¼ teaspoon ground cinnamon

Preheat the oven to 350°F.

Combine the flour, lemon rind, and salt in a bowl and make a depression in the center; add the cooled butter, sugar, eggs, and milk, and gradually work in to form a smooth mixture. Spread over the base of a well-greased 9-inch-square cake pan. Place the sliced peaches in a layer over the surface.

Topping: Combine the egg yolks, sugar, cream cheese, cream, and cornstarch, and beat briskly until smooth. Fold in the stiffly beaten egg whites. Spoon the topping over the peaches.

Bake for 20 minutes. Quickly scatter the almonds and cinnamon over the surface, reduce the oven temperature to 300°F, and continue baking for another 30 to 35 minutes. Allow to cool slightly, mark into squares, then cool and chill before serving.

Sour-Cherry Cream Pudding

Yield: 5 or 6 servings

¾ cup powdered sugar

½ stick butter or margarine, softened

2 eggs, separated

1 cup flour

1 teaspoon baking powder

¼ teaspoon salt

¼ to ⅓ cup milk

1 can (15 ounces) sour red cherries

additional ¼ cup sugar

½ cup cherry syrup

whipped cream, for serving

Preheat the oven to 350°F.

Beat the sugar and butter until creamy; add the egg yolks and beat well. Sift the flour, baking powder, and salt over the sugar–egg mixture. Drizzle ¼ cup of milk down one side of the bowl and lightly fold in; add extra milk, if required, to make a soft cake batter.

Whisk the egg whites until soft peaks form. Carefully fold into the cake batter—do not overmix. Spoon the mixture into a well-greased casserole.

Heat the cherries, extra sugar, and cherry syrup until boiling, and carefully pour over the cake mixture.

Bake for 30 to 35 minutes. Remove from the oven and allow to cool slightly. Serve warm, with whipped cream, if desired.

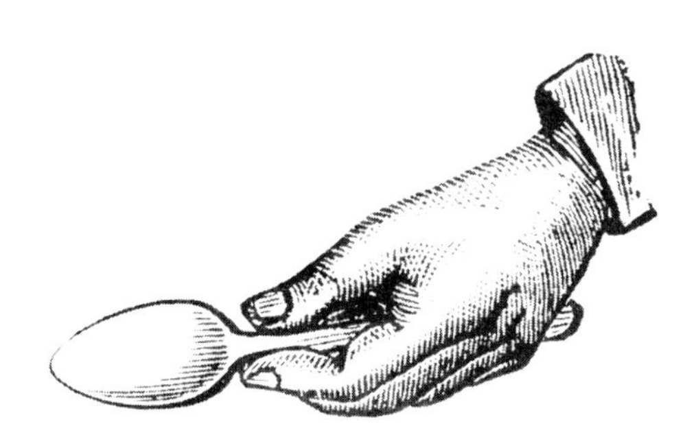

Mocha Walnut Pudding

Yield: 5 to 6 servings

1 package chocolate cake mix

egg and water (less 1 tablespoon), as directed

¼ cup brown sugar

¼ cup white sugar

½ cup chopped walnuts

¼ cup chopped raisins

1 tablespoon cocoa powder

1 cup hot black coffee

Preheat the oven to 350°F.

Prepare the chocolate cake mix with the egg as directed on the package but use less water than specified. Spoon into a well-greased casserole.

Combine the sugars with the walnuts, raisins, and cocoa, and scatter over the cake mixture. Carefully pour the hot coffee over the surface.

Bake for 35 to 40 minutes. Serve hot or warm.

One-Two-Three Chocolate Pudding

Yield: 4 or 5 servings

1 cup self-rising flour

¾ cup sugar

¼ teaspoon salt

2 tablespoons cocoa powder

½ cup milk

1 to 1½ tablespoons corn oil

1 teaspoon vanilla extract

½ cup chopped raisins

¼ cup chopped walnuts

¾ cup brown sugar

additional ¼ cup cocoa powder

1¾ cups very hot water

Preheat the oven to 325°F.

Sift the first four ingredients into a bowl. Add the next five ingredients, and mix well. Pour into a well-greased casserole. Combine the brown sugar and extra cocoa, and sprinkle it over the mixture. Carefully pour the hot water over the surface.

Bake for 40 to 45 minutes. Serve warm.

Baked Pancakes Jubilee

Yield: 4 servings

Filling:
2 green cooking apples, peeled, cored, and sliced

½ stick butter or margarine

¼ cup raisins

¼ teaspoon ground cinnamon

¼ teaspoon ground nutmeg

Pancakes:
¼ cup flour

⅛ teaspoon salt

1 egg, beaten

1½ tablespoons strong coffee

1½ tablespoons milk

¾ stick butter or margarine, melted

confectioners' sugar, for sprinkling

ice cream, for serving

Filling: Cook the sliced apples in the heated butter over low heat until just softened. Add the raisins and spices, and mix. Keep the filling warm.

Pancakes: Preheat the oven to 450°F.

Sift the flour and salt into a bowl; add the egg, coffee, and milk and whisk lightly for 2 to 3 minutes.

Pour half of the melted butter into each of two deep 9-inch enamel pie plates; tilt the plates to coat the bases and sides. Heat the pie plates over a very low heat; when the butter is gently sizzling, pour half of the pancake batter into each plate.

Immediatley place into the preheated oven and bake for 10 to 12 minutes. After 2 or 3 minutes the batter will begin to bubble and puff up, so quickly open the oven door and prick or puncture with a skewer or fork; repeat this process once or twice more as the batter puffs up. Then reduce the oven temperature to 350°F and continue baking for another 8 to 10 minutes. The batter will gradually creep up the sides of the plates during the baking. When golden brown and crisp around the edges, remove from the oven and carefully drain off any surplus butter.

To assemble the pancakes: Spoon half of the filling down the center of each pancake and fold the sides over the center; dust each liberally with confectioners' sugar. Cut each roll in half. Serve with ice cream if desired.

Lemon Honey Sponge

Yield: 4 or 5 servings

¾ stick butter or margarine, softened

1 cup powdered sugar

1 tablespoon honey

3 teaspoons grated lemon rind

¼ cup lemon juice

3 eggs, separated

1½ cups milk (at room temperature)

⅓ cup self-rising flour

¼ cup cornstarch

Preheat the oven to 300°F.

Beat the butter and sugar until white and creamy. Add the honey, lemon rind, and lemon juice, and beat well. Add the egg yolks and gradually beat in the milk (the mixture will "curdle" slightly). Fold in the sifted flour and cornstarch.

Beat the egg whites until well foamed but not stiff; carefully fold into the batter mixture (pieces of egg white should still remain visible). Spoon the mixture into a well-greased casserole.

Bake for 55 to 60 minutes.

Note: The pudding can be baked at a slightly higher or lower temperature while a main-course roast is in the oven; adjust the timing as required. Serve warm, with ice cream if desired.

Lemon Apple Sponge

Yield: 4 or 5 servings

1 stick butter or margarine, softened

¼ cup powdered sugar

2 eggs, separated

3 teaspoons grated lemon rind

½ cup lemon juice

2 cups stale sponge-cake pieces

1 teaspoon baking powder

⅓ cup sugar

1 large apple

Preheat the oven to 325°F.

Beat the butter and powdered sugar until creamy; add the egg yolks and lemon rind and beat well. Mix in the lemon juice and sponge-cake pieces. Scatter the baking powder over the surface and mix.

Turn into a well-greased shallow casserole and place in the oven; loosely cover with a sheet of aluminum foil.

Bake for 30 to 35 minutes. (When cooked, remove from the oven and increase the oven temperature to 400°F.)

Beat the egg whites until stiff and glossy; gradually add the sugar, beating well after each addition. Core the apple but do not peel; grate it coarsely and fold into the meringue mixture. Carefully spoon the meringue over the top of the lemon sponge and return it to the hotter oven to set the surface (about 7 minutes). Serve hot or warm.

Upside-Down Pudding

Yield: 5 or 6 servings

Butterscotch Layer:
½ cup brown sugar

¾ stick butter, softened

fruits and nuts—see below

Cake Layer:
¾ stick butter or margarine, softened

⅓ cup powdered sugar

1 teaspoon vanilla extract

2 eggs, beaten

¼ cup milk

1½ cups self-rising flour

Butterscotch layer: Preheat the oven to 350°F.

Cream the brown sugar and butter together, and spread over the base of a well-greased 8-inch-round or -square cake pan. Arrange the fruits and nuts over the surface in a pattern.

Cake layer: Beat the butter, sugar, and vanilla extract together until creamy. Add the eggs and milk, and beat well. Fold in the sifted flour, and carefully spread over the arranged fruits and nuts.

Bake for 30 to 35 minutes. Allow to stand in the pan for 6 to 8 minutes, then invert onto a serving platter so that the fruit and nut pattern is uppermost. Serve hot in wedges or squares, with hot custard or ice cream as desired.

Fruits and Nuts:
- Dried apricots, prunes, and walnuts—lightly soaked, and seeded as required.
- Pineapple, ginger, and pecans—sliced—with candied ginger pieces.
- Peaches, cherries, and almonds—sliced—with halved candied cherries.

Right: **Upside-Down Pudding (see above).**

Chocolate Bread Pudding

Yield: 6 to 8 servings

3 cups milk
1 cup cream
1½ cups soft white bread crumbs
4 ounces baking chocolate, grated
additional 2 cups milk
½ cup sugar
½ cup raisins
1 teaspoon vanilla extract
4 eggs, separated

Heat the milk and cream in a nonstick saucepan until scalding. Add the bread crumbs and set aside, loosely covered, for 30 minutes.

Preheat the oven to 300°F.

Melt the chocolate in the top half of a double boiler, then add the extra milk and the sugar and stir over low heat until blended.

Stir the raisins into the bread-crumb mixture, add the vanilla and egg yolks, and beat well, gradually adding the chocolate milk.

Whisk the egg whites until well foamed and fold into the breaded milk. Carefully pour into a well-greased casserole. Place the casserole dish on a cookie sheet.

Bake for 1 to 1¼ hours or until set. Remove from the oven, allow to stand for 10 to 15 minutes. Serve warm.

Speedy Chocolate-Fudge Dessert

Yield: 6 to 8 servings

1 package chocolate cake mix
1 package chocolate-flavored instant pudding mix
1 cup water, lukewarm
¼ cup vegetable oil
whipped cream or creamy custard, for serving
shaved chocolate, for decoration

Empty the cake and pudding mixes into a bowl, and make a well in the center. Add the water and oil, and beat on the medium speed of an electric mixer for 4 minutes.

Line and generously grease a 10-inch microwave-safe ring pan (or place a small glass in the center of a cake pan; pour the mixture into the pan and cook in a microwave oven on medium heat (or according to manufacturer's directions for cake cooking) for 15 minutes.

Remove from the oven and cover loosely with a cloth; allow to stand for 15 minutes, then turn out. Serve warm, with whipped cream or custard as desired and a decoration of shaved chocolate.

Swiss Apricot Trifle

Yield: 6 servings

¾ cup dried apricots
½ cup sweet sherry, warmed
1 sponge jelly roll, homemade or purchased
3 eggs, separated
1½ tablespoons custard powder
½ cup sugar
1 teaspoon vanilla extract
2½ cups milk
½ teaspoon grated nutmeg
candied cherries, for decoration
candied angelica, for decoration
whipped cream, for serving

Generously brush the apricots all over with the warmed sherry. Let them stand for 15 to 20 minutes, re-brushing from time to time.

Preheat the oven to 350°F.

Cut the jelly roll into slices and line the base and sides of a well-greased, shallow casserole. Place the apricots over the sponge slices; sprinkle any remaining sweet sherry over the top.

Beat the egg yolks with the custard powder, half of the sugar, the vanilla, and with sufficient milk to blend to a creamy mixture. Heat the remaining milk in a nonstick saucepan until scalding. Gradually stir in the egg mixture and the nutmeg, and continue stirring over very low heat until thickened. Carefully spoon over the apricots and sponge slices.

Beat the egg whites and remaining sugar until it is the consistency of a meringue. Spoon it roughly over the custard.

Bake for 15 to 20 minutes. Press a few candied cherries and angelica pieces into the meringue for decoration, and allow to stand for 15 to 20 minutes. Serve warm, with whipped cream if desired.

Chocolate Snowdrift

Yield: 4 or 5 servings

1 cup flour
1 teaspoon baking powder
2 tablespoons butter or margarine
3 cups boiling milk
¼ cup sugar
2 eggs, separated
1 teaspoon vanilla extract
3 ounces baking chocolate, coarsely grated
whipped cream, for serving

Preheat the oven to 400° F.

Sift the flour and baking powder into a heatproof bowl, and rub in the butter. Make a well in the center, and pour in the boiling milk, whisking quickly and constantly.

Add the sugar, egg yolks, and vanilla and beat well. Beat the egg whites until stiff and fold into the mixture—do not overmix. Spoon the mixture into a well-greased casserole and sprinkle the chocolate over the surface.

Bake for 15 to 17 minutes or until the mixture sets. Remove from the oven; allow to stand for 5 or 6 minutes. Serve warm with whipped cream if desired.

Old-Fashioned Roly Poly

Yield: 8 servings

2 cups self-rising flour
½ teaspoon salt
1½ tablespoons sugar
1 tablespoon powdered milk
4 ounces shredded suet (or shredded chilled margarine)
water to mix, chilled
½ to ¾ cup raspberry jam (jelly)
2 or 3 firm bananas
creamy custard, for serving

Preheat the oven to 425°F.

Place the flour, salt, and sugar into a bowl with the powdered milk and suet, and toss to mix well. Using a knife for mixing, add sufficient water to mix to a soft pliable dough. Turn onto a floured board and knead very lightly. Pat out to a rectangle about 1 inch thick.

Spread the raspberry jam over the surface to within 1 inch of the edge. Place the peeled bananas along one side; loosely roll up the dough, and lift onto a well-greased cookie sheet. Using a sharp knife, make three or four slashes along the surface of the roll; brush the surface with water.

Bake for 30 to 40 minutes. Serve hot, cut into slices, with creamy custard.

Sweet Syrup Puffs

Yield: 4 or 5 servings

1¼ cups self-rising flour, sifted
1 teaspoon grated lemon rind
¼ teaspoon salt
3 tablespoons butter or margarine
1 egg, beaten
3 tablespoons milk
¾ cup brown sugar
additional ½ stick butter or margarine
2 tablespoons light corn syrup
2 cups boiling water
whipped cream, for serving

Combine the flour, lemon rind, and salt in a bowl, and rub in the butter. Add the combined egg and milk, and mix to a soft dough. Turn onto a floured board and knead lightly. Shape into a long roll and cut into 8 to 10 slices; place these on a plate and chill for 10 to 15 minutes.

Preheat the oven to 375°F.

Combine the brown sugar, butter, corn syrup, and boiling water in a small baking pan.

Bake for 5 to 7 minutes. Lift out, carefully drop in each of the dough slices, and quickly baste the pan liquid over them; return to the oven for 17 to 20 minutes.

Serve the puffs hot, with the syrup spooned over and an accompanying bowl of whipped cream for individual use.

Fruited Muesli Dessert

Yield: 6 servings

4 eggs, separated
1½ cups milk
¾ cup sweetened condensed milk
1½ tablespoons cornstarch
3 or 4 bananas
1 cup raisins
1½ cups toasted muesli cereal
⅓ cup sugar

Preheat the oven to 350°F. Grease a casserole.

Combine the egg yolks with the milk, condensed milk, and cornstarch in a nonstick saucepan. Cook over low heat, stirring constantly, until the consistency is that of a thin custard.

Peel the bananas and cut into slices; arrange them in layers in the greased casserole with the raisins and the muesli cereal. Spoon hot custard between each layer.

Beat the egg whites until stiff and glossy; gradually add the sugar, beating well between each addition. Spoon roughly over the layers of dessert in the casserole.

Bake until the meringue is tipped with golden brown (17 to 20 minutes). Serve warm or cold.

Note: If preparing the first section of the dessert ahead of time, place it in the oven to heat through before topping with the meringue.

Almond-Cream Roll

Yield: 8 servings

3 eggs (at room temperature)
½ cup powdered sugar, slightly warmed
1 cup self-rising flour
¼ teaspoon almond extract
2 to 3 tablespoons milk or water
Filling: ***1 stick butter or margarine, softened***
½ cup powdered sugar
2 eggs, separated
1 cup ground almonds
¼ cup heavy cream, whipped
Topping: ***2 to 3 tablespoons sweet sherry***
1 tablespoon orange juice
1 cup heavy cream, chilled
2 to 3 teaspoons confectioners' sugar
2 to 3 teaspoons grated orange rind

Preheat the oven to 375°F. Prepare a 14 × 10-inch jelly-roll pan by lining it with greaseproof paper and greasing thoroughly.

Place the eggs and sugar into a bowl and beat until very thick—about 12 to 15 minutes. Fold in the sifted flour, and add the almond extract with sufficient milk to mix to a soft sponge batter. Spread into the prepared pan.

Bake for 12 to 15 minutes. Turn out onto greaseproof paper (lightly dusted with powdered sugar), then carefully roll the sponge up with the greaseproof paper. Leave for 2 to 3 minutes, then carefully unroll and remove the paper. Loosely re-roll, and allow to cool.

Filling: Cream the butter and sugar well. Gradually beat in the egg yolks; then add the ground almonds, mixing well.

Beat the egg whites until well foamed; add the cream and fold through. Carefully fold into the butter mixture. Unroll the sponge and spread the filling over; re-roll.

Topping: Combine the sweet sherry and orange juice, and sprinkle it over the outside of the sponge. Chill for 30 minutes.

Whip the cream until stiff. Add the confectioners' sugar and orange rind. Spread over the outside of the sponge roll, swirling to form an attractive design on the surface. Chill until ready to slice and serve.

***Right:* Fruited Muesli Dessert (see above left).**

Passion-Fruit Pavlova

Yield: 8 to 10 servings

6 egg whites (at room temperature)

⅛ teaspoon cream of tartar

1 cup sugar

1 tablespoon cornstarch

2 teaspoons white vinegar

cornstarch, for dusting

Topping:
1¼ cups heavy cream, chilled

1 teaspoon vanilla extract

2 teaspoons confectioners' sugar

pulp of 4 large passion fruits (or ½ to ¾ cup canned passion-fruit pulp)

Preheat the oven to 400°F.

Beat the egg whites (preferably in a large glass bowl) until stiff and glossy. Combine the cream of tartar, sugar, and cornstarch, and gradually add to the egg whites, beating well after each addition. Sprinkle the vinegar over the surface and fold in lightly—do not overmix.

Grease the base and sides of an 8-inch springform pan and dust with cornstarch; shake off any excess. Pile the meringue into the pan, spreading to form a slight depression in the center.

Place into the preheated oven, close the door, and immediately reduce the oven temperature to 250°F, and bake for 1¼ to 1½ hours.

Open the oven door and leave the meringue standing in the oven for 15 minutes, before removing to a draft-free area; carefully loosen the springform-pan rim and allow to cool. (The meringue may sink slightly in the center.) Carefully lift the meringue onto a flat platter, removing the pan base.

Topping: Whip the cream, vanilla, and confectioners' sugar until thickened and firm. Spoon onto the meringue; lightly spread it. Spoon the passion-fruit pulp over the cream, and chill until ready to serve.

Notes: For ease of slicing, use a large knife constantly dipped into hot water.

Where passion fruit is unavailable, substitute sliced kiwi fruit.

Hazelnut Meringue

Yield: 8 servings

4 egg whites

1 cup powdered sugar

½ teaspoon vinegar

1 teaspoon instant coffee powder

1 cup ground hazelnuts

Topping:
1¼ cups heavy cream, chilled

2 teaspoons confectioners' sugar

2 ounces grated chocolate

1 to 2 tablespoons whiskey cream liqueur

2 ounces chocolate, melted

whole hazelnuts, for decoration

Preheat the oven to 375°F.

Beat the egg whites until stiff and glossy. Gradually add the sugar, beating constantly; then add the vinegar and coffee powder, and beat. Fold in the ground hazlenuts. Spoon the mixture into two 8-inch greased springform pans (or cake pans with removable bases).

Bake for 35 to 40 minutes. Remove from the oven, loosen the springform rings, and allow to cool.

Topping: Whip the cream until stiff. Sweeten with the confectioners' sugar and fold in the grated chocolate.

To assemble the meringue: Drizzle the whiskey cream liqueur over each of the hazelnut meringues. Spread each with the whipped chocolate cream, and sandwich together. Drizzle the melted chocolate over the top layer of cream, and decorate with whole hazelnuts. Chill well before serving.

Right: **Hazelnut Meringue (see above); Passion-Fruit Pavlova (see above left).**

Orange Date Squares

Yield: 8 servings

3 cups chopped dates
¼ cup sugar
½ cup water
¾ cup orange juice
2 to 3 teaspoons grated orange rind
1½ sticks butter or margarine, softened
1 cup brown sugar
1 egg
1 teaspoon vanilla extract
2 cups self-rising flour, sifted
1½ cups quick-cooking oats
¼ teaspoon mixed spices
warm custard, for serving

Combine the dates with the sugar, water, orange juice, and orange rind in a saucepan; heat slowly, stirring constantly, until bubbling, then lower the heat and simmer for 2 to 3 minutes. Allow to cool.

Preheat the oven to 375°F. Thoroughly grease an 8- or 9-inch-square cake pan.

Beat the butter and brown sugar until creamy. Add the egg and vanilla and mix well. Add the flour, oats, and spices, and stir thoroughly.

Press about two-thirds of the mixture into the prepared cake pan and spread the cooled date mixture over. Crumble the remaining oat mixture over the surface; press lightly.

Bake for 30 to 35 minutes. Cut into squares while still hot. Serve warm, with custard spooned over each square.

Glazed Fruit Shortcake

Yield: 8 to 10 servings

Shortcake:
1½ sticks butter or margarine, softened
¾ cup powdered sugar
2 eggs, beaten
2¼ cups self-rising flour, sifted
rind and juice of 1 small orange

Topping:
½ cup candied cherries, chopped
½ cup raisins, chopped
½ cup slivered almonds
⅓ cup brown sugar
¼ cup self-rising flour
½ stick butter or margarine, melted
¼ cup light corn syrup, warmed

Preheat the oven to 350°F.

Shortcake: Cream the butter and sugar together well. Add the eggs and beat thoroughly. Fold in the sifted flour. Then add the orange rind and sufficient orange juice to form a firm cake mixture. Spread into a well-greased 8-inch springform pan.

Bake for 45 to 50 minutes.

Topping: Combine the cherries, raisins, almonds, sugar, and flour in a bowl. Drizzle the melted butter over, and mix well.

Without removing the cake from the oven, carefully coat the surface with the fruit–nut mixture; drizzle the corn syrup over the top, and continue baking for another 15 to 20 minutes.

Remove from the oven, allow to stand for 3 to 4 minutes, then lift off the springform ring and continue cooling for 10 to 15 minutes. Serve warm, with ice cream or custard.

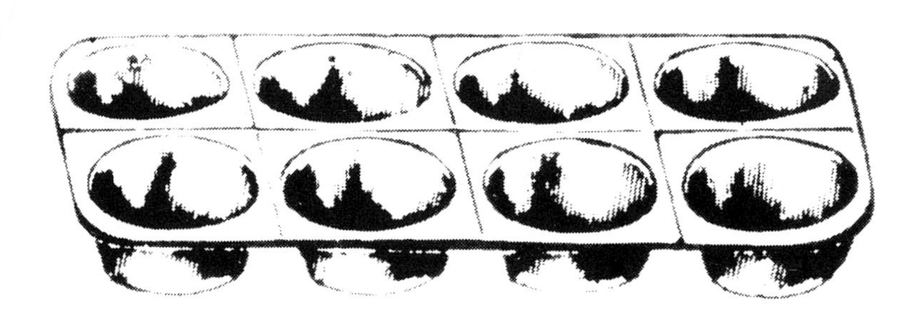

Peach-Kuchen Squares

Yield: 9 servings

1 package yellow cake mix
½ cup flaked coconut
1 stick butter or margarine, chopped
1 can (1 pound 13 ounces) sliced peaches, well drained
¼ cup brown sugar
½ teaspoon cinnamon
1¼ cups sour cream
2 eggs, beaten
additional 1 tablespoon brown sugar, for topping
additional flaked coconut, for topping

Preheat the oven to 350°F.

Mix the contents of the cake mix package with the coconut. Cut in the butter until the mixture resembles coarse bread crumbs, and press over the base of a well-greased 9-inch-square cake pan.

Bake for 15 to 20 minutes. Remove from the oven and allow to cool slightly. (Leave the oven on.)

Arrange the peach slices over the partially baked base; sprinkle the combined brown sugar and cinnamon over the top. Beat the sour cream and eggs together until just blended; spoon over the peaches. Sprinkle the additional brown sugar and coconut over the surface.

Return to the oven and bake for another 10 to 15 minutes, until the topping is set. Serve warm, cut into squares.

One-Egg Meringue

Yield: 6 servings

1 egg white
1 cup powdered sugar
2 tablespoons boiling water
1 teaspoon vanilla extract
2 teaspoons baking powder
cornstarch, for dusting
Filling: ***1½ to 2 cups chopped fruit salad, well drained***
1¼ cups heavy cream, chilled
1 to 2 teaspoons confectioners' sugar

Lightly mix the egg white and all but 2 teaspoons of the sugar in the small bowl of an electric mixer. Cover loosely and set aside for several hours or overnight.

Next day: Re-beat the sugared egg white in the mixer for 2 minutes on medium speed; add the boiling water and vanilla, and beat on high speed for 15 minutes. Remove the beaters, sift the baking powder over the surface and fold in very lightly but thoroughly.

Preheat the oven to 250°F.

Prepare a cookie sheet by greasing and dusting lightly with cornstarch. Mark a 7-inch circle in the center and roughly cover with the meringue. Form a slight depression in the center of the meringue, and dust the edges with the reserved 2 teaspoons of sugar.

Bake for 1 to 1¼ hours. Allow to stand in the oven with the door ajar for 30 minutes; then remove and allow to cool.

Filling: Just before serving, spoon the fruit salad onto the center, and cover with whipped cream that has been sweetened with the sugar.

Cut into wedges to serve.

Butterscotch Meringue Sponge

Yield: 6 servings

1 8-inch sponge cake

1 to 2 tablespoons sweet sherry

2 tablespoons cornstarch

½ cup brown sugar

2 eggs, separated

1¼ cups whole milk

½ cup sugar

½ stick butter

½ teaspoon vanilla extract

½ cup chopped almonds or walnuts

whipped cream, for serving

Cut the sponge horizontally into halves, and sprinkle the sweet sherry over each half. Place the bottom half onto an ovenproof platter about 3 inches wider than the cake.

Blend the cornstarch, brown sugar, egg yolks, and milk in a nonstick saucepan and cook over low heat, stirring constantly, until thickened and boiling; simmer for 1 minute. Remove from the heat, and cover tightly to avoid a skin forming on the surface.

Place half the sugar with the butter and vanilla into a small pan; heat until the mixture is bubbling and beginning to brown, then quickly beat it into the hot custard. Allow the butterscotch to cool.

Preheat the oven to 400°F.

Spread the cooled butterscotch over the bottom sponge layer and place the top layer over to form a sandwich. Scatter the chopped almonds over the surface.

Beat the egg whites until stiff and glossy; gradually add the remaining sugar, beating well between each addition to form a meringue. Spoon the meringue over the top and sides of the filled sponge, swirling to form an attractive design. Place the platter onto a cookie sheet in the hot oven.

Bake for 4 to 5 minutes or until the meringue crust is crisp. Remove from the oven, and carefully cut into wedges. Serve with whipped cream.

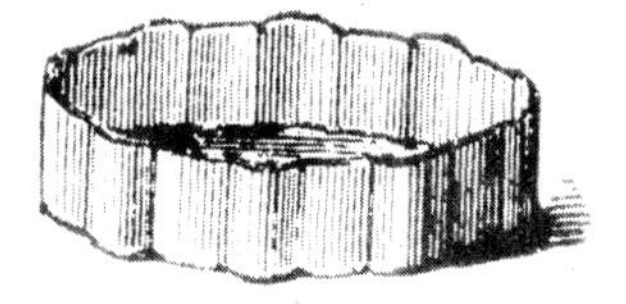

Choc-Coffee Torte

Yield: 8 to 10 servings

5 egg whites (at room temperature)

1 cup powdered sugar

2 teaspoons cornstarch

1 6-ounce package chocolate chips

1 teaspoon coffee extract

Filling:
4 ounces baking chocolate, chopped

2 egg yolks

¼ cup sugar

1 cup half-coffee, half-milk

1 to 2 tablespoons coffee liqueur

1 cup heavy cream, chilled

1 to 2 teaspoons confectioners' sugar

Preheat the oven to 275°F.

Beat the egg whites until stiff and glossy. Sprinkle one-third of the sugar over the surface, and beat again for 3 to 5 minutes. Combine the remaining sugar and the cornstarch; sprinkle over the egg whites and fold in very gently but thoroughly—do not overmix. Fold in the chocolate chips and coffee extract.

Cover a cookie sheet with aluminum foil. Mark out a circle about 8 to 9 inches round and brush this area with oil. Pile the meringue onto the greased foil, slightly depressing the center of it to form a pastry shell.

Bake in the preheated oven for 30 minutes, then reduce the oven temperature to 225°F and bake for another 40 to 45 minutes. Remove to a draft-free area to cool.

Filling: Melt the chocolate in the top half of a double boiler over hot—not boiling—water. Combine the beaten egg yolks, sugar, and milk–coffee; add this to the chocolate and cook, stirring constantly, until it is of a custard consistency. Flavor with the liqueur and set aside to cool.

Whip the cream and sweeten it with the confectioners' sugar.

To assemble: Carefully peel the aluminum foil away from the base of the meringue and place it on a flat platter. Spoon the chocolate filling into the center, and decorate with the whipped cream. Chill until ready to serve.

Right: **Strawberry Crêpes Royale** **(see p. 268).**

White-Mountain Meringue

Yield: 8 to 10 servings

Meringue:
4 egg whites (at room temperature)
¼ teaspoon salt
¼ teaspoon cream of tartar or ½ teaspoon lemon juice
1¼ cups powdered sugar
1 teaspoon vanilla extract
cornstarch, for dusting
Topping:
1 can (1 pound) chestnut puree
2 tablespoons brandy liqueur
1 cup heavy cream, chilled
1 tablespoon confectioners' sugar
2 ounces baking chocolate, coarsely grated, or ¼ cup chopped walnuts

Preheat the oven to 300°F.

Meringue: Whisk the egg whites with the salt until stiff and glossy but not dry. Beat in the cream of tartar (or lemon juice). Gradually add the sugar, a tablespoon at a time, beating well after each addition until about two-thirds has been added and the mixture resembles a thick marshmallow. Fold in all but 1 tablespoon of the remaining sugar, and the vanilla.

Cover a cookie sheet with aluminum foil and lightly grease the area of a 7-inch circle; dust over the circle with cornstarch. Spoon the meringue into a large piping bag fitted with a fluted or rose tube. Fill the prepared circle with a spiral of meringue. Then continue to pipe decreasing sizes of spiral circles—one on top of the other—until a cone shape is formed and the meringue is all used.

Place in the preheated oven and bake for 20 minutes. Lower the oven temperature to 250°F and continue baking for another 45 to 50 minutes. Carefully remove the meringue from the foil while it is still warm and place onto a serving plate to cool.

Topping: Combine the chestnut puree with the brandy liqueur, beating well. Whip the cream with the confectioners' sugar until it is thick yet still soft, then chill well.

Drizzle the chestnut puree mixture from the top of the meringue cone so that it runs unevenly down the sides. Spoon the cream over in the same fashion but do not entirely cover the puree. Scatter the chocolate or walnuts over the top and serve.

Pavlova Plus

Yield: 8 servings

Meringue:
5 egg whites
¼ teaspoon salt
1 cup sugar
2 teaspoons cornstarch
2 teaspoons vinegar
Filling:
1¼ cups heavy cream, chilled
2 to 3 teaspoons confectioners' sugar
1 teaspoon vanilla extract
Topping:
1 cup chopped canned fruits
1 cup chopped dried fruits
1 cup canned fruit syrup
½ cup jam (jelly) or marmalade
¼ to ⅓ cup brandy

Preheat the oven to 300°F.

Meringue: Beat the egg whites with the salt until stiff and glossy. Add half of the sugar in small amounts, beating well after each addition. Combine the remaining sugar and cornstarch, and fold in the egg whites. Sprinkle the vinegar over the surface, and fold in—do not overbeat.

Place a 9- to 10-inch round of aluminum foil or greaseproof paper onto a cookie sheet; grease lightly and dust a little cornstarch over the surface. Spread the meringue over the foil or paper, scooping out the center slightly to resemble a pie shell.

Bake for 60 to 70 minutes. Open the oven door and allow the meringue to cool slowly for 15 to 20 minutes, then remove to a draft-free area to stand until completely cold.

Filling: Whip the cream until thickened, add sugar (to taste) with the vanilla, and chill until required.

Topping: Combine the fruits, fruit syrup, and jam or marmalade in a saucepan, and bring slowly to a boil over low heat; simmer for 3 to 4 minutes, then remove from the heat. Add the brandy, and stir. Allow to cool, and chill until required.

To assemble the dessert: Carefully peel the foil or paper away from the base of the meringue; place on a flat serving plate. Spoon the cream filling into the recessed section of the meringue, and drizzle the brandied fruit sauce over the surface. Cut into slices for serving.

Note: Canned apricots, peaches, pineapple, etc., can be mixed with dried apricots, raisins, prunes, etc., in varying proportions as desired.

Mocha Macaroon Parfaits

Yield: 5 or 6 servings

Macaroons:
3 egg whites, unchilled

1 cup sugar

½ cup instant potato flakes, dry

1 cup flaked coconut

⅛ teaspoon salt

1 teaspoon instant coffee powder

Mocha Parfaits:
¼ to ⅓ cup marsala wine, coffee-flavored

1¼ cups cream

3 ounces semisweet chocolate, grated

1 teaspoon instant coffee powder

1 tablespoon confectioners' sugar

Macaroons: Preheat the oven to 350°F.

Beat the egg whites until stiff and glossy. Gradually add the sugar, beating well after each addition. Lightly fold in the potato flakes, coconut, salt and coffee powder. Place the mixture in heaped teaspoonfuls onto greased cookie sheets.

Bake for 20 to 22 minutes. Allow to cool on wire racks.

Mocha Parfaits: Coarsely crush the macaroons and mix with the marsala wine. Whip the cream until firm; divide in half, flavoring one half with the grated chocolate and coffee powder, and the other with confectioners' sugar.

Spoon alternate amounts of crushed macaroons, chocolate cream, and sweetened cream into parfait glasses. Chill until ready to serve.

Orange Meringue Loaf

Yield: 6 to 8 servings

6 egg whites (at room temperature)

¼ teaspoon cream of tartar

¼ teaspoon salt

1 cup sugar

½ teaspoon orange extract

½ teaspoon brandy extract

Orange Sauce:
1 cup sugar

⅛ teaspoon salt

3 tablespoons cornstarch

2 teaspoons grated lemon rind

1 cup orange juice

3 egg yolks, lightly beaten

1 tablespoon butter or margarine

1 cup heavy cream, chilled

flaked toasted almonds, for topping

Preheat the oven to 350°F.

Beat the egg whites until stiff and glossy. Add the cream of tartar and salt, and beat. Gradually add the sugar, beating well after each addition. Flavor with the extracts.

Spoon the mixture into a greased and cornstarch-dusted 9 × 5 × 3-inch loaf pan. Set the pan in a baking pan containing 3 to 4 cups hot water.

Bake for 55 to 60 minutes. Remove from the oven and place the loaf pan on a wire rack in a draft-free area to cool.

Orange Sauce: Combine the sugar, salt, cornstarch and lemon rind in the top half of a double boiler; blend in the orange juice and egg yolks, and cook over boiling water until the sauce is of a thick custard consistency. Add the butter, brushing it across the surface to prevent a skin forming on the custard while it cools. Chill.

To finish the meringue: Whip the cream until soft peaks form; fold into the orange custard. Carefully turn the meringue onto a serving plate and spoon the Orange Sauce over. Scatter the almonds over the top. Cut into slices for serving.

Sauce Variations: Use pineapple juice, crushed and sieved strawberries, or apricot or peach puree in place of the orange juice.

Apricot Almond Soufflé

Yield: 5 or 6 servings

8 ounces dried apricots
1½ cups water
2 tablespoons lemon juice
⅓ cup sugar
2 eggs, separated
3 egg whites
½ cup chopped, toasted almonds
extra sugar, for dusting
whipped cream, for serving

Cover the dried apricots with the water and lemon juice and let stand for 30 minutes.

Preheat the oven to 350°F.

Bring the apricots slowly to a boil, then simmer until the apricots are softened. Remove from the heat, allow to stand for 10 minutes, then puree in a food processor or press through a fine sieve. While still warm, add half of the sugar and the egg yolks and beat well.

Whisk the 5 egg whites until soft peaks form. Add the remaining sugar and whisk well, then lightly fold into the apricot puree with the almonds—do not overmix.

Prepare a soufflé dish or straight-sided casserole by greasing well and dusting with extra sugar. Add the apricot mixture, being careful not to disturb the coating on the dish. Dust a little sugar over the surface.

Bake for 30 to 35 minutes. Serve at once, with whipped cream.

Miniature Fruit Soufflés

Yield 6 to 8 servings

8 ounces ripe pitted fruit—peaches, apricots, etc.
½ cup powdered sugar
6 egg whites (at room temperature)
cookie crumbs, for coating
2 tablespoons brandy fruit liqueur
1 to 2 tablespoons confectioners' sugar

Preheat the oven to 425°F.

Peel and chop the fruit coarsely, and rub through a sieve for a final weight of 6 ounces. Mix with the powdered sugar. Beat the egg whites until very stiff and glossy. Fold in the sweetened fruit puree as lightly as possible.

Grease six to eight small soufflé dishes, and dust the insides with fine cookie crumbs. Spoon equal portions of the fruit mixture into each one. Place the dishes onto a cookie sheet.

Bake for 8 to 9 minutes. Remove from the oven. Serve hot or cold with a sprinkling of brandy liqueur and a dusting of confectioners' sugar over the top.

Note: If using canned fruits, drain well (both before and after sieving) and decrease the sugar slightly for the sweetened varities.

Hazelnut Puffs

Yiled: 4 or 5 servings

3 eggs, separated
⅛ teaspoon salt
½ cup sugar
3 ounces baking chocolate, melted
1 teaspoon brandy or rum extract
1 cup finely chopped hazelnuts
¼ cup chopped candied cherries
additional finely chopped hazelnuts, for coating
whipped cream, for decoration
chocolate curls, for decoration

Preheat the oven to 350°F.

Whisk the egg whites until stiff and glossy. Gradually add the salt and sugar, beating well after each addition.

Beat the egg yolks until thickened. Fold in the cooled chocolate, extract, hazelnuts, and cherries; then lightly fold in the egg-white mixture.

Prepare 4 or 5 custard cups or straight-sided molds by greasing and then dusting with finely chopped hazelnuts. Divide the dessert mixture into each one, being careful not to disturb the sides. Arrange the custard cups in a baking pan and pour 2 to 3 cups of hot water into the base.

Carefully place in the oven, cover loosely with aluminum foil, and bake for 15 to 17 minutes. Serve warm, with a topping of whipped cream and chocolate curls for decoration.

Right: **Miniature Fruit Soufflés (see left).**

Fruit Pasta Pudding

Yield: 6 to 8 servings

1½ to 2 cups cooked and drained fruit—see the variations below
½ teaspoon ground cinnamon or nutmeg
¼ cup chopped pecans or walnuts
1½ to 2 cups cooked pasta shapes (⅔ cup uncooked)
½ stick butter or margarine, melted
½ cup sour cream
1 cup cottage cheese, sieved
2 eggs, beaten
½ cup fruit syrup—from the cooked fruit
2 tablespoons brown sugar
additional ½ teaspoon cinnamon or nutmeg

Preheat the oven to 350°F.

Combine the fruit, spice, and nuts and spread over the base of a well-greased casserole.

Toss the cooked pasta and melted butter together. Combine the sour cream, cottage cheese, eggs, and fruit syrup, and mix into the pasta. Spoon the mixture into the casserole and sprinkle the combined brown sugar and extra spice over the surface.

Bake for 30 to 35 minutes. Remove from the oven and allow to stand for 10 minutes before serving hot. Can be served cold, but not chilled.

Fruit Variations: One of the following: apples, rhubarb, apricots, peaches, quinces, or berries—add sugar for desired sweetening.

Combine apples with chopped dates, figs, prunes, raisins, or currants.

Mock Strawberry Crisp

Yield: 6 servings

½ cup sugar
3 tablespoons cornstarch
⅛ teaspoon cardamom
⅛ teaspoon cloves
3½ to 4 cups diced rhubarb
2 to 3 teaspoons strawberry extract
¼ cup orange juice
¾ cup brown sugar
¾ cup quick-cooking oats
1 tablespoon flaked coconut
½ cup self-rising flour, sifted
¾ stick butter or margarine, melted
2 egg whites, stiffly beaten
ice cream or cream, for serving

Preheat the oven to 350°F.

Combine the sugar, cornstarch, and spices, and toss with the rhubarb; place into a well-greased casserole and mix in the combined strawberry extract and orange juice.

Bake the rhubarb until it is softened; stir occasionally to distribute the thickening syrup.

Meanwhile combine the brown sugar, oats, coconut, and sifted flour in a bowl; mix in the melted butter, then lightly fold in the beaten egg whites.

Roughly spoon this over the rhubarb mixture and return to the oven for 20 to 25 minutes, until the topping is crisp. Serve warm, with ice cream if desired.

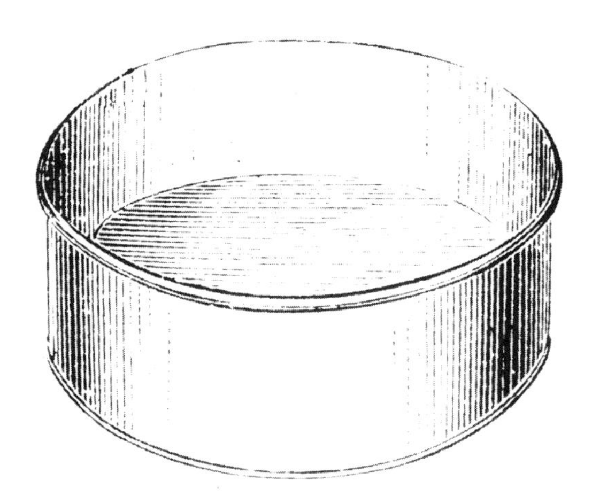

Apricot Rice Caramel

Yield: 5 or 6 servings

4 ounces dried apricots

water to cover

½ stick butter or margarine, melted

½ cup brown sugar

1½ cups cooked rice (⅔ cup uncooked)

1½ cups milk, warmed

3 eggs, beaten

¼ cup sugar

½ teaspoon vanilla extract

½ cup cream

¼ teaspoon ground nutmeg

whipped cream, for serving

Place the apricots into a small saucepan and just cover with water. Cover the pan, and cook slowly until just tender; then remove from heat, cool, and drain.

Preheat the oven to 350°F.

Combine the melted butter and brown sugar, and spread over the base and about one-third of the way up the sides of an ovenproof pudding bowl. Press the apricots over the surface, and then press the cooked rice over the apricots.

To the warm milk, add the beaten eggs, sugar, and vanilla; then beat in the cream. Carefully pour the mixture into the center of the pudding bowl, and sprinkle the nutmeg over the surface.

Lift the bowl into a baking pan containing 1 to 2 cups of hot water; place in the oven.

Bake for 1 hour or until set. Remove, allow to cool, and then chill well. Turn onto a serving platter. Serve with whipped cream.

Golden Custard Slice

Yield: 8 to 10 servings

8 ounces gingersnaps

½ cup flaked coconut

1½ sticks butter or margarine, melted

Custard:
½ cup light corn syrup

1 teaspoon mixed spices

1½ cups cooked and mashed pumpkin (12 ounces raw)

½ cup raisins

3 eggs, separated

2 tablespoons sweet sherry

1 cup sour cream

whipped cream, for serving

Crush the gingersnaps to fine crumbs, and combine with the coconut and cooled butter. Press onto the base and about halfway up the sides of a well-greased 8-inch springform pan. Chill for 30 minutes.

Preheat the oven to 400°F.

Custard: Combine the corn syrup, spices, cold pumpkin, raisins, egg yolks, and sweet sherry; mix well. Gradually add the sour cream. Then fold in stiffly beaten egg whites, mixing very lightly. Carefully pour into the crumb crust.

Bake in the preheated oven for 10 minutes, then reduce the oven temperature to 325°F and bake for another 50 to 55 minutes or until the custard is set. Remove, allow to cool, and chill. For serving, cut into slices. Serve with whipped cream.

Old-Fashioned Baked Custard

Yield: 6 servings

3 eggs, beaten

¼ cup sugar

1 tablespoon whole-milk powder

1 teaspon vanilla extract

2½ cups milk, warmed

½ teaspoon grated nutmeg

Preheat the oven to 325°F.

Beat the eggs, sugar, powdered milk, and vanilla, only until well blended but not frothy in appearance. Add the milk, and mix.

Strain into a well-greased casserole and place the casserole into a baking pan containing 2 to 3 cups of hot water. Sprinkle the nutmeg over the surface.

Bake for 50 to 60 minutes, or until a knife inserted in the center of the custard comes away clean. Remove; allow to cool.

Note: If baking the custard with other foods in the oven, the temperature can be varied slightly. Do not bake at a temperature higher than 350°F, or the custard may separate or curdle.

Variations:

Rice Custard: Add 2 to 3 tablespoons of partially cooked, drained rice—omitting 1 egg.

Pasta Custard: Add 2 to 3 tablespoons of partially cooked, drained pasta—omitting 1 egg.

Chocolate Custard: Add ½ cup of grated chocolate or 2 tablespoons of drinking chocolate.

Dried-Fruit Custard: Add ½ cup of raisins or currants, or chopped dried apricots or dates, to the basic mixture.

Caramel Custard: Line the base of the casserole with a boiled caramel—1 cup sugar and ½ cup water—before pouring the custard mixture over. Unmold before serving.

Bread and Butter Custard: Arrange 2 or 3 slices of buttered bread over the surface of the custard before baking. Scatter extra sugar over the top if desired.

Golden Cream Custard: Replace 1 cup of the milk with evaporated milk or cream, and substitute light corn syrup for the sugar.

Honey Spice Custard: Use honey in place of the sugar, and stir 1 teaspoon mixed spices into the custard before baking.

Coconut Superb Custard: Substitute condensed sweetened milk for the sugar and add 2 to 3 tablespoons flaked coconut to the milk mixture.

Custard Brûlée: Bake the custard in a flameproof casserole as usual; allow to cool and then chill well. Sprinkle a generous layer of sugar over the top of the custard and place under a hot broiler until the sugar melts and forms a toffee glaze. Serve at once.

Note: Insulate the edge of the casserole with a multiple layer of crushed aluminum foil if required.

Right: **From top: Caramel Baked Custard (see above); Old-Fashioned Baked Custard (see above left); Spiced Orange Delight (see p. 261).**

C

D